Hell Girl

2

Miyuki Eto

Created by The Jigoku Shoujo Project

Translated and adapted by Gemma Collinge
Lettered by North Market Street Graphics

Ballantine Books · New York

A Del Rey Manga/Kodansha Trade Paperback Original

Hell Girl volume 2 copyright © 2006 by Miyuki Eto/The Jigoku Shoujo Project
English translation copyright © 2008 by Miyuki Eto/The Jigoku Shoujo Project

Published in the United States by Del Rey Books, an imprint of The Random House Publishing Group, a division of Random House, Inc., New York.

DEL REY is a registered trademark and the Del Rey colophon is a trademark of Random House, Inc.

Publication rights arranged through Kodansha Ltd.

First published in Japan in 2006 by Kodansha Ltd., Tokyo

ISBN 978-0-345-50416-6

Printed in the United States of America

www.delreymanga.com

9 8 7 6 5 4 3 2 1

Translator/adapter: Gemma Collinge
Lettering: North Market Street Graphics

Contents

Honorifics Explained

Throughout the Del Rey Manga books, you will find Japanese honorifics left intact in the translations. For those not familiar with how the Japanese use honorifics and, more important, how they differ from American honorifics, we present this brief overview.

Politeness has always been a critical facet of Japanese culture. Ever since the feudal era, when Japan was a highly stratified society, use of honorifics—which can be defined as polite speech that indicates relationship or status—has played an essential role in the Japanese language. When addressing someone in Japanese, an honorific usually takes the form of a suffix attached to one's name (example: "Asuna-san"), is used as a title at the end of one's name, or appears in place of the name itself (example: "Negi-sensei," or simply "Sensei!").

Honorifics can be expressions of respect or endearment. In the context of manga and anime, honorifics give insight into the nature of the relationship between characters. Many English translations leave out these important honorifics and therefore distort the feel of the original Japanese. Because Japanese honorifics contain nuances that English honorifics lack, it is our policy at Del Rey not to translate them. Here, instead, is a guide to some of the honorifics you may encounter in Del Rey Manga.

-san: This is the most common honorific and is equivalent to Mr., Miss, Ms., or Mrs. It is the all-purpose honorific and can be used in any situation where politeness is required.

-sama: This is one level higher than "-san" and is used to confer great respect.

-dono: This comes from the word "tono," which means "lord." It is an even higher level than "-sama" and confers utmost respect.

-kun: This suffix is used at the end of boys' names to express familiarity or endearment. It is also sometimes used by men among friends, or when addressing someone younger or of a lower station.

-chan: This is used to express endearment, mostly toward girls. It is also used for little boys, pets, and even among lovers. It gives a sense of childish cuteness.

Bozu: This is an informal way to refer to a boy, similar to the English terms "kid" and "squirt."

Sempai/
Senpai: This title suggests that the addressee is one's senior in a group or organization. It is most often used in a school setting, where underclassmen refer to their upperclassmen as "sempai." It can also be used in the workplace, such as when a newer employee addresses an employee who has seniority in the company.

Kohai: This is the opposite of "sempai" and is used toward underclassmen in school or newcomers in the workplace. It connotes that the addressee is of a lower station.

Sensei: Literally meaning "one who has come before," this title is used for teachers, doctors, or masters of any profession or art.

-[blank]: This is usually forgotten in these lists, but it is perhaps the most significant difference between Japanese and English. The lack of honorific means that the speaker has permission to address the person in a very intimate way. Usually, only family, spouses, or very close friends have this kind of permission. Known as *yobisute*, it can be gratifying when someone who has earned the intimacy starts to call one by one's name without an honorific. But when that intimacy hasn't been earned, it can be very insulting.

Hell Girl

Miyuki Eto

Created by
The Jigoku Shoujo Project

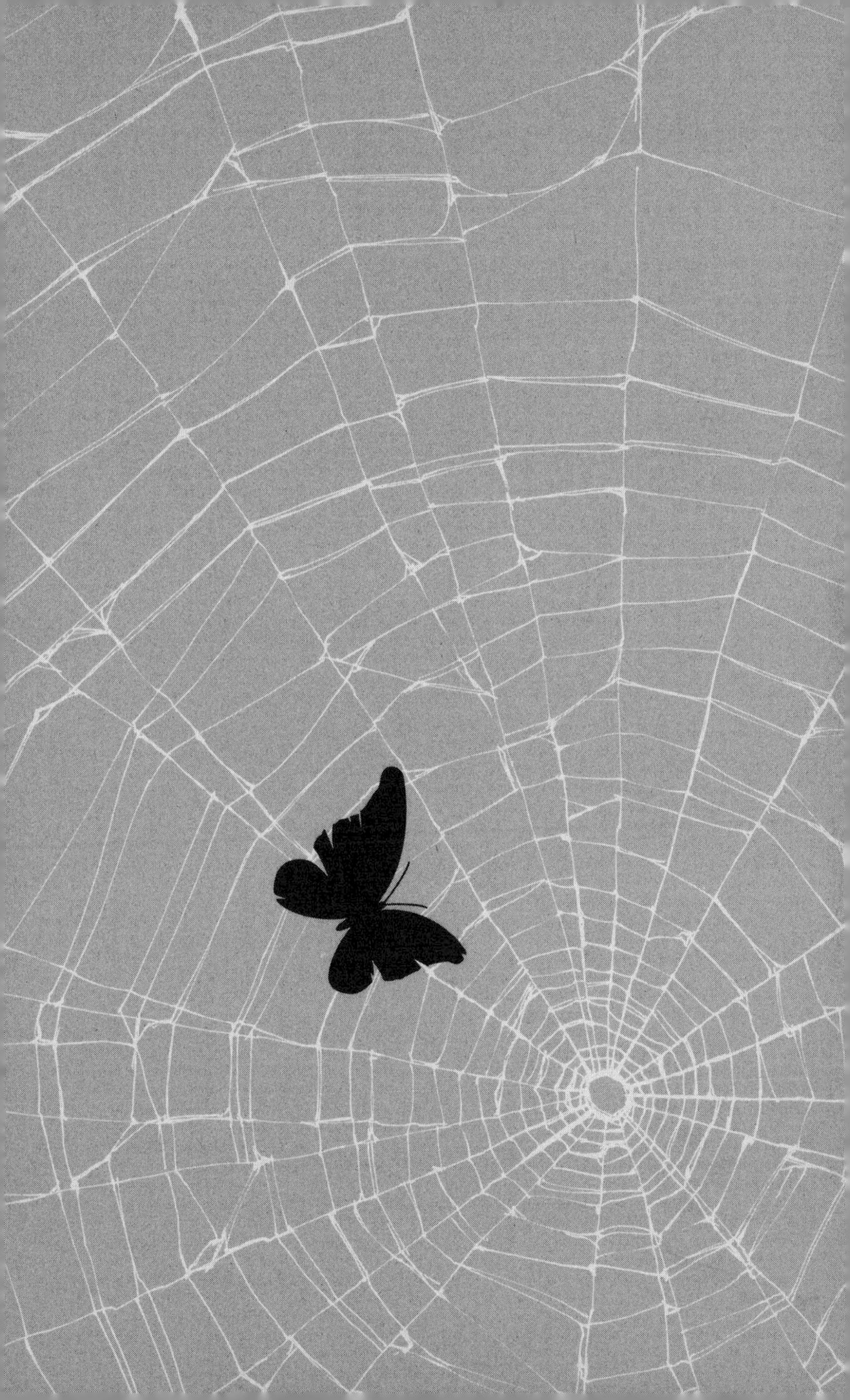

Chapter Six: Ice Shadows

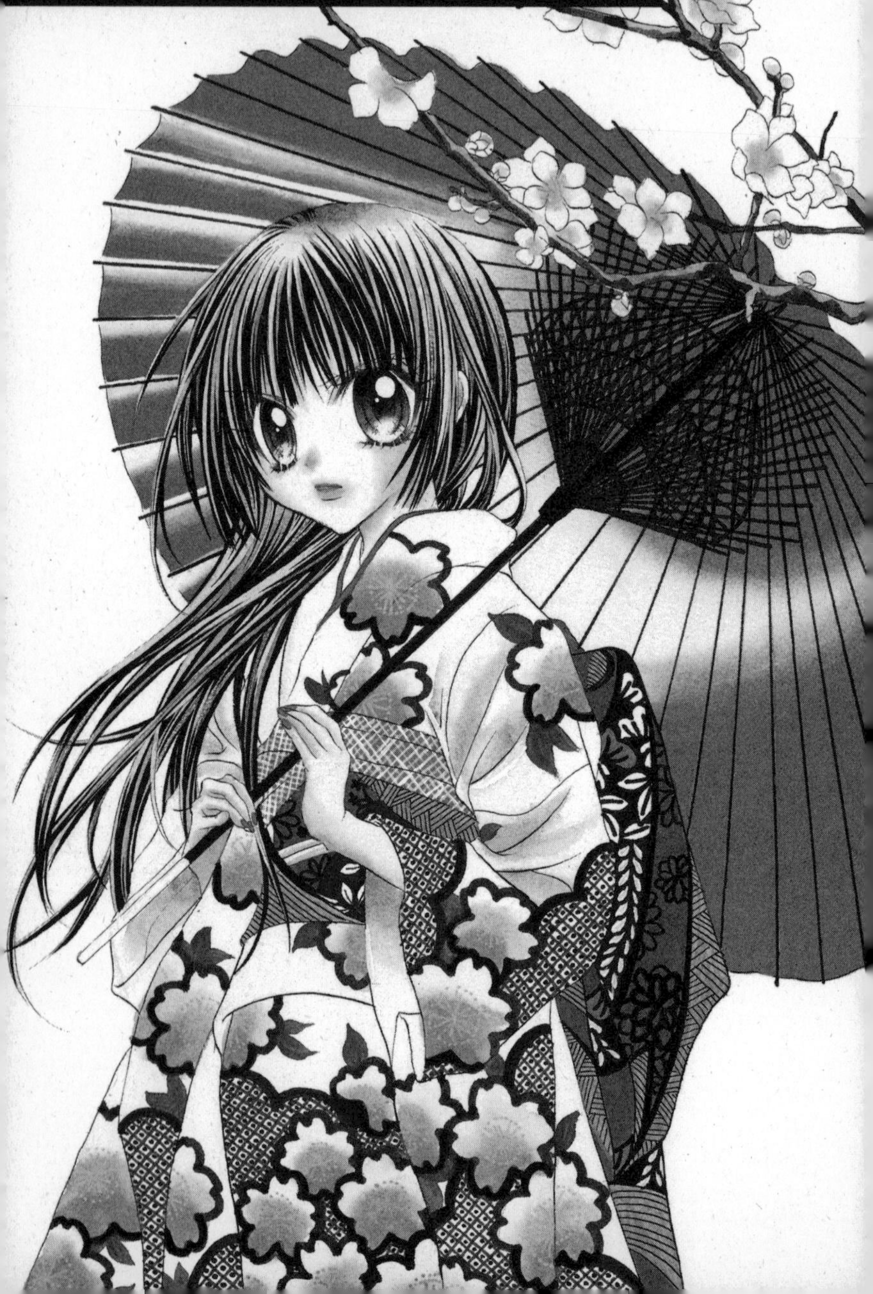

# Greetings!

Hello. This is Miyuki Etô. Thank you so much
for buying volume two of *Hell Girl*. In the first
volume, I left out the part of the anime where
they untie the thread on the straw doll to
complete the contract, so from chapter five on
I've included it. I'm still getting used to it.

I'm so happy that it's been officially
confirmed that there'll be a second
season of the anime. I hope you enjoy both
the anime and manga versions of *Hell Girl*.

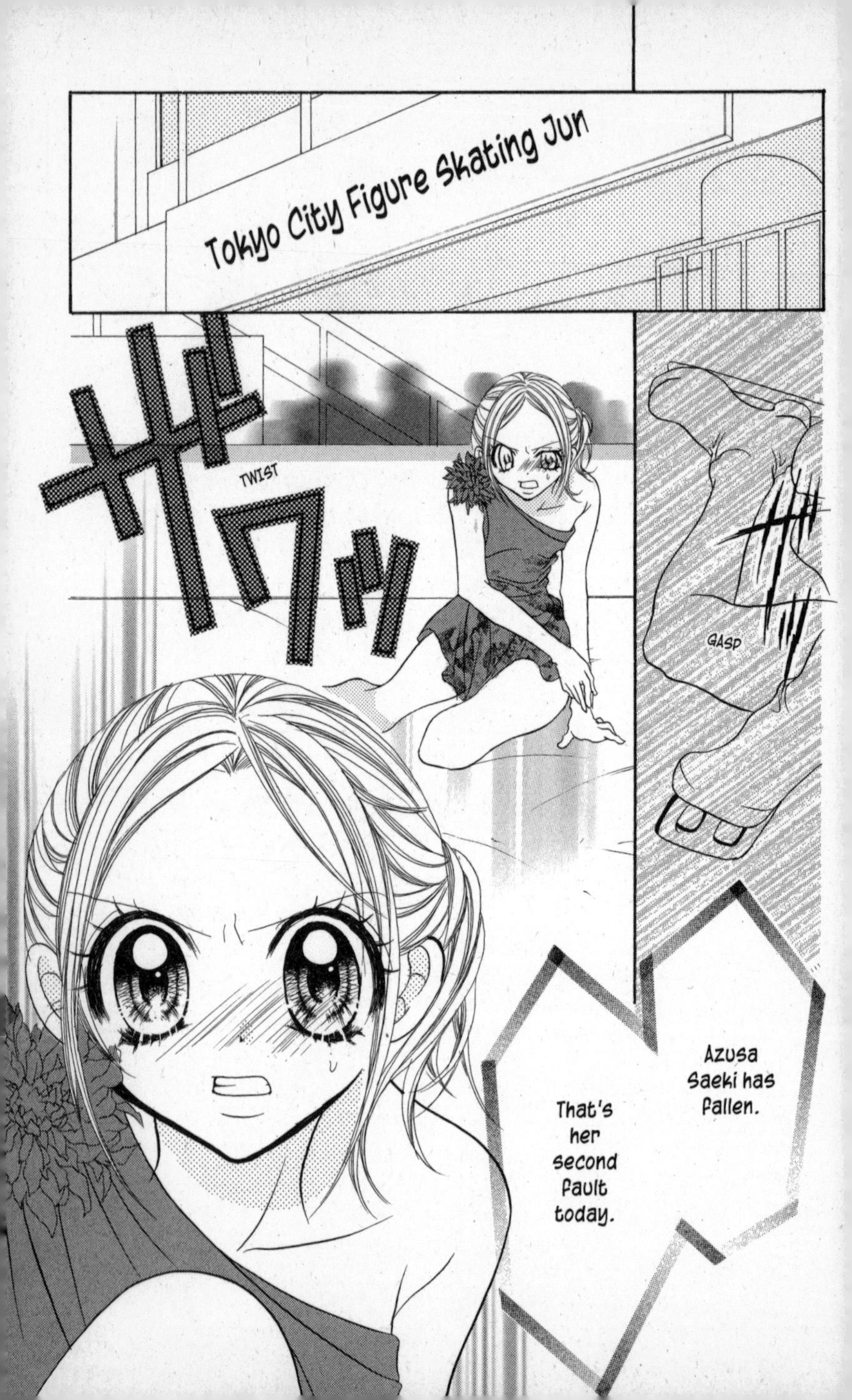
Tokyo City Figure Skating Jun
GASP
サワッ
TWIST
Azusa Saeki has fallen.
That's her second fault today.

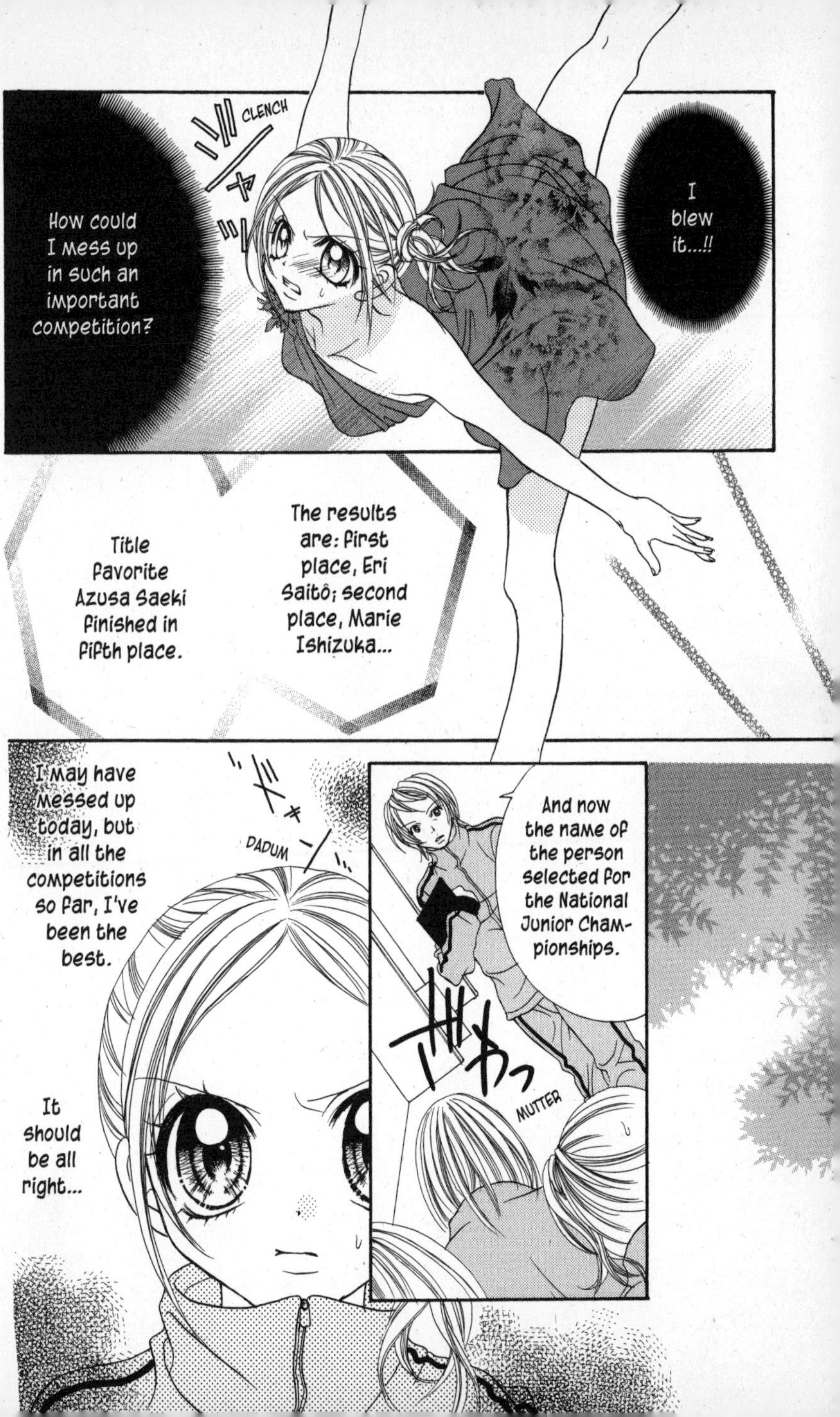
I blew it...!!
CLENCH
How could I mess up in such an important competition?
The results are: first place, Eri Saitô; second place, Marie Ishizuka...
Title favorite Azusa Saeki finished in fifth place.
And now the name of the person selected for the National Junior Championships.
MUTTER
DADUM
I may have messed up today, but in all the competitions so far, I've been the best.
It should be all right...

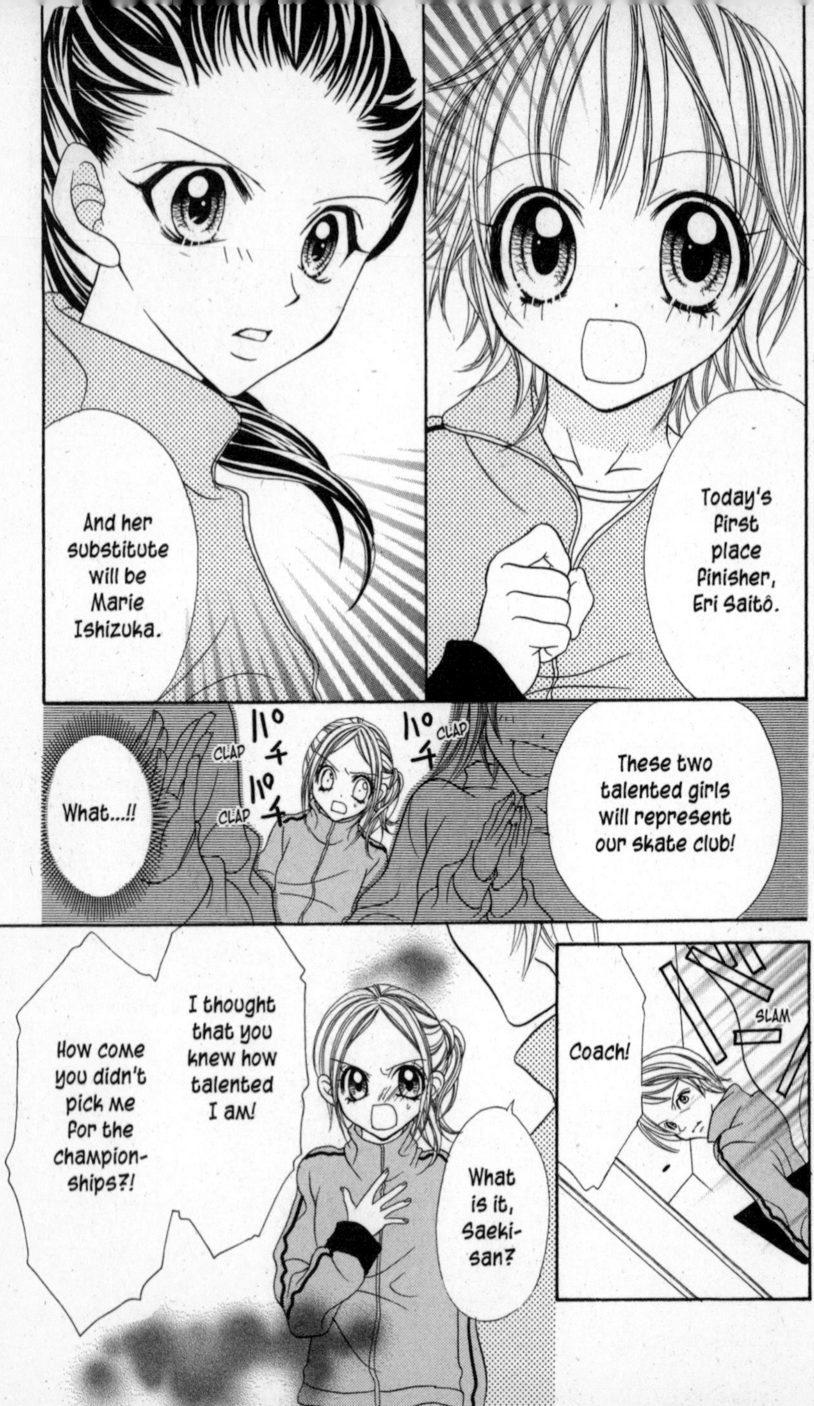
Today's first place finisher, Eri Saitô.
And her substitute will be Marie Ishizuka.
These two talented girls will represent our skate club!
パチ CLAP
パチ CLAP
パチ CLAP
What...!!
SLAM
Coach!
What is it, Saeki-san?
I thought that you knew how talented I am!
How come you didn't pick me for the championships?!

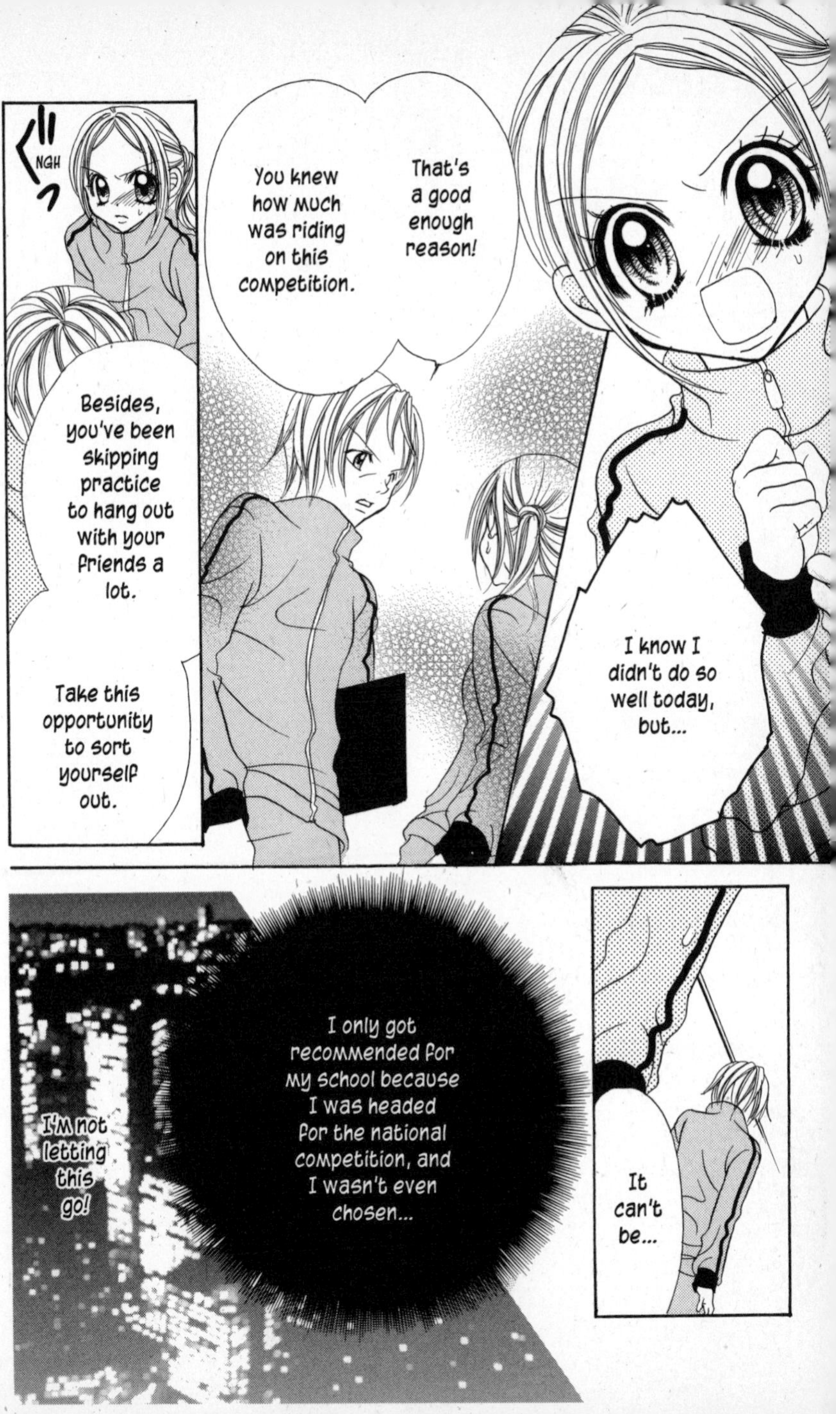
I know I didn't do so well today, but...
That's a good enough reason!
You knew how much was riding on this competition.
NGH
Besides, you've been skipping practice to hang out with your friends a lot.
Take this opportunity to sort yourself out.
It can't be...
I only got recommended for my school because I was headed for the national competition, and I wasn't even chosen...
I'm not letting this go!

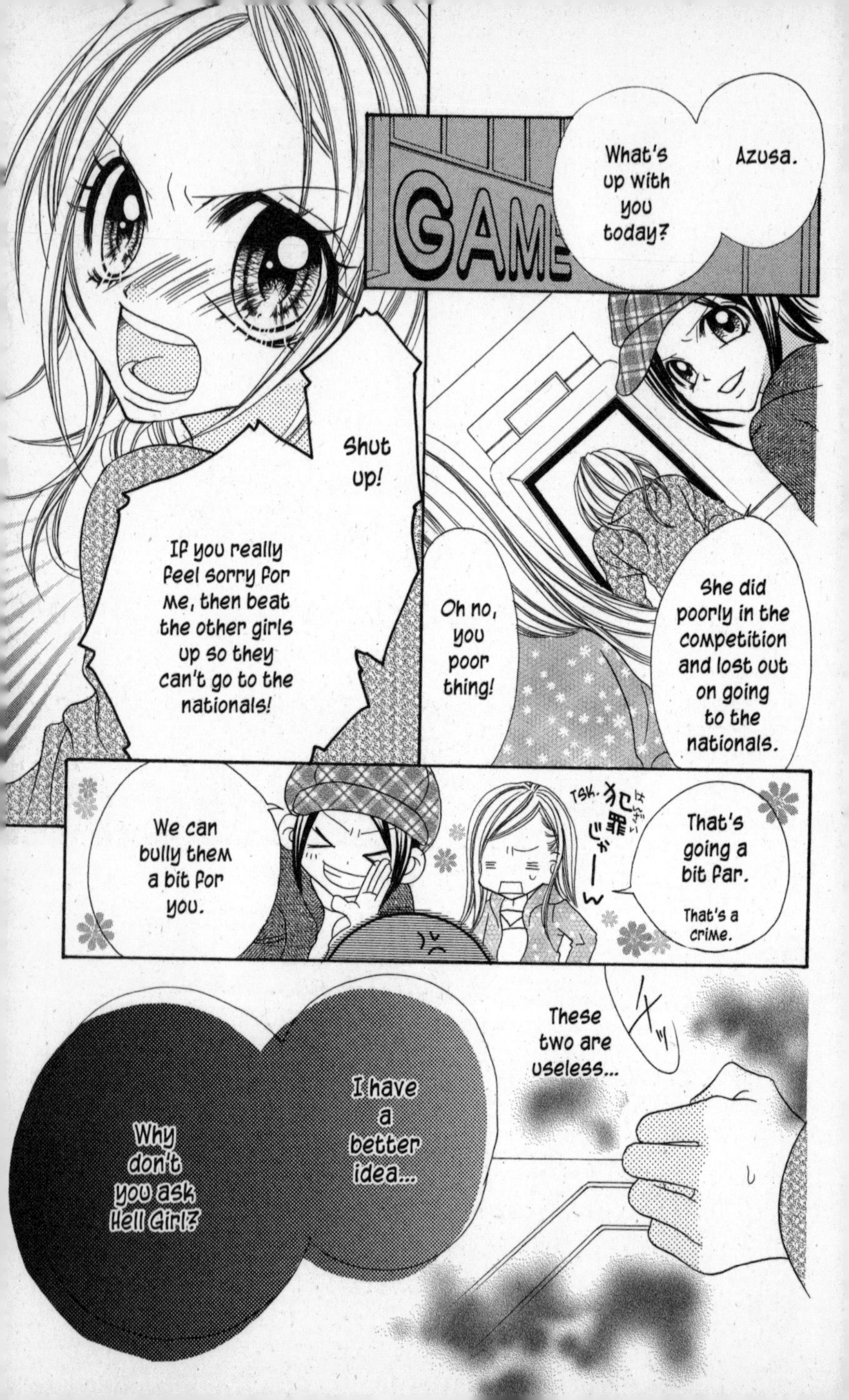
Azusa.
What's up with you today?
She did poorly in the competition and lost out on going to the nationals.
Oh no, you poor thing!
Shut up!
If you really feel sorry for me, then beat the other girls up so they can't go to the nationals!
That's going a bit far.
That's a crime.
TSK.
犯罪じゃーん
We can bully them a bit for you.
These two are useless...
I have a better idea...
Why don't you ask Hell Girl?

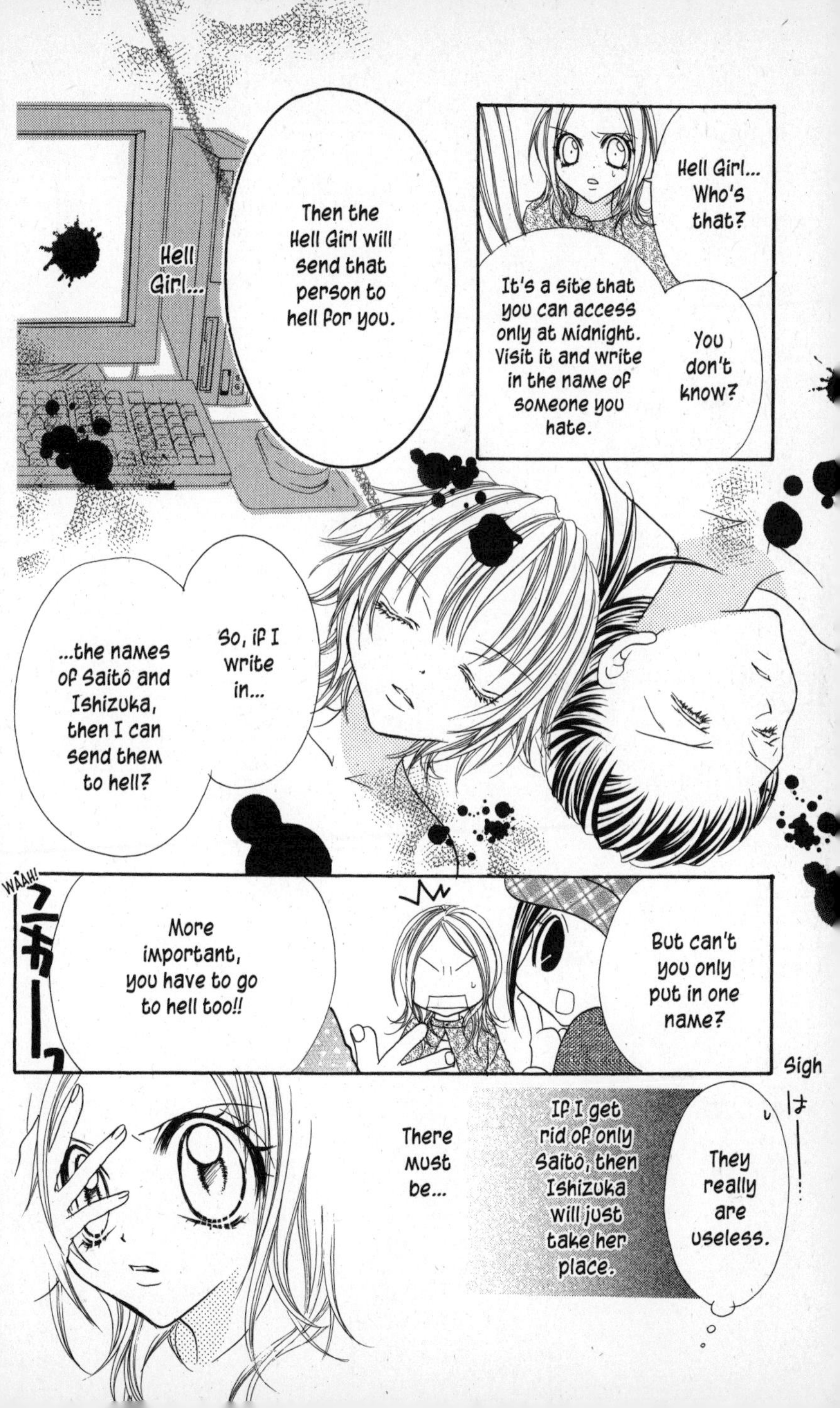
Hell Girl... Who's that?
You don't know?
It's a site that you can access only at midnight. Visit it and write in the name of someone you hate.
Then the Hell Girl will send that person to hell for you.
Hell Girl...
So, if I write in...
...the names of Saitô and Ishizuka, then I can send them to hell?
But can't you only put in one name?
More important, you have to go to hell too!!
WÂAH!
Sigh
They really are useless.
If I get rid of only Saitô, then Ishizuka will just take her place.
There must be...

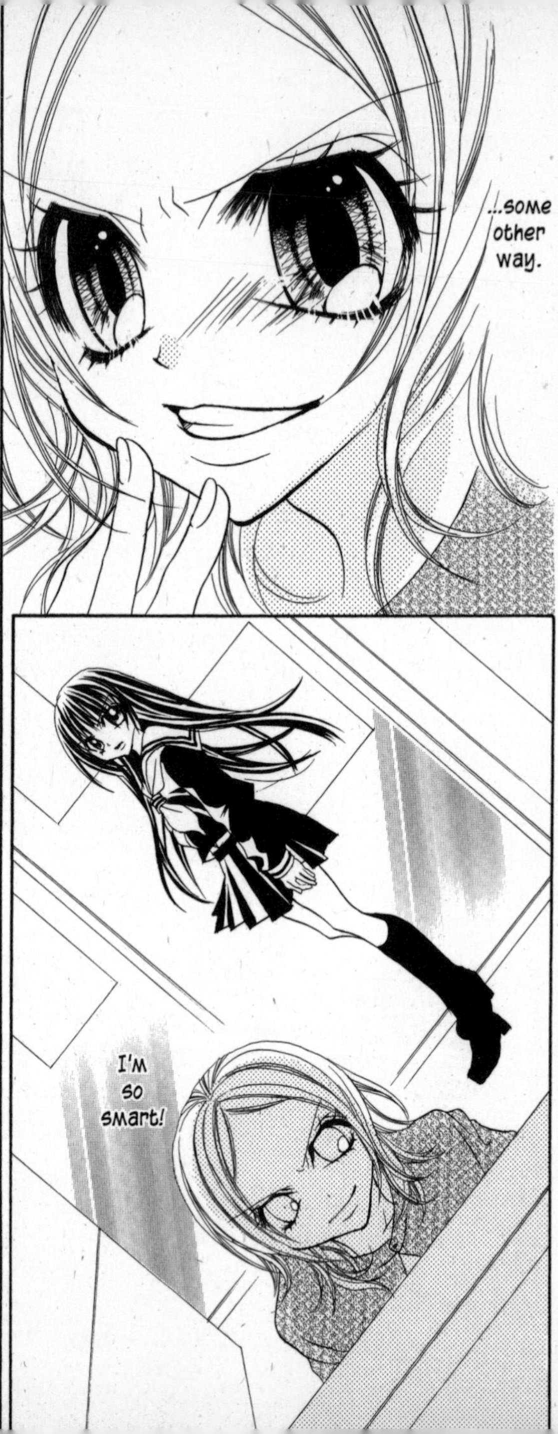
...some other way.
I'm so smart!

Author's Note

What our business meeting looks like

I seem to have more work than everyone else.

This idiot is too quiet. They need to have attitude.

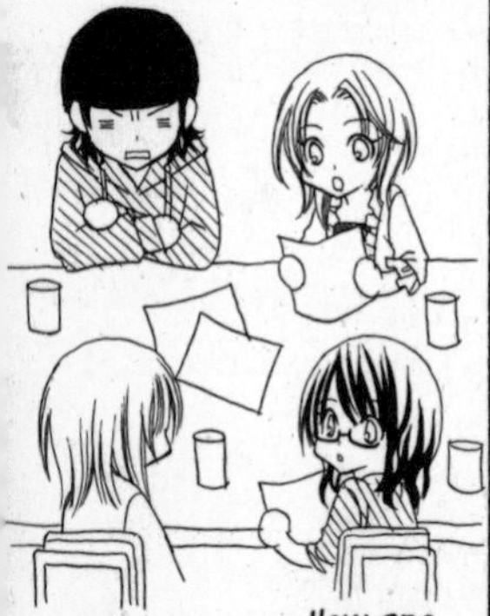

Let's put in a picture of them counting the cold hard cash.

How are they going to find out about what she did?

Lots of things that you wouldn't expect from a *Nakayoshi* manga!

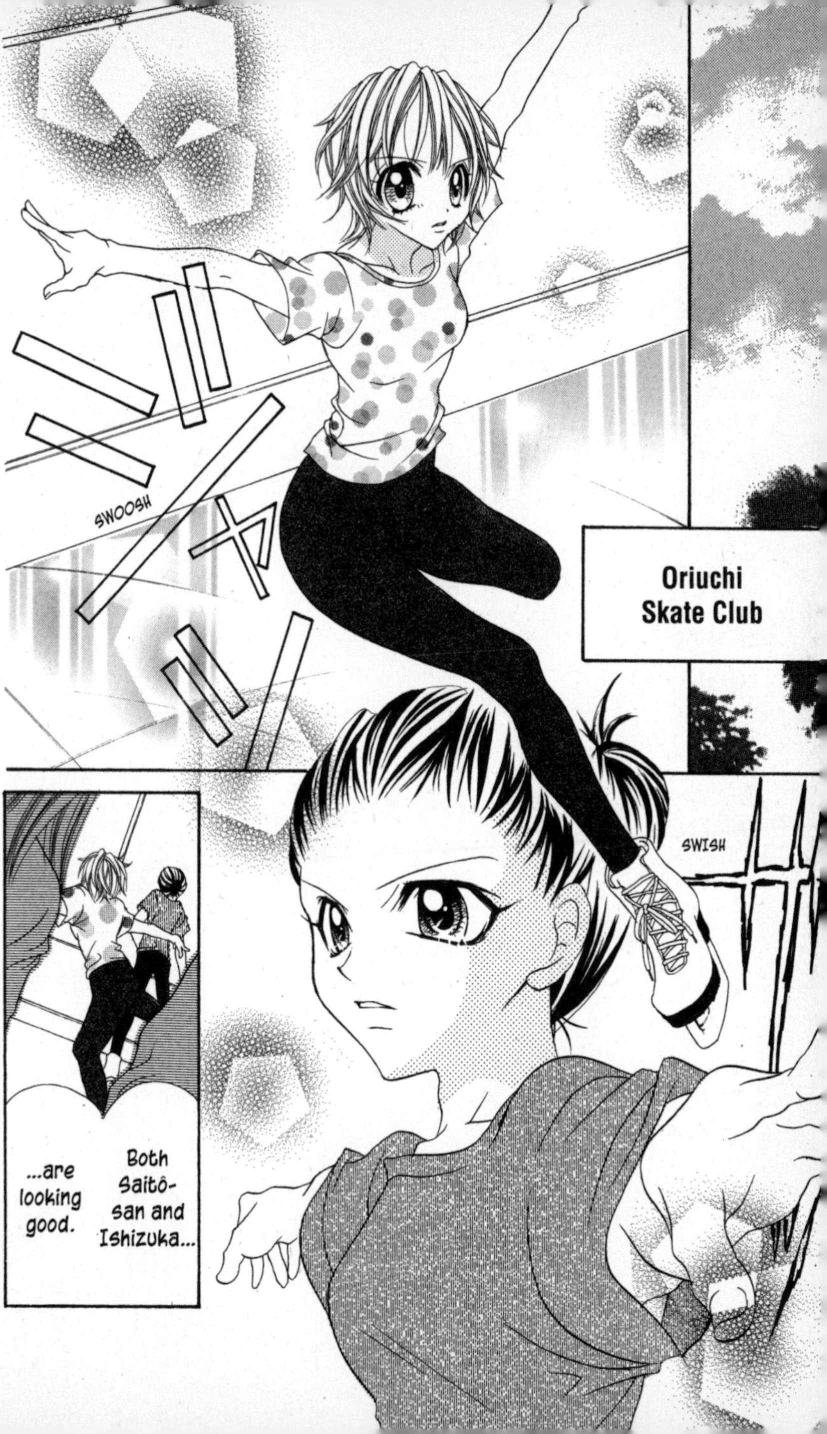
Oriuchi Skate Club
SWOOSH
SWISH
Both Saitô-san and Ishizuka...
...are looking good.

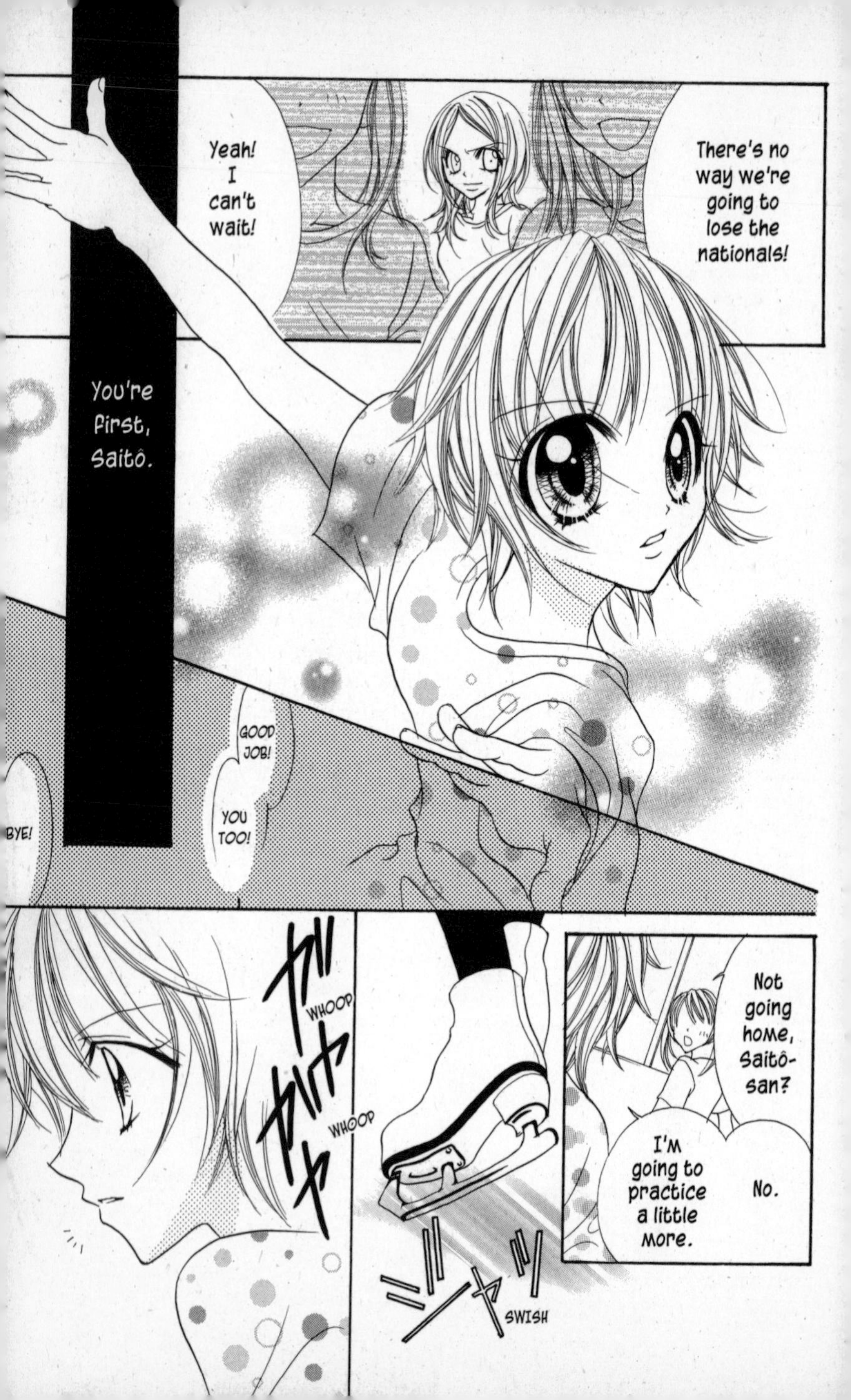
There's no way we're going to lose the nationals!
Yeah! I can't wait!
You're first, Saitô.
GOOD JOB!
YOU TOO!
BYE!
Not going home, Saitô-san?
No.
I'm going to practice a little more.
SWISH
WHOOP
WHOOP

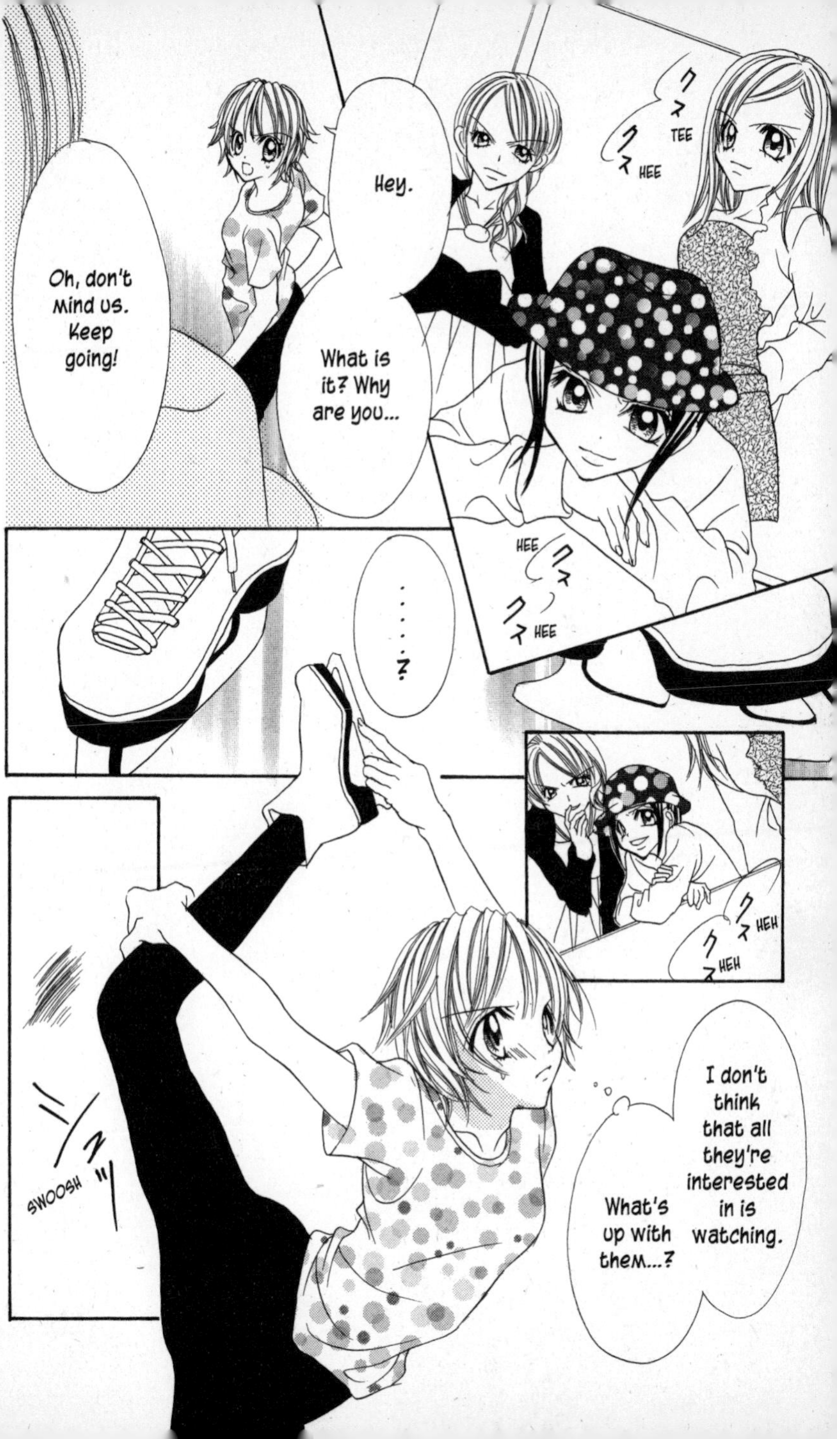
TEE
HEE
Hey.
What is it? Why are you...
Oh, don't mind us. Keep going!
HEE
HEE
......?
HEH
HEH
I don't think that all they're interested in is watching.
What's up with them...?
SWOOSH

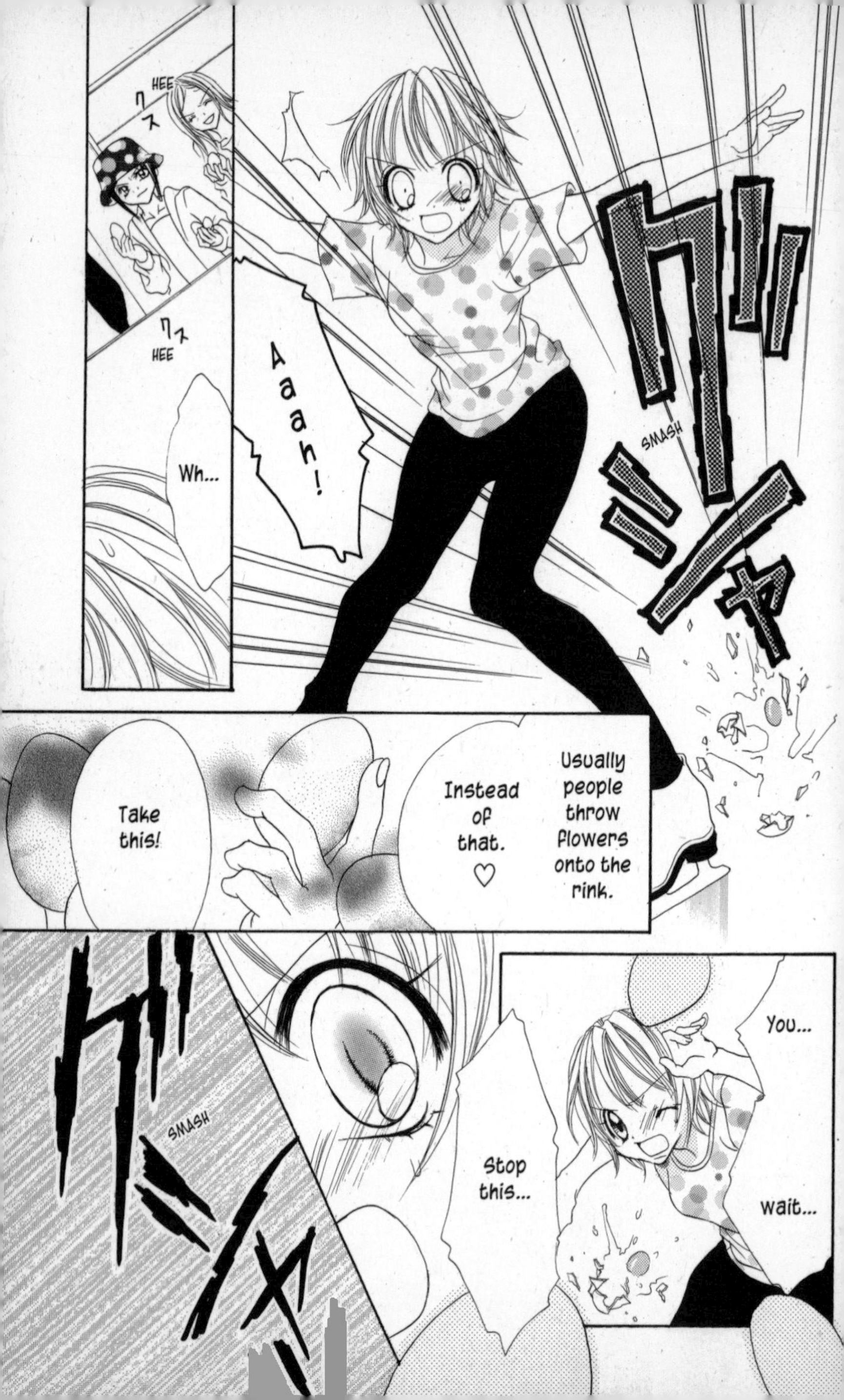
Aaah!
SMASH
HEE
HEE
Wh...
Usually people throw flowers onto the rink.
Instead of that. ♡
Take this!
You...
wait...
Stop this...
SMASH

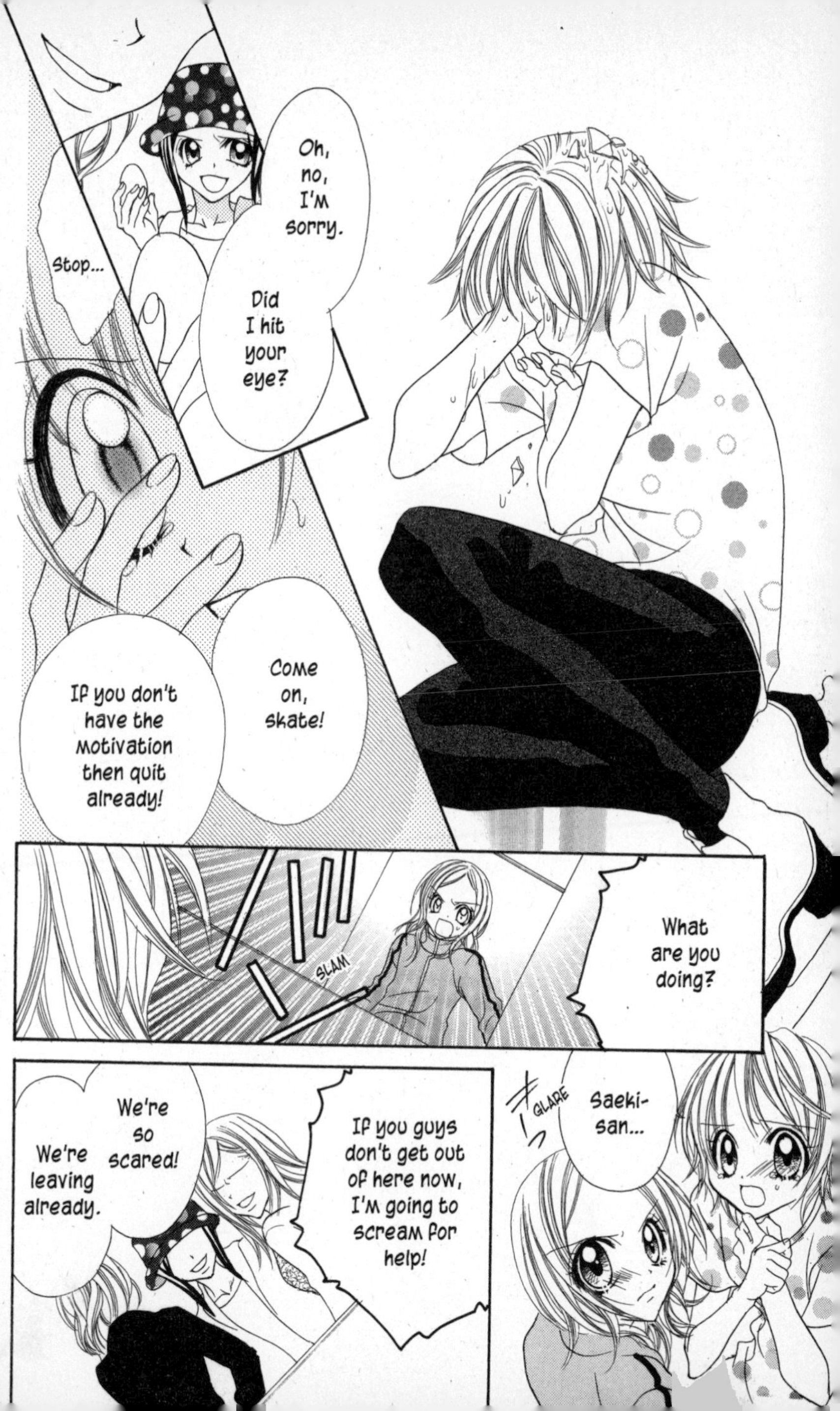

Oh, no, I'm sorry.
Did I hit your eye?
Stop...
Come on, skate!
If you don't have the motivation then quit already!
What are you doing?
SLAM
GLARE
Saeki-san...
If you guys don't get out of here now, I'm going to scream for help!
We're so scared!
We're leaving already.

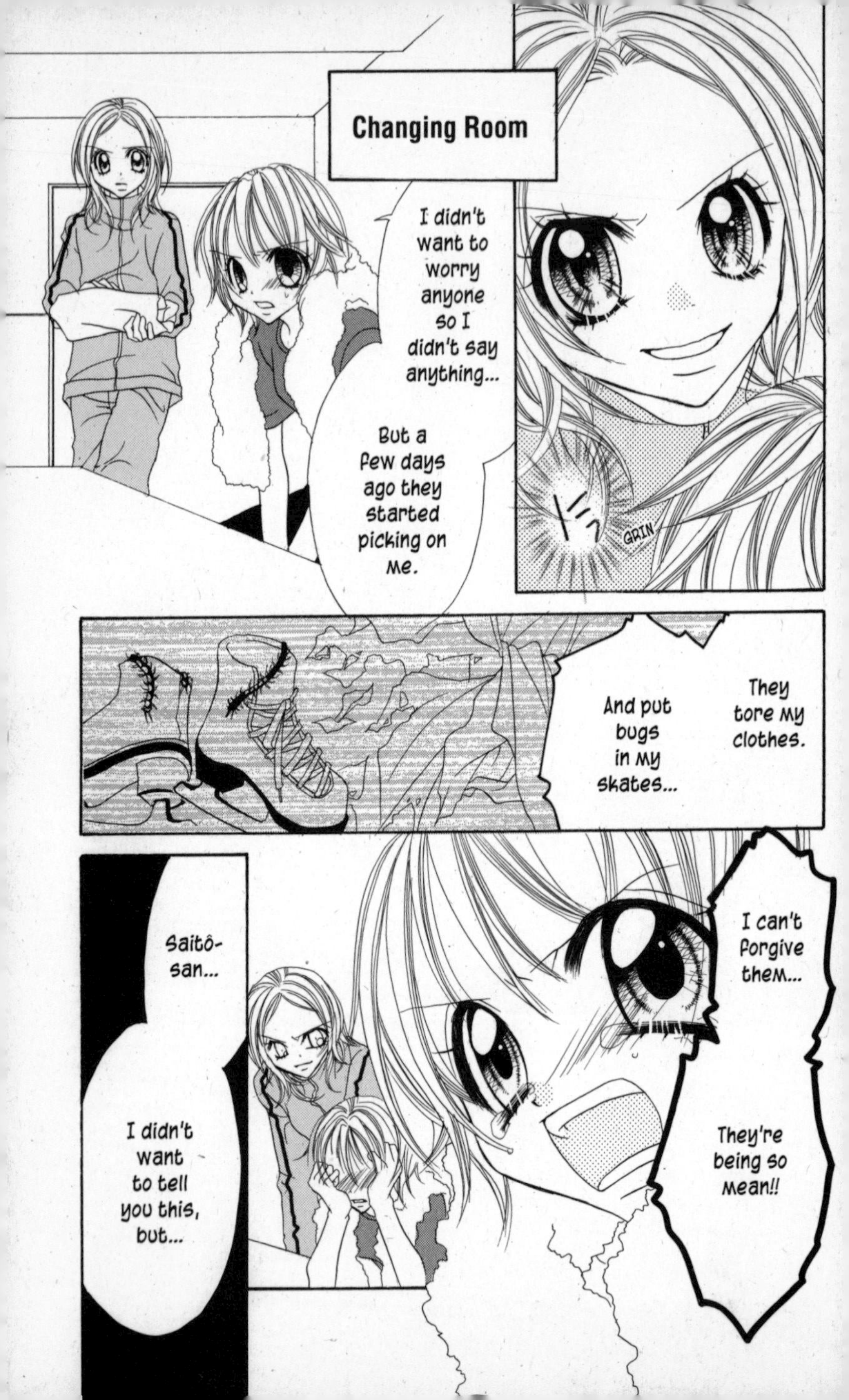
GRIN
Changing Room
I didn't want to worry anyone so I didn't say anything...
But a few days ago they started picking on me.
They tore my clothes.
And put bugs in my skates...
I can't forgive them...
They're being so mean!!
Saitô-san...
I didn't want to tell you this, but...

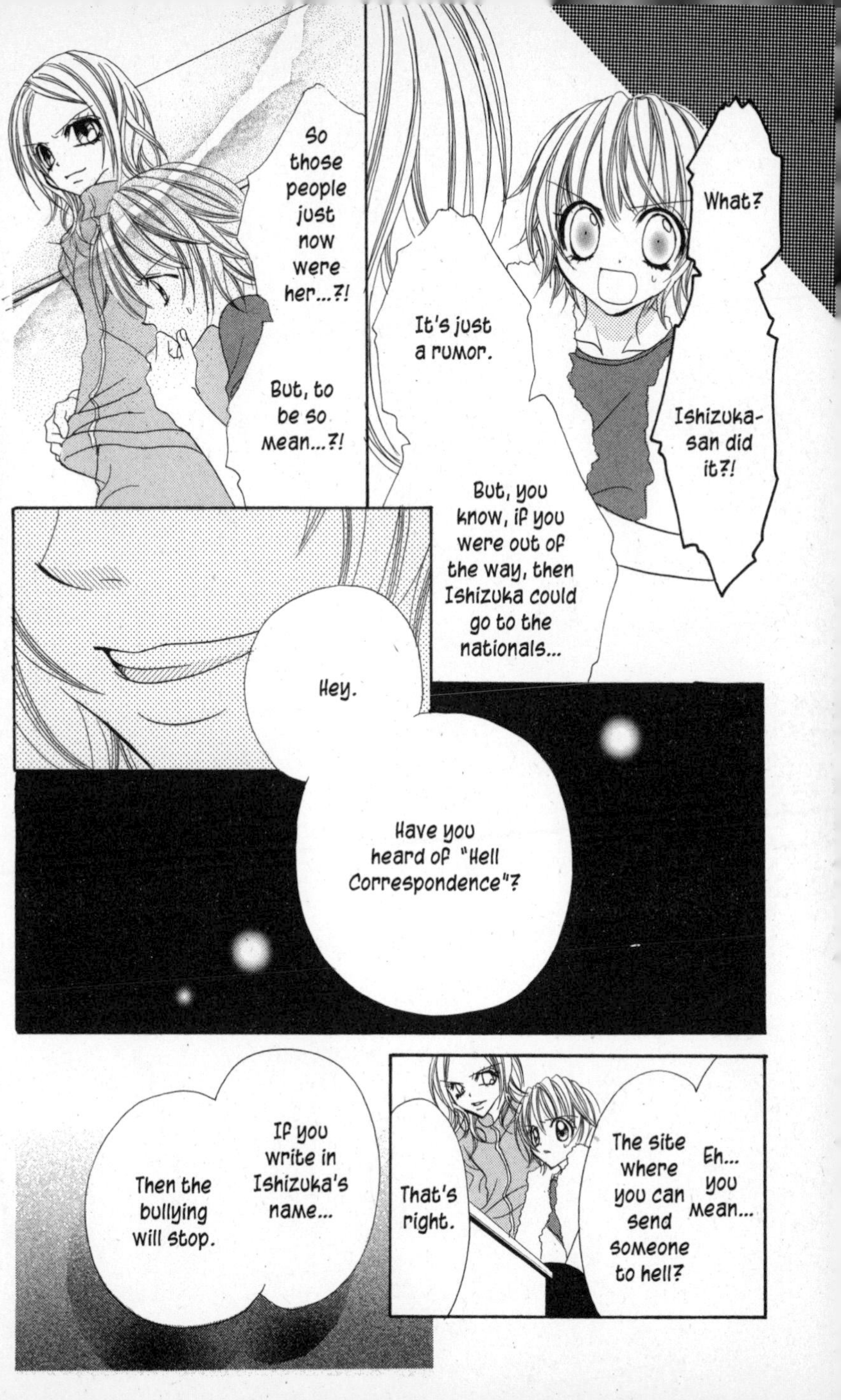
What?
Ishizuka-san did it?!
It's just a rumor.
But, you know, if you were out of the way, then Ishizuka could go to the nationals...
So those people just now were her...?!
But, to be so mean...?!
Hey.
Have you heard of "Hell Correspondence"?
Eh... you mean...
The site where you can send someone to hell?
That's right.
If you write in Ishizuka's name...
Then the bullying will stop.

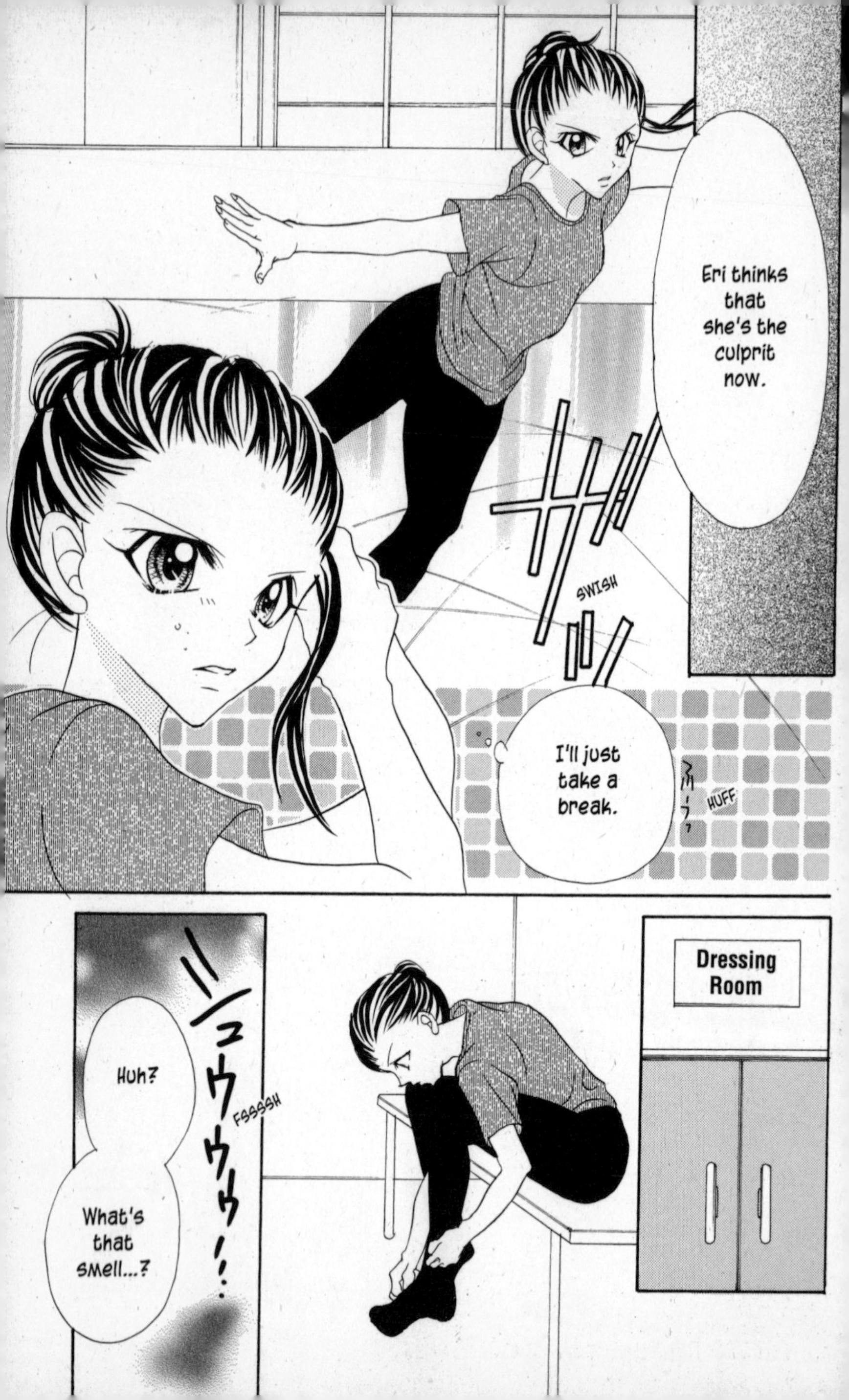
Eri thinks that she's the culprit now.
SWISH
I'll just take a break.
HUFF
Dressing Room
FSSSSH
Huh?
What's that smell...?

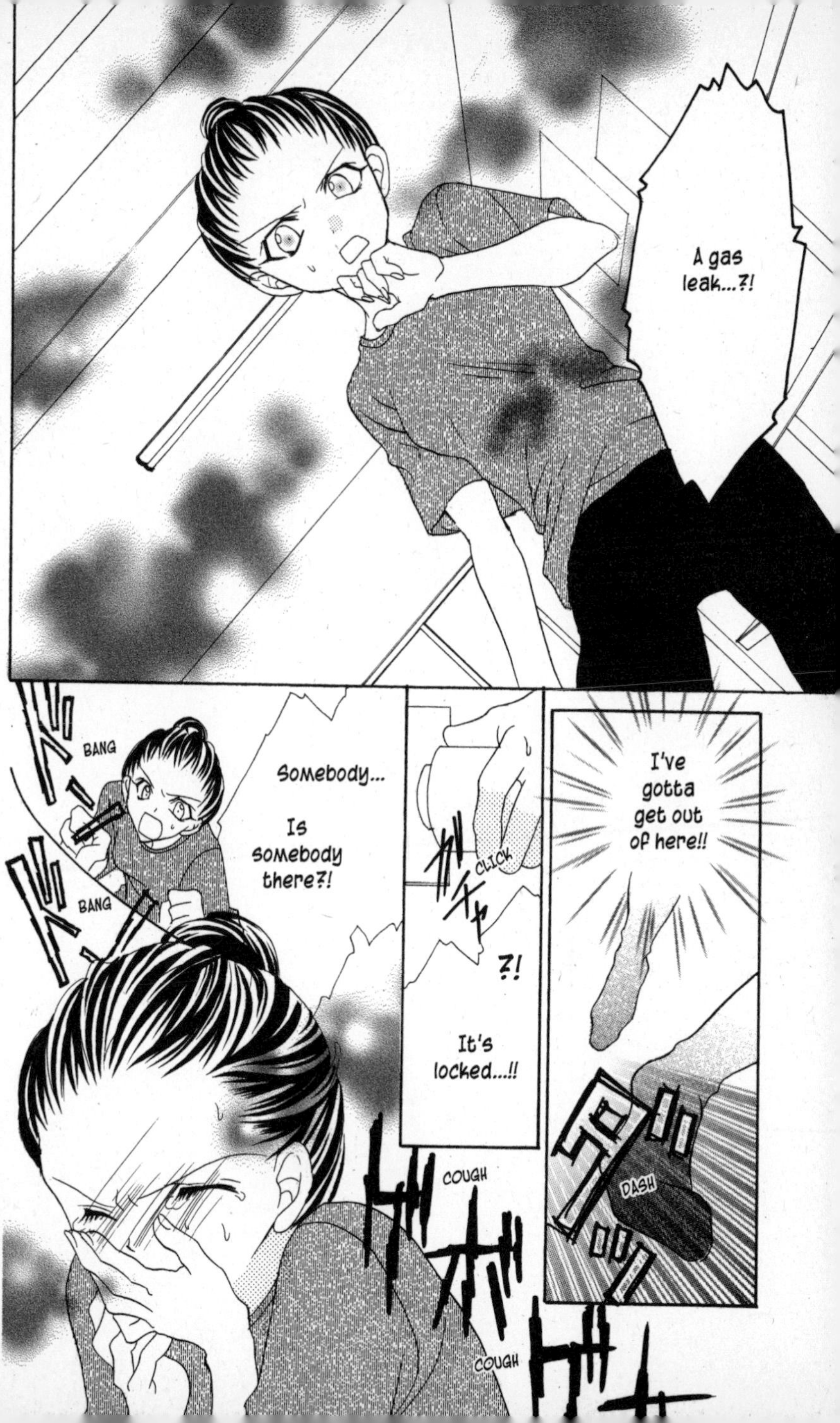
A gas leak...?!
I've gotta get out of here!!
DASH
CLICK
?!
It's locked...!!
Somebody...
Is somebody there?!
BANG
BANG
COUGH
COUGH

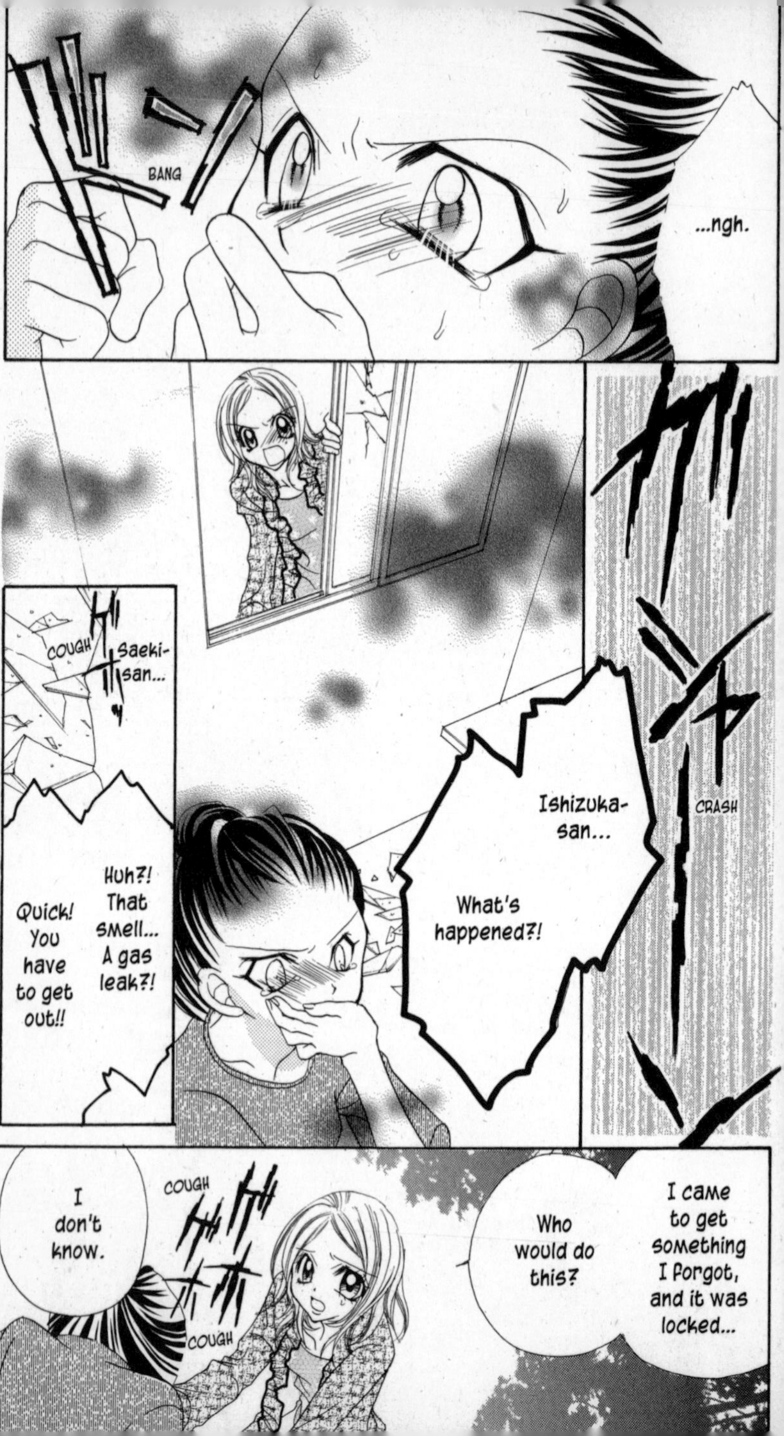
...ngh.
BANG
CRASH
Ishizuka-san...
What's happened?!
COUGH
Saeki-san...
Huh?! That smell... A gas leak?!
Quick! You have to get out!!
I came to get something I forgot, and it was locked...
Who would do this?
COUGH
COUGH
I don't know.

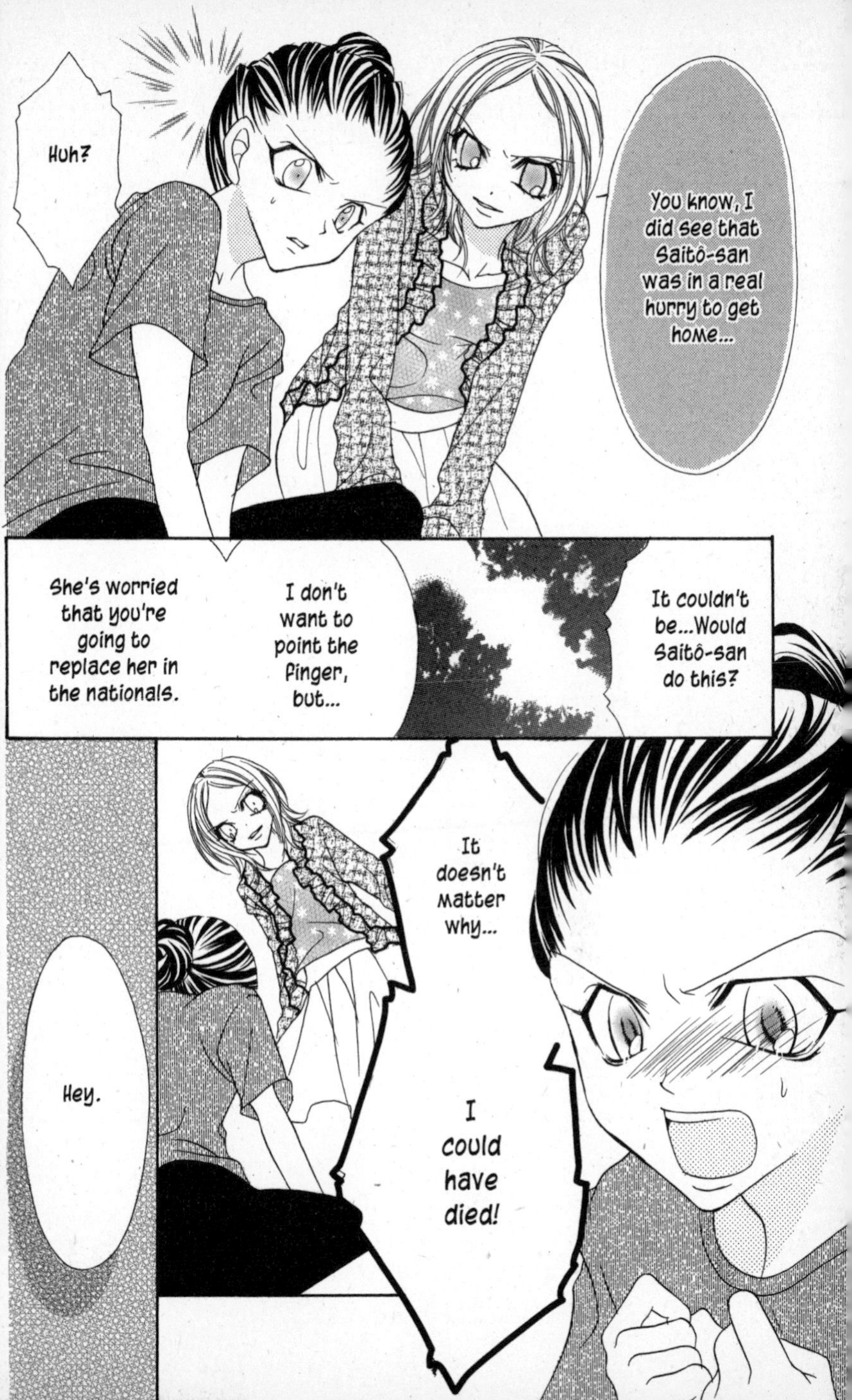
You know, I did see that Saitô-san was in a real hurry to get home...
Huh?
It couldn't be...Would Saitô-san do this?
I don't want to point the finger, but...
She's worried that you're going to replace her in the nationals.
It doesn't matter why...
I could have died!
Hey.

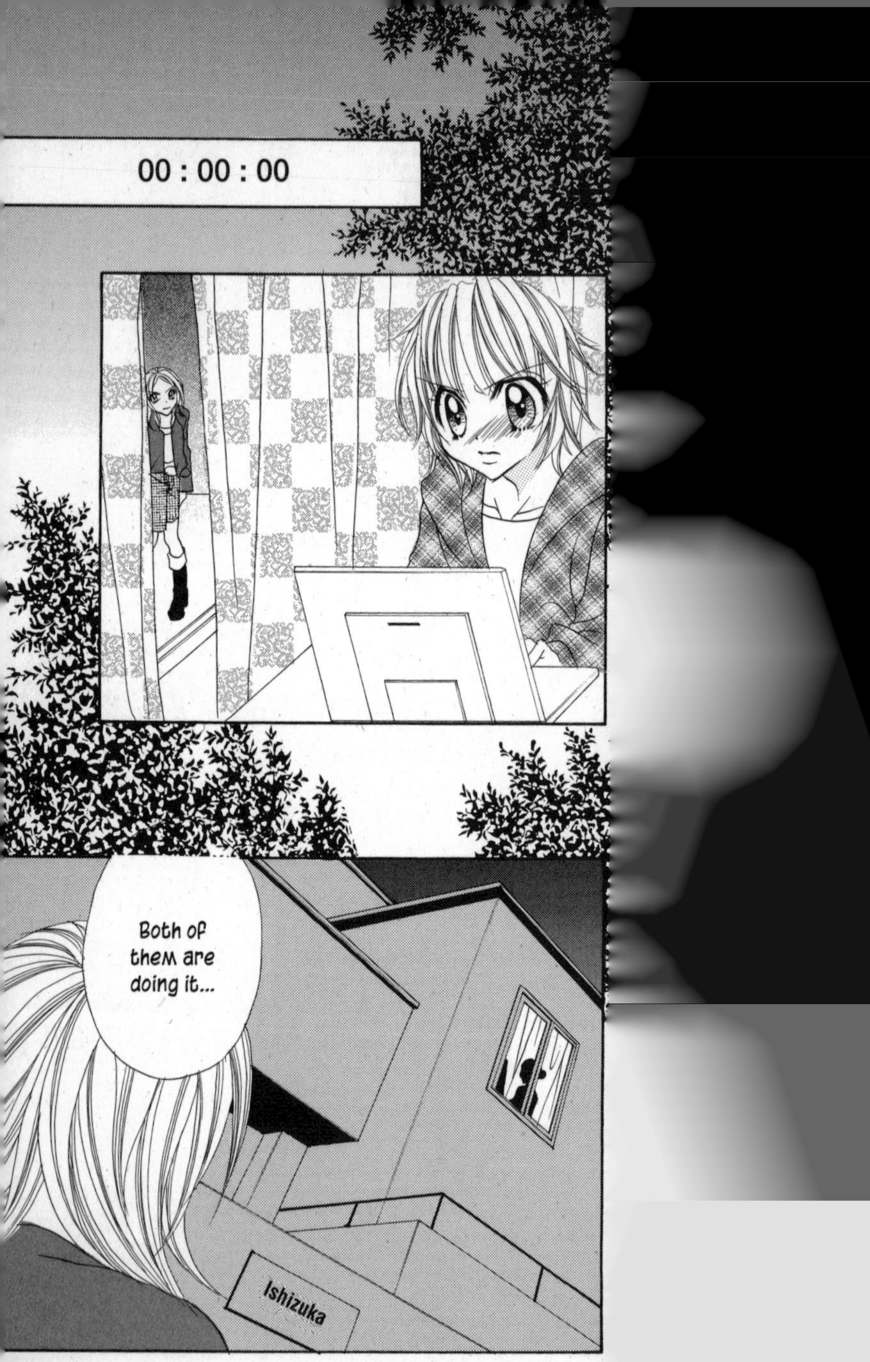
00 : 00 : 00
Both of them are doing it...
Ishizuka

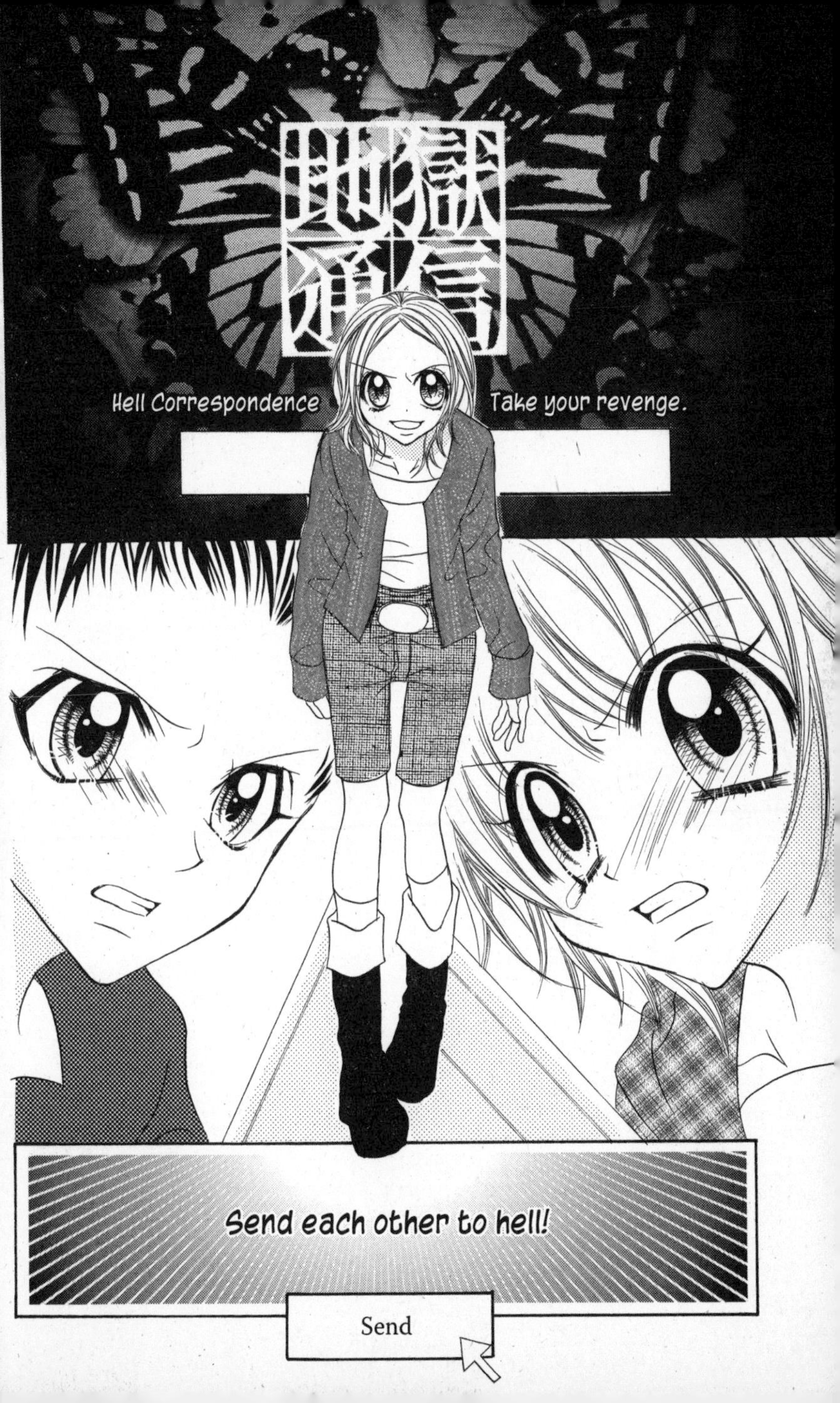
地獄通信
Hell Correspondence
Take your revenge.
Send each other to hell!
Send

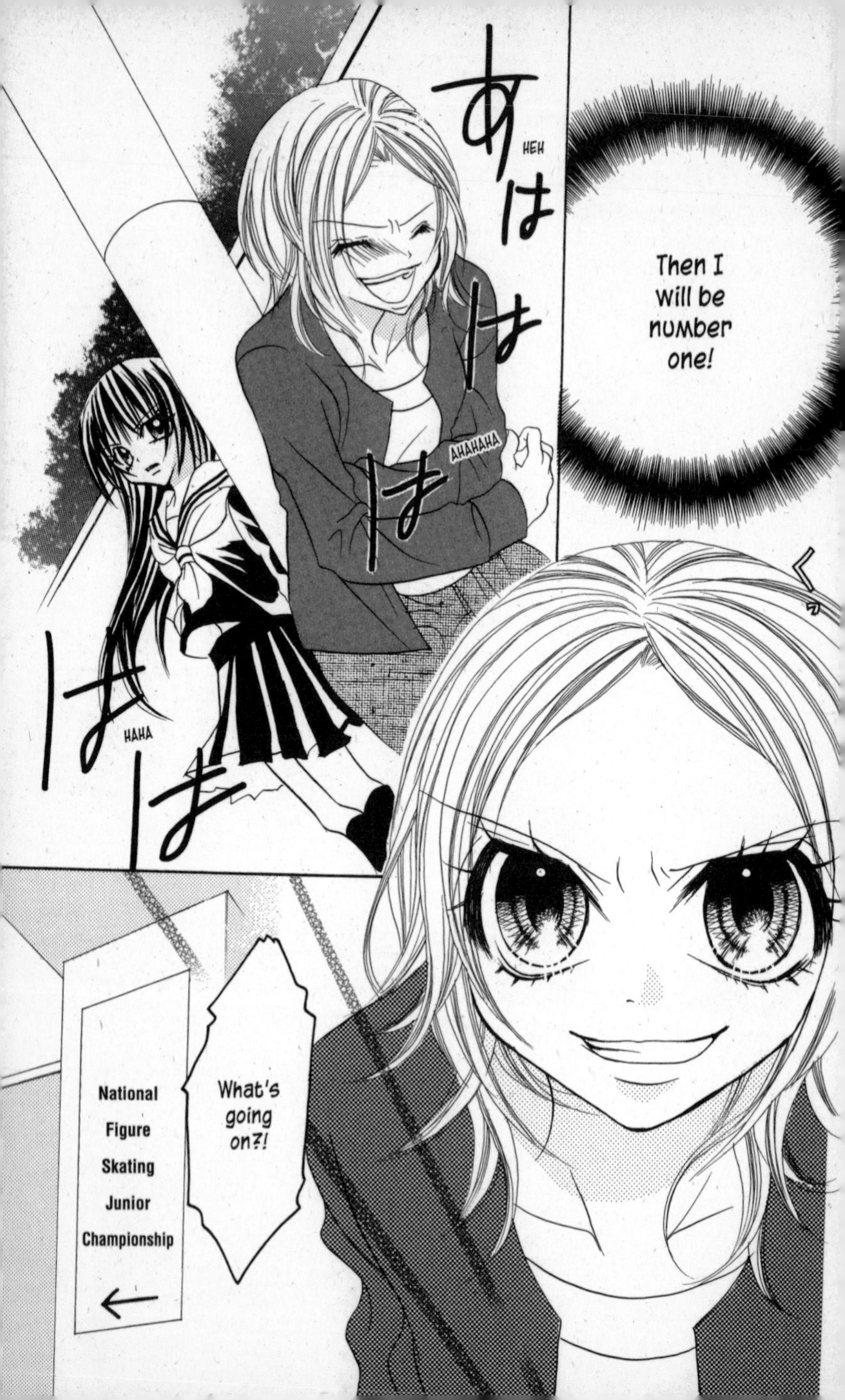

Then I will be number one!
あは
HEH
はは
AHAHAHA
はは
HAHA
What's going on?!
National Figure Skating Junior Championship ←

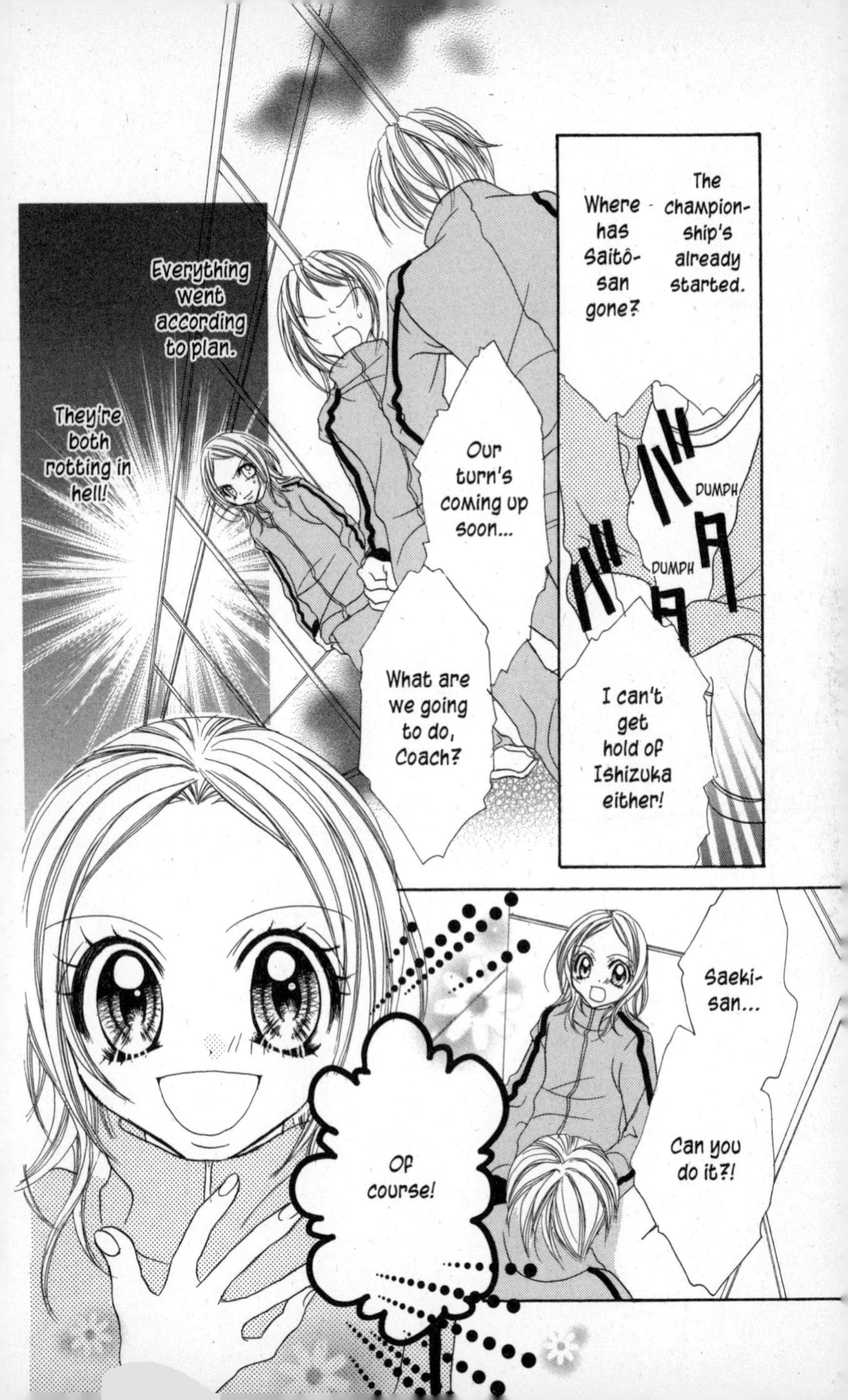
The championship's already started.
Where has Saitô-san gone?
バタ
DUMPH
バタ
DUMPH
I can't get hold of Ishizuka either!
Our turn's coming up soon...
What are we going to do, Coach?
Everything went according to plan.
They're both rotting in hell!
Saeki-san...
Can you do it?!
Of course!

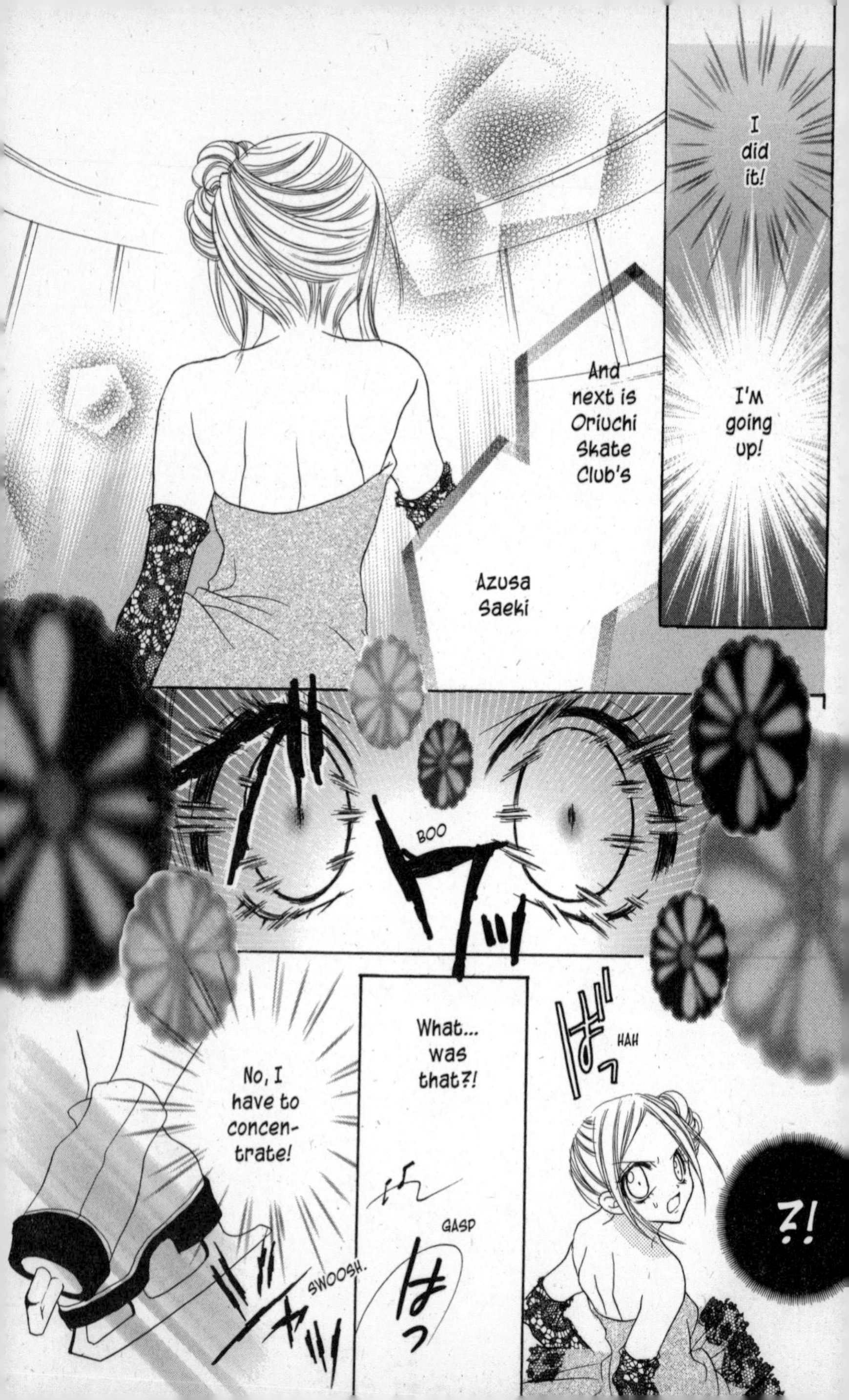

I did it!
I'm going up!
And next is Oriuchi Skate Club's
Azusa Saeki
BOO
?!
HAH
What... was that?!
GASP
はっ
No, I have to concentrate!
SWOOSH.

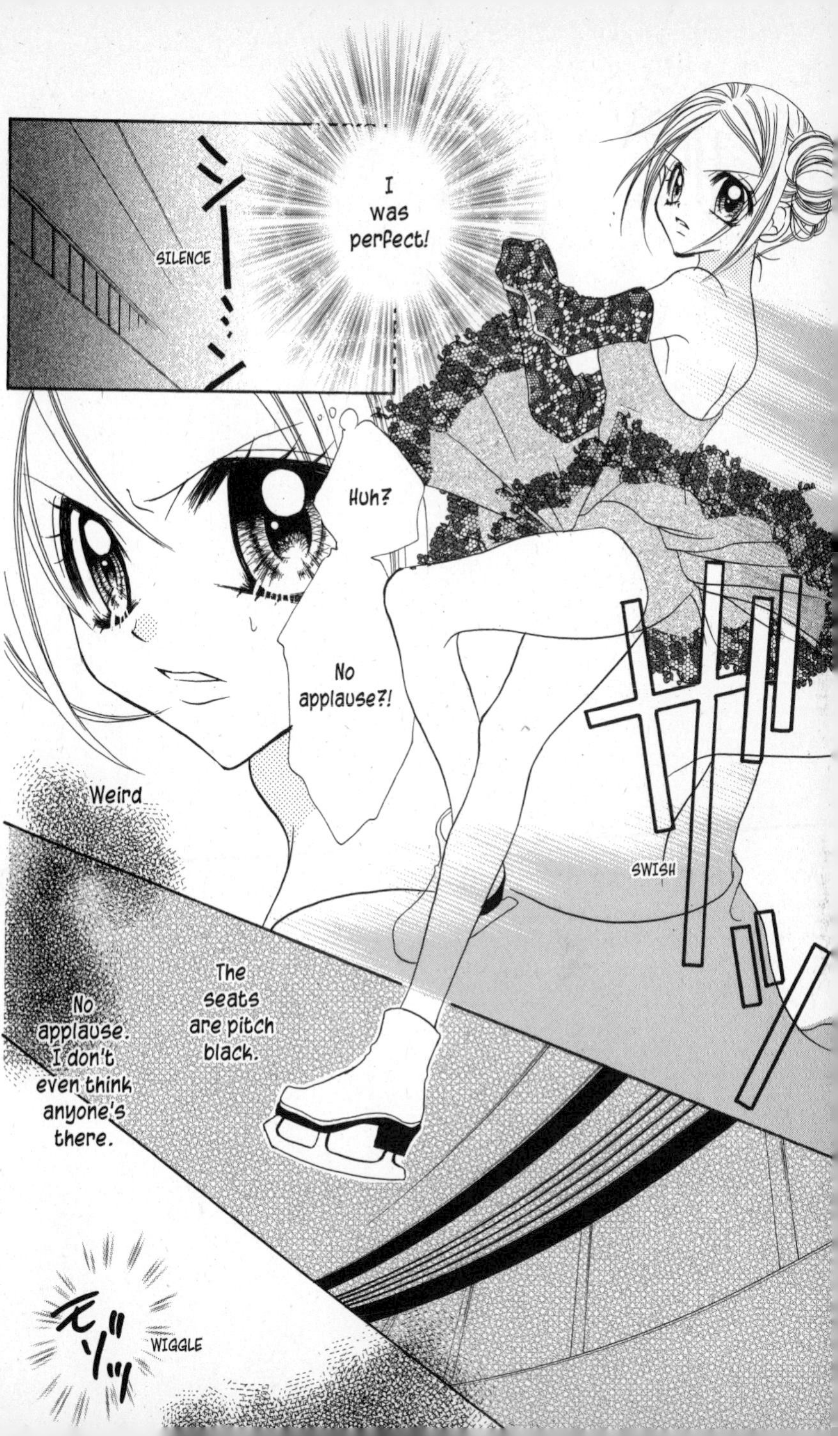
I was perfect!
SWISH
SILENCE
Huh?
No applause?!
Weird
The seats are pitch black.
No applause. I don't even think anyone's there.
WIGGLE

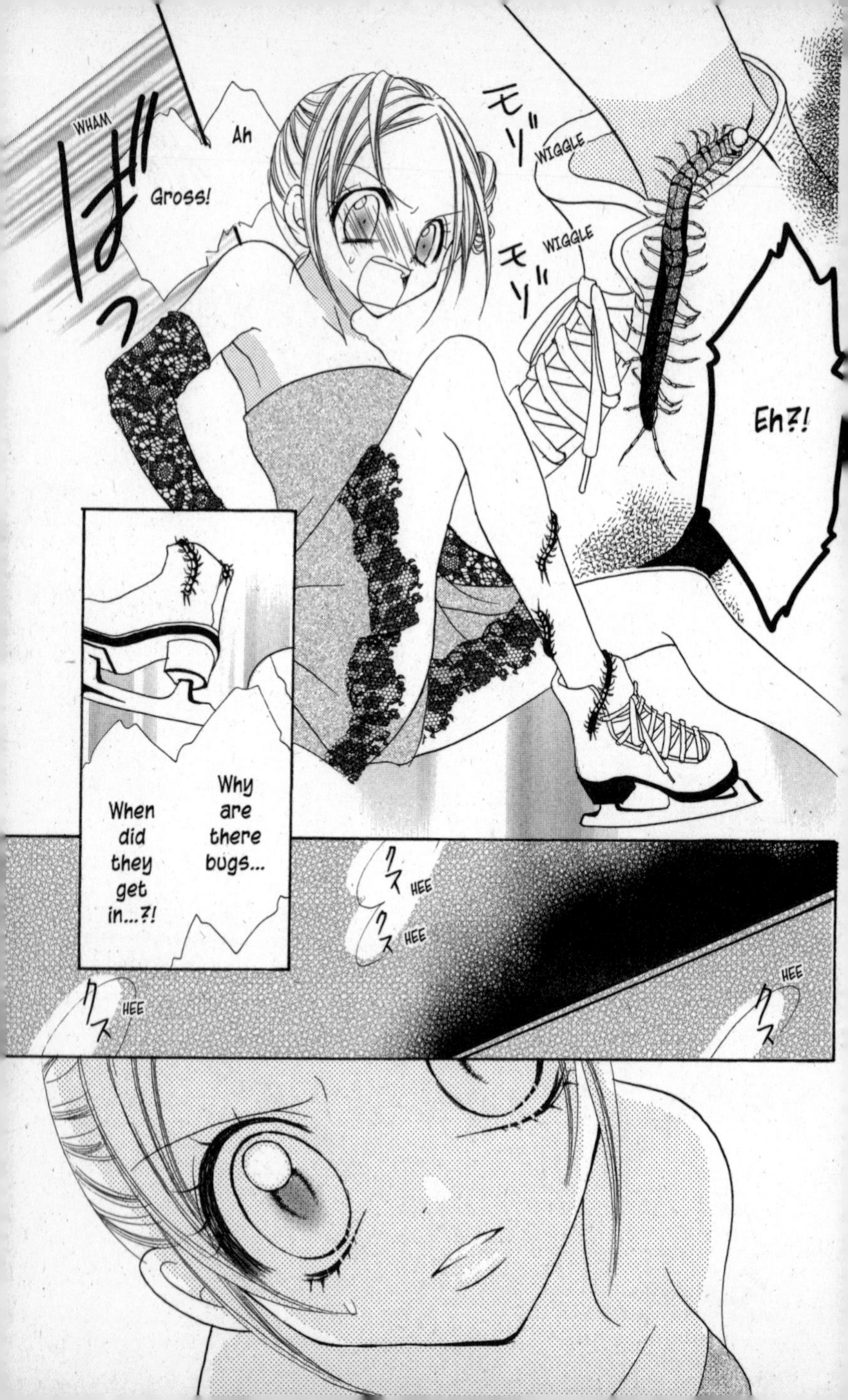
モゾ WIGGLE
モゾ WIGGLE
Ah
Gross!
ばっ WHAM
Eh?!
Why are there bugs...
When did they get in...?!
クス HEE
クス HEE
クス HEE
クス HEE

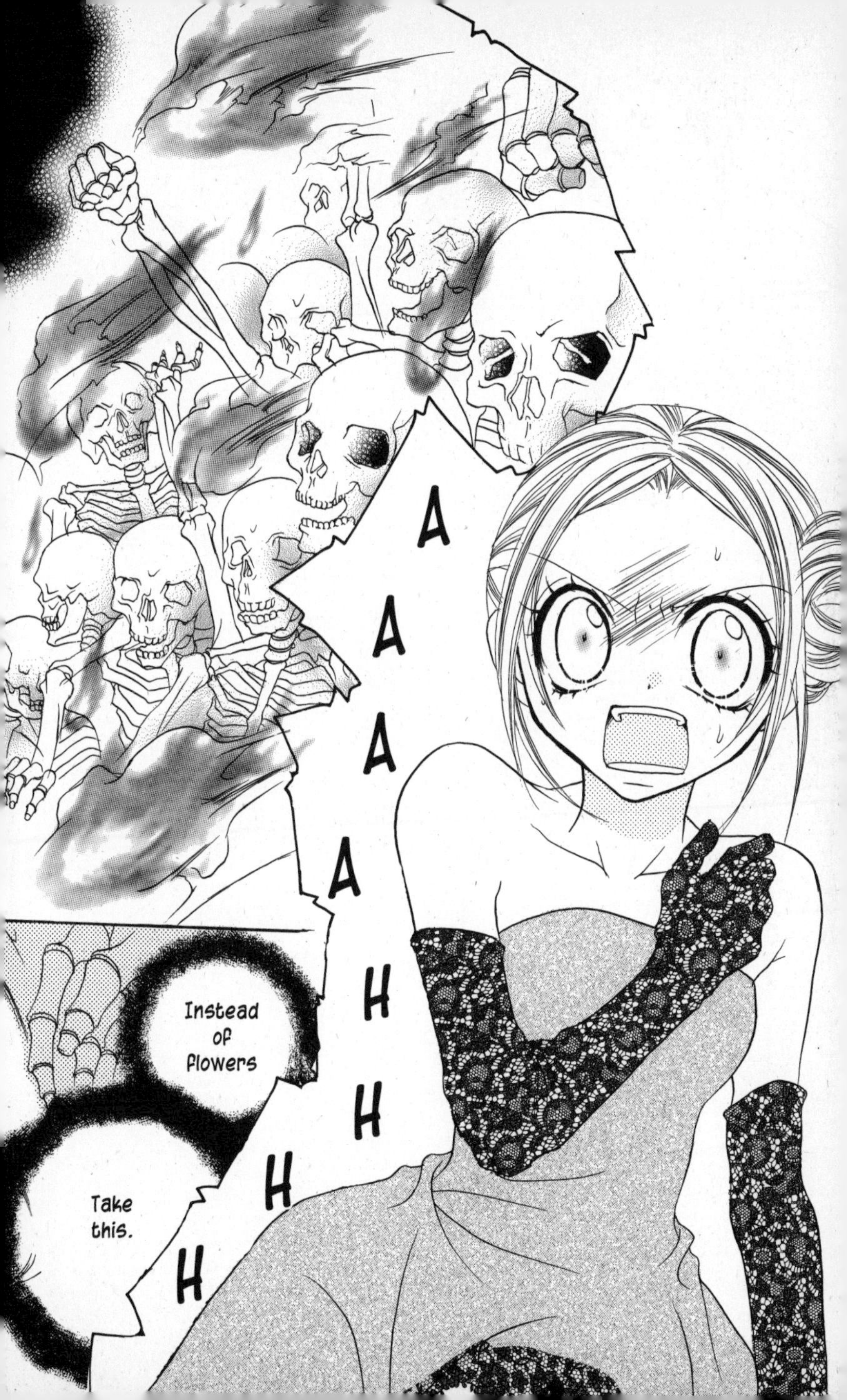
AAAAHHHH
Instead of flowers
Take this.

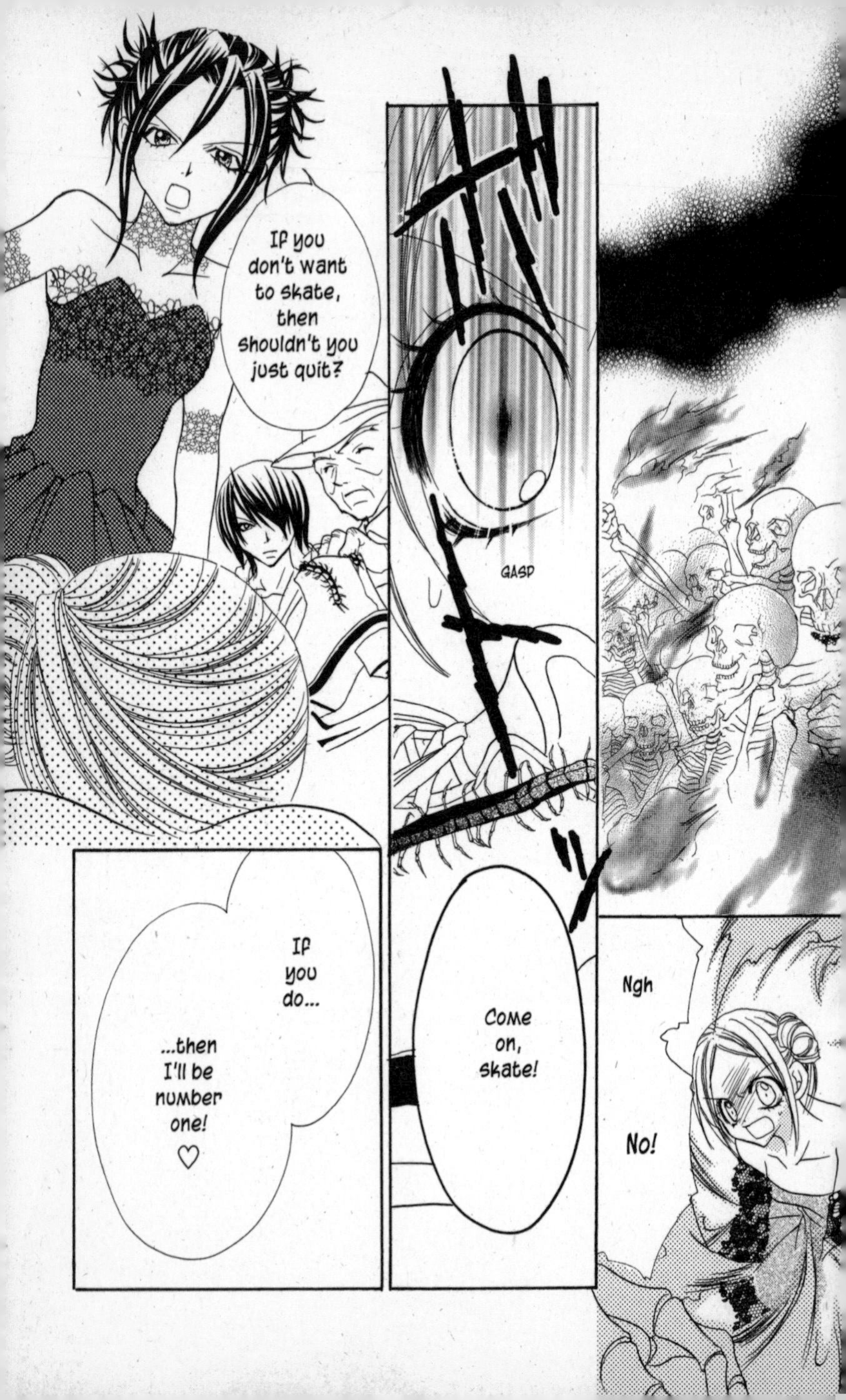
Ngh
No!
GASP
Come on, skate!
If you don't want to skate, then shouldn't you just quit?
If you do...
...then I'll be number one! ♡

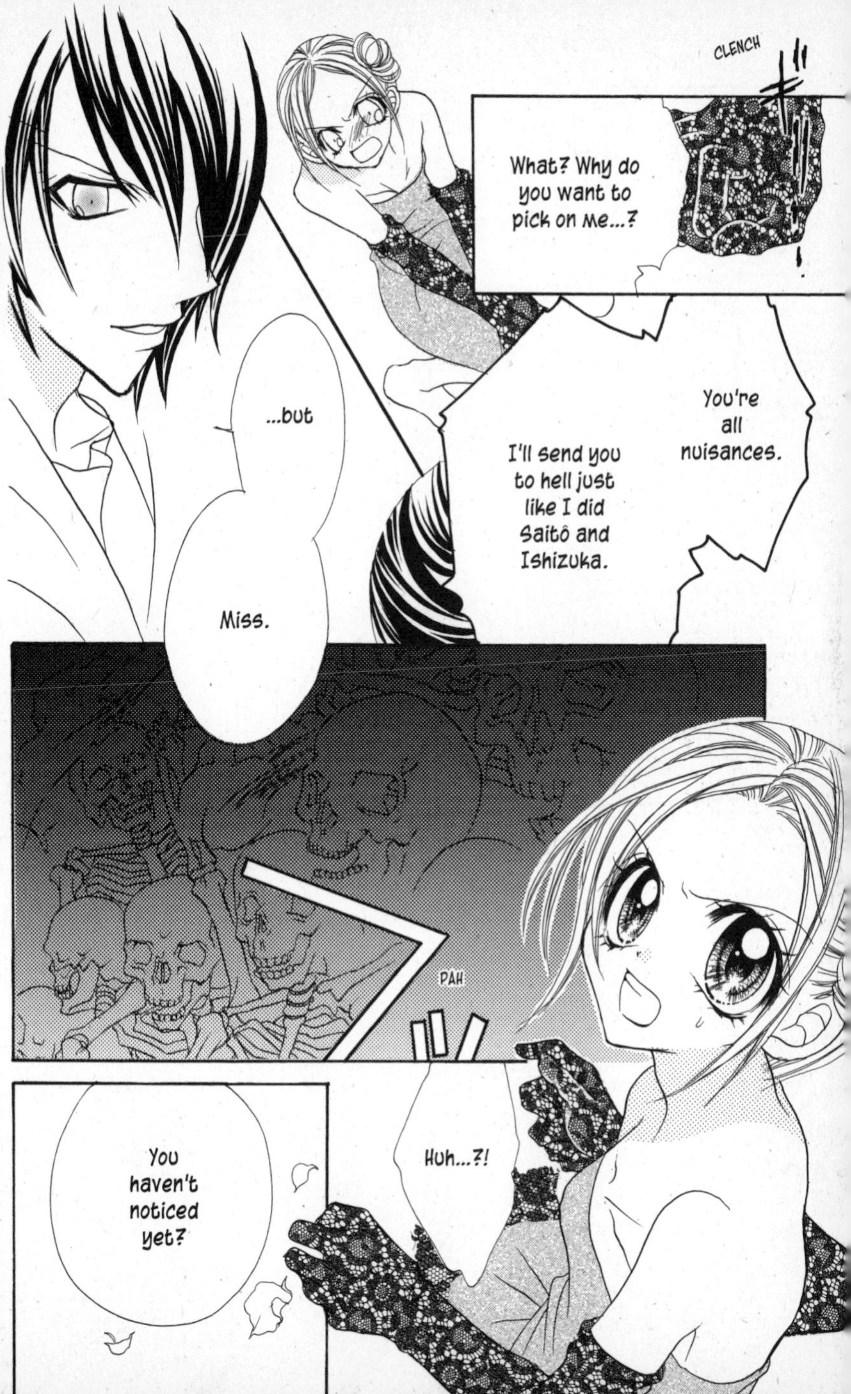
CLENCH
What? Why do you want to pick on me...?
You're all nuisances.
I'll send you to hell just like I did Saitô and Ishizuka.
...but
Miss.
PAH
Huh...?!
You haven't noticed yet?

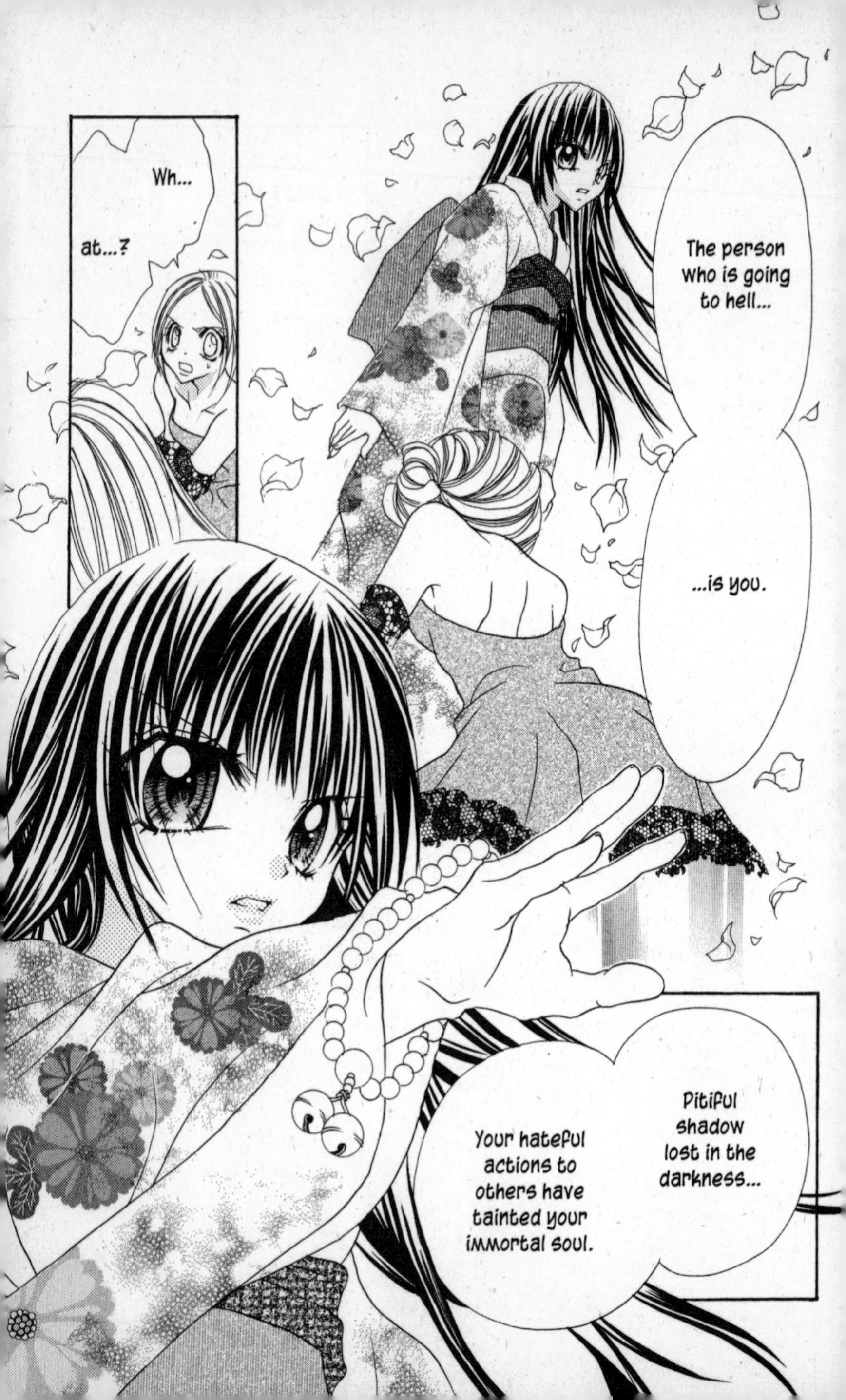
The person who is going to hell...
...is you.
Wh...
at...?
Pitiful shadow lost in the darkness...
Your hateful actions to others have tainted your immortal soul.

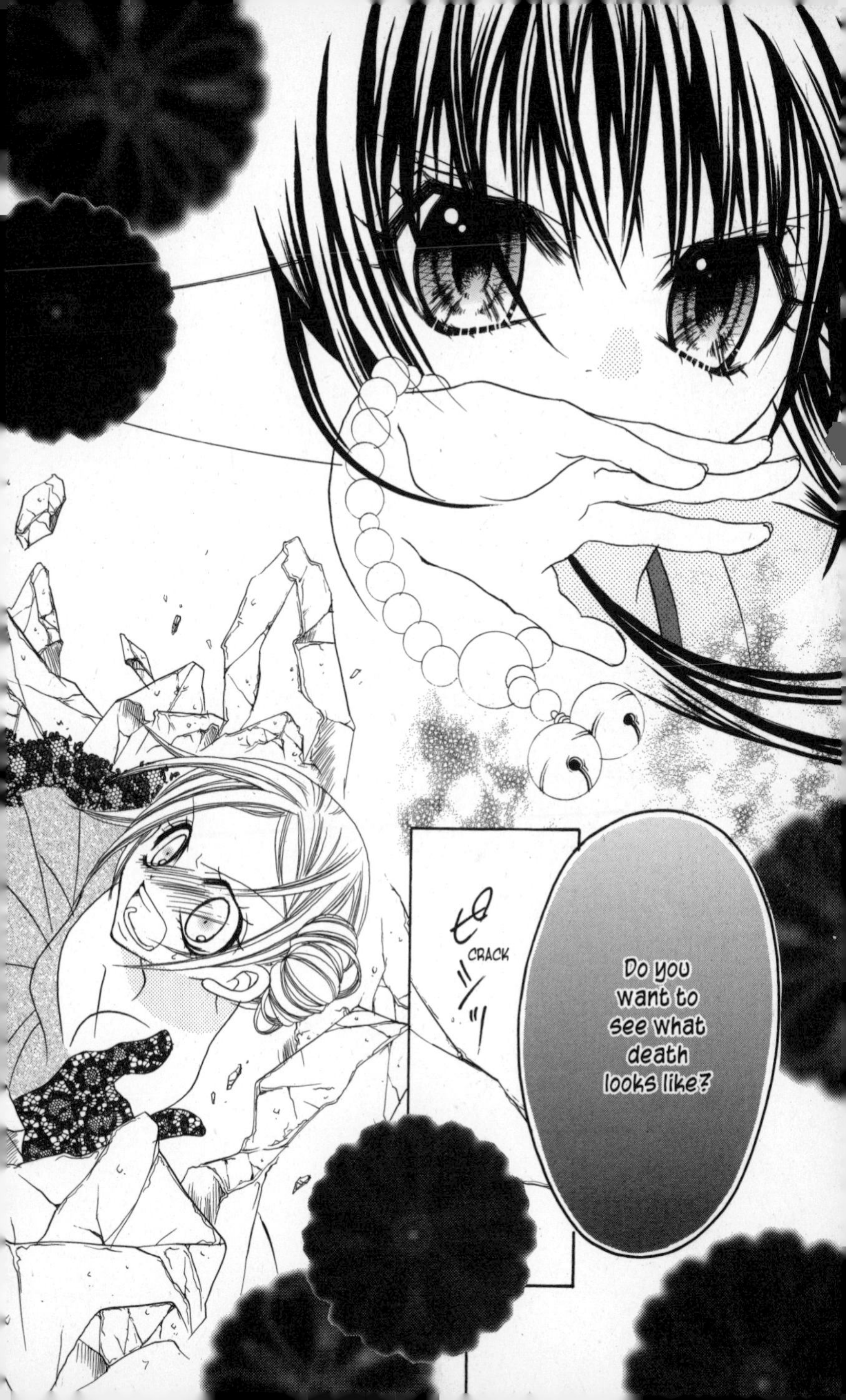
Do you want to see what death looks like?
CRACK

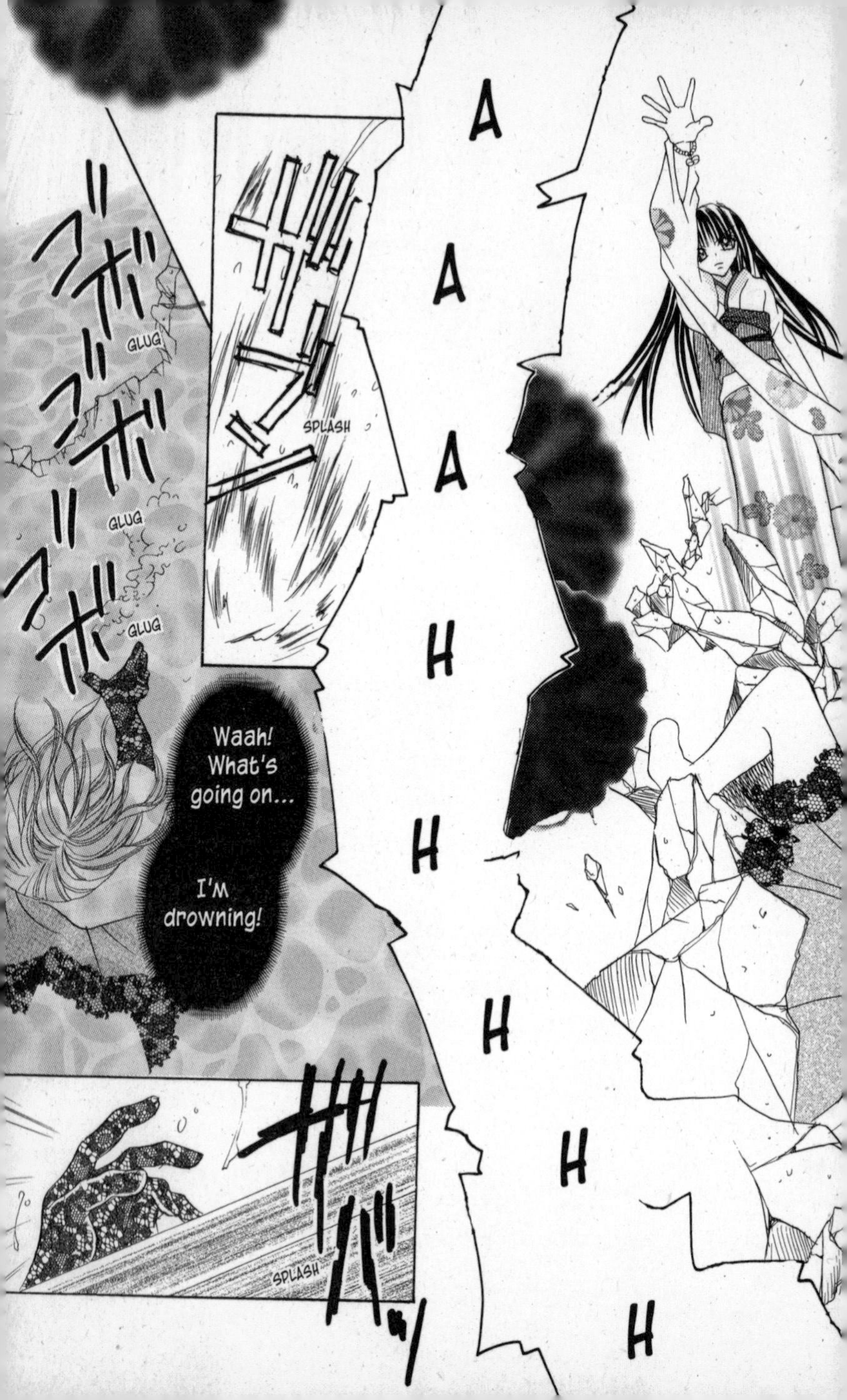

AAAHHHHHH
SPLASH
GLUG
GLUG
GLUG
Waah! What's going on...
I'M drowning!
SPLASH

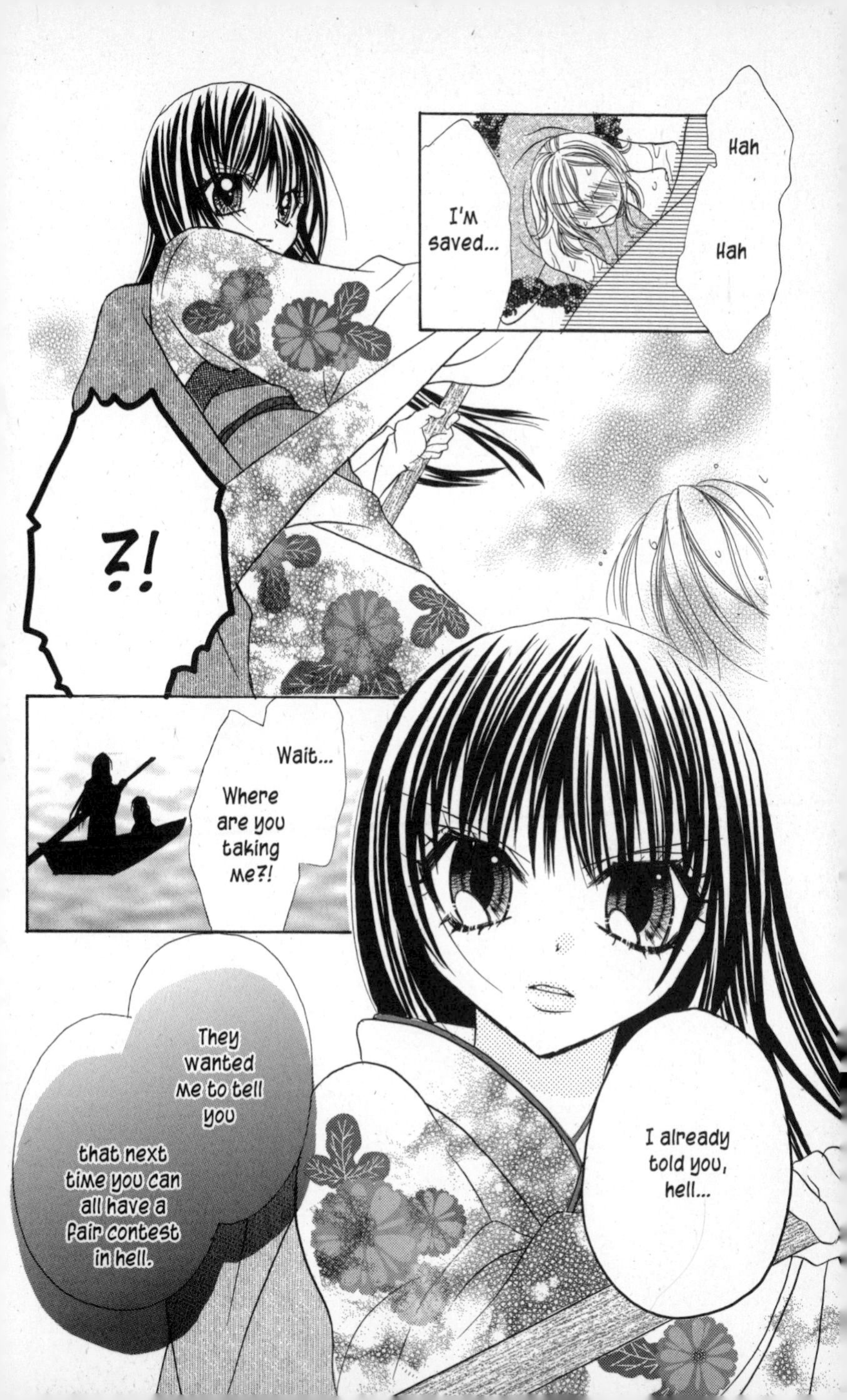
Hah
Hah
I'm saved...
?!
Wait...
Where are you taking me?!
I already told you, hell...
They wanted me to tell you
that next time you can all have a fair contest in hell.

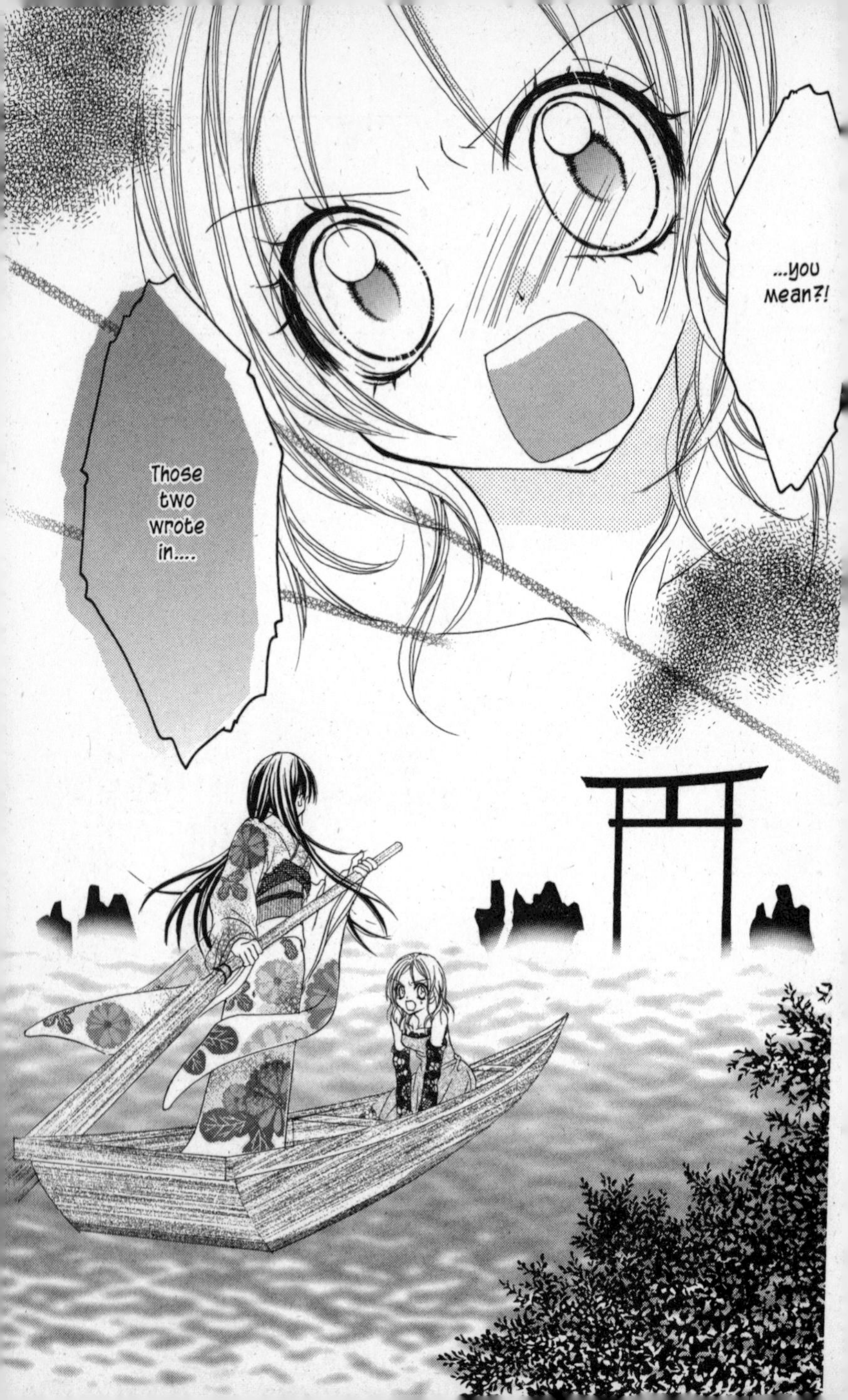
Those two wrote in....
...you mean?!

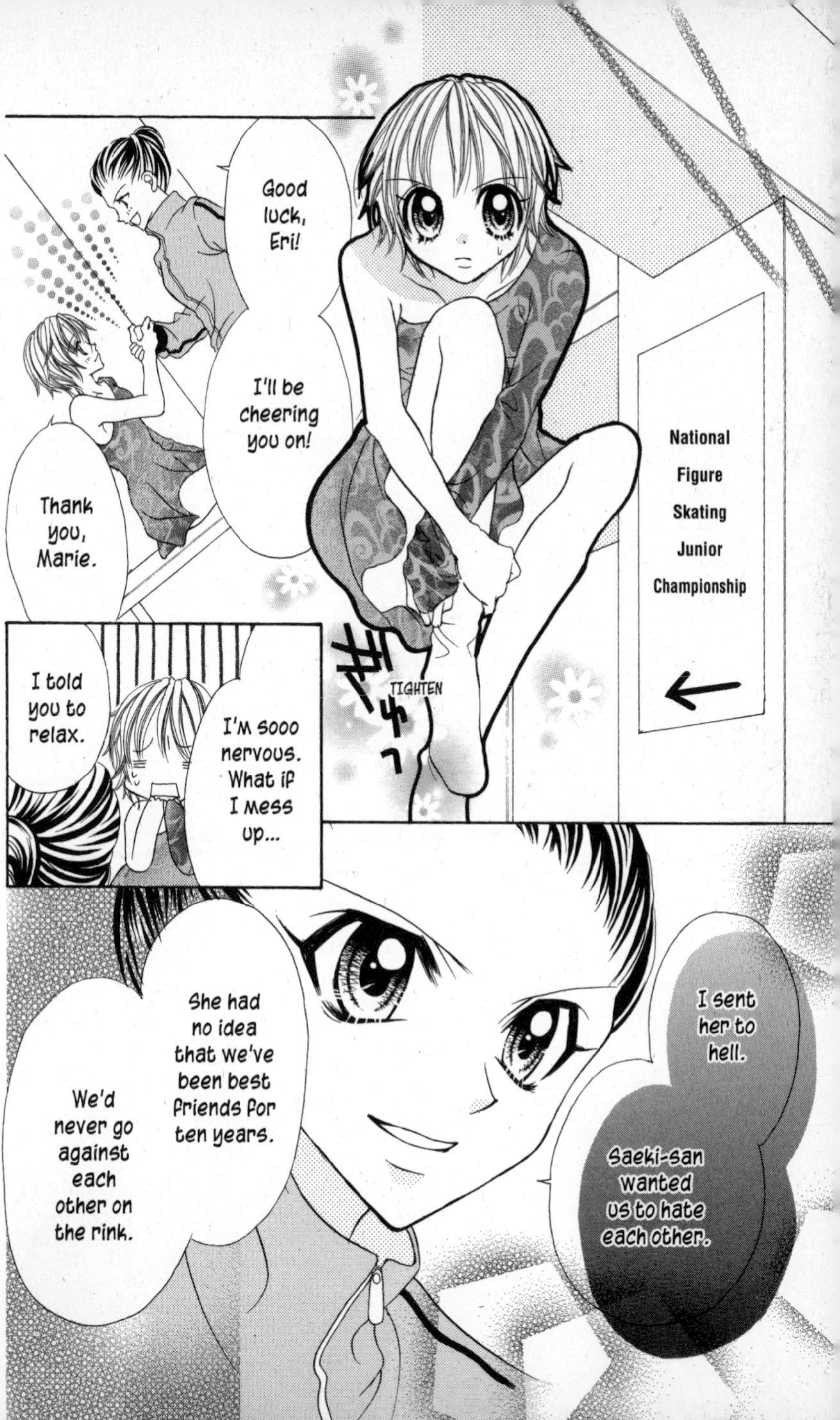
National Figure Skating Junior Championship
TIGHTEN
Good luck, Eri!
I'll be cheering you on!
Thank you, Marie.
I'm sooo nervous. What if I mess up...
I told you to relax.
I sent her to hell.
Saeki-san wanted us to hate each other.
She had no idea that we've been best friends for ten years.
We'd never go against each other on the rink.

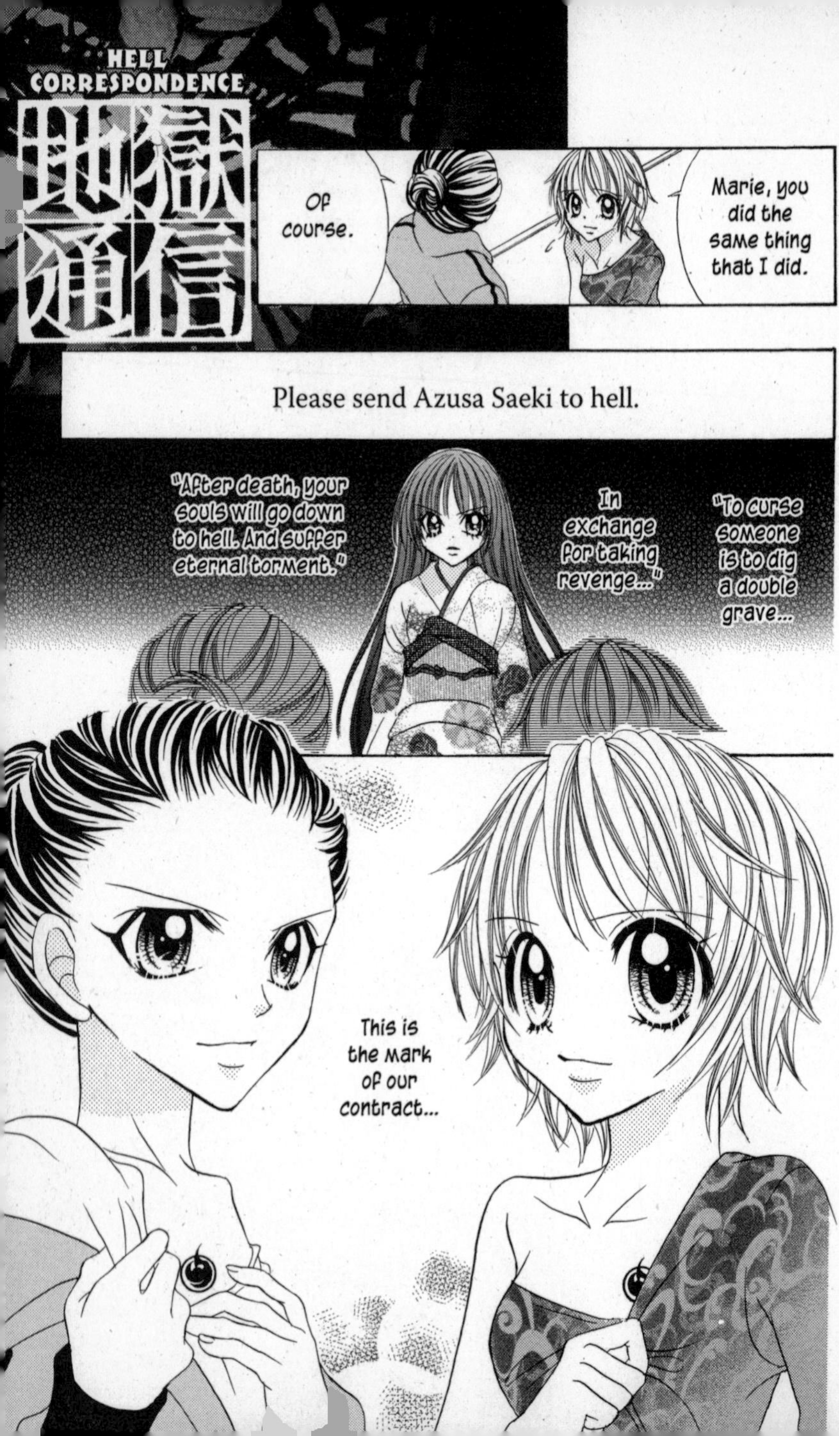
Marie, you did the same thing that I did.
Of course.
HELL CORRESPONDENCE
地獄通信
Please send Azusa Saeki to hell.
"To curse someone is to dig a double grave...
In exchange for taking revenge..."
"After death, your souls will go down to hell. And suffer eternal torment."
This is the mark of our contract...

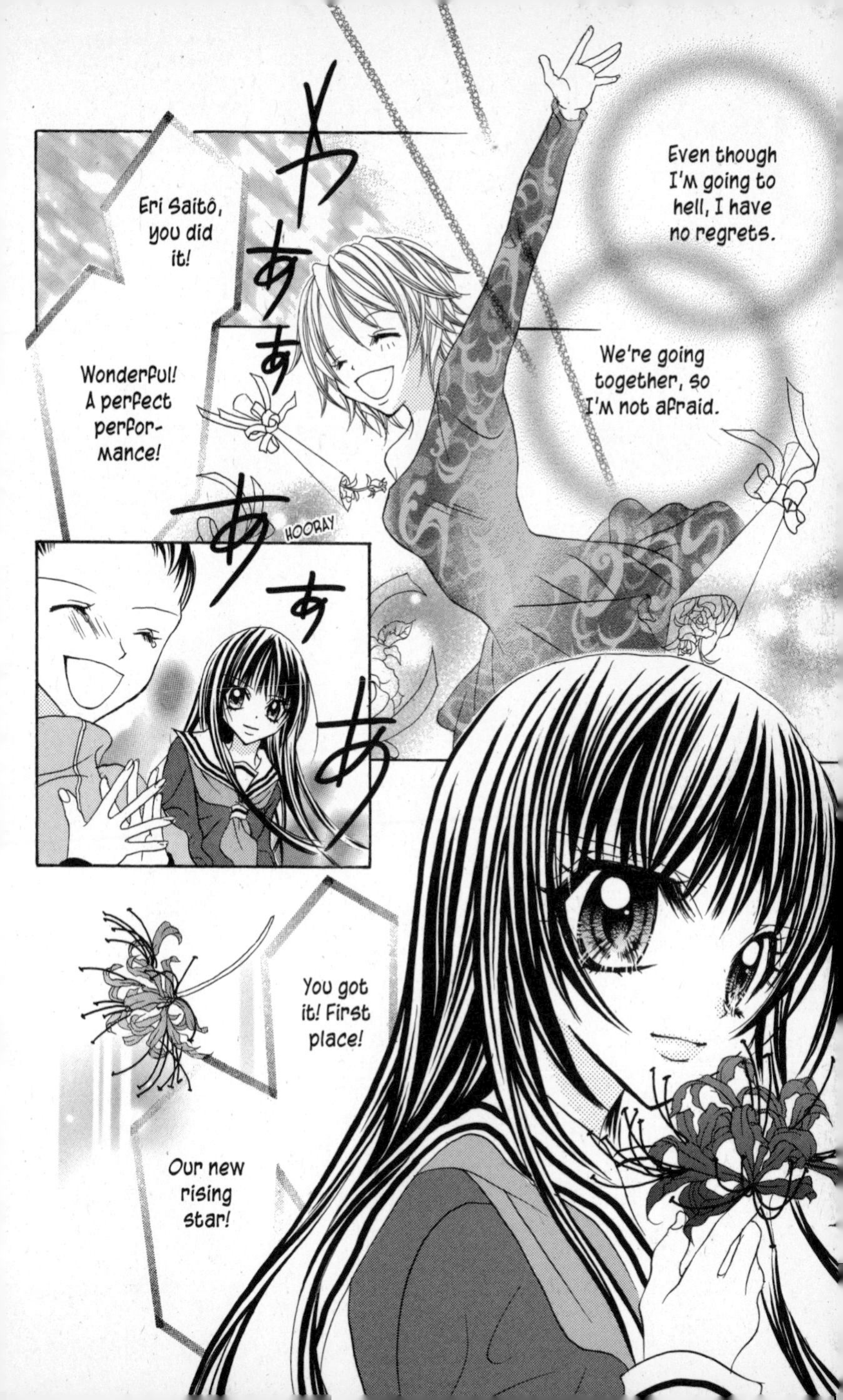
Even though I'm going to hell, I have no regrets.
Eri Saitô, you did it!
We're going together, so I'm not afraid.
Wonderful! A perfect performance!
わあぁあぁあ
HOORAY
You got it! First place!
Our new rising star!

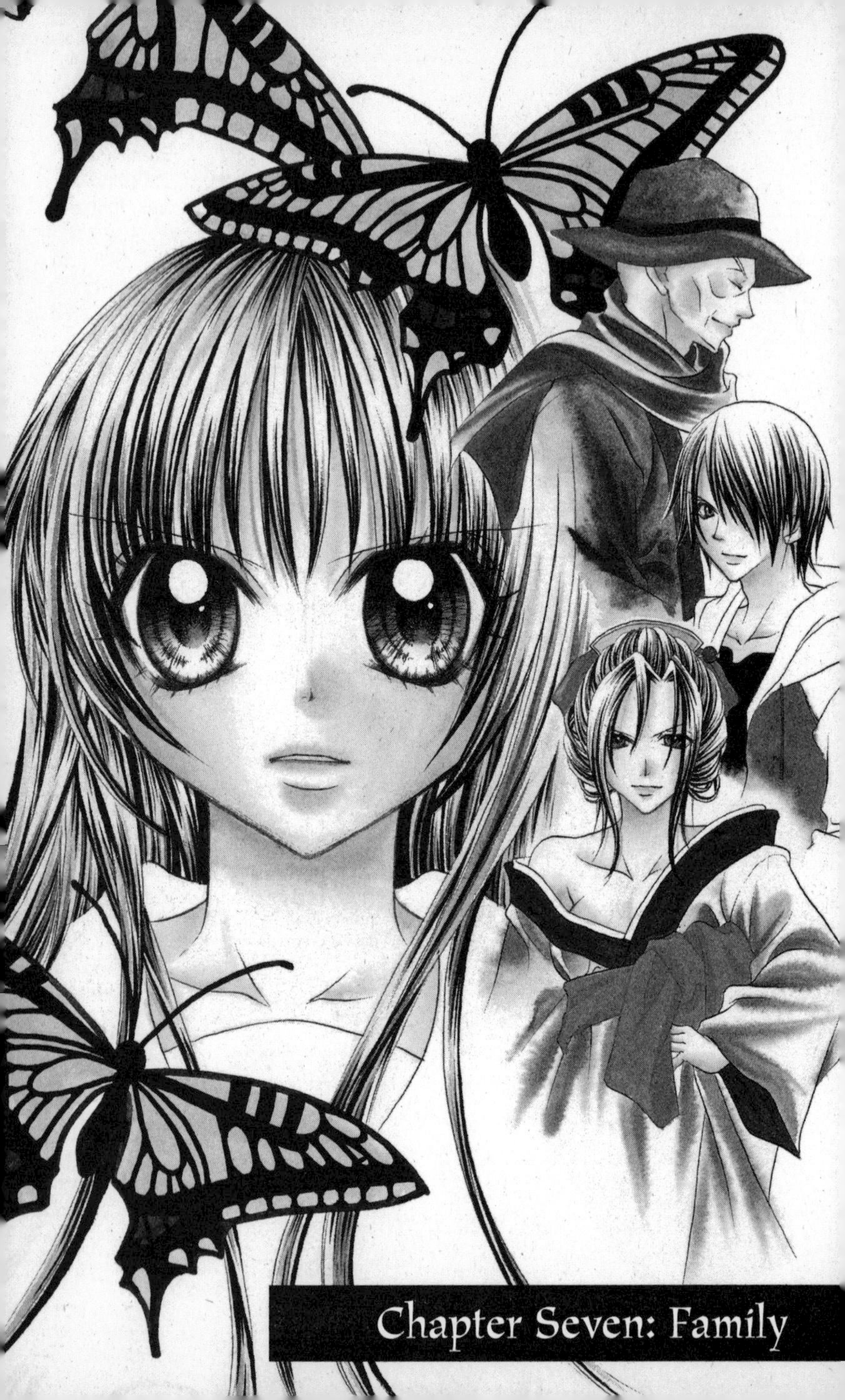

Chapter Seven: Family

Author's Note

Explanation and nonsense

(Mostly stupid) Eh...

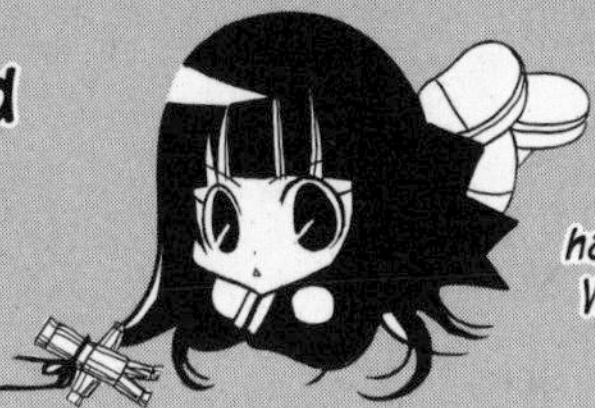

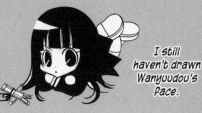

I still haven't drawn Wanyuudou's face.

Chapter Six "Ice Shadows"

"A clash on the sports field" was the vague theme. I don't really watch sports much (I don't understand the rules), so I tried watching baseball. From there I looked at the Olympics. That was how I reached ice-skating. A gold medal! And then I threw down the remote, it was so difficult to watch. When I'm doing the cleaning while I'm tired, the same tragic scene often occurs.

Chapter Seven "Family"

We were trying to get new *Nakayoshi* readers at that time, so I endeavored to make this story easy to understand. Because the pen twisted around a lot, I've started using a pen nib attached to a chopstick instead. When I try to use a regular pen now it feels weird.

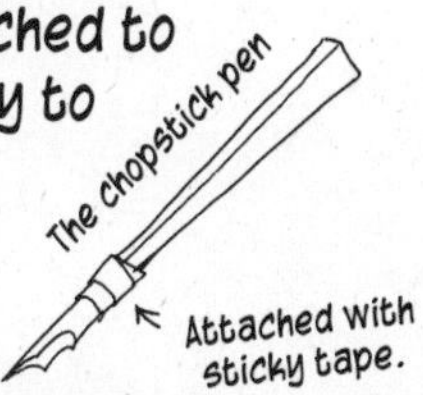
The chopstick pen
Attached with sticky tape.

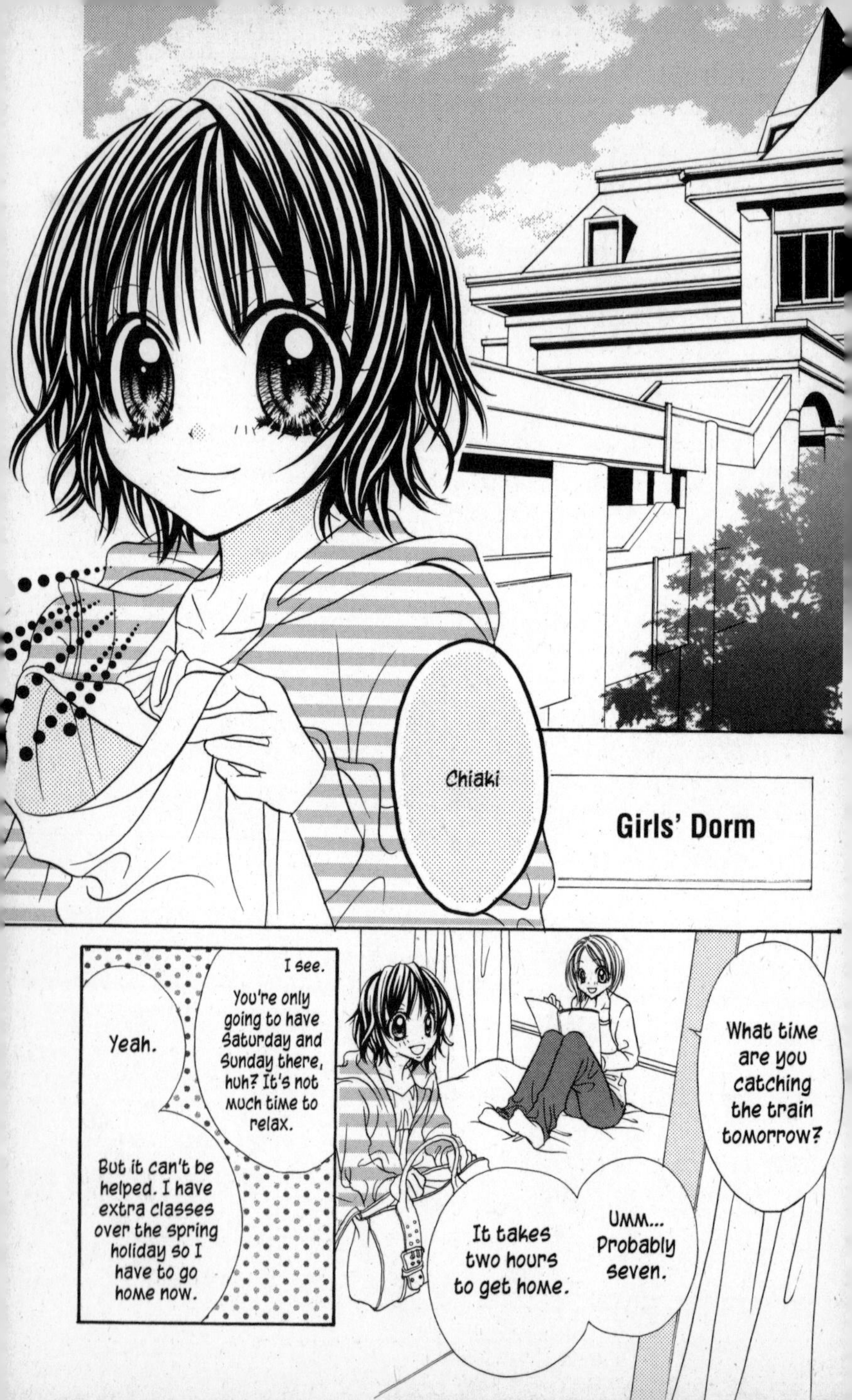
Girls' Dorm
Chiaki
What time are you catching the train tomorrow?
Umm... Probably seven.
It takes two hours to get home.
I see. You're only going to have Saturday and Sunday there, huh? It's not much time to relax.
Yeah.
But it can't be helped. I have extra classes over the spring holiday so I have to go home now.

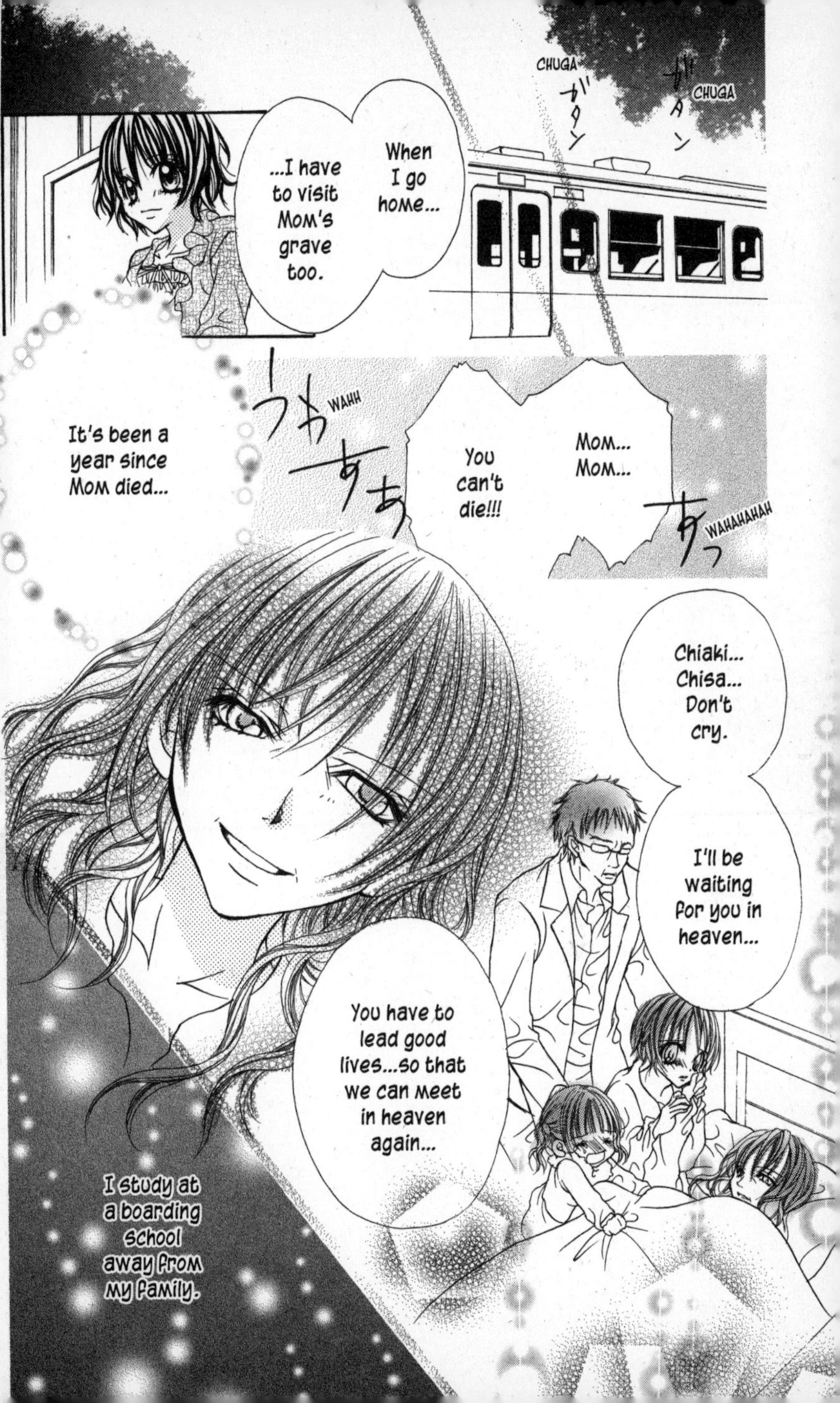
CHUGA
CHUGA
When I go home...
...I have to visit Mom's grave too.
It's been a year since Mom died...
Mom... Mom...
You can't die!!!
WAHAHAHAH
WAHH
Chiaki... Chisa... Don't cry.
I'll be waiting for you in heaven...
You have to lead good lives...so that we can meet in heaven again...
I study at a boarding school away from my family.

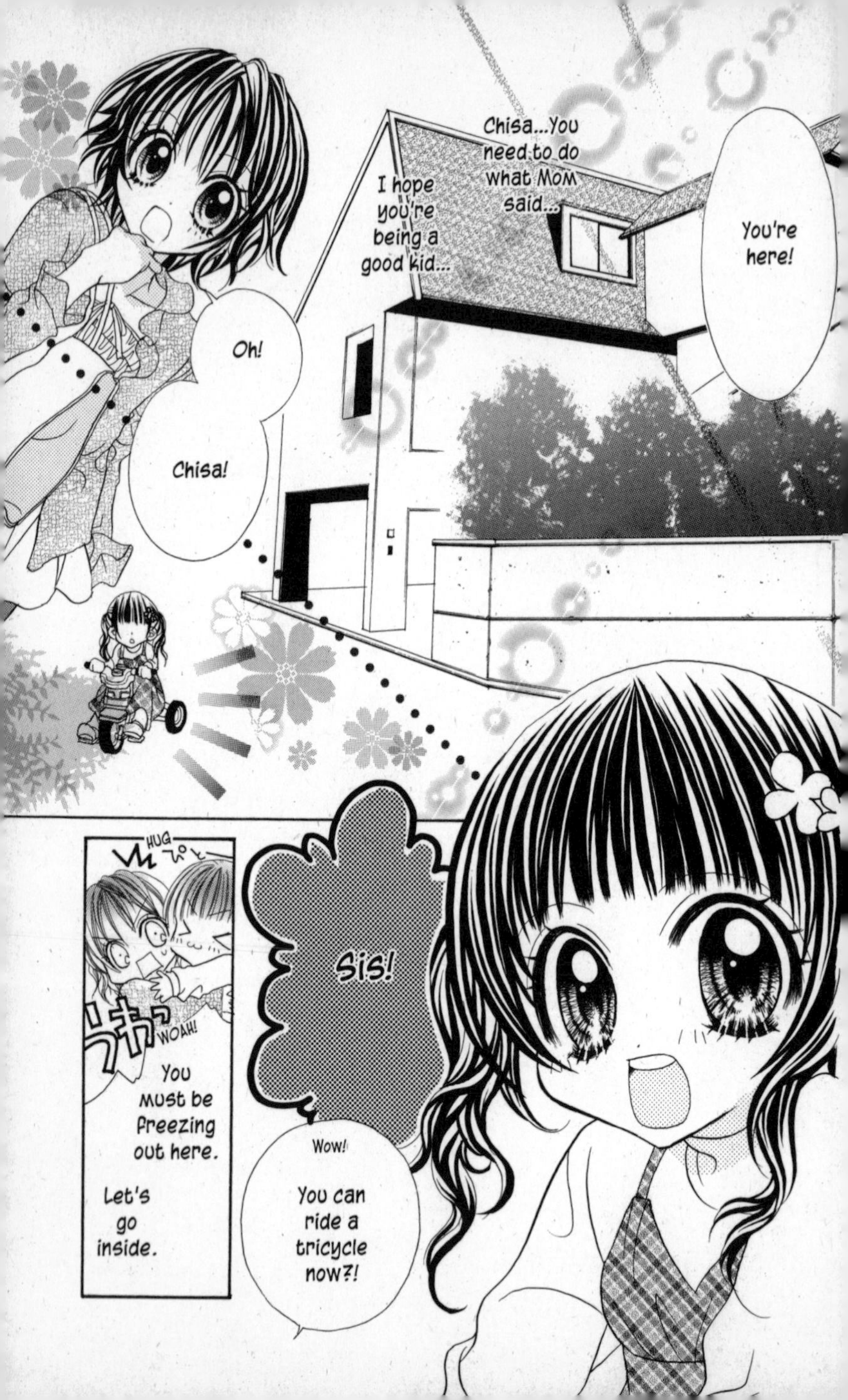

You're here!
Chisa...You need to do what Mom said...
I hope you're being a good kid...
Oh!
Chisa!
Sis!
Wow!
You can ride a tricycle now?!
HUG
WOAH!
You must be freezing out here.
Let's go inside.

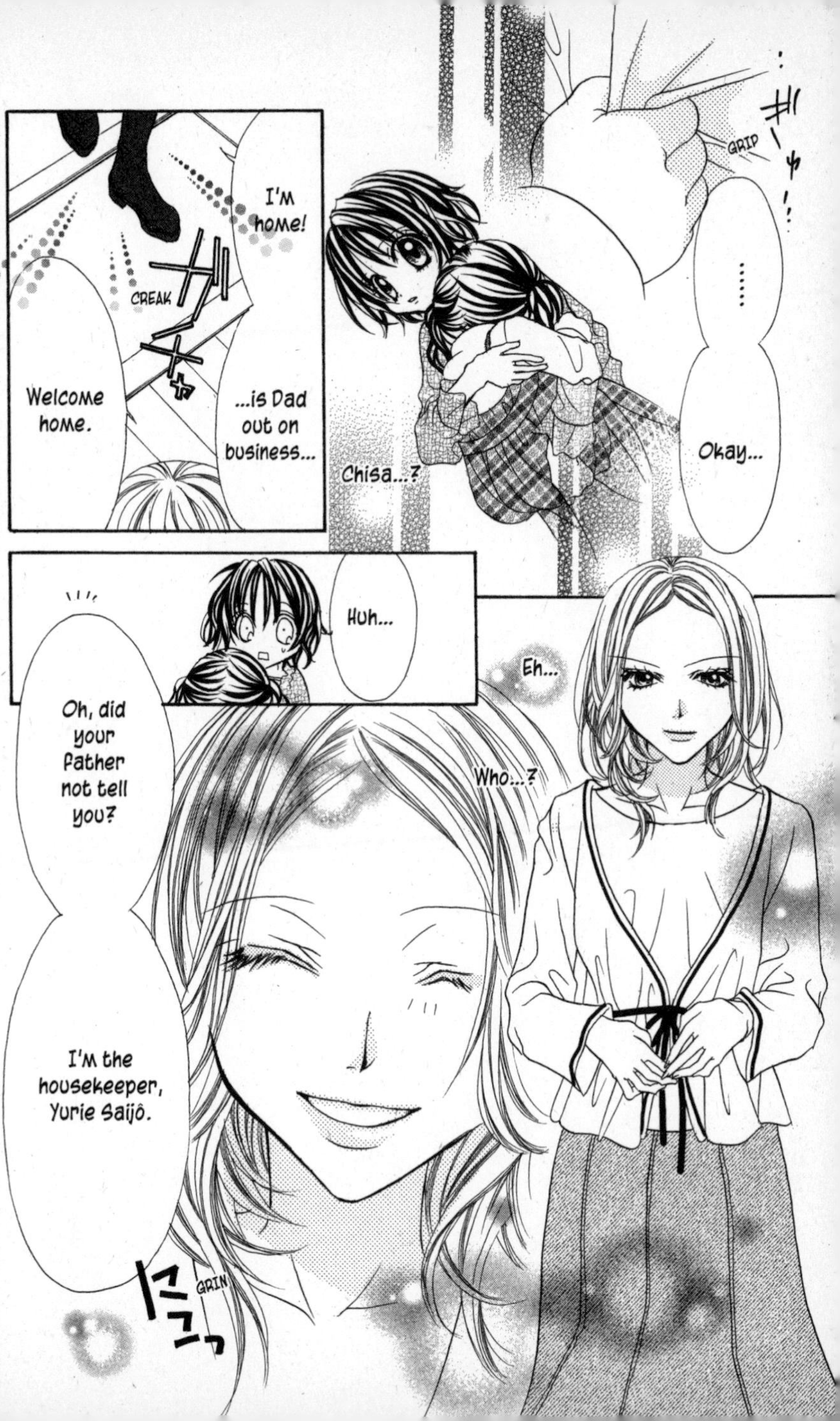
GRIP
......
Okay...
Chisa...?
I'm home!
CREAK
...is Dad out on business...
Welcome home.
Huh...
Eh...
Who...?
Oh, did your father not tell you?
I'm the housekeeper, Yurie Saijô.
GRIN

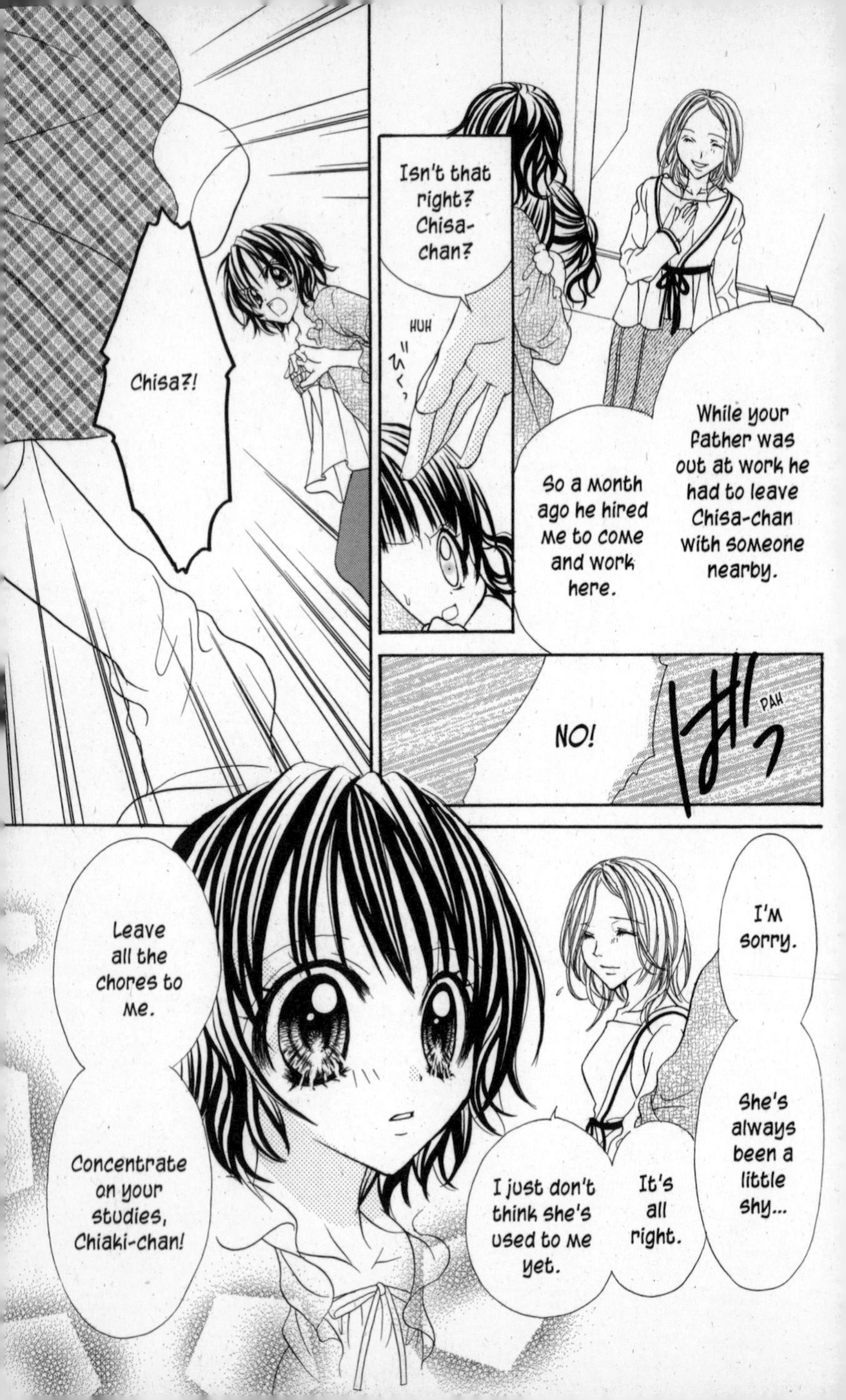
While your father was out at work he had to leave Chisa-chan with someone nearby.
So a month ago he hired me to come and work here.
Isn't that right? Chisa-chan?
HUH
ひくっ
NO!
はっ
PAH
Chisa?!
I'm sorry.
She's always been a little shy...
It's all right.
I just don't think she's used to me yet.
Leave all the chores to me.
Concentrate on your studies, Chiaki-chan!

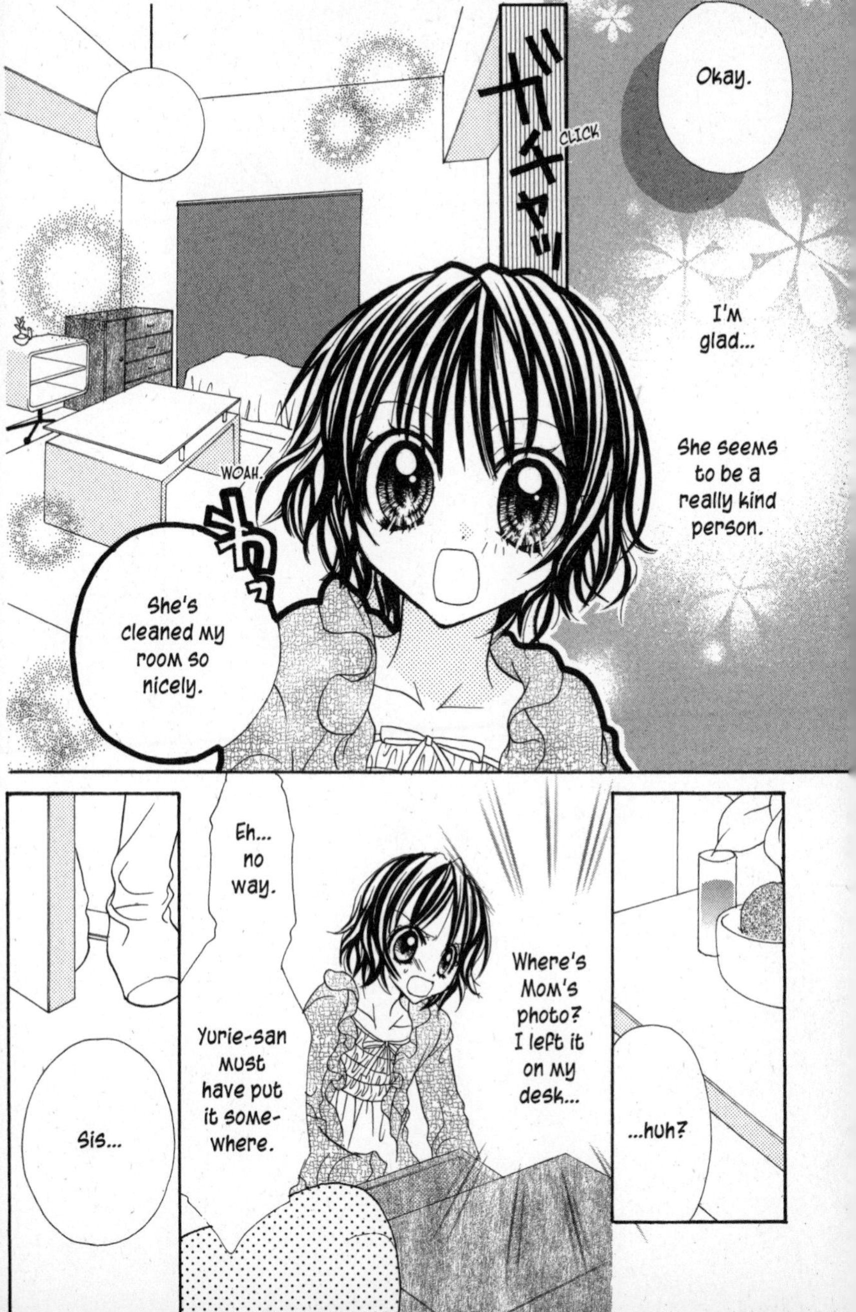
Okay.
ガチャッ
CLICK
I'm glad...
She seems to be a really kind person.
WOAH.
She's cleaned my room so nicely.
...huh?
Where's Mom's photo? I left it on my desk...
Eh... no way.
Yurie-san must have put it somewhere.
Sis...

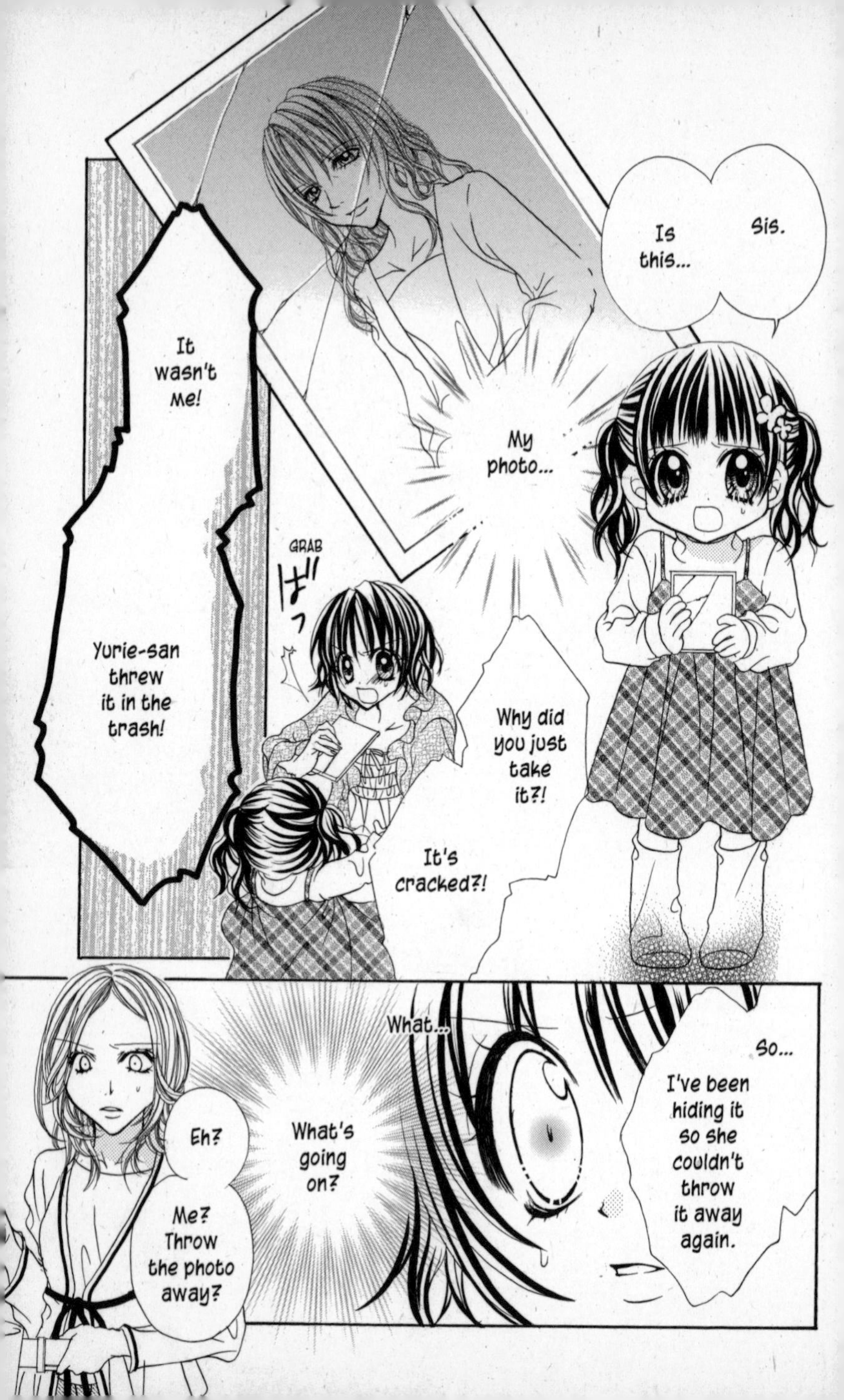
Sis.
Is this...
My photo...
GRAB
ばっ
Why did you just take it?!
It's cracked?!
It wasn't me!
Yurie-san threw it in the trash!
So...
I've been hiding it so she couldn't throw it away again.
What...
What's going on?
Eh?
Me? Throw the photo away?

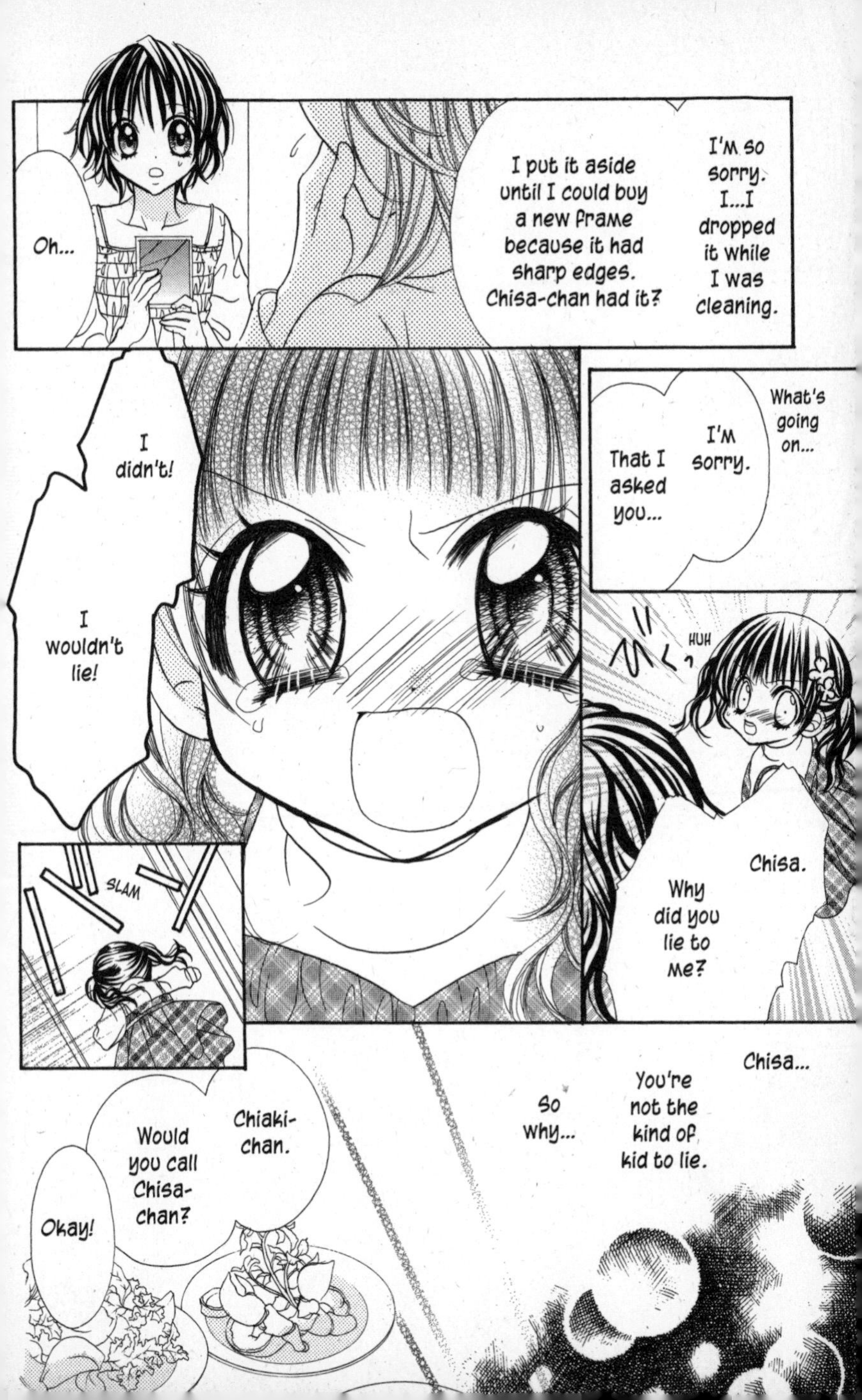
I'm so sorry. I...I dropped it while I was cleaning.
I put it aside until I could buy a new frame because it had sharp edges. Chisa-chan had it?
Oh...
What's going on...
I'm sorry.
That I asked you...
HUH
Chisa.
Why did you lie to me?
I didn't!
I wouldn't lie!
SLAM
Chisa...
You're not the kind of kid to lie.
So why...
Chiaki-chan.
Would you call Chisa-chan?
Okay!

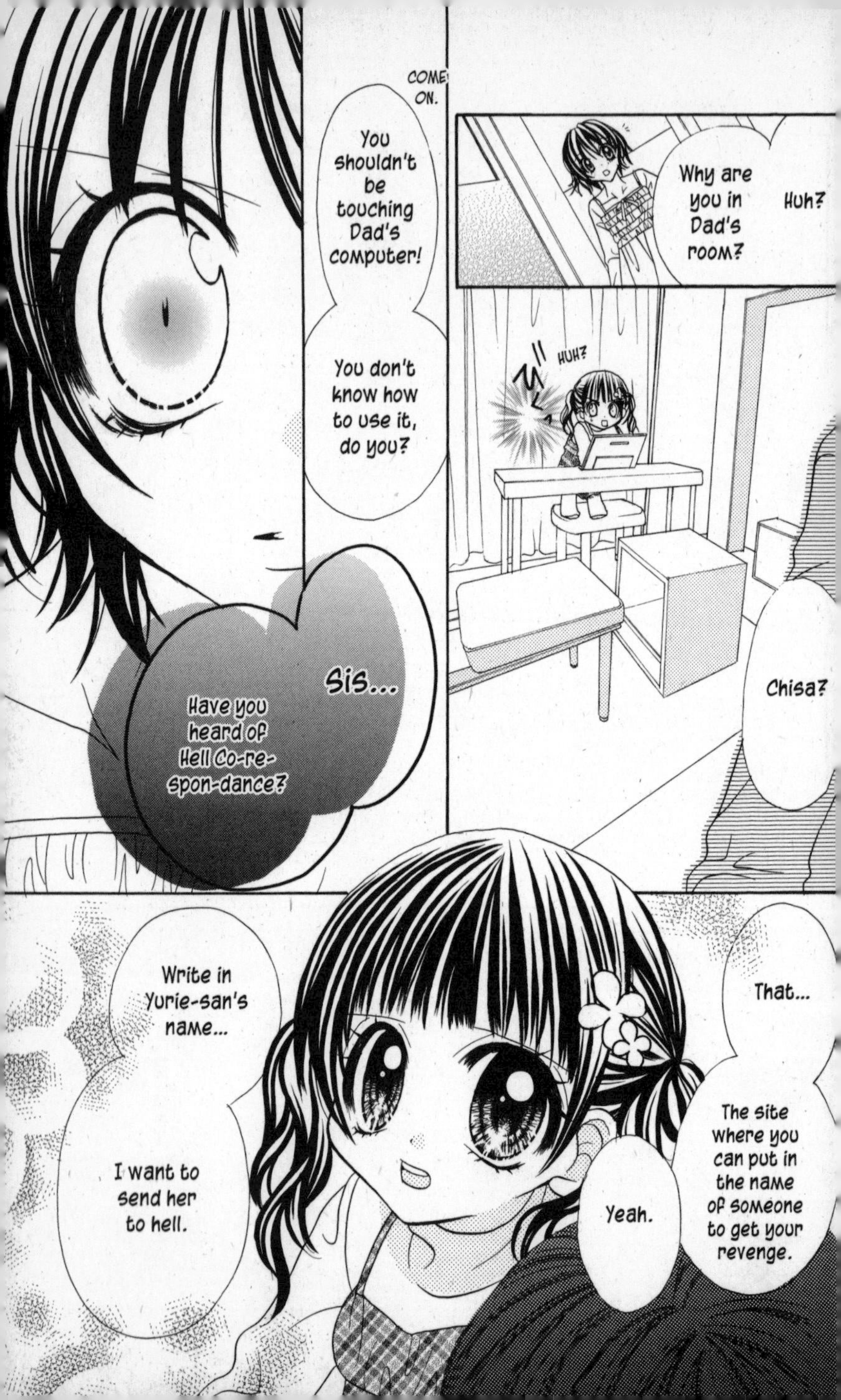
Huh?
Why are you in Dad's room?
Chisa?
HUH?
COME ON.
You shouldn't be touching Dad's computer!
You don't know how to use it, do you?
Sis...
Have you heard of Hell Co-re-spon-dance?
That...
The site where you can put in the name of someone to get your revenge.
Yeah.
Write in Yurie-san's name...
I want to send her to hell.

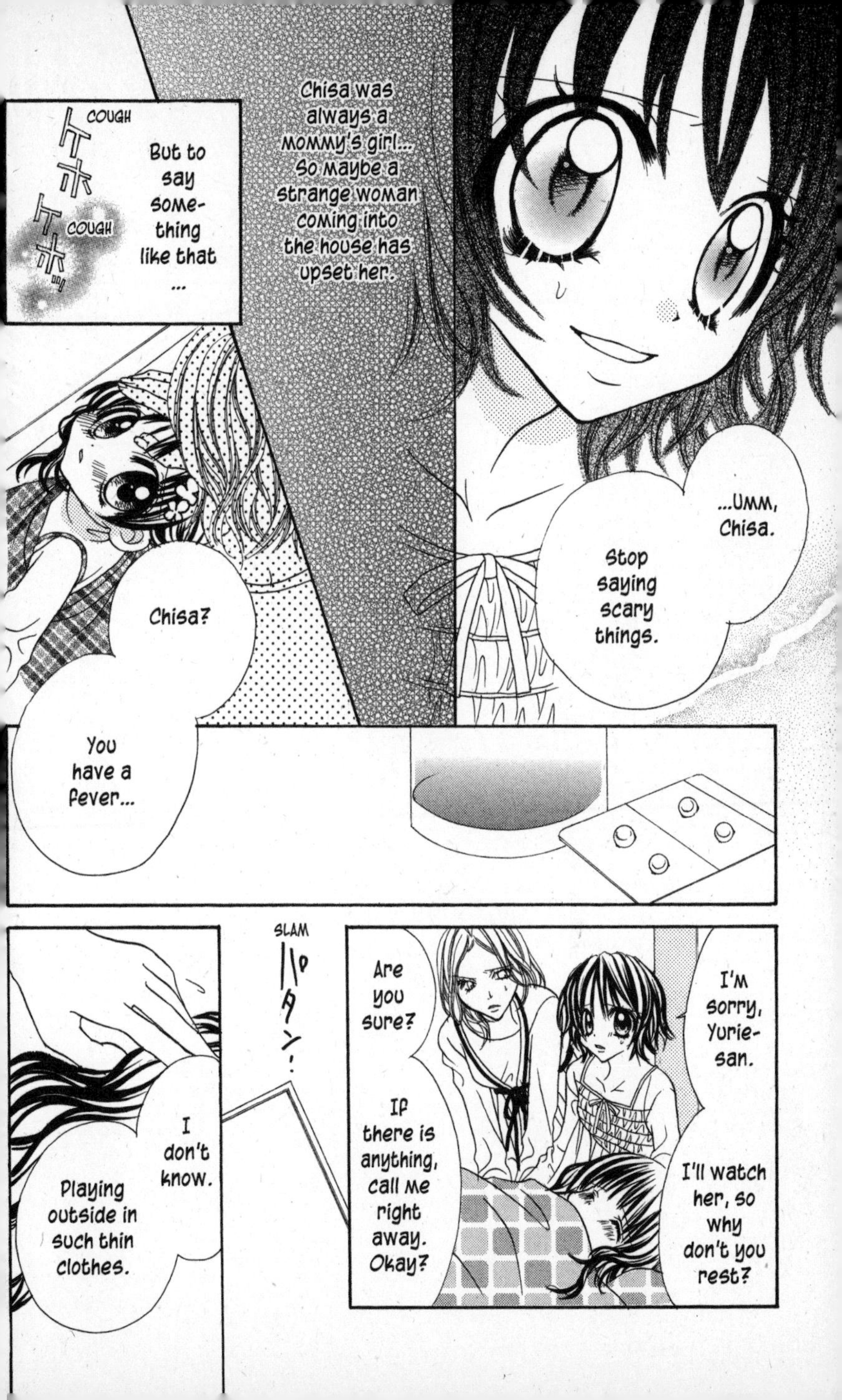
...Umm, Chisa.
Stop saying scary things.
Chisa was always a mommy's girl... So maybe a strange woman coming into the house has upset her.
But to say some-thing like that ...
COUGH
ケホ
COUGH
ケホ
Chisa?
You have a fever...
I'm sorry, Yurie-san.
I'll watch her, so why don't you rest?
Are you sure?
If there is anything, call me right away. Okay?
SLAM
バタン
I don't know.
Playing outside in such thin clothes.

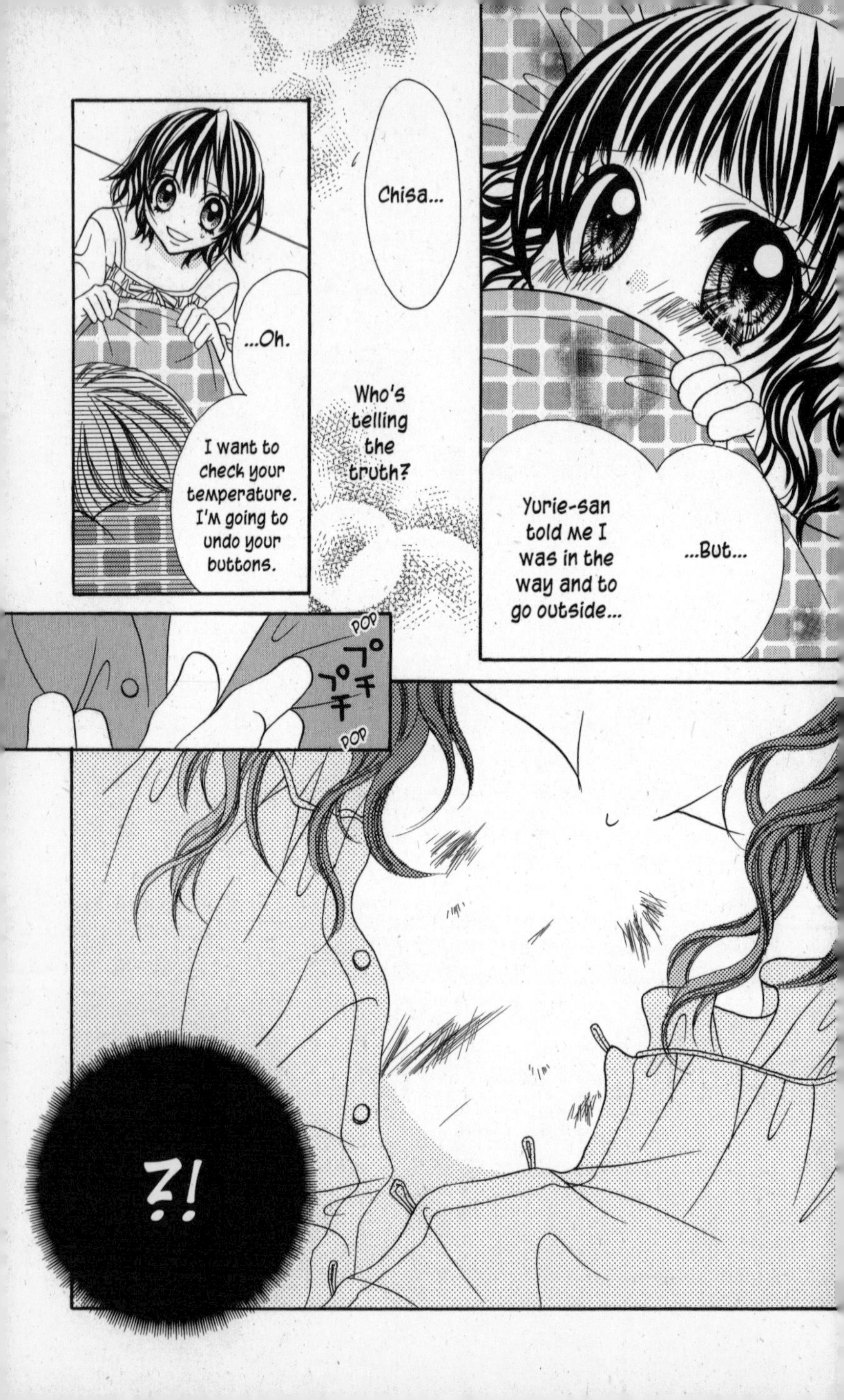
Yurie-san told me I was in the way and to go outside...
...But...
Chisa...
Who's telling the truth?
...Oh.
I want to check your temperature. I'm going to undo your buttons.
POP
プチ
プチ
POP
?!

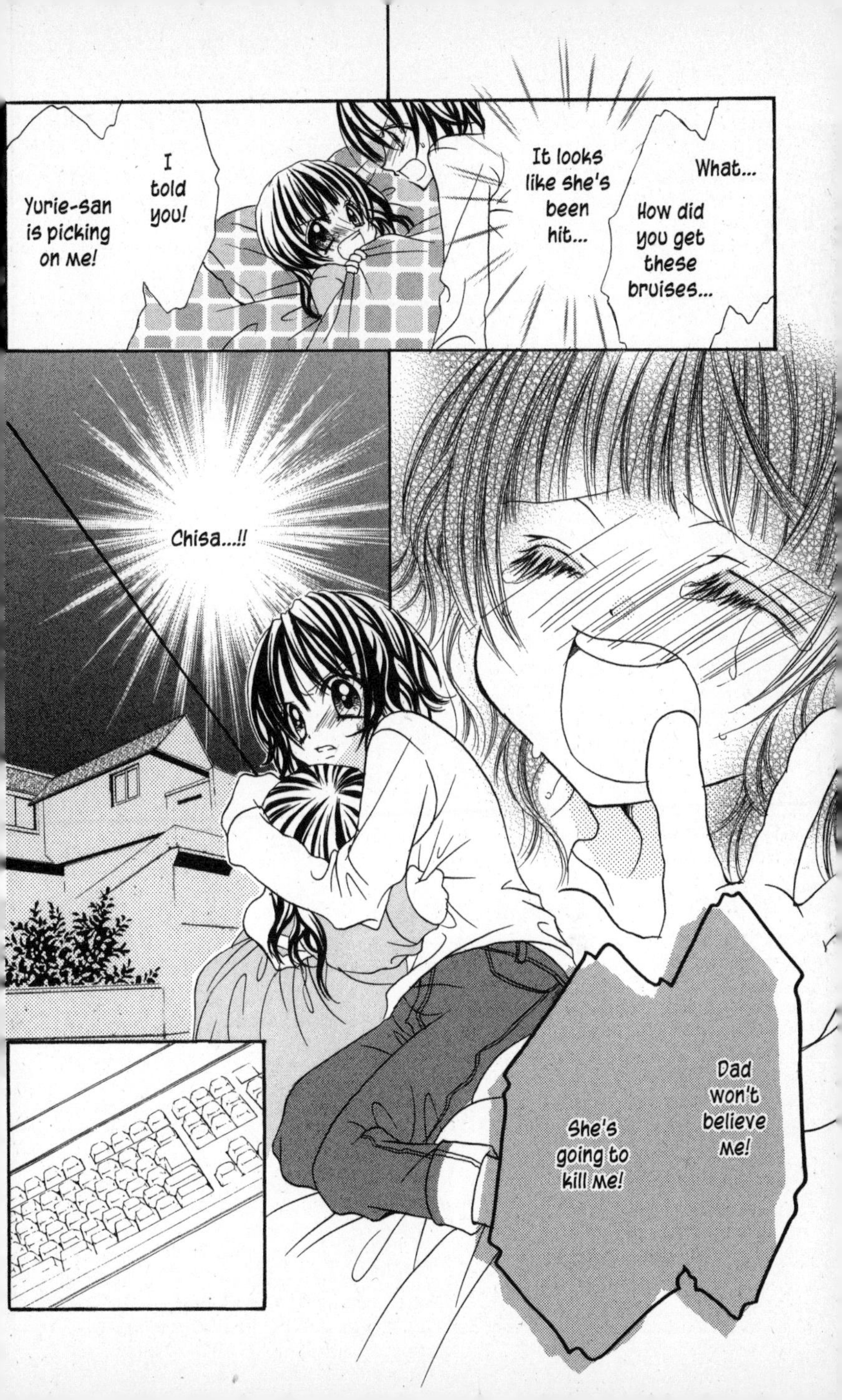
What...
How did you get these bruises...
It looks like she's been hit...
I told you!
Yurie-san is picking on me!
Dad won't believe me!
She's going to kill me!
Chisa...!!

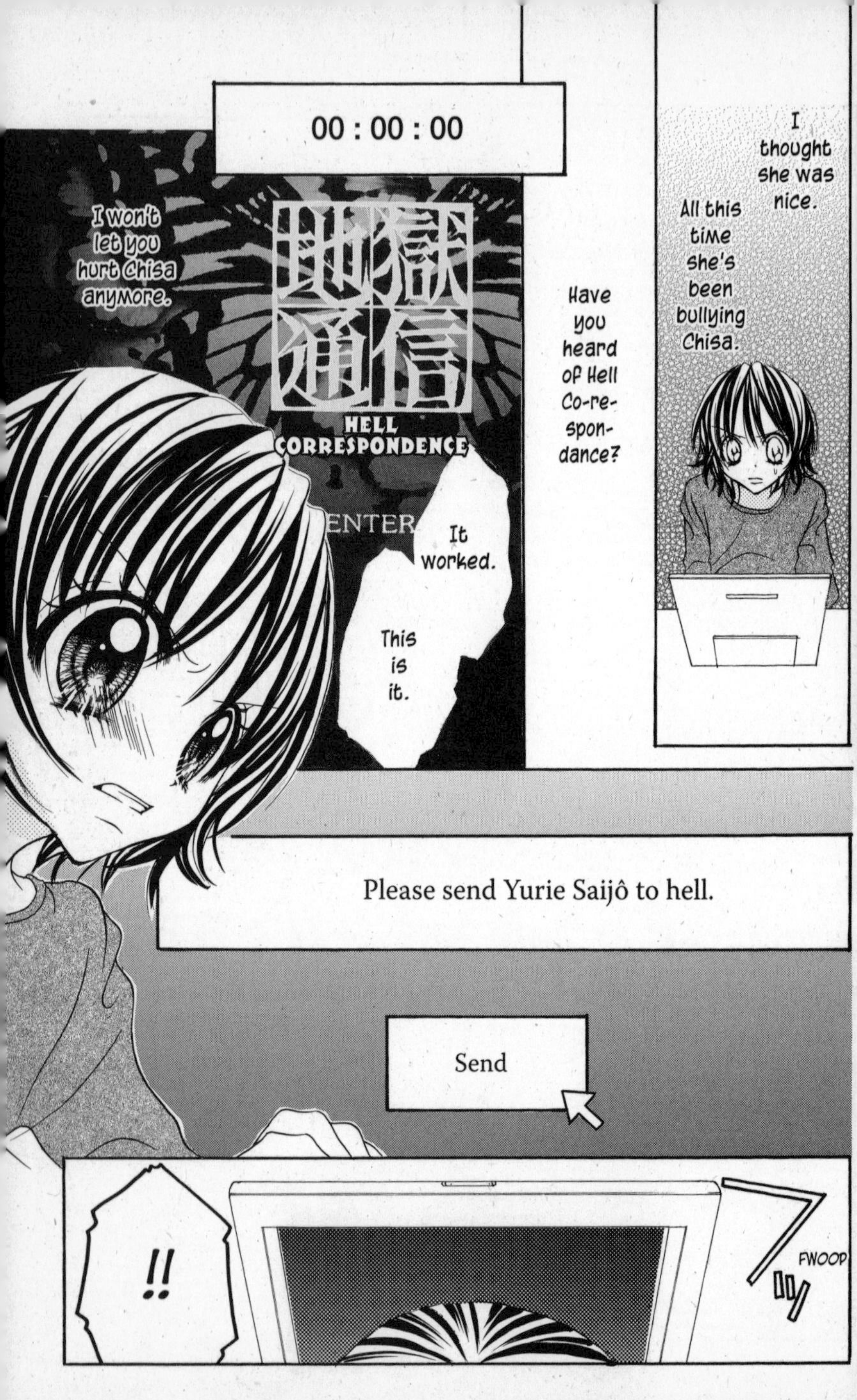
I thought she was nice.
All this time she's been bullying Chisa.
Have you heard of Hell Co-re-spon-dance?
00 : 00 : 00
地獄通信
HELL CORRESPONDENCE
ENTER
It worked.
This is it.
I won't let you hurt Chisa anymore.
Please send Yurie Saijô to hell.
Send
FWOOP
!!

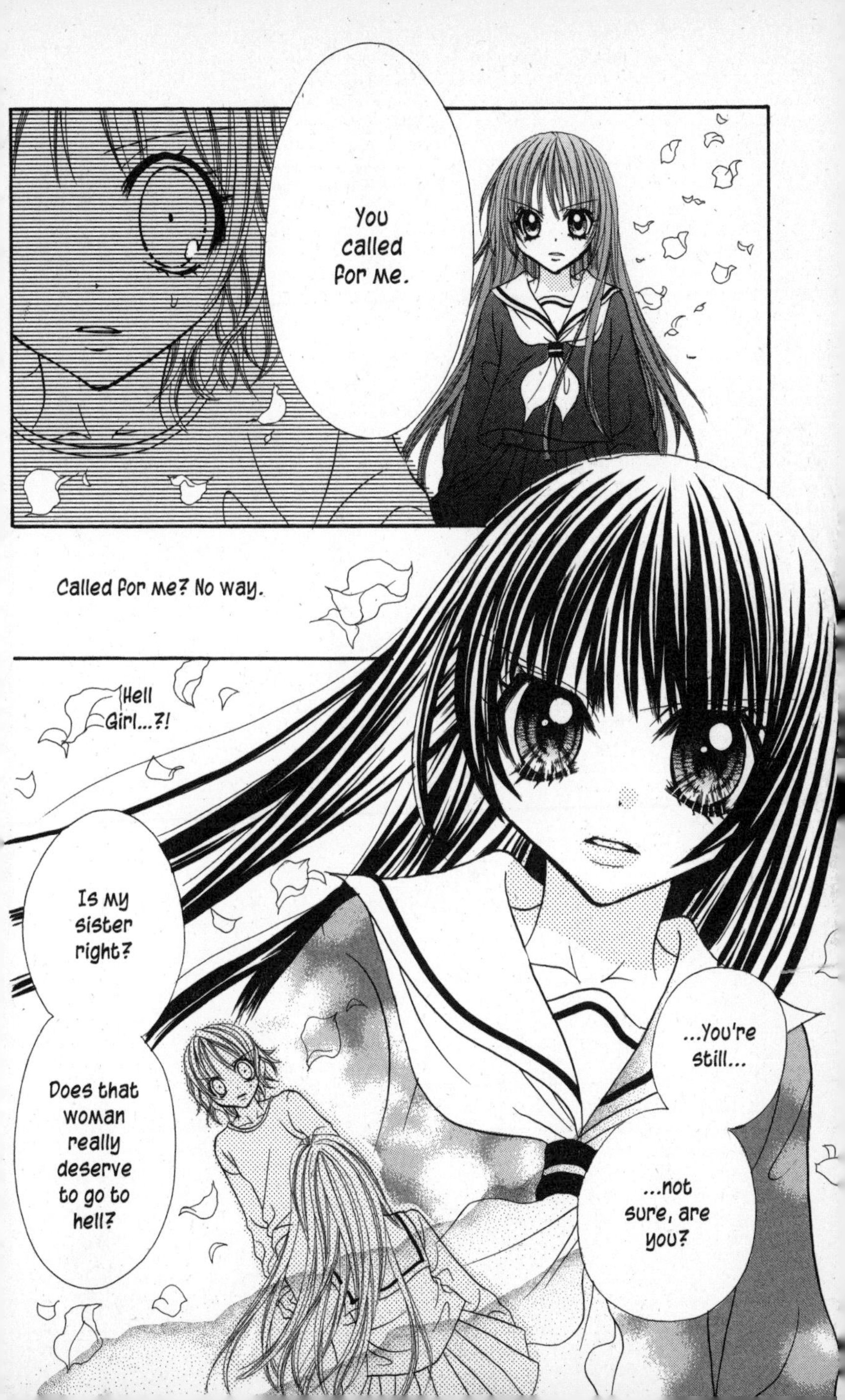
You called for me.
Called for me? No way.
Hell Girl...?!
Is my sister right?
Does that woman really deserve to go to hell?
...You're still...
...not sure, are you?

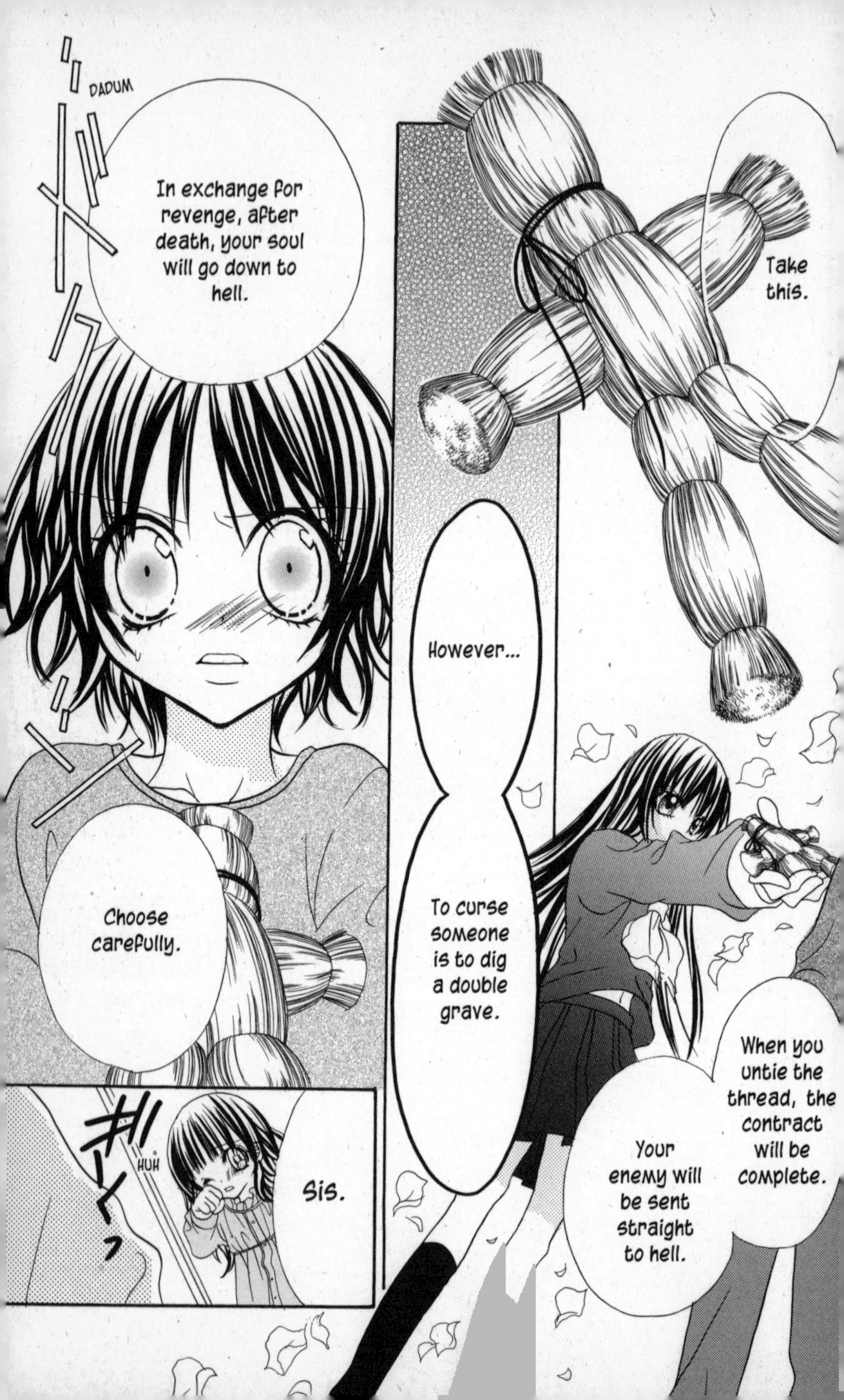

Take this.
However...
To curse someone is to dig a double grave.
When you untie the thread, the contract will be complete.
Your enemy will be sent straight to hell.
DADUM
In exchange for revenge, after death, your soul will go down to hell.
Choose carefully.
HUH
Sis.

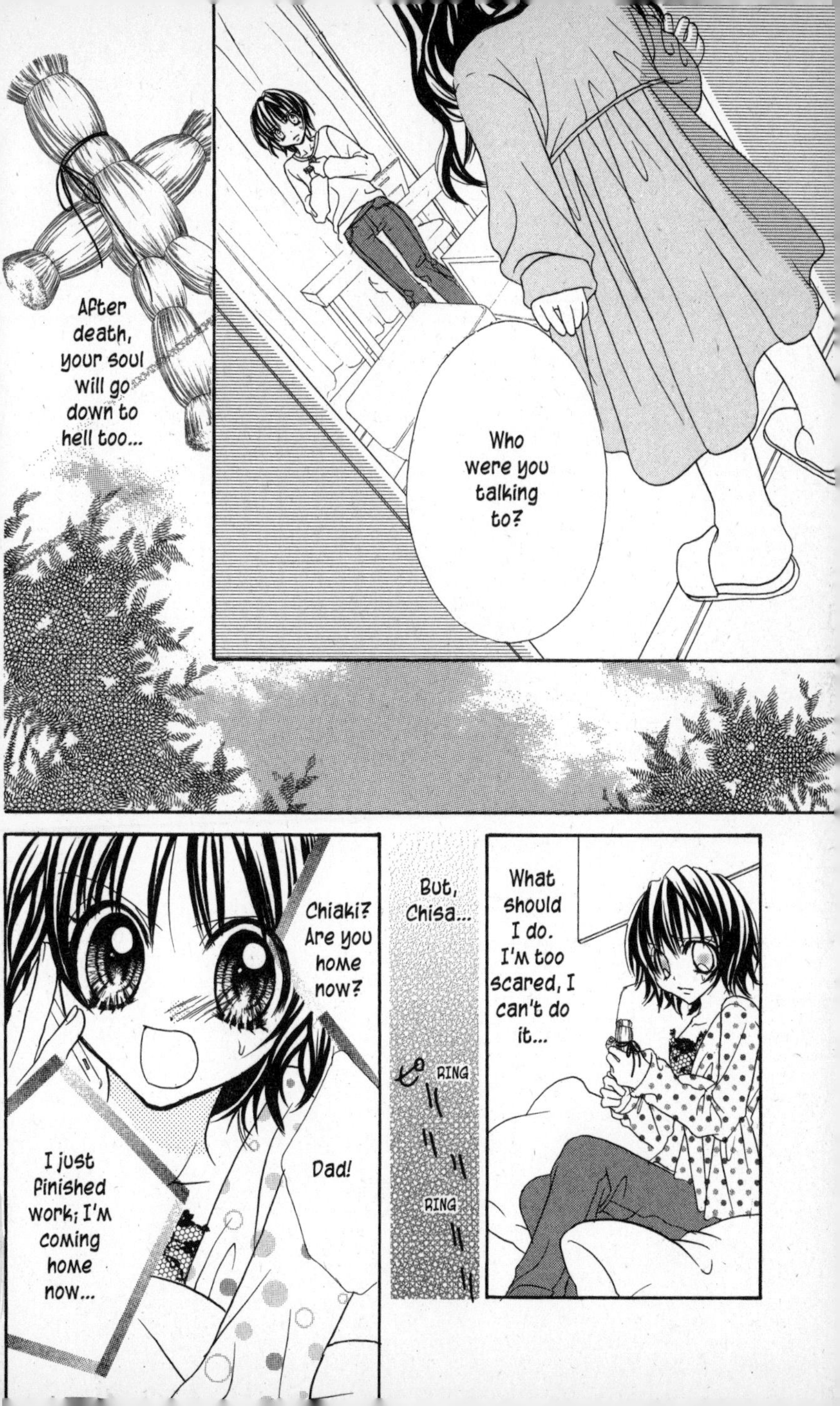
Who were you talking to?
After death, your soul will go down to hell too...
What should I do. I'm too scared, I can't do it...
But, Chisa...
RING
RING
Chiaki? Are you home now?
Dad!
I just finished work; I'm coming home now...

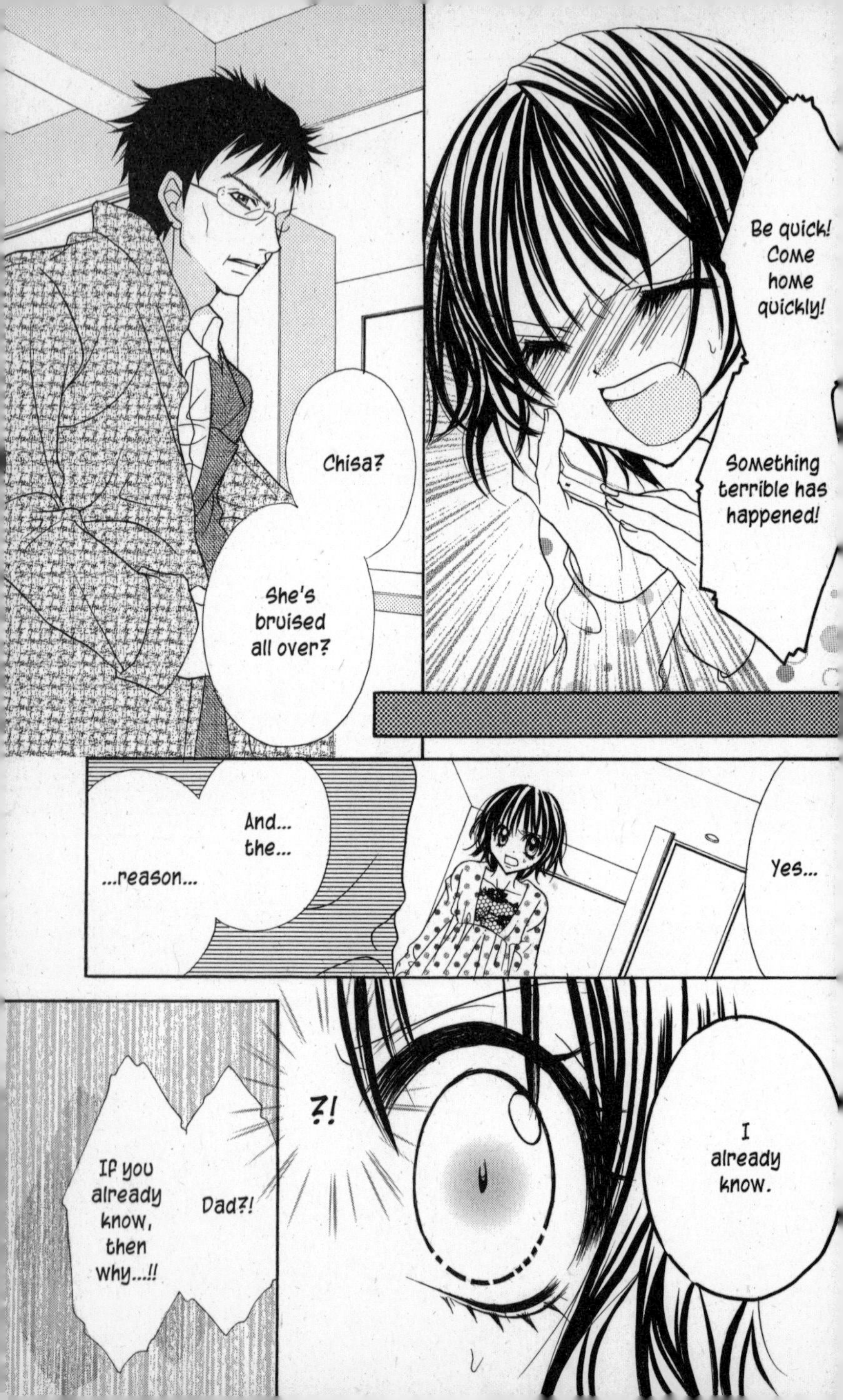
Be quick! Come home quickly!
Something terrible has happened!
Chisa?
She's bruised all over?
Yes...
And... the...
...reason...
I already know.
?!
Dad?!
If you already know, then why...!!

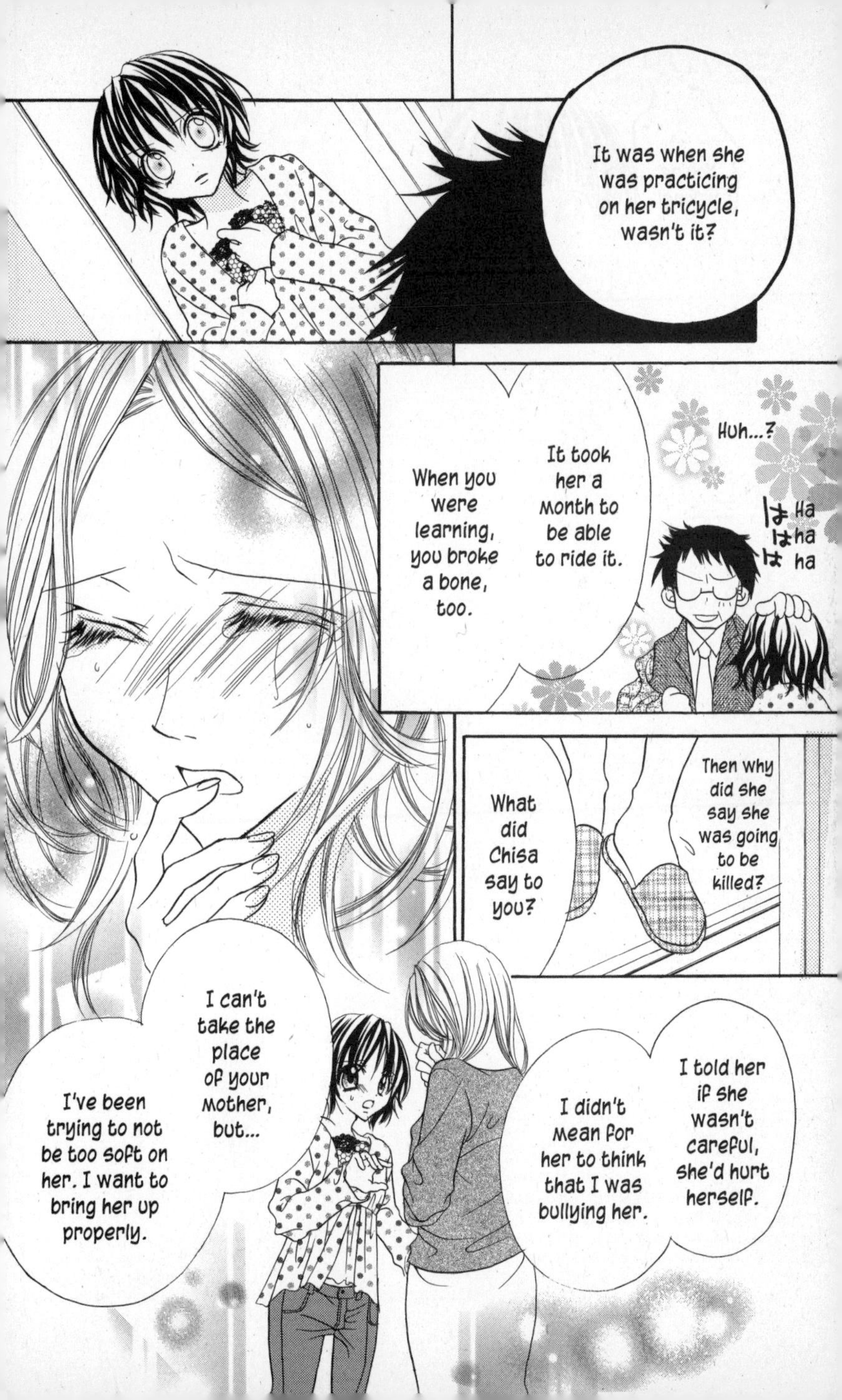
It was when she was practicing on her tricycle, wasn't it?
Huh...?
ははは
Ha ha ha
It took her a month to be able to ride it.
When you were learning, you broke a bone, too.
Then why did she say she was going to be killed?
What did Chisa say to you?
I told her if she wasn't careful, she'd hurt herself.
I didn't mean for her to think that I was bullying her.
I can't take the place of your mother, but...
I've been trying to not be too soft on her. I want to bring her up properly.

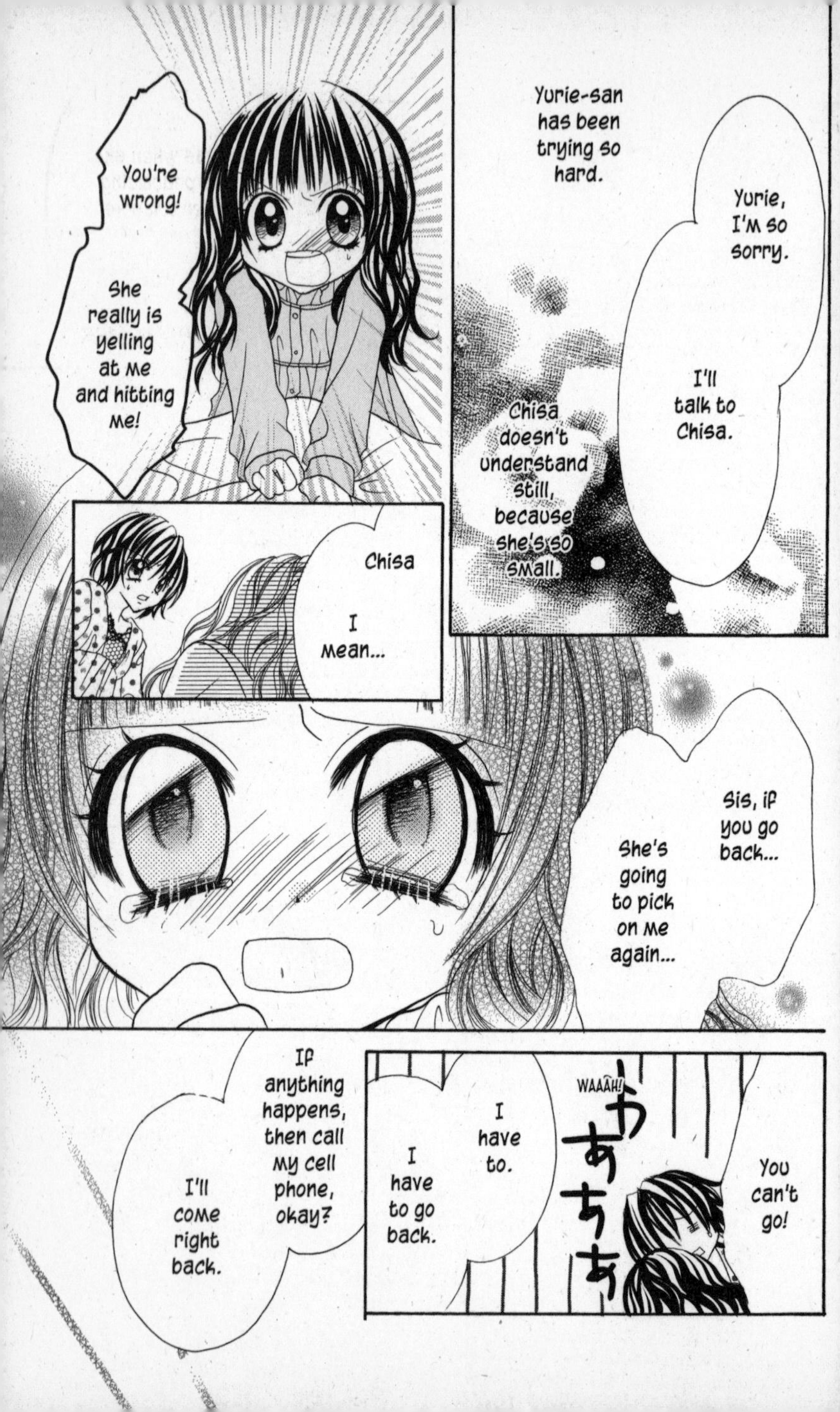

Yurie, I'm so sorry.
I'll talk to Chisa.
Yurie-san has been trying so hard.
Chisa doesn't understand still, because she's so small.
You're wrong!
She really is yelling at me and hitting me!
Chisa
I mean...
Sis, if you go back...
She's going to pick on me again...
You can't go!
WAAAH!
I have to.
I have to go back.
If anything happens, then call my cell phone, okay?
I'll come right back.

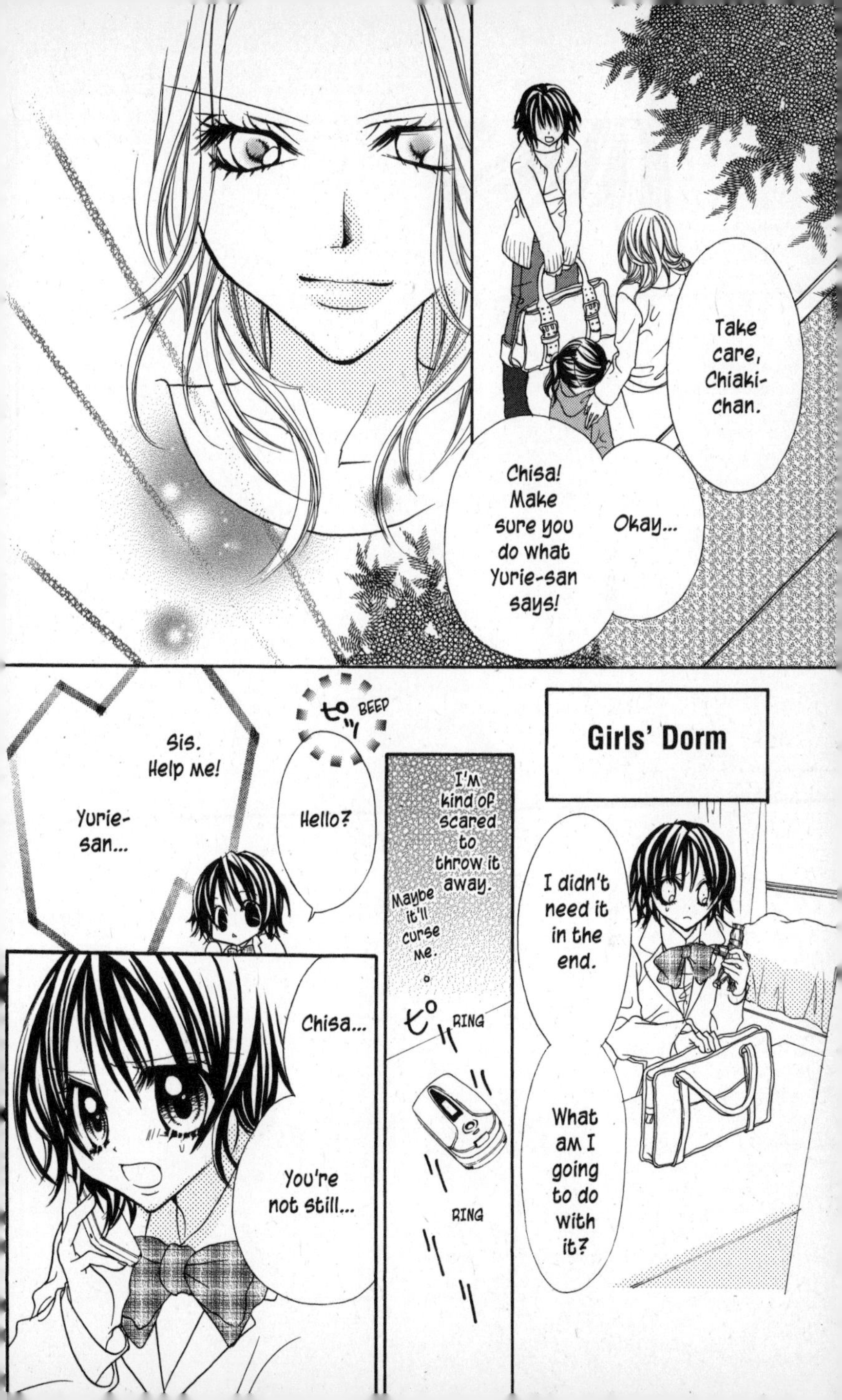

Take care, Chiaki-chan.
Chisa! Make sure you do what Yurie-san says!
Okay...
Girls' Dorm
I didn't need it in the end.
What am I going to do with it?
I'm kind of scared to throw it away.
Maybe it'll curse me.
RING
RING
BEEP
Hello?
Yurie-san...
Sis. Help me!
Chisa...
You're not still...

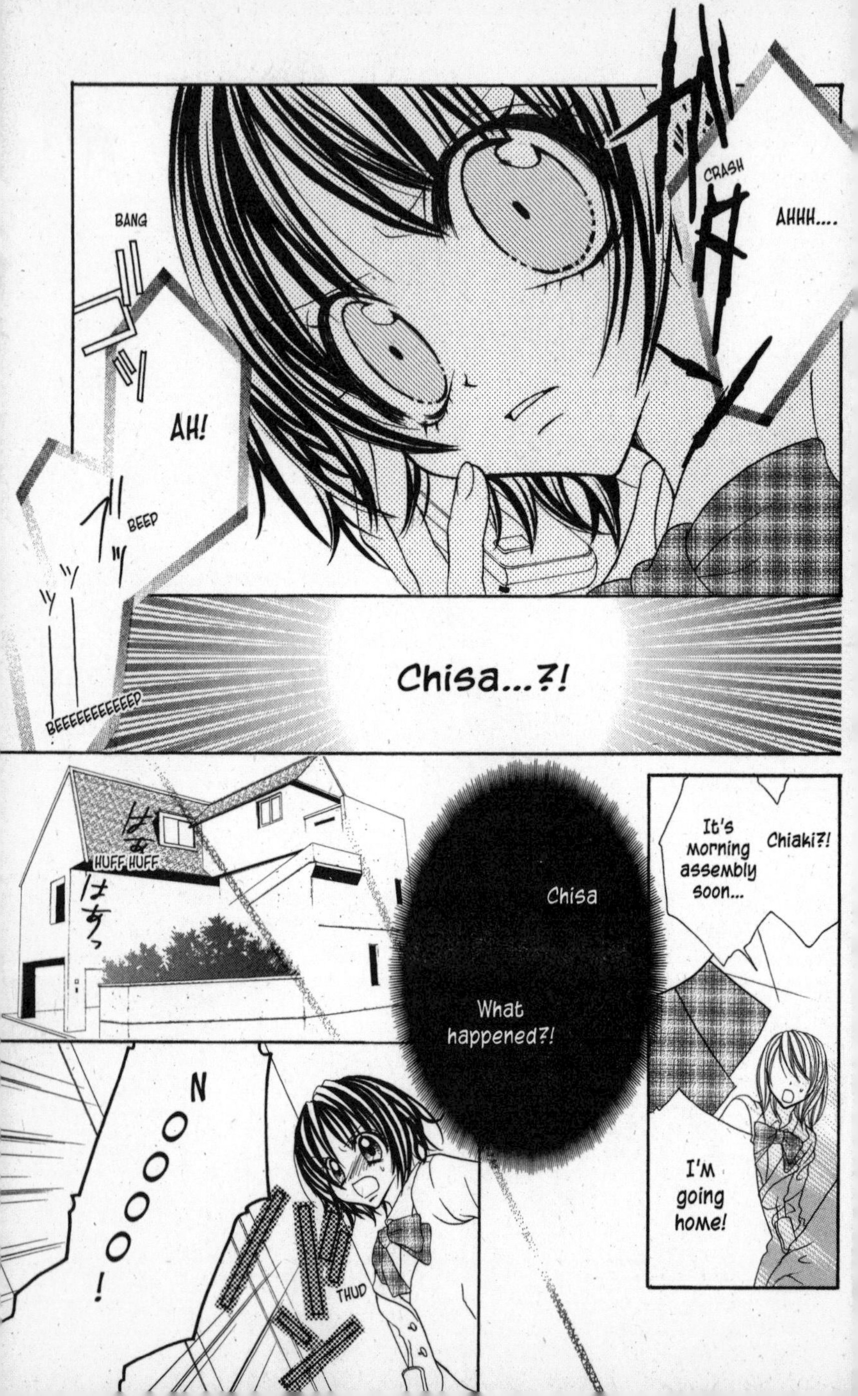
CRASH
AHHH....
BANG
AH!
BEEP
BEEEEEEEEEEEP
Chisa...?!
Chiaki?!
It's morning assembly soon...
I'M going home!
はぁ
HUFF HUFF
はあっ
Chisa
What happened?!
NOOOOOO!
THUD

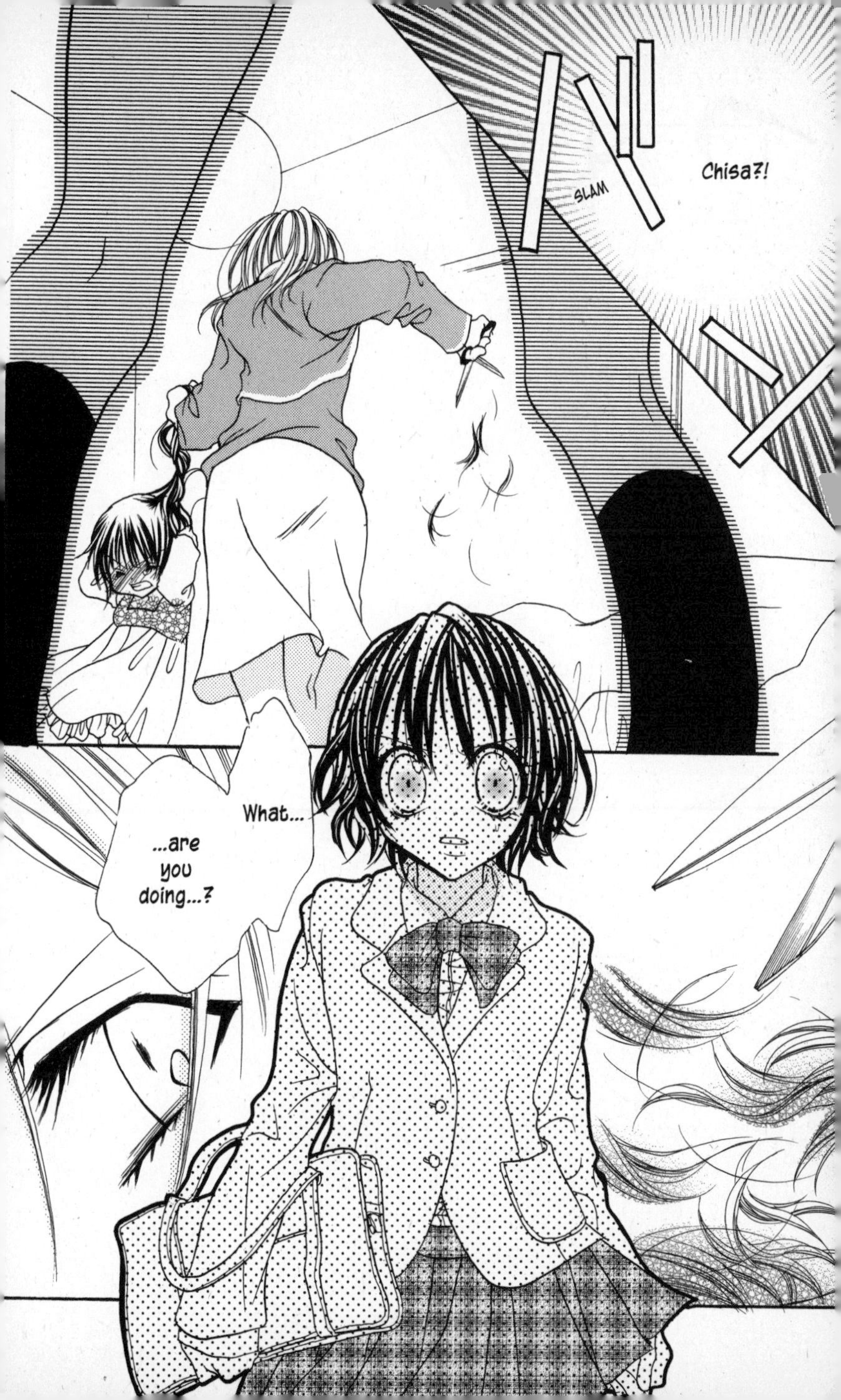
SLAM
Chisa?!
What...
...are you doing...?

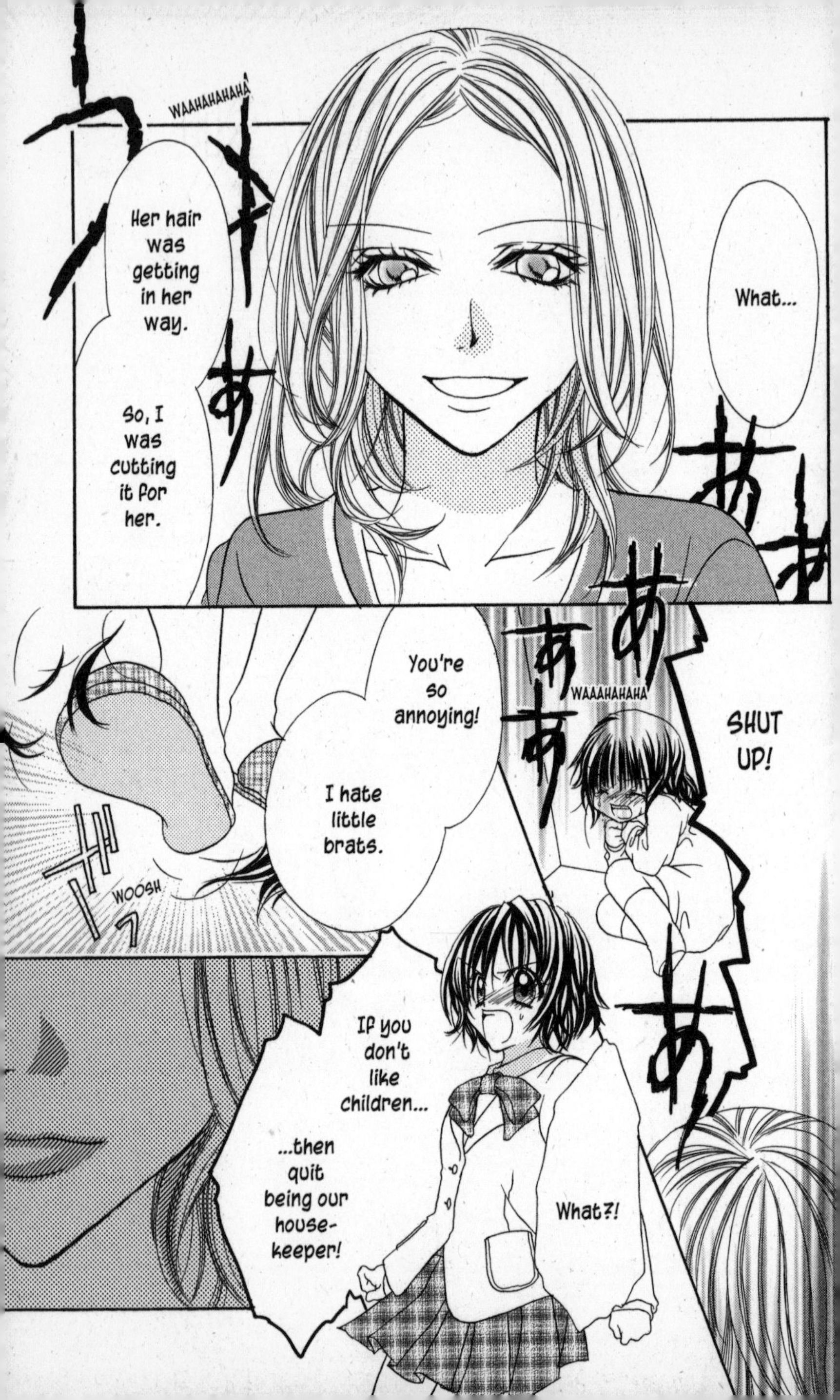
What...
WAAAHAHAHAHA
Her hair was getting in her way.
So, I was cutting it for her.
SHUT UP!
WAAAHAHAHA
You're so annoying!
I hate little brats.
WOOSH
What?!
If you don't like children...
...then quit being our housekeeper!

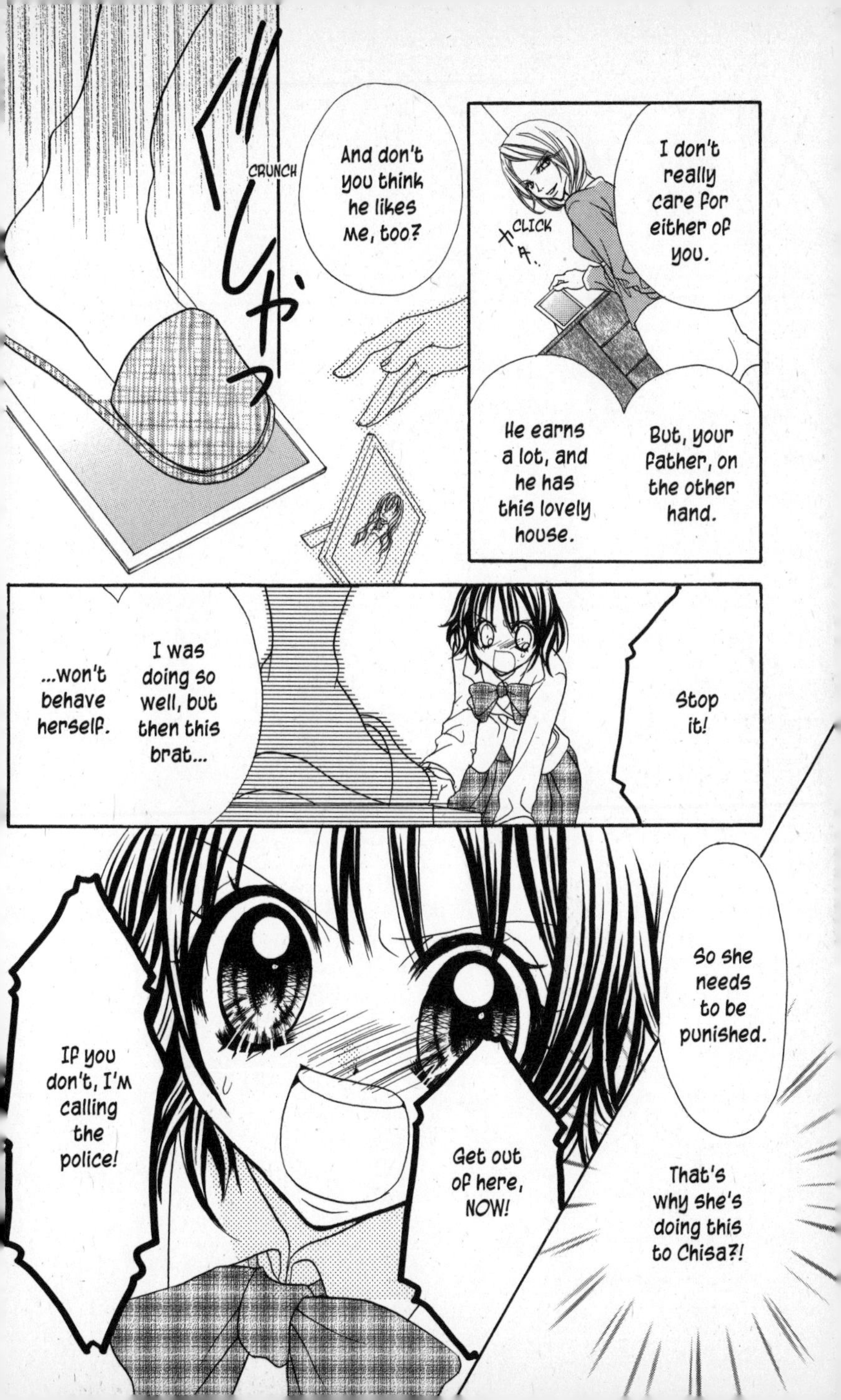
I don't really care for either of you.
CLICK
But, your father, on the other hand.
He earns a lot, and he has this lovely house.
And don't you think he likes me, too?
CRUNCH
Stop it!
I was doing so well, but then this brat...
...won't behave herself.
So she needs to be punished.
That's why she's doing this to Chisa?!
Get out of here, NOW!
If you don't, I'm calling the police!

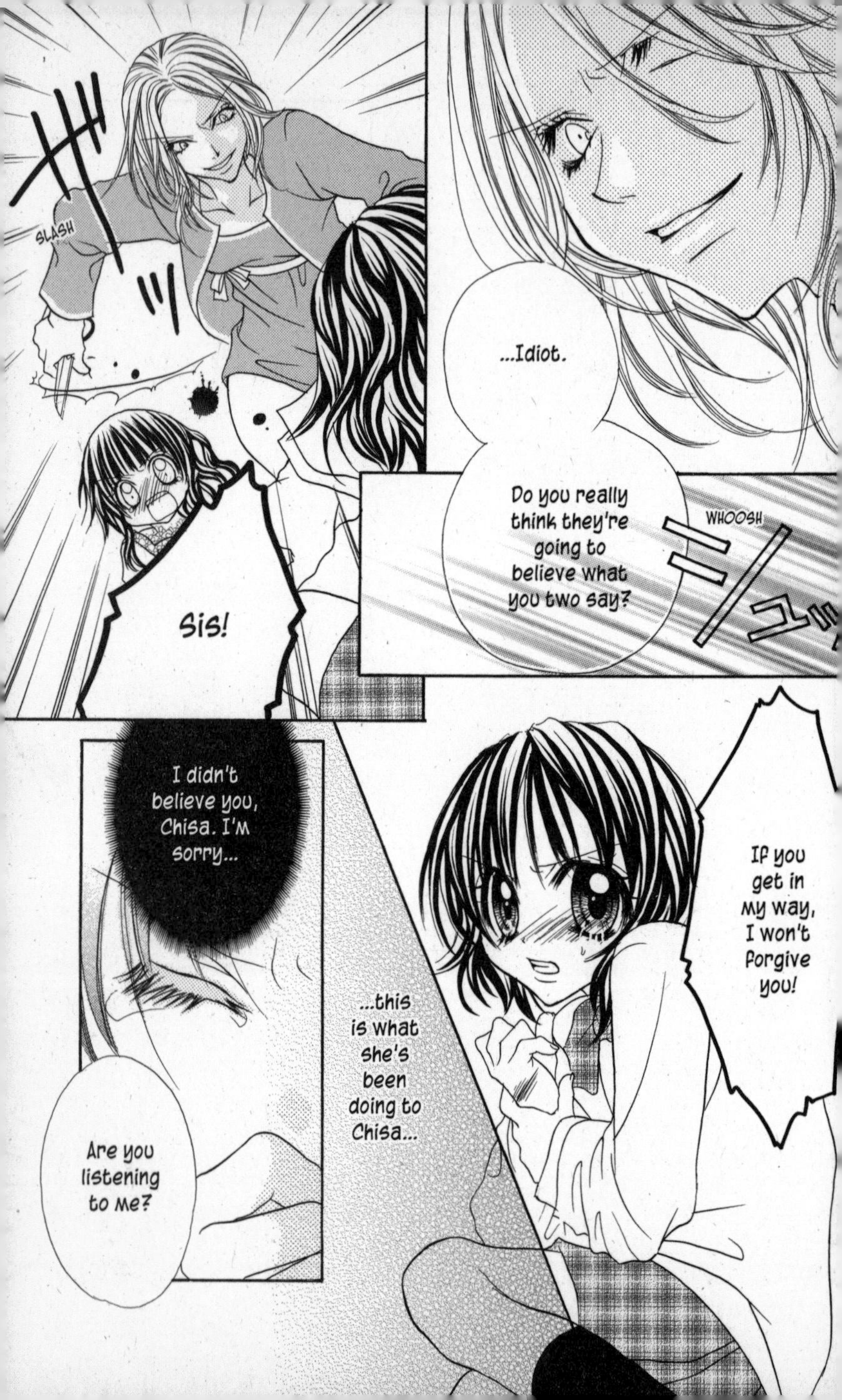
...Idiot.
Do you really think they're going to believe what you two say?
WHOOSH
SLASH
Sis!
If you get in my way, I won't forgive you!
...this is what she's been doing to Chisa...
I didn't believe you, Chisa. I'm sorry...
Are you listening to me?

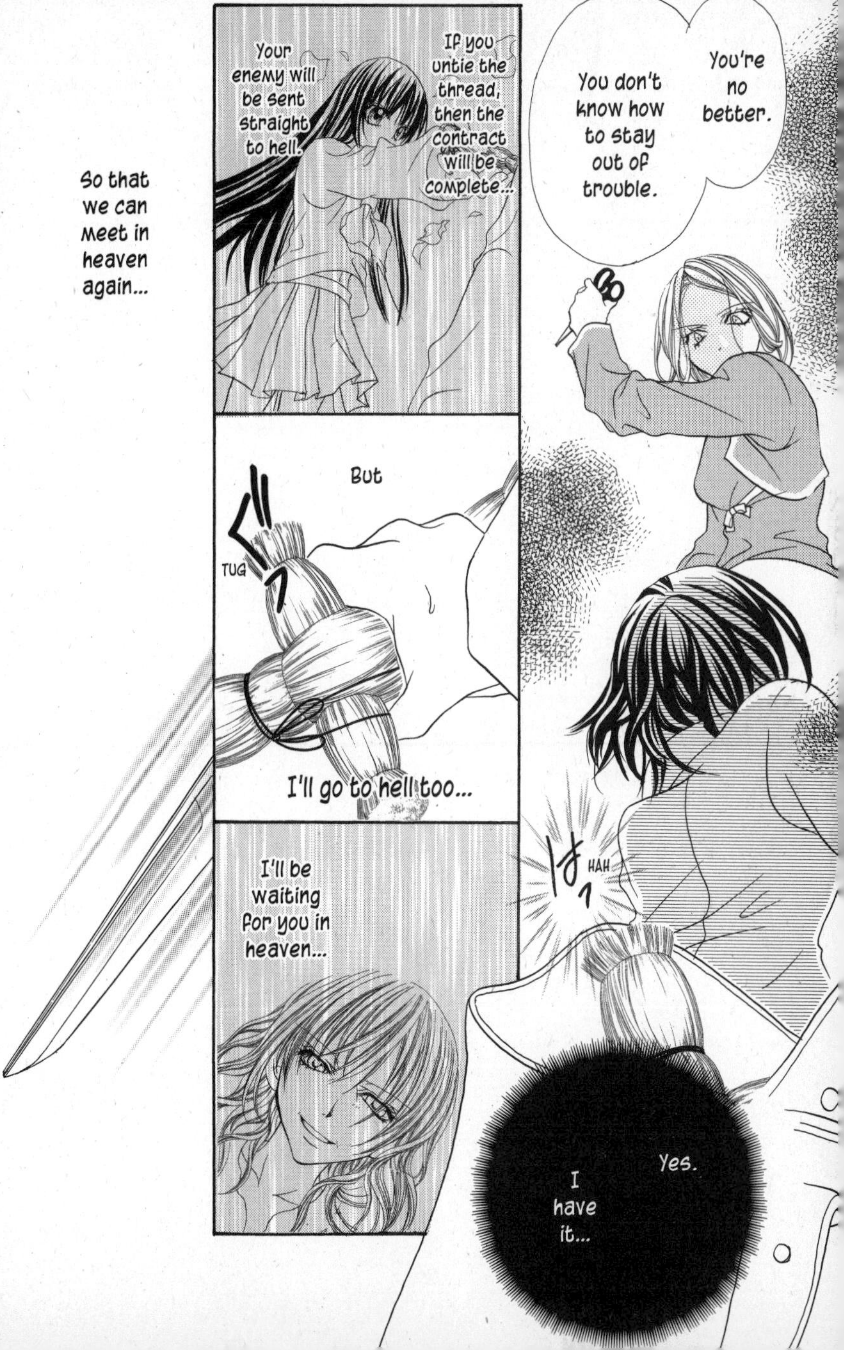
You're no better.
You don't know how to stay out of trouble.
HAH
Yes.
I have it...
If you untie the thread, then the contract will be complete...
Your enemy will be sent straight to hell.
But
TUG
I'll go to hell too...
I'll be waiting for you in heaven...
So that we can meet in heaven again...

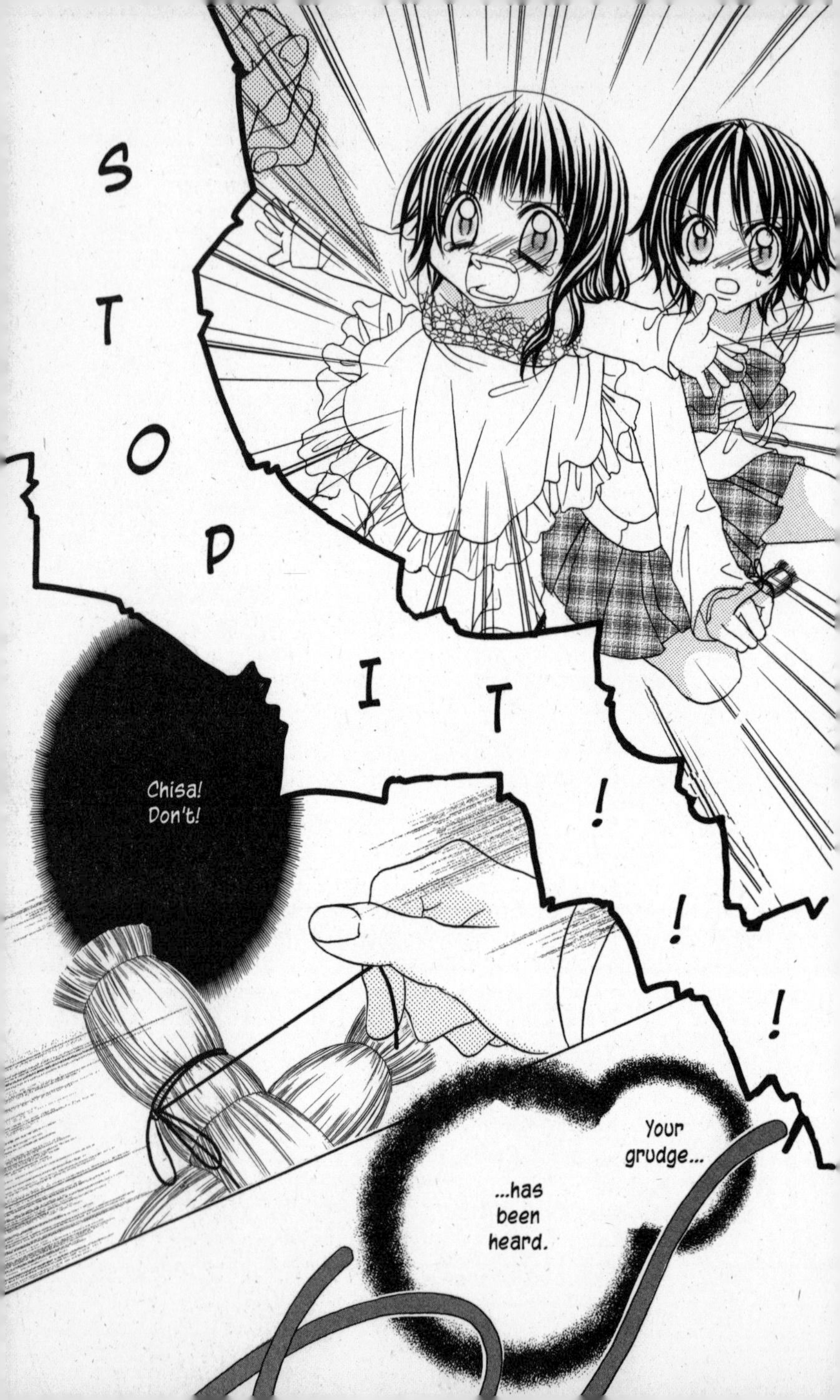
STOP IT!!!
Chisa! Don't!
Your grudge...
...has been heard.

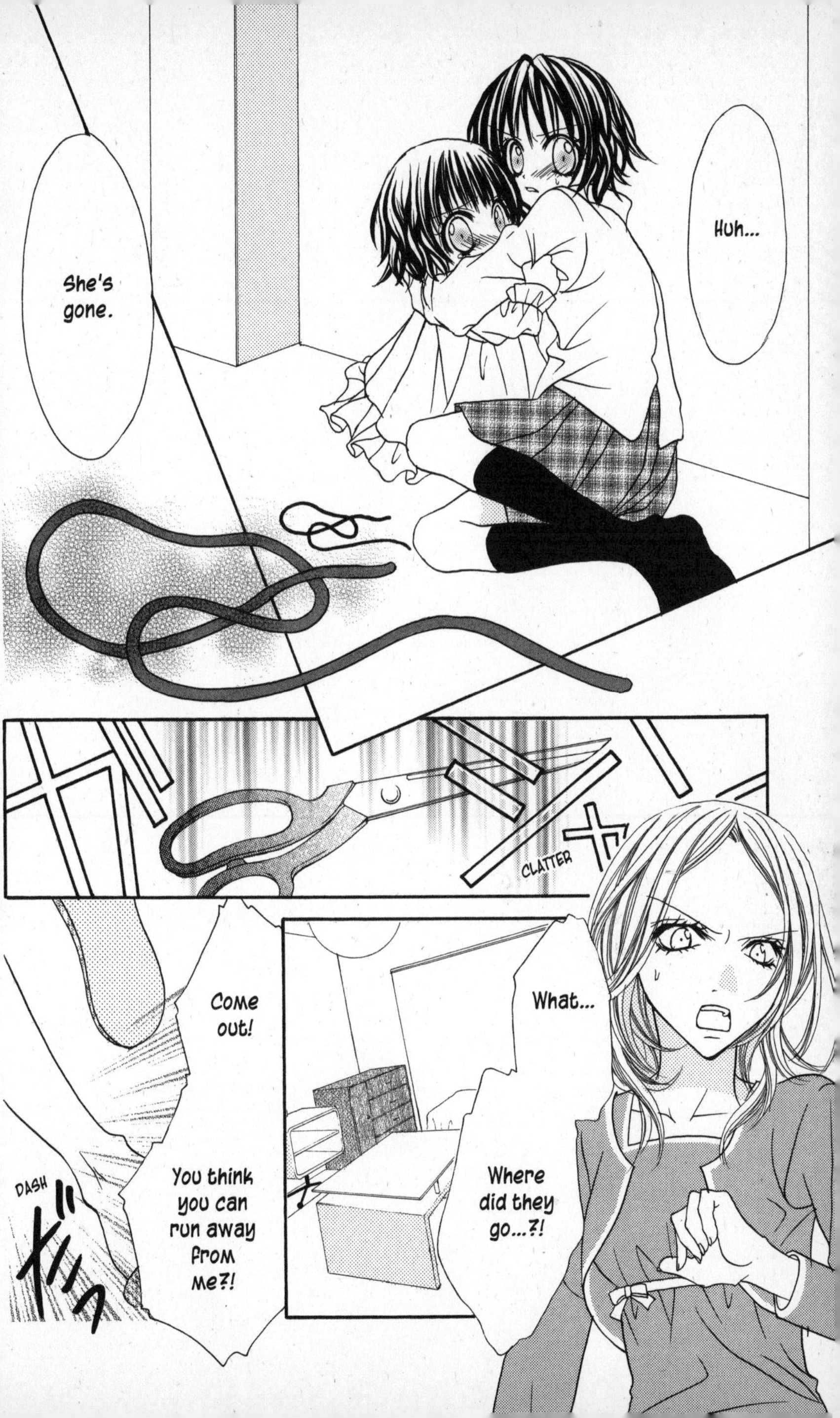
Huh...
She's gone.
CLATTER
What...
Where did they go...?!
Come out!
You think you can run away from me?!
DASH

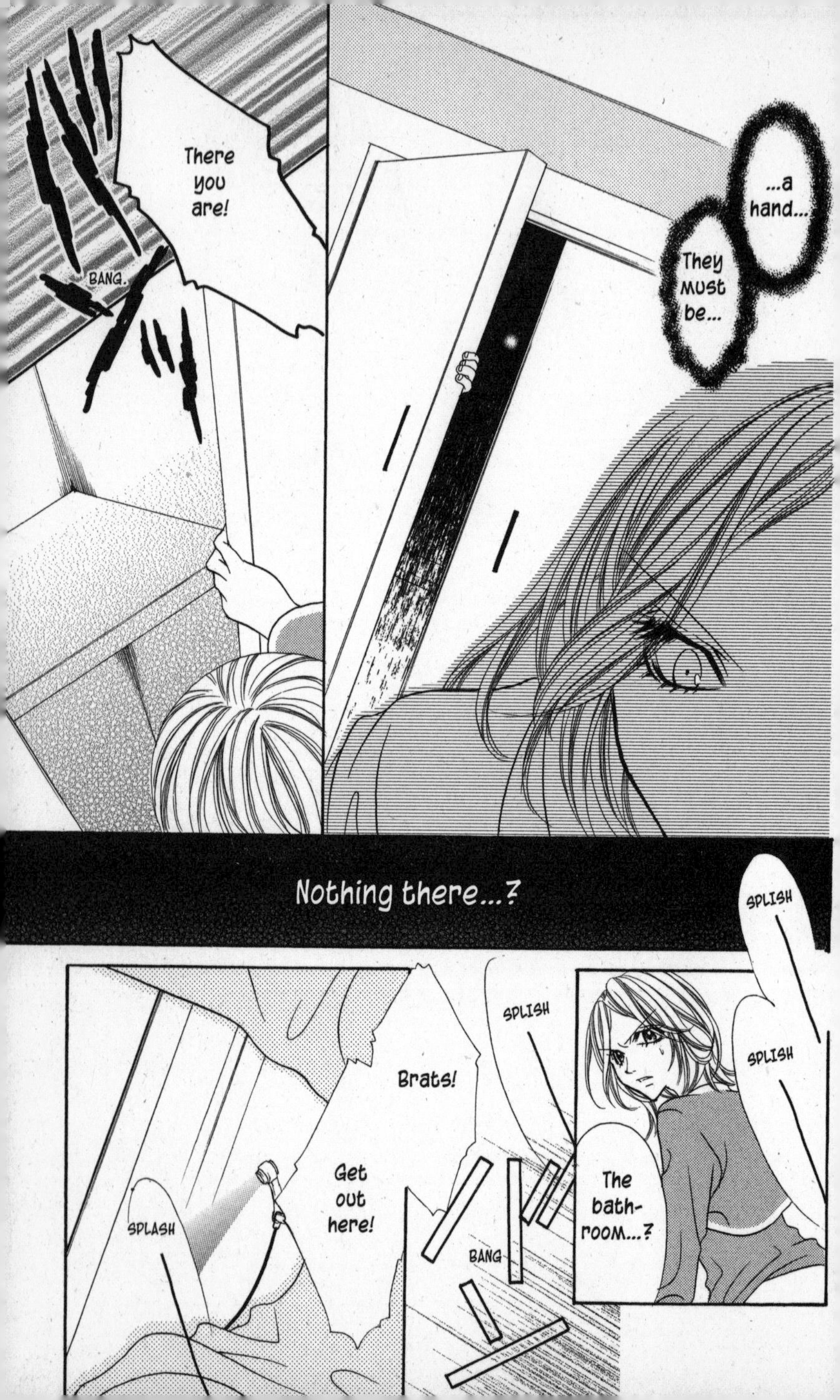

...a hand...
They must be...
There you are!
BANG.
Nothing there...?
SPLISH
SPLISH
The bath-room...?
SPLISH
Brats!
Get out here!
BANG
SPLASH

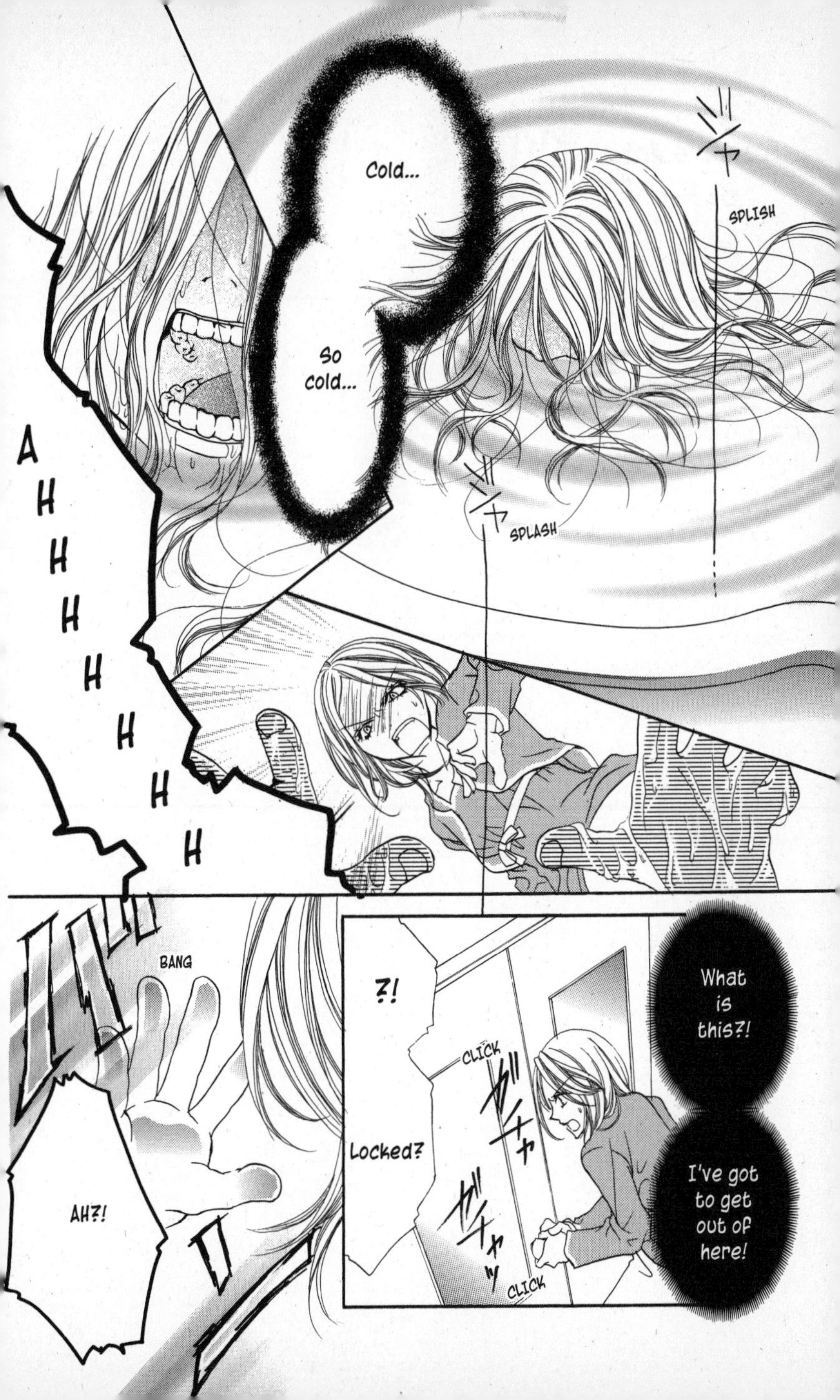

SPLISH
Cold...
So cold...
SPLASH
AHHHHHHHH
What is this?!
I've got to get out of here!
?!
CLICK
Locked?
CLICK
BANG
AH?!

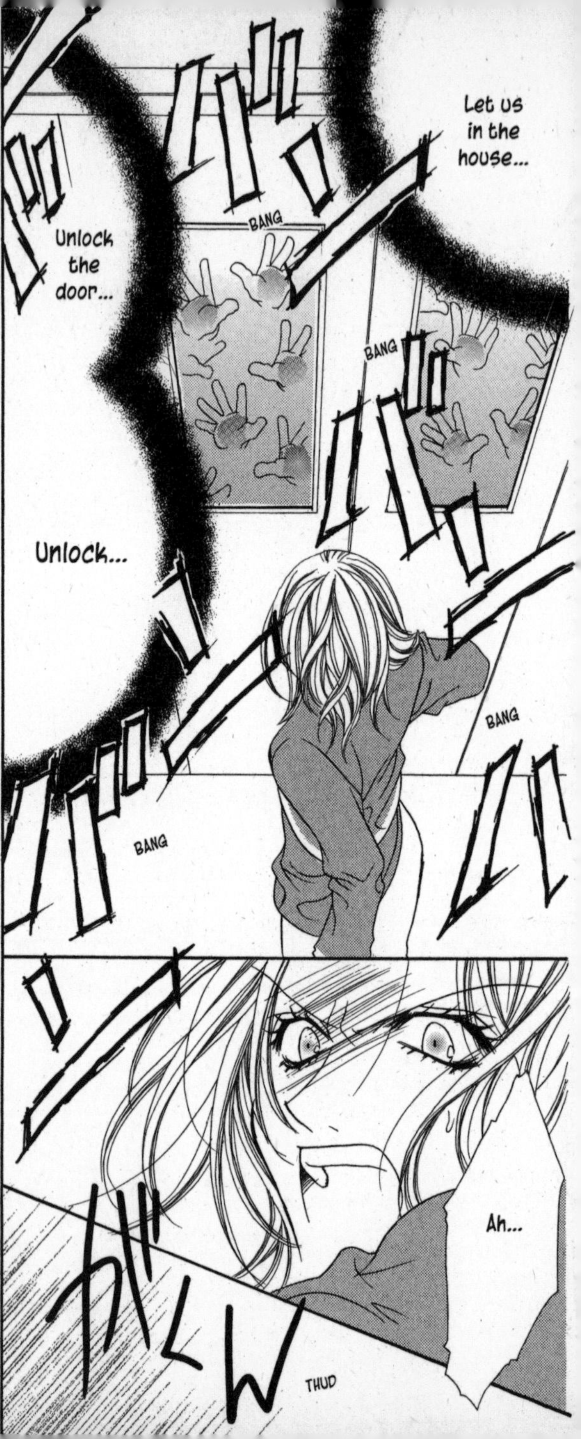
Let us in the house...
BANG
Unlock the door...
BANG
Unlock...
BANG
BANG
Ah...
THUD

Author's Note

The anime scriptwriter has apparently seen a really scary ghost. No jokes. I don't have a strong feeling for the supernatural, I don't have any experiences like that, but, sometimes, in the middle of the night, when I'm working on this manuscript, I hear this "Ahhh" sound in my ear. I get in this big panic thinking that there is a ghost there.

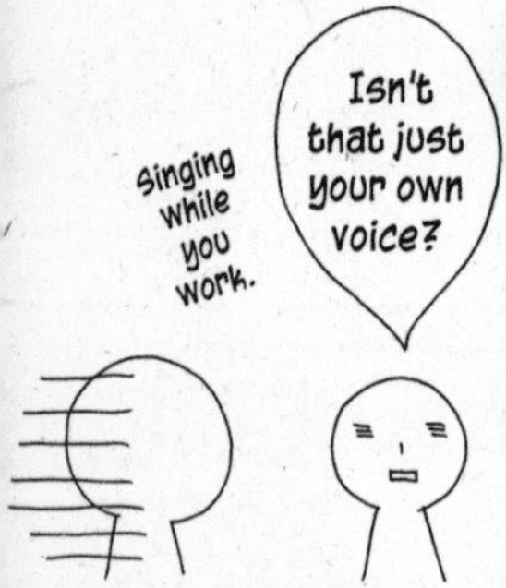
Isn't that just your own voice?
Singing while you work.

People make fun of me!

But maybe they're right.

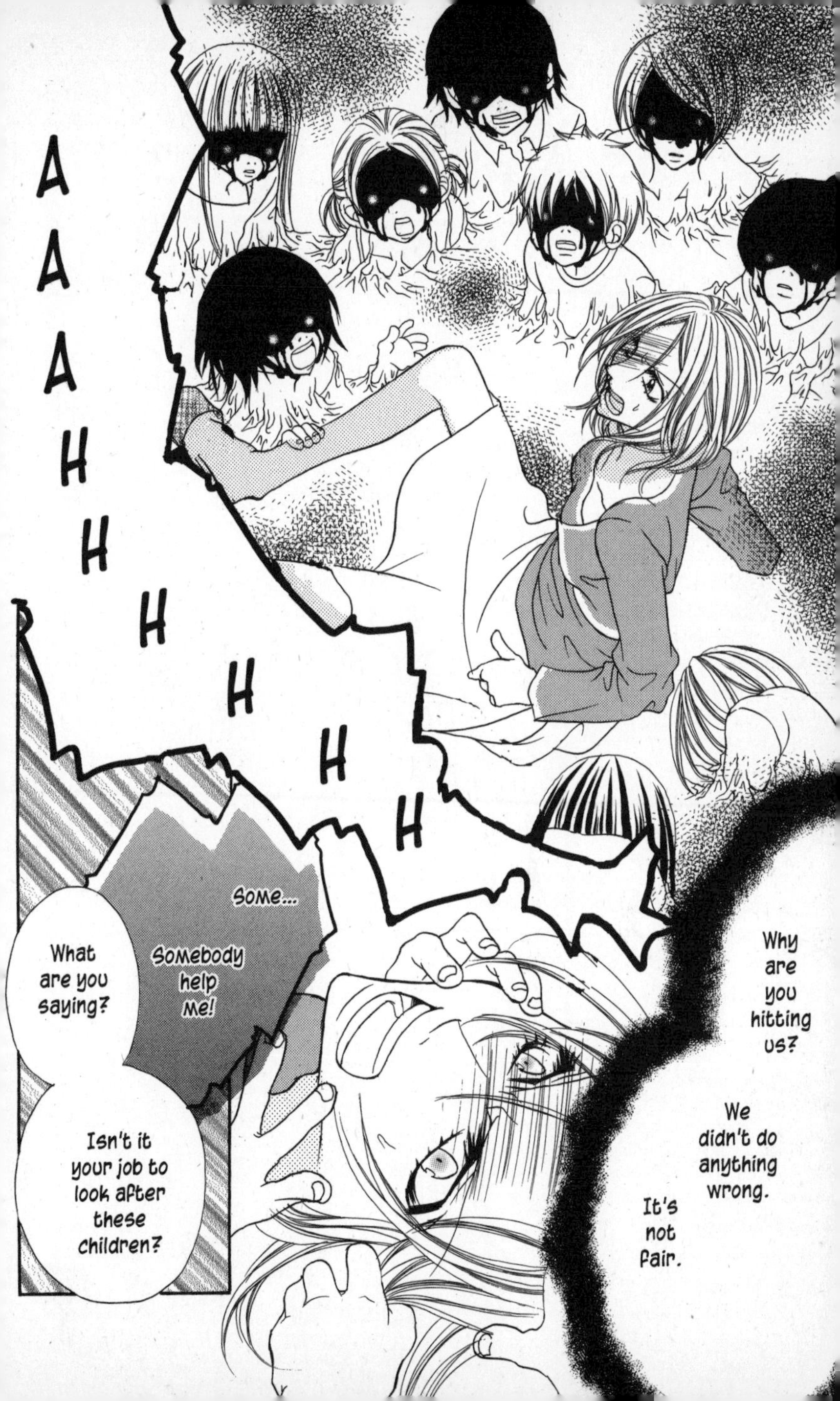
AAAHHHHHH
Why are you hitting us?
We didn't do anything wrong.
It's not fair.
Some...
Somebody help me!
What are you saying?
Isn't it your job to look after these children?

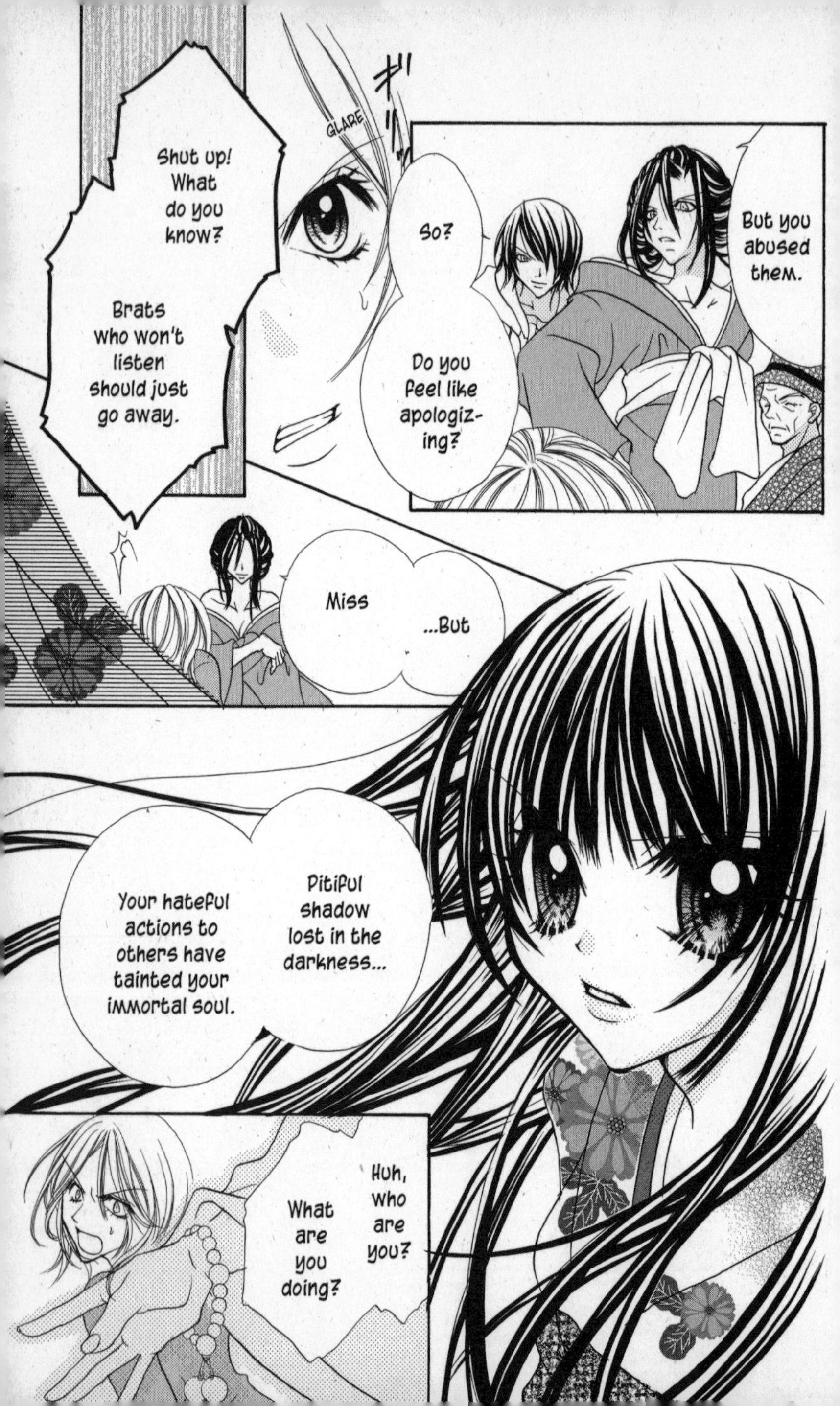

But you abused them.
So?
Do you feel like apologizing?
ギリ
GLARE
Shut up! What do you know?
Brats who won't listen should just go away.
Miss
...But
Pitiful shadow lost in the darkness...
Your hateful actions to others have tainted your immortal soul.
Huh, who are you?
What are you doing?

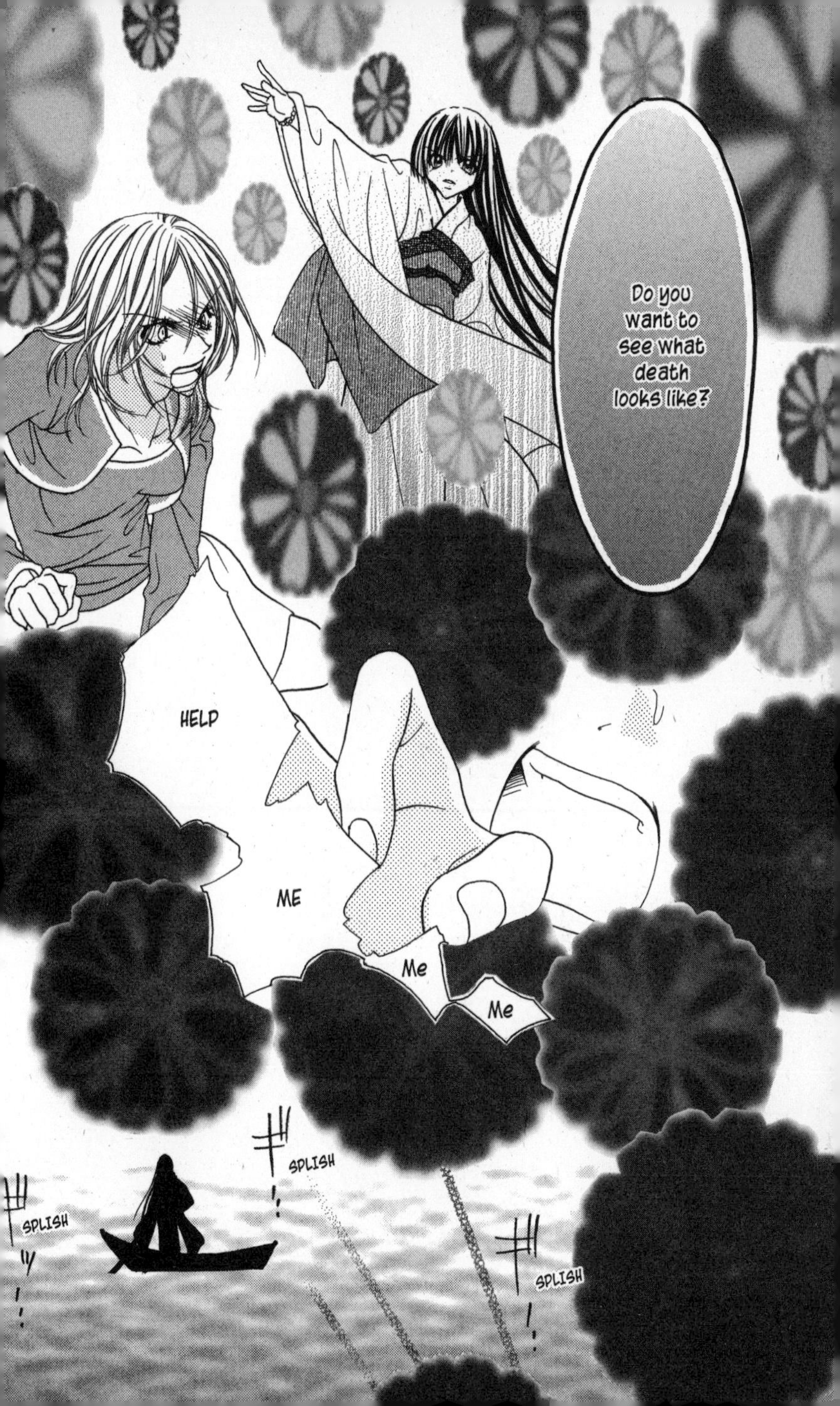
Do you want to see what death looks like?
HELP
ME
Me
Me
SPLISH
SPLISH
SPLISH

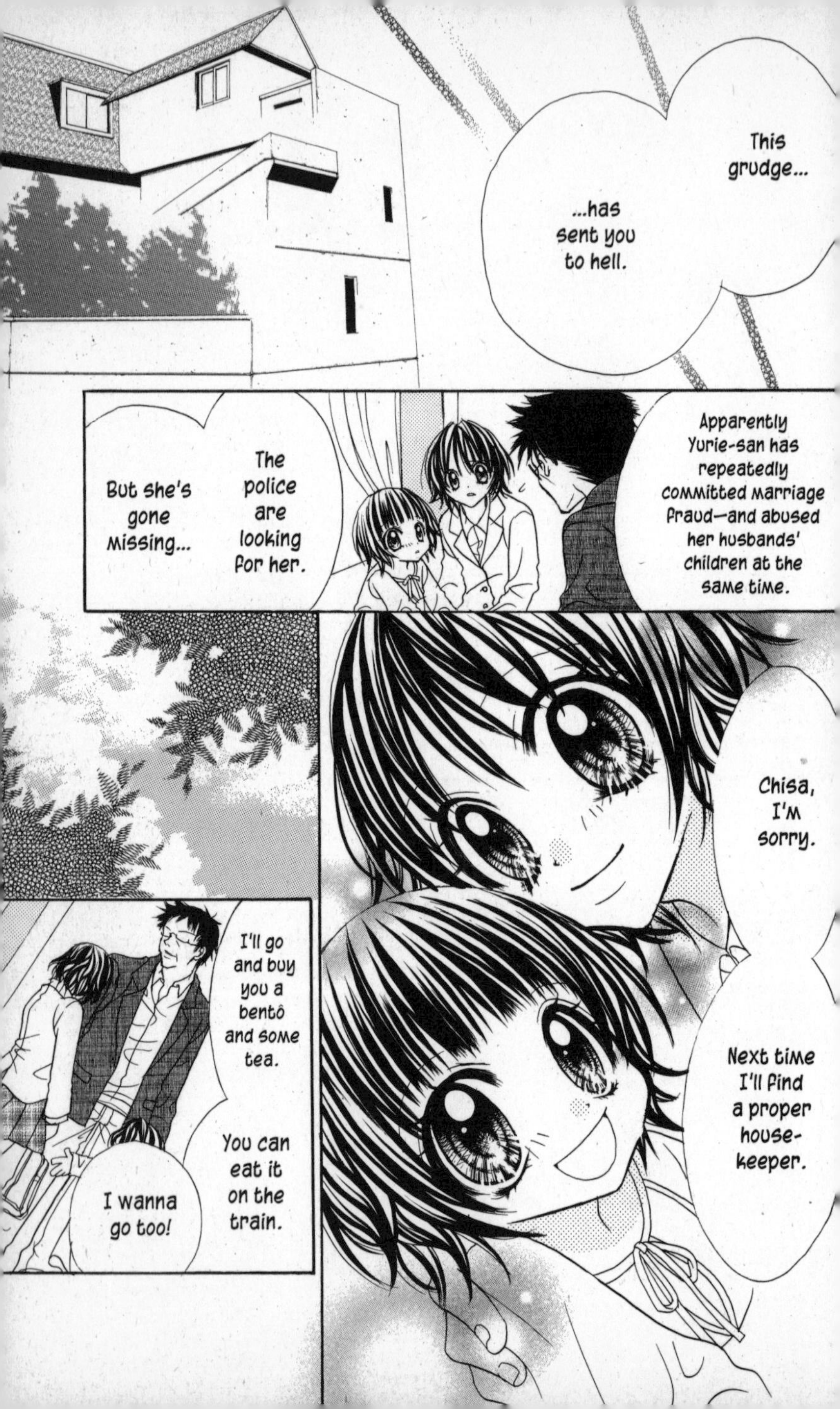
This grudge...
...has sent you to hell.
Apparently Yurie-san has repeatedly committed marriage fraud—and abused her husbands' children at the same time.
The police are looking for her.
But she's gone missing...
Chisa, I'm sorry.
Next time I'll find a proper house-keeper.
I'll go and buy you a bentô and some tea.
You can eat it on the train.
I wanna go too!

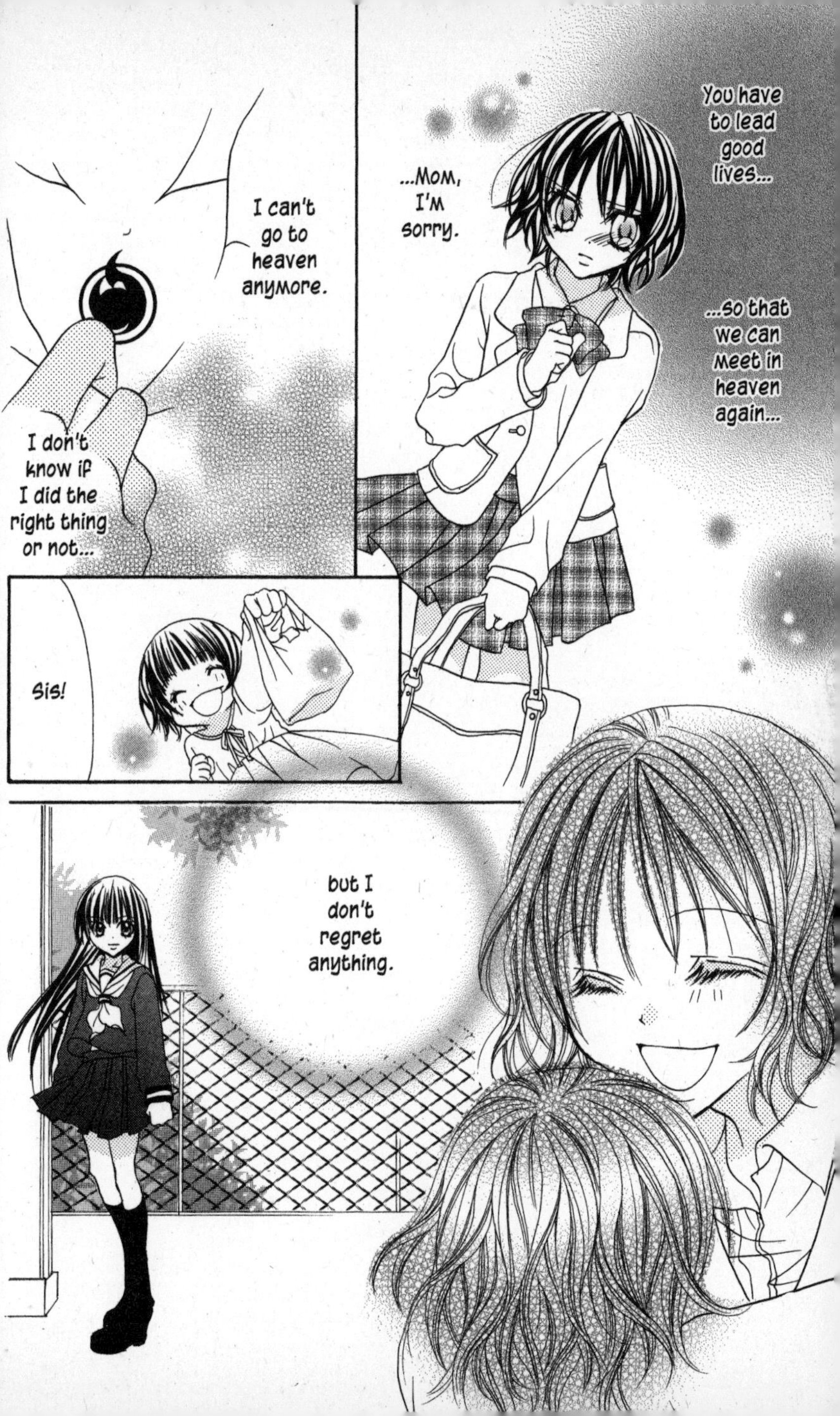

You have to lead good lives...
...so that we can meet in heaven again...
...Mom, I'm sorry.
I can't go to heaven anymore.
I don't know if I did the right thing or not...
Sis!
but I don't regret anything.

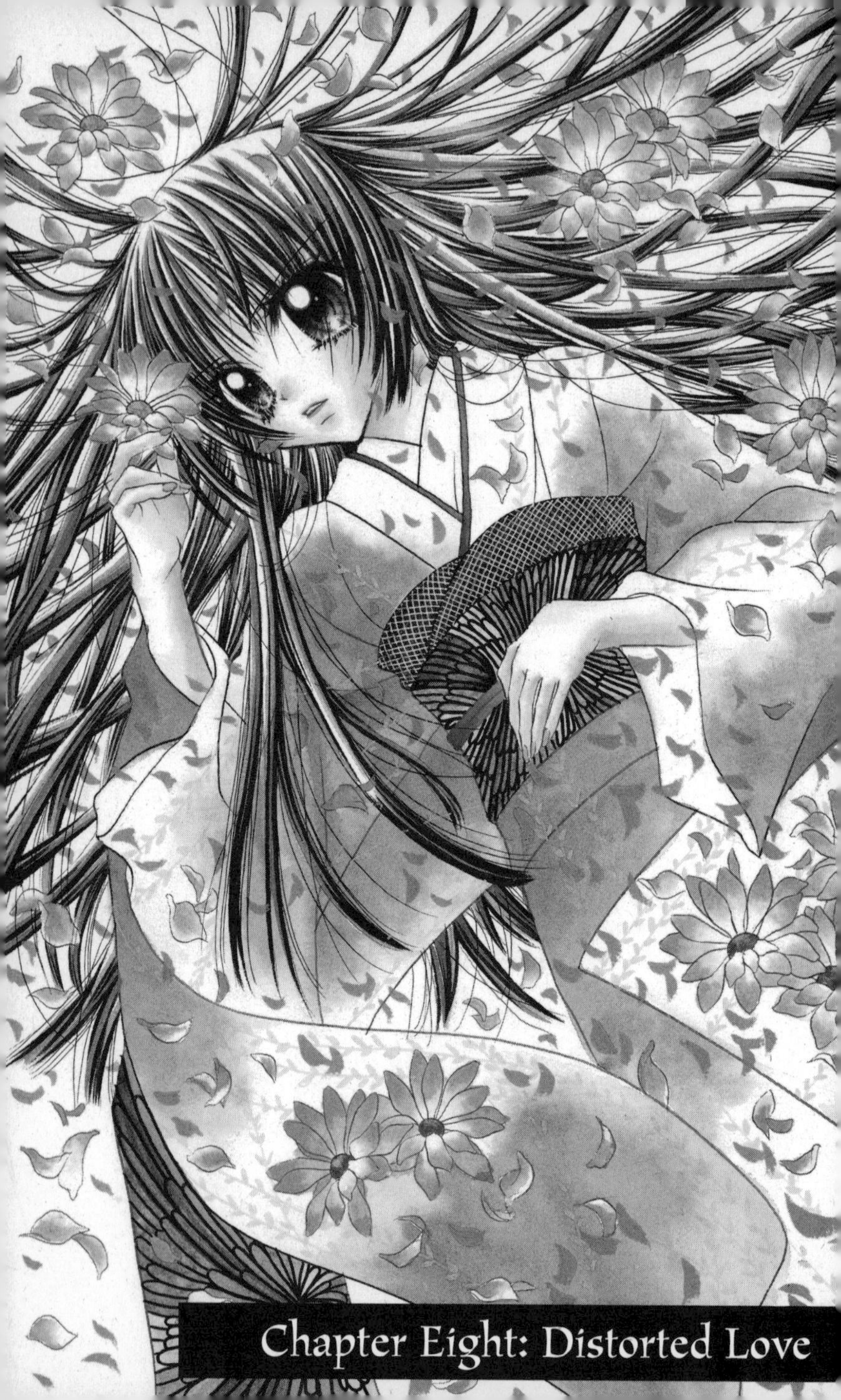

Chapter Eight: Distorted Love

Chapter Eight "Distorted Love"

It was supposed to have a creepy feel to it. I really like flowers, but I'm very bad at looking after them. My flowers always get flies and mold. I did have one tough plant that even ate flies, but it got eaten by fungi in the end. Sorry...

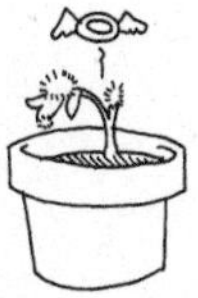

Chapter Nine "Lost Cat"

The scene where she goes to hell with the teacher in a bag was quite difficult to make look good like my editors asked. I didn't get it right. I like eating fish, but I can't eat the eyeballs. And squid eyes are so scary!

Chapter Ten "Friends"

This is another version of the anime episode "Friends." I really liked this story. I went to the launch party of the anime while I was drawing up the manuscript. I got lost and a supervisor had to help me out. The doll I was given when I left was so cute. I recommend it.

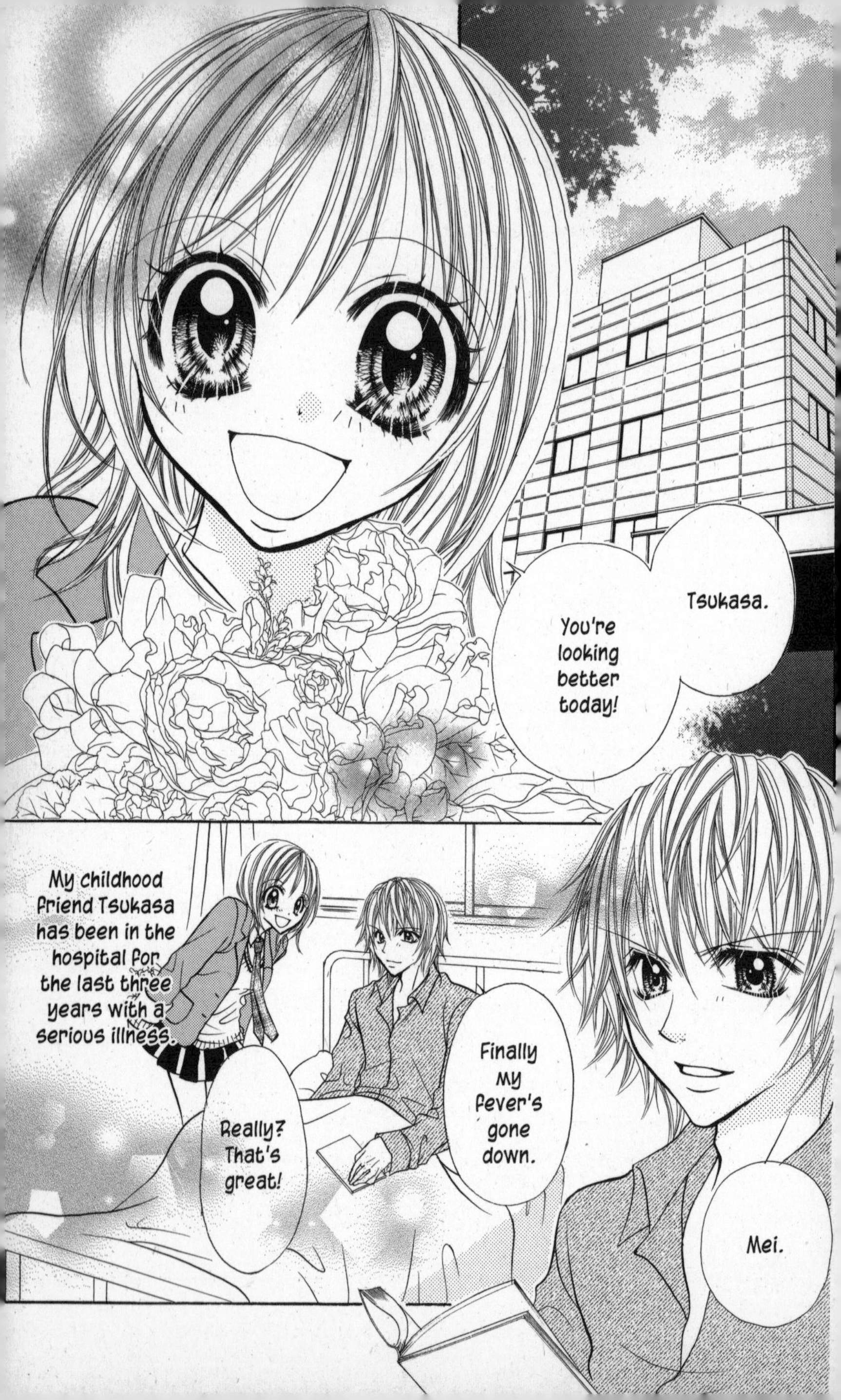
Tsukasa.
You're looking better today!
Mei.
Finally my fever's gone down.
Really? That's great!
My childhood friend Tsukasa has been in the hospital for the last three years with a serious illness.

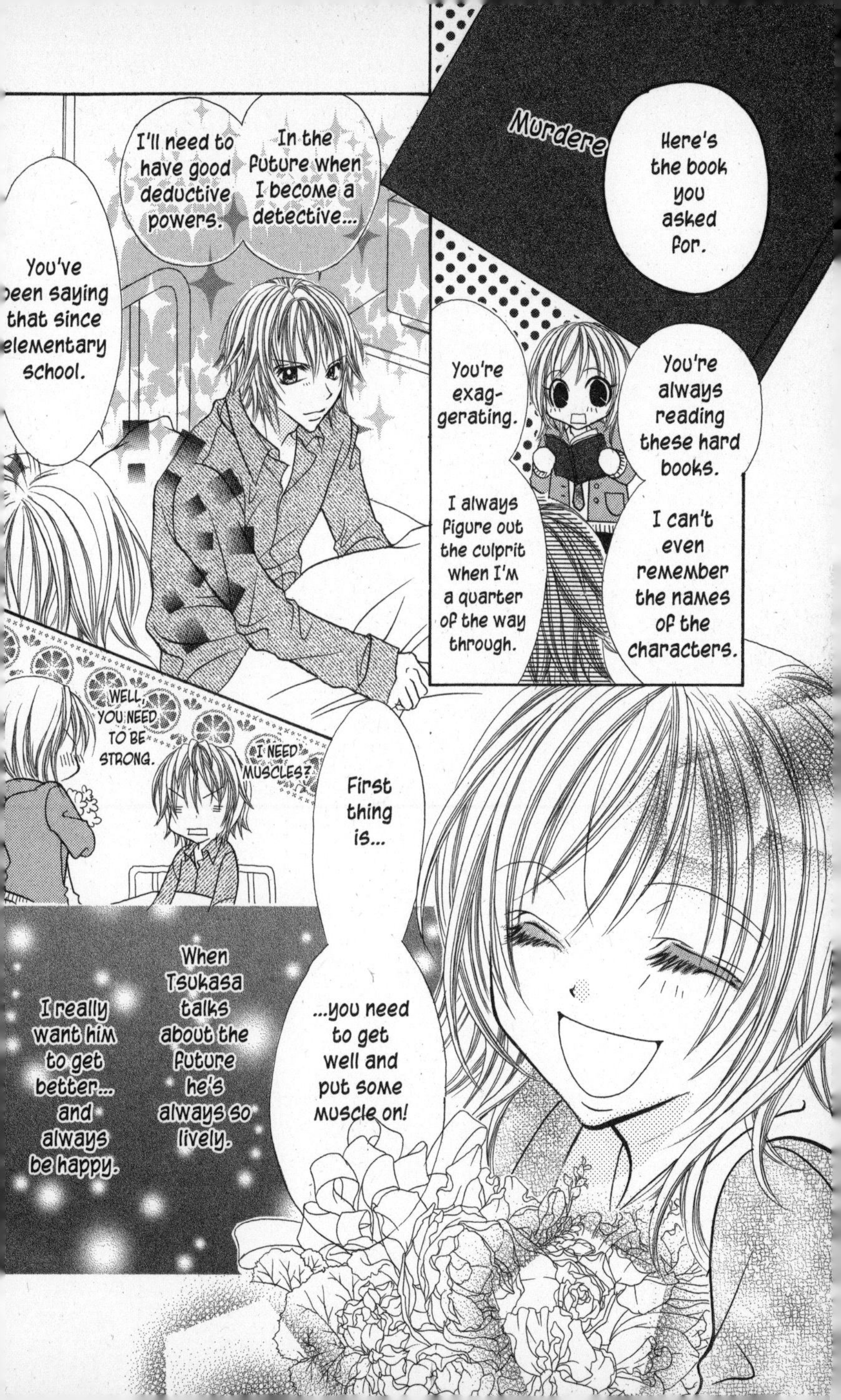
Murdere
Here's the book you asked for.
You're always reading these hard books.
I can't even remember the names of the characters.
You're exag-gerating.
I always figure out the culprit when I'm a quarter of the way through.
In the future when I become a detective...
I'll need to have good deductive powers.
You've been saying that since elementary school.
First thing is...
...you need to get well and put some muscle on!
WELL, YOU NEED TO BE STRONG.
I NEED MUSCLES?
When Tsukasa talks about the future he's always so lively.
I really want him to get better... and always be happy.

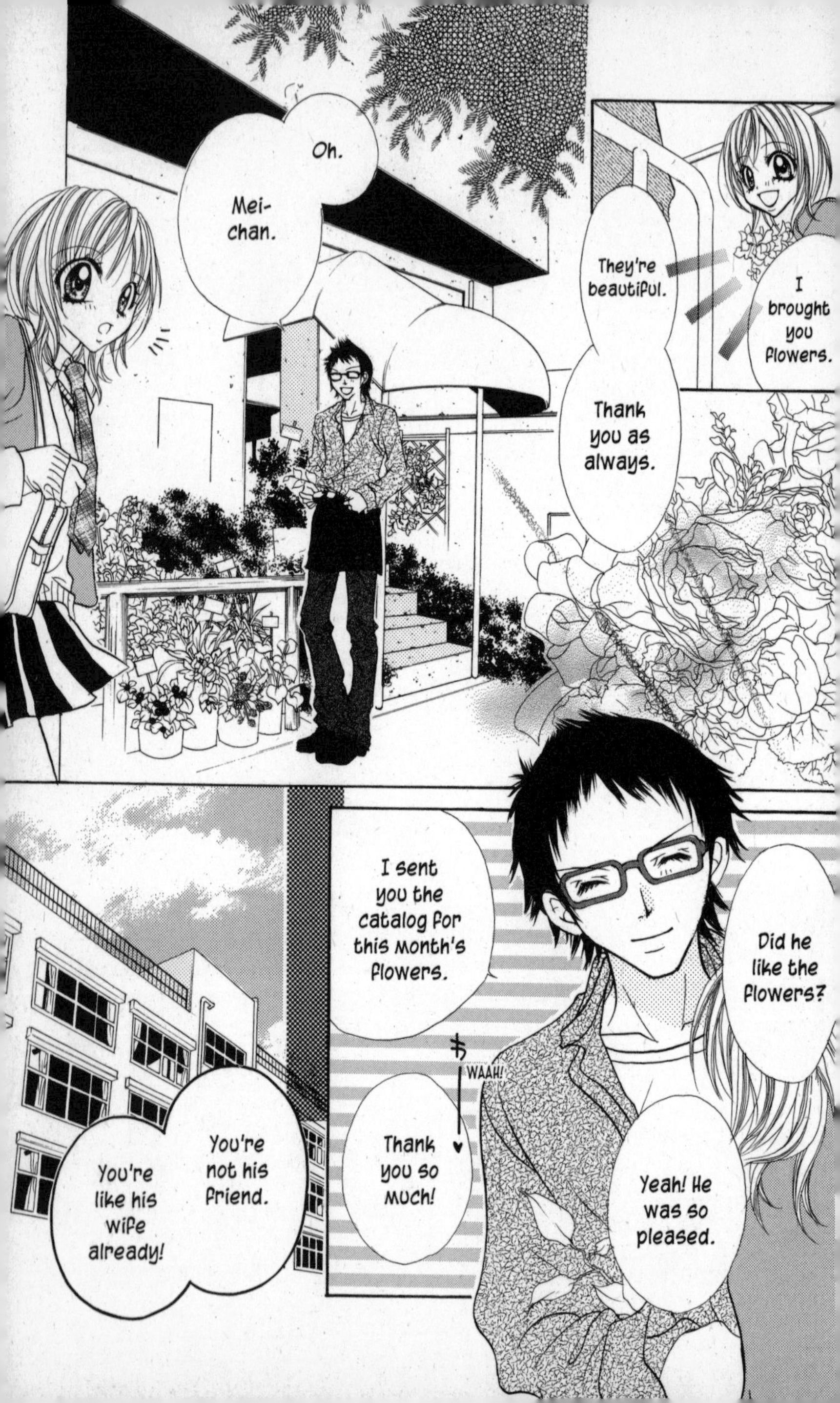
I brought you flowers.
They're beautiful.
Thank you as always.
Oh.
Mei-chan.
Did he like the flowers?
Yeah! He was so pleased.
I sent you the catalog for this month's flowers.
WAAH!
Thank you so much!
You're not his friend.
You're like his wife already!

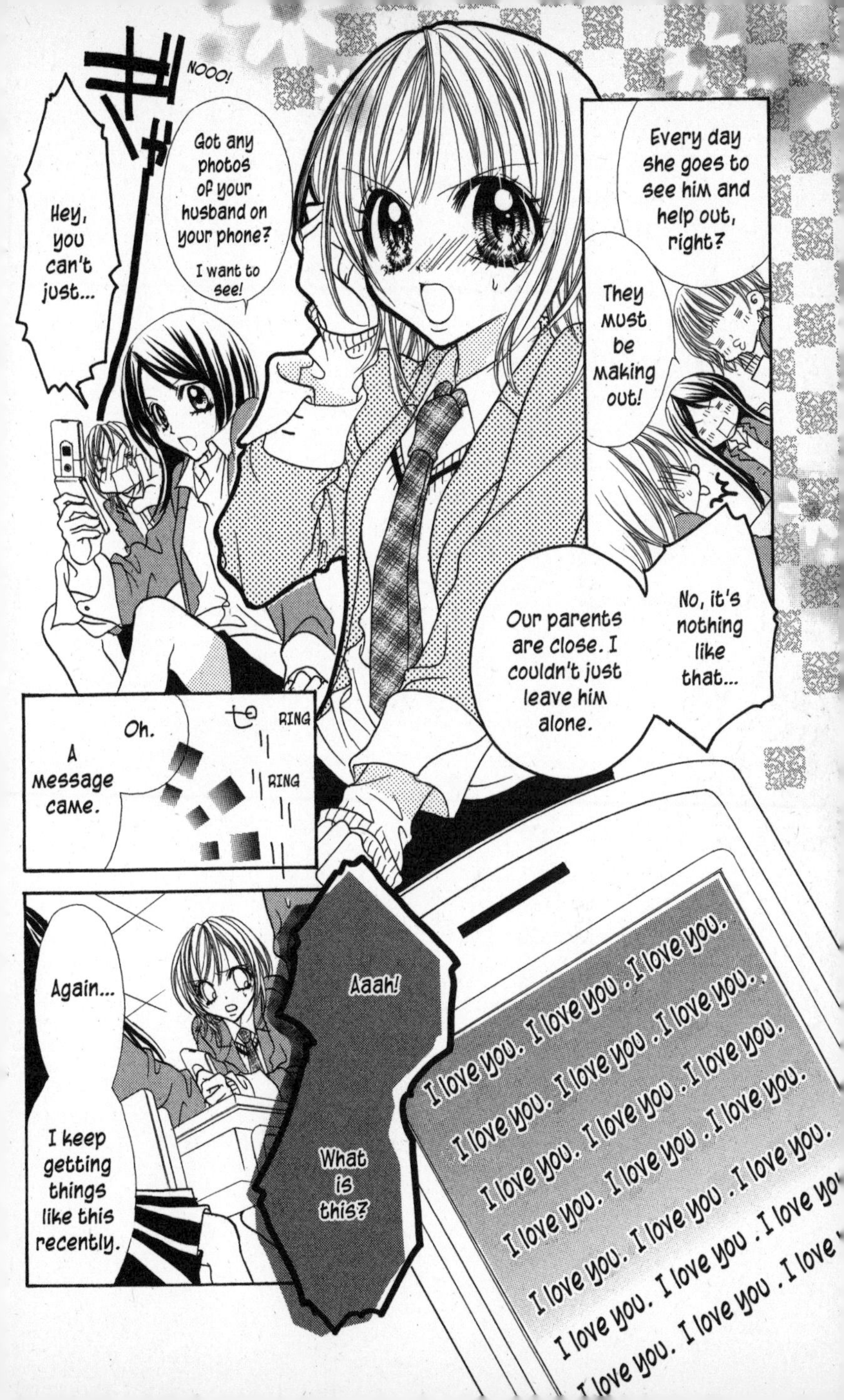
Every day she goes to see him and help out, right?
They must be making out!
No, it's nothing like that...
Our parents are close. I couldn't just leave him alone.
Got any photos of your husband on your phone?
I want to see!
NOOO!
Hey, you can't just...
RING
RING
Oh.
A message came.
I love you. I love you . I love you.
I love you. I love you . I love you. .
I love you. I love you . I love you.
I love you. I love you . I love you.
I love you. I love you . I love you.
I love you. I love you . I love you
I love you. I love you . I love
I love you. I love you.
Aaah!
What is this?
Again...
I keep getting things like this recently.

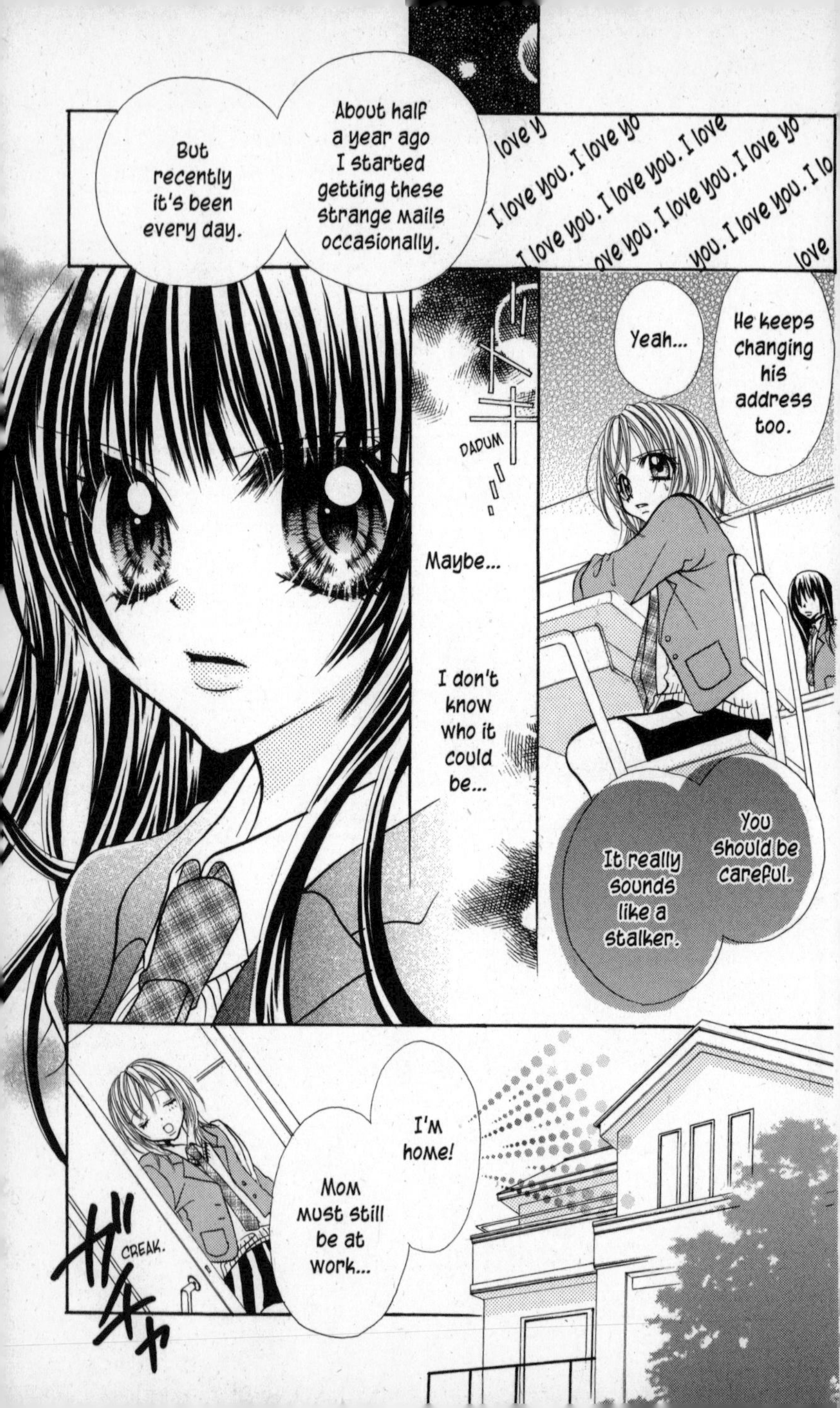
love y
I love you. I love yo
I love you. I love you. I love
ove you. I love you. I love you. I love yo
you. I love you. I lo
love
About half a year ago I started getting these strange mails occasionally.
But recently it's been every day.
He keeps changing his address too.
Yeah...
You should be careful.
It really sounds like a stalker.
DADUM
Maybe...
I don't know who it could be...
I'm home!
Mom must still be at work...
CREAK.

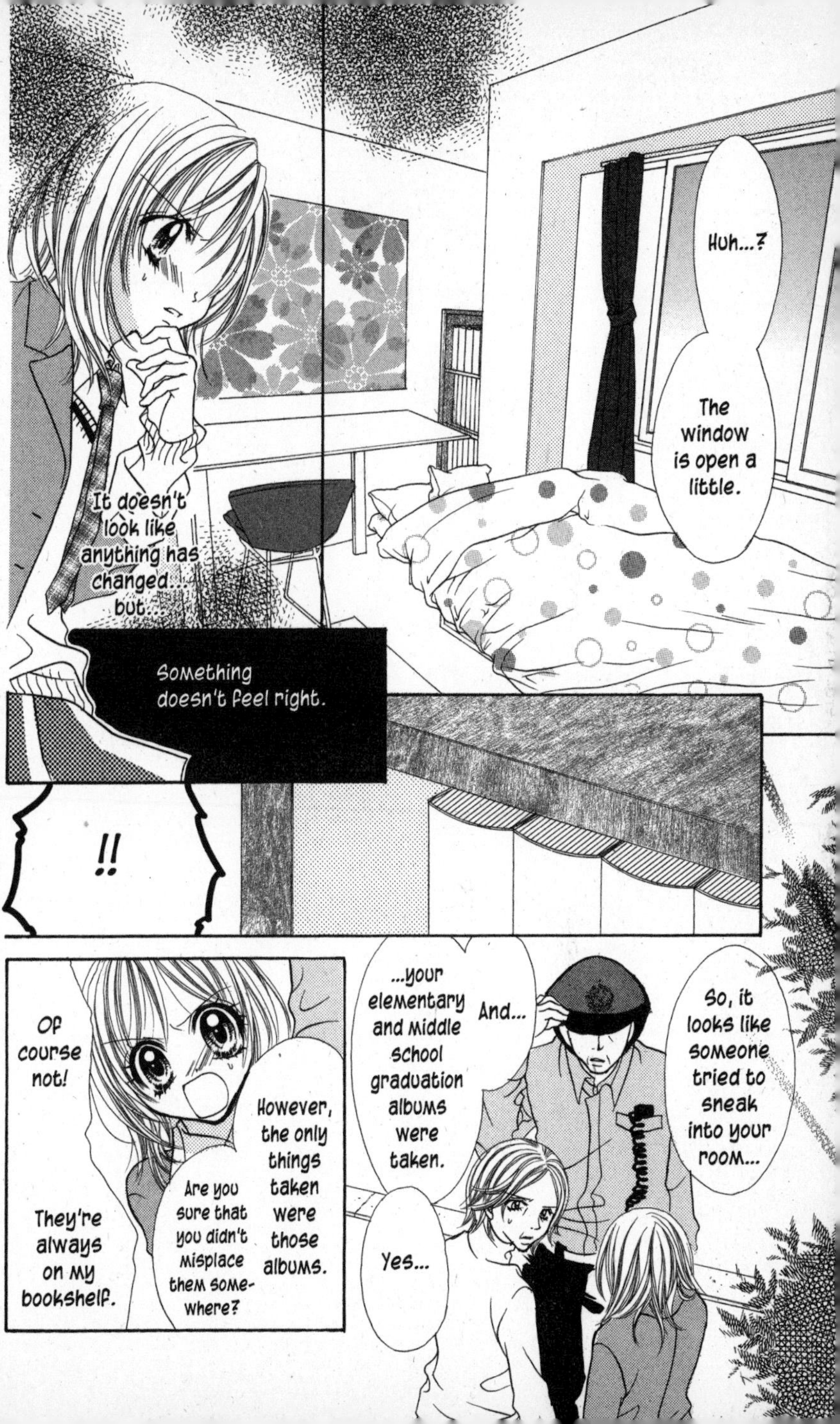
Huh...?
The window is open a little.
It doesn't look like anything has changed... but...
Something doesn't feel right.
!!
So, it looks like someone tried to sneak into your room...
And...
...your elementary and middle school graduation albums were taken.
Yes...
However, the only things taken were those albums.
Are you sure that you didn't misplace them some-where?
Of course not!
They're always on my bookshelf.

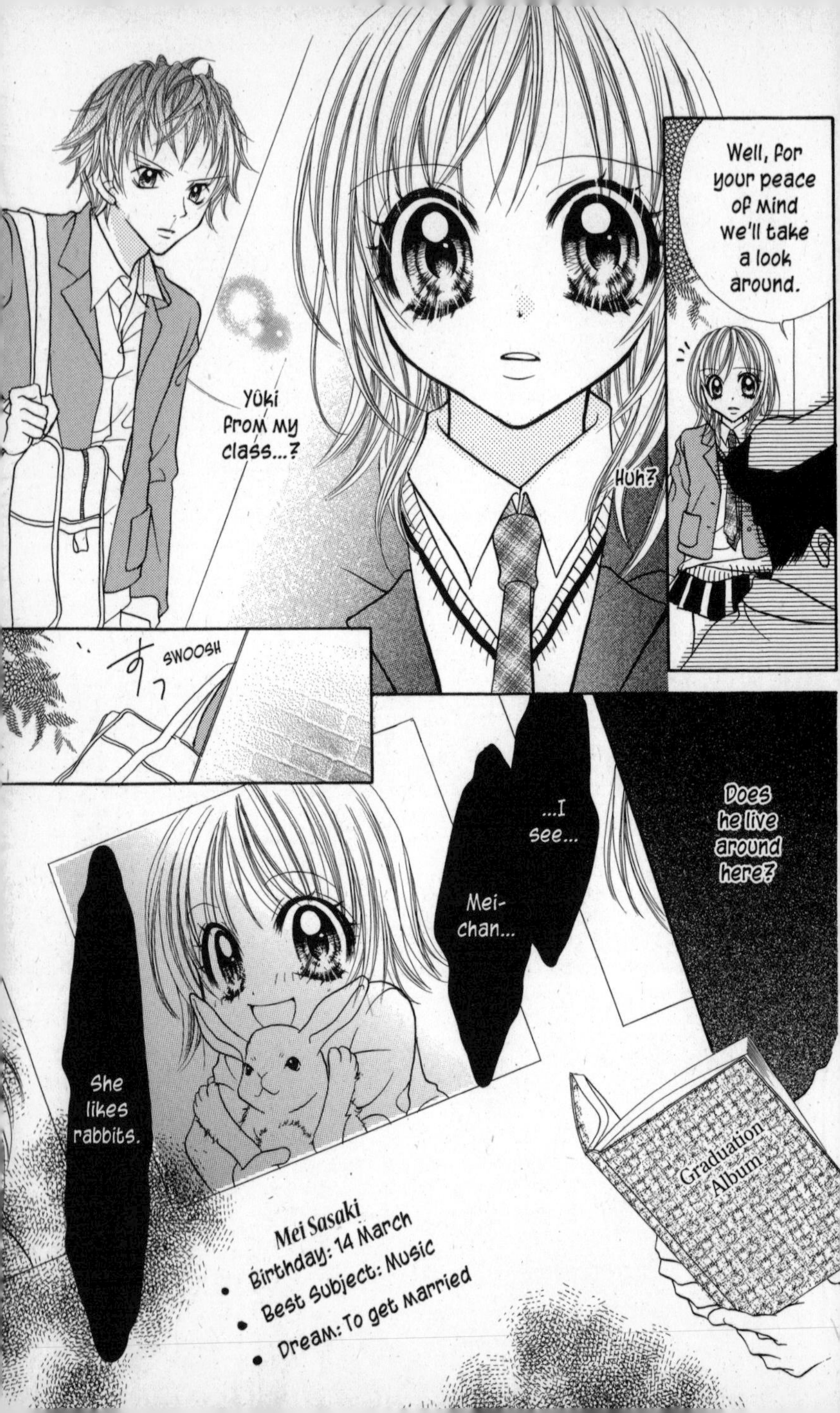
Well, for your peace of mind we'll take a look around.
Huh?
Yūki from my class...?
すっ
SWOOSH
Does he live around here?
...I see...
Mei-chan...
She likes rabbits.
Graduation Album
Mei Sasaki
• Birthday: 14 March
• Best Subject: Music
• Dream: To get Married

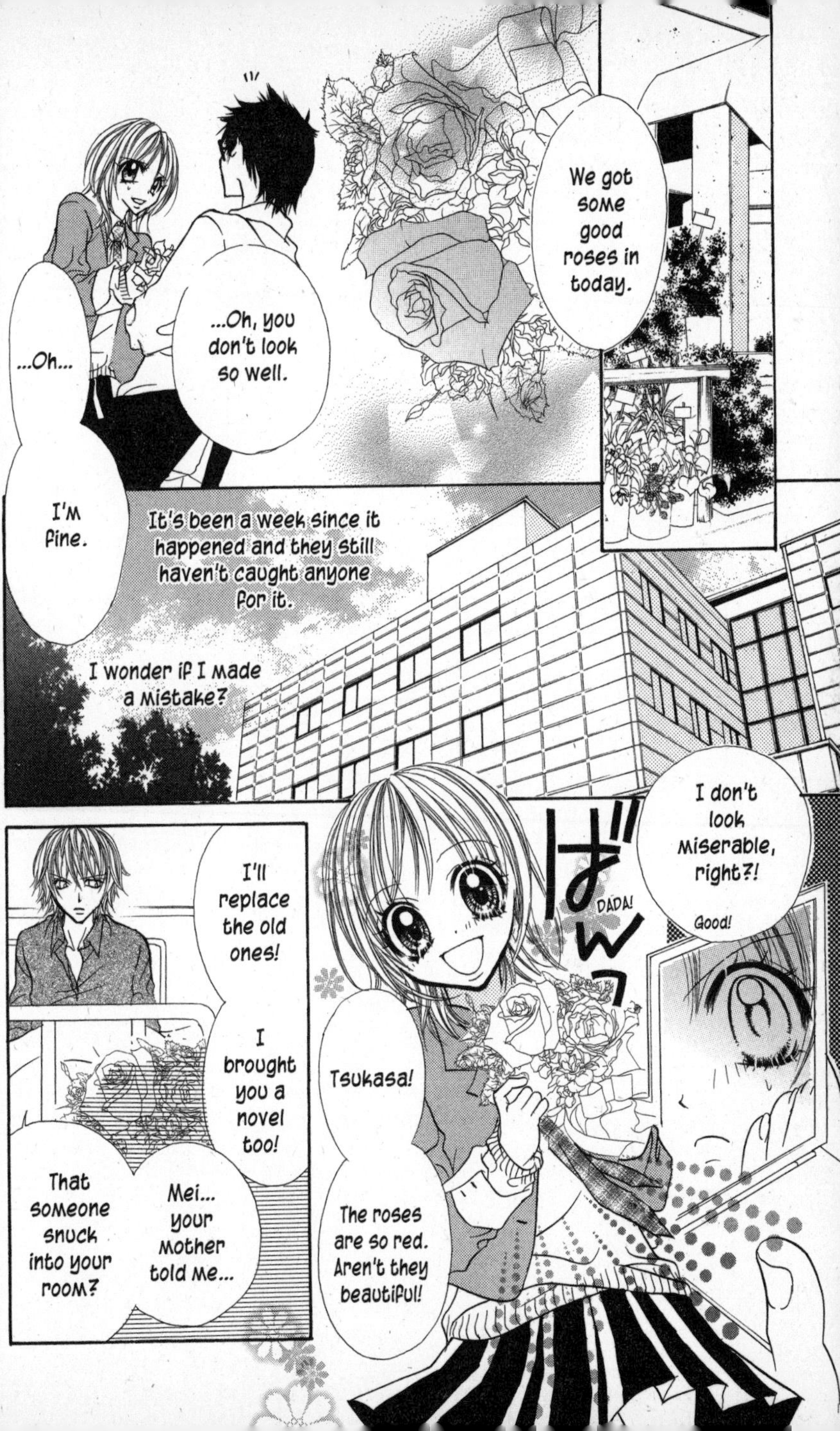

We got some good roses in today.
...Oh, you don't look so well.
...Oh...
I'm fine.
It's been a week since it happened and they still haven't caught anyone for it.
I wonder if I made a mistake?
I don't look miserable, right?!
Good!
ばっ
DADA!
Tsukasa!
The roses are so red. Aren't they beautiful!
I'll replace the old ones!
I brought you a novel too!
Mei... your mother told me...
That someone snuck into your room?

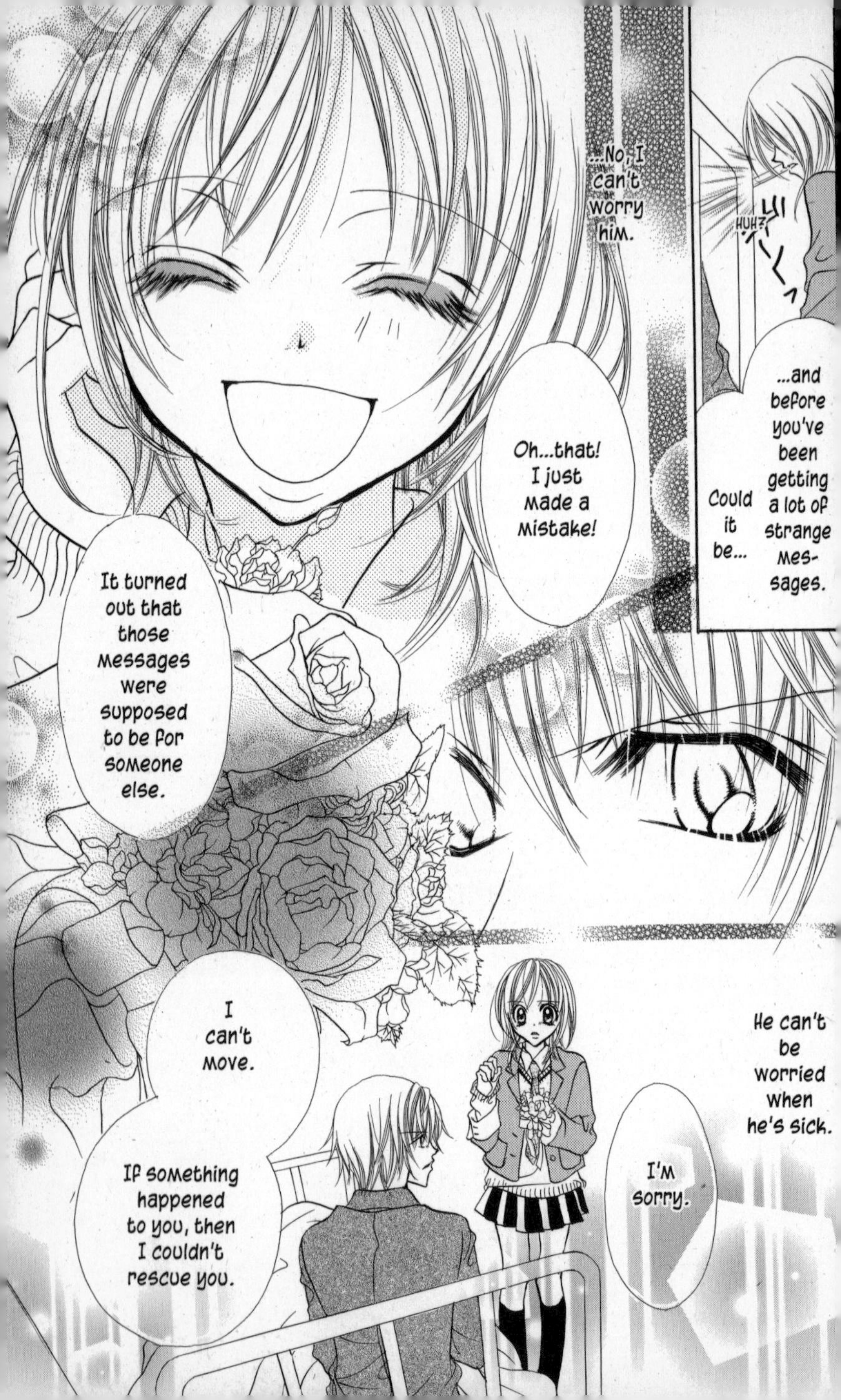
HUH?
...and before you've been getting a lot of strange messages.
Could it be...
...No, I can't worry him.
Oh...that! I just made a mistake!
It turned out that those messages were supposed to be for someone else.
He can't be worried when he's sick.
I'm sorry.
I can't move.
If something happened to you, then I couldn't rescue you.

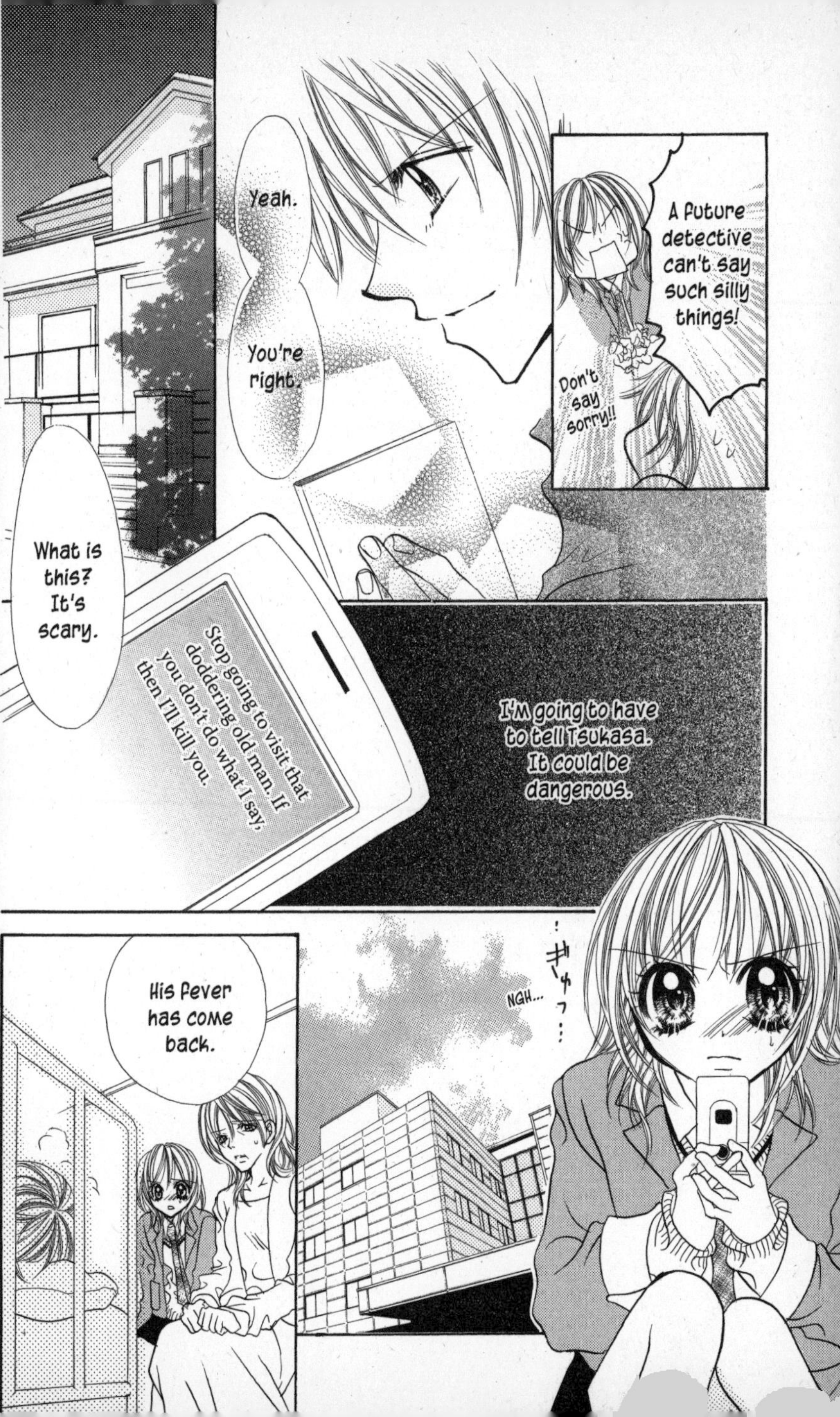
A future detective can't say such silly things!
Don't say sorry!!
Yeah.
You're right.
I'm going to have to tell Tsukasa. It could be dangerous.
Stop going to visit that doddering old man. If you don't do what I say, then I'll kill you.
What is this? It's scary.
NGH...
His fever has come back.

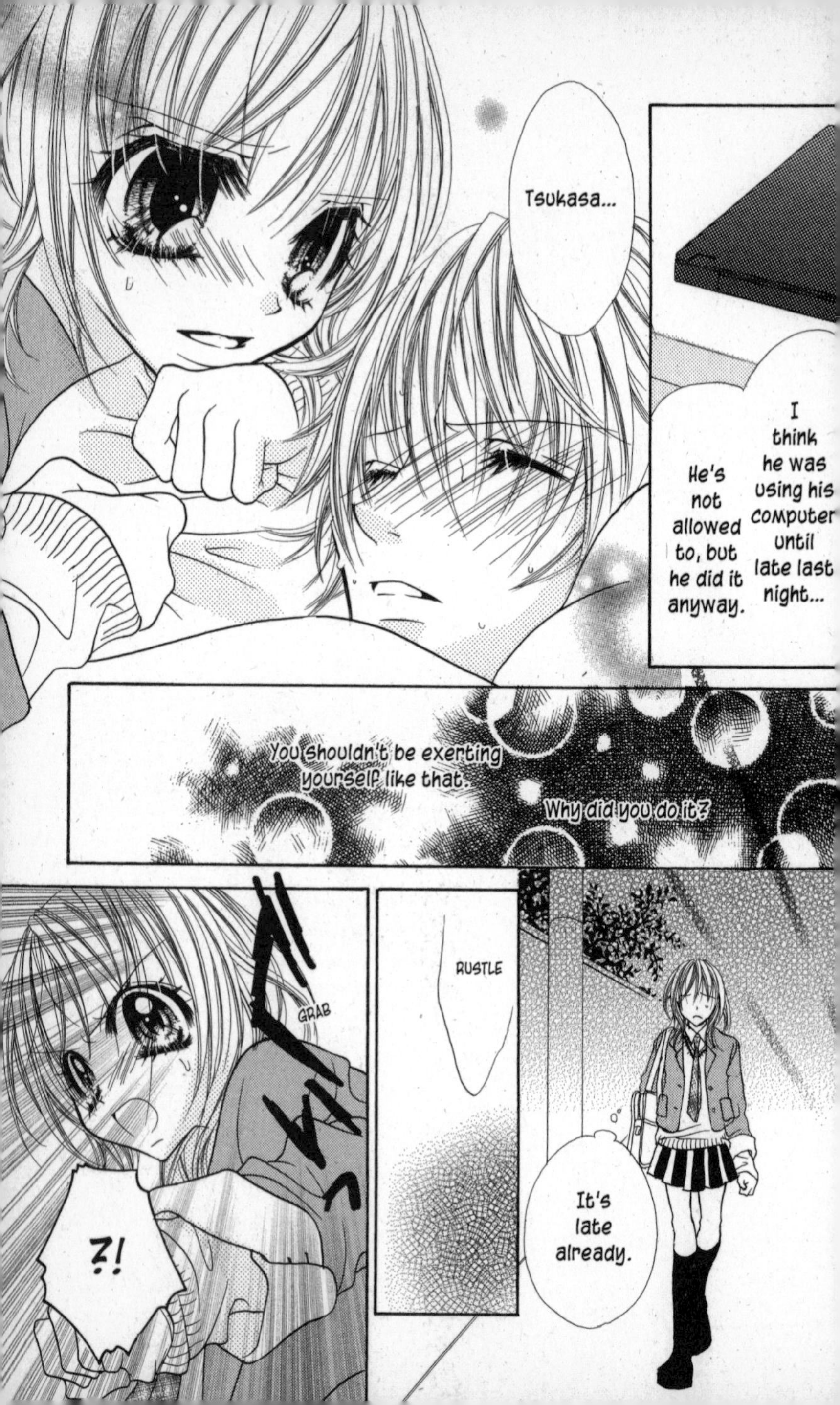
I think he was using his computer until late last night...
He's not allowed to, but he did it anyway.
Tsukasa...
You shouldn't be exerting yourself like that.
Why did you do it?
It's late already.
RUSTLE
GRAB
?!

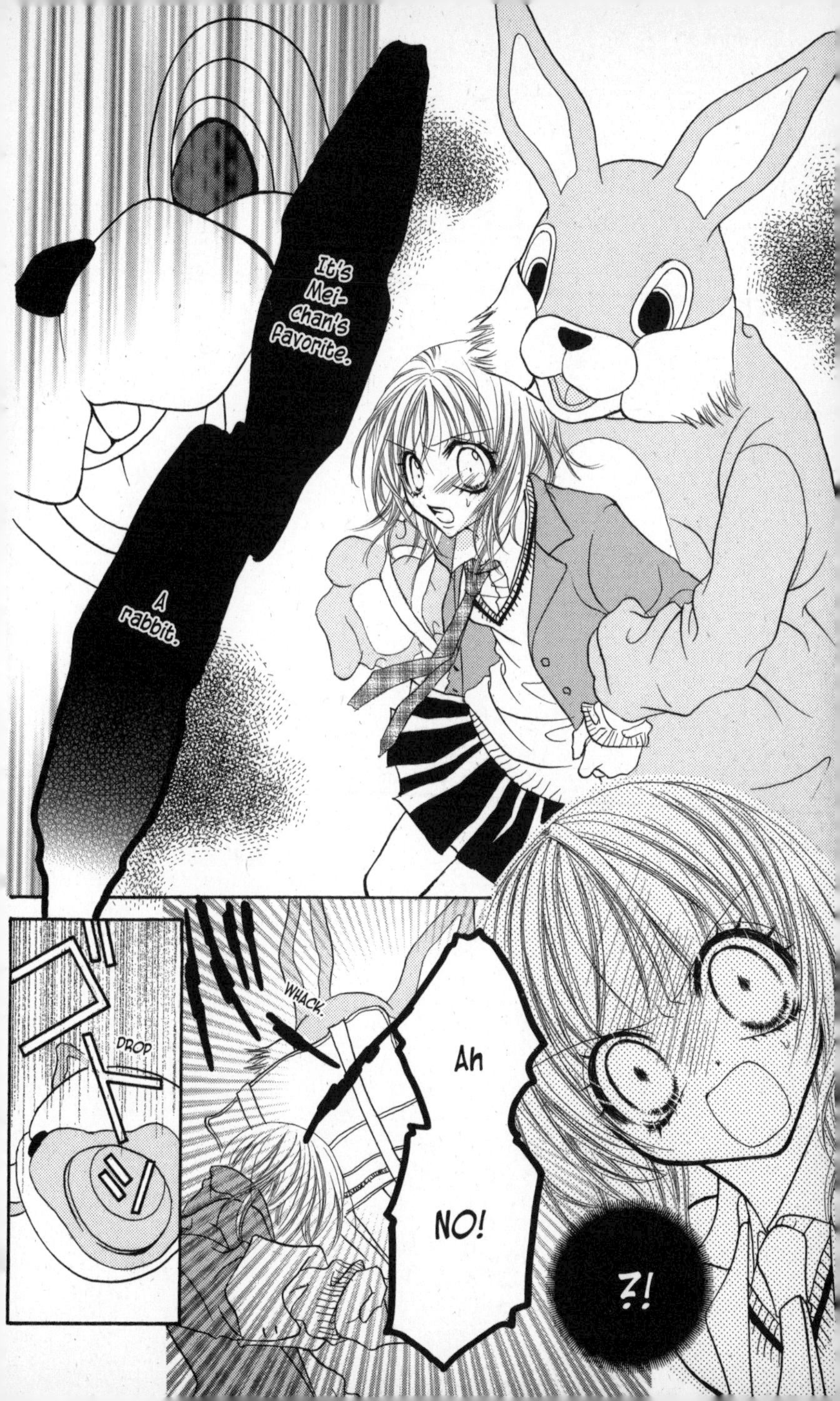
It's Mei-chan's favorite.
A rabbit.
?!
Ah
NO!
WHACK.
DROP

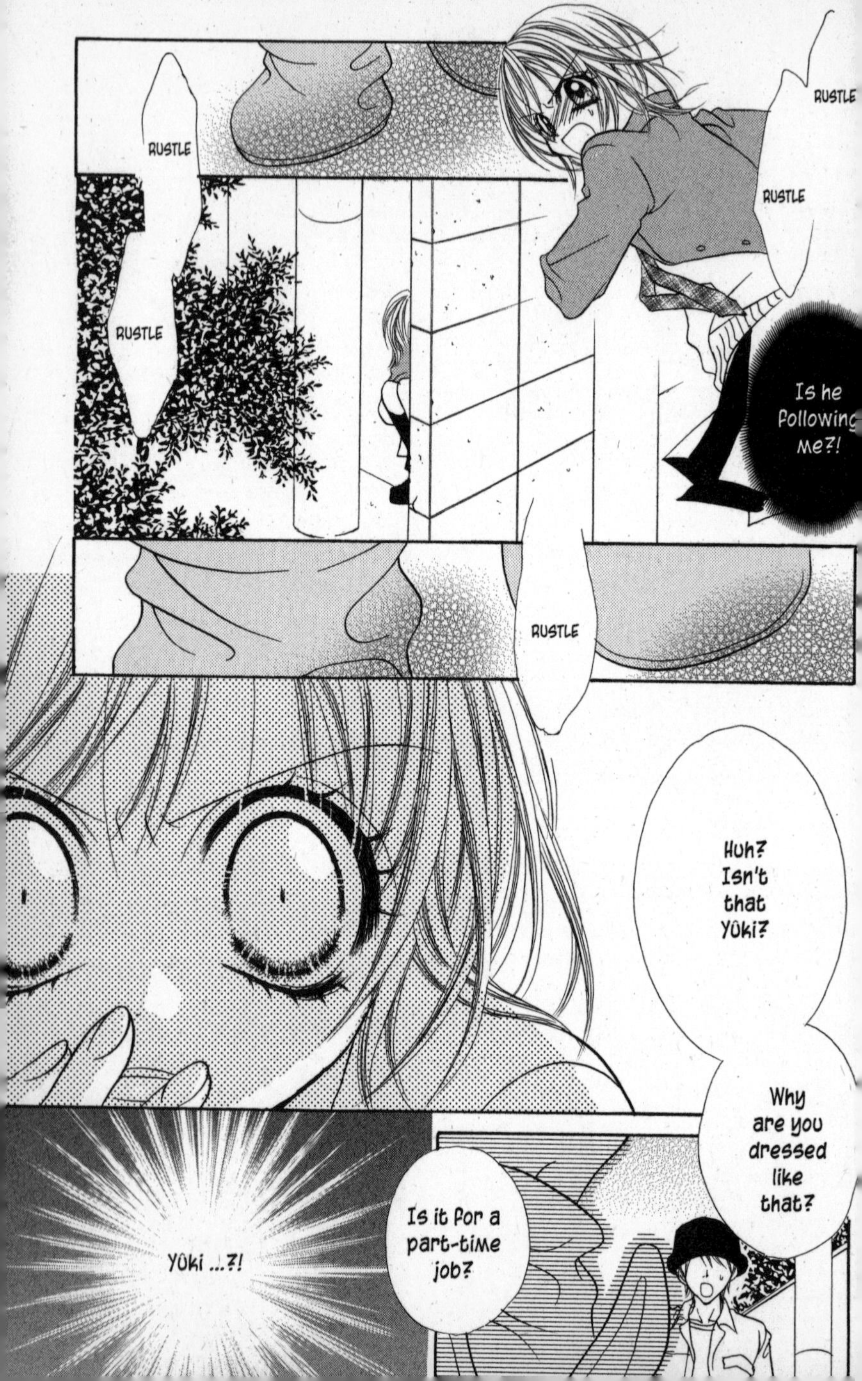
RUSTLE
RUSTLE
Is he following me?!
RUSTLE
RUSTLE
RUSTLE
Huh? Isn't that Yûki?
Why are you dressed like that?
Is it for a part-time job?
Yûki ...?!

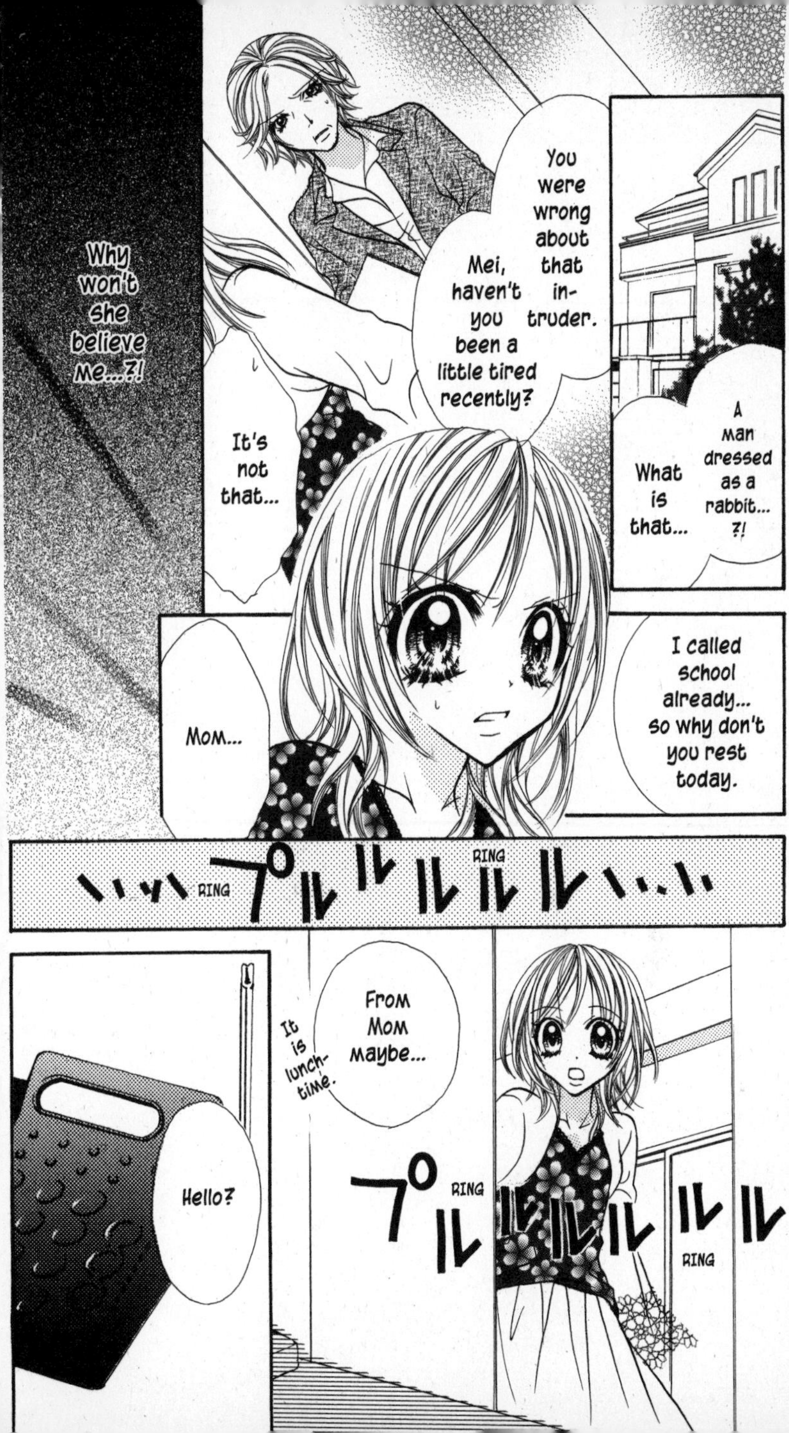
A man dressed as a rabbit...?!
What is that...
You were wrong about that intruder.
Mei, haven't you been a little tired recently?
It's not that...
I called school already... so why don't you rest today.
Mom...
Why won't she believe me...?!
RING
RING
RING
RING
From Mom maybe...
It is lunch-time.
Hello?

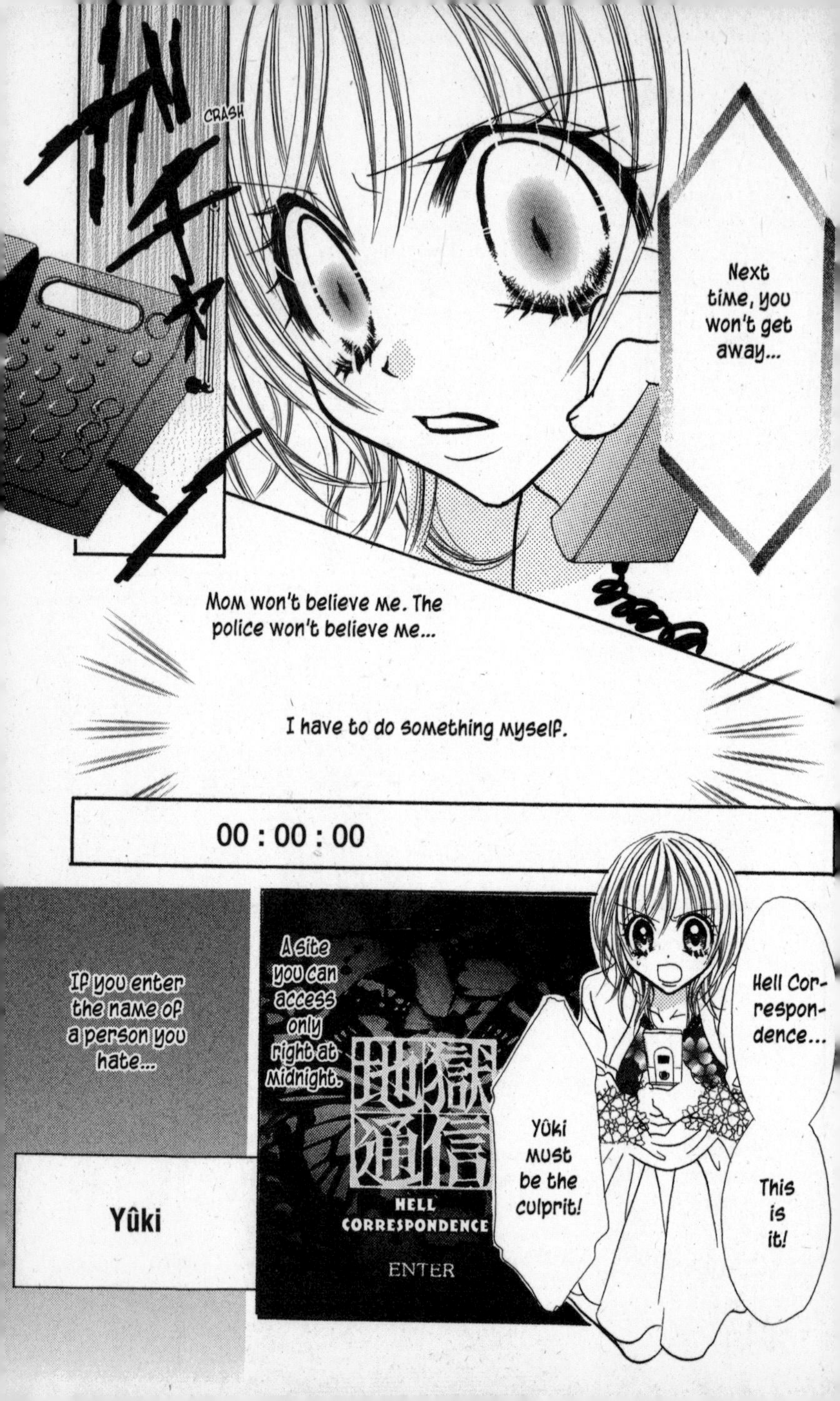

Next time, you won't get away...
CRASH
Mom won't believe me. The police won't believe me...
I have to do something myself.
00 : 00 : 00
Hell Correspondence...
This is it!
Yûki must be the culprit!
A site you can access only right at midnight.
地獄通信
HELL CORRESPONDENCE
ENTER
If you enter the name of a person you hate...
Yûki

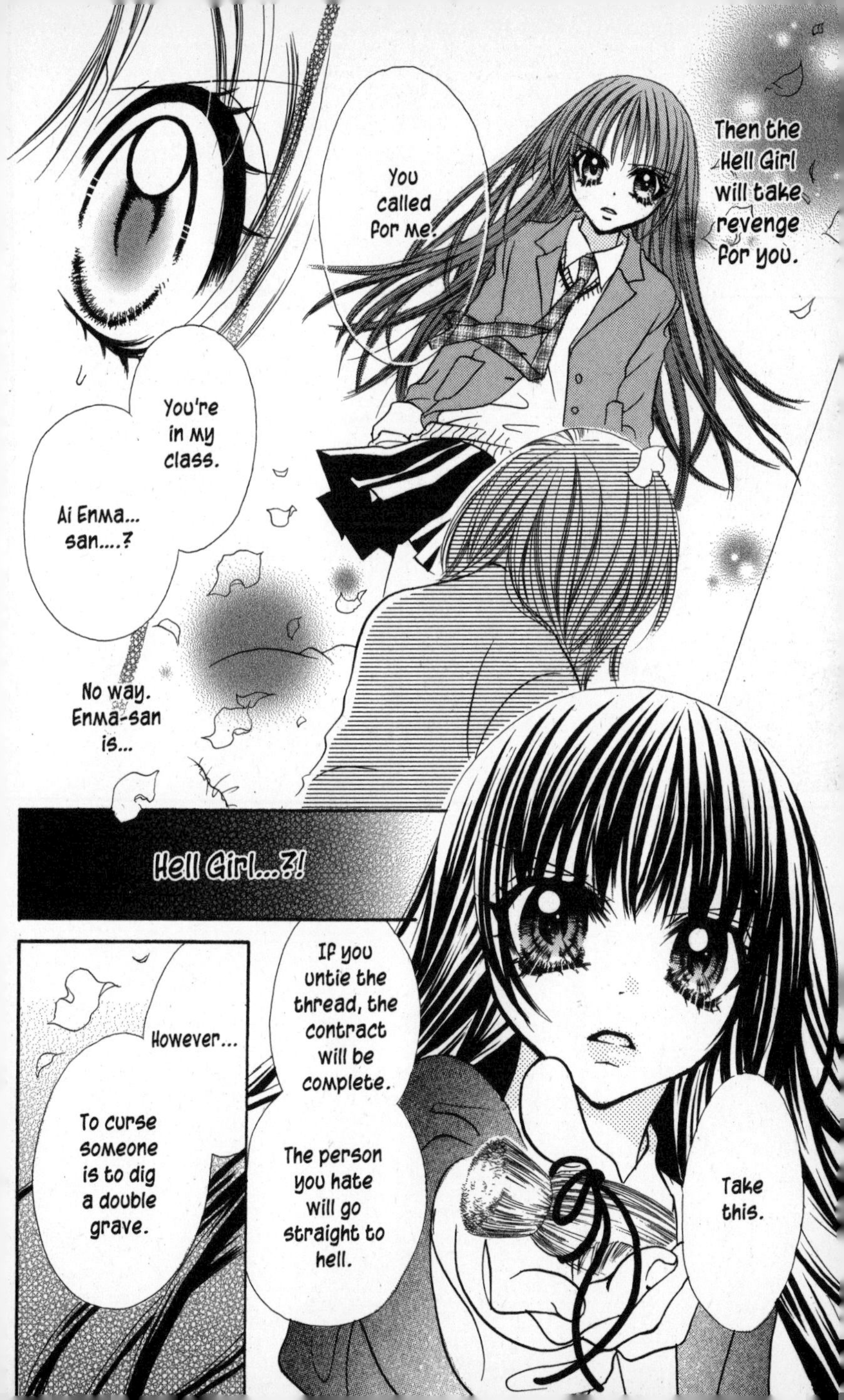

Then the Hell Girl will take revenge for you.
You called for me.
You're in my class.
Ai Enma... san....?
No way. Enma-san is...
Hell Girl...?!
Take this.
If you untie the thread, the contract will be complete.
The person you hate will go straight to hell.
However...
To curse someone is to dig a double grave.

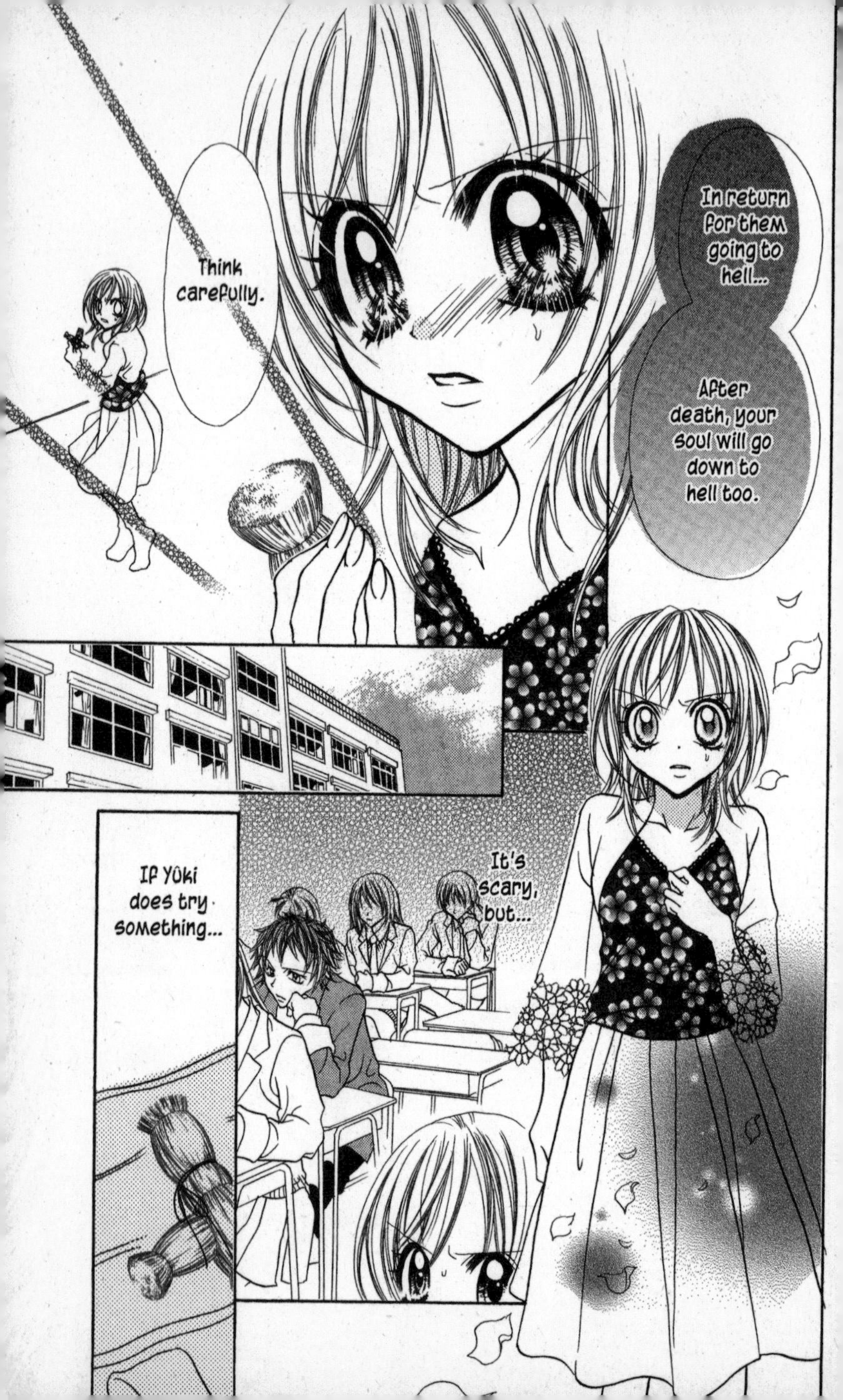
In return for them going to hell...
After death, your soul will go down to hell too.
Think carefully.
It's scary, but...
If Yûki does try something...

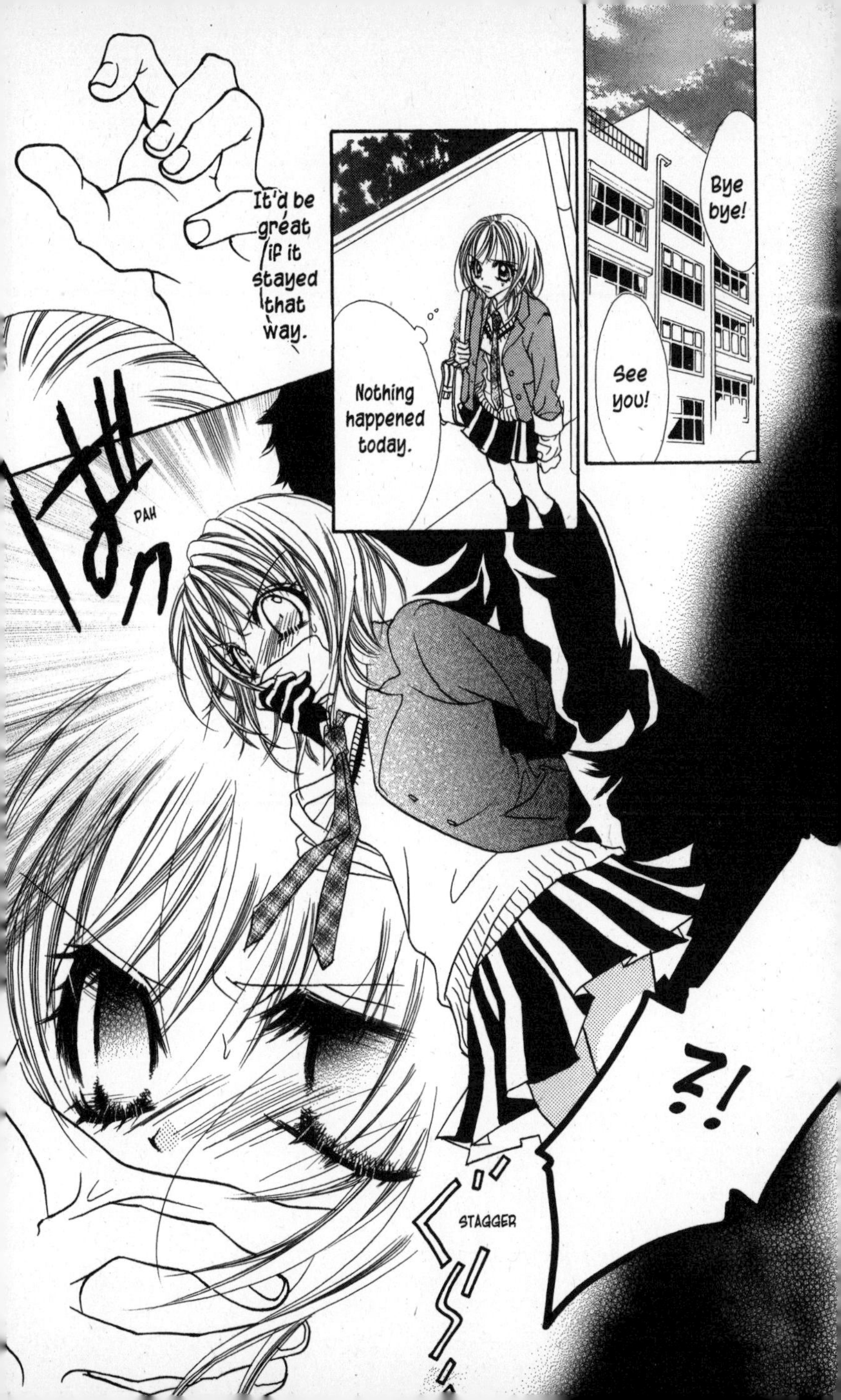

Bye bye!
See you!
Nothing happened today.
It'd be great if it stayed that way.
PAH
?!
STAGGER

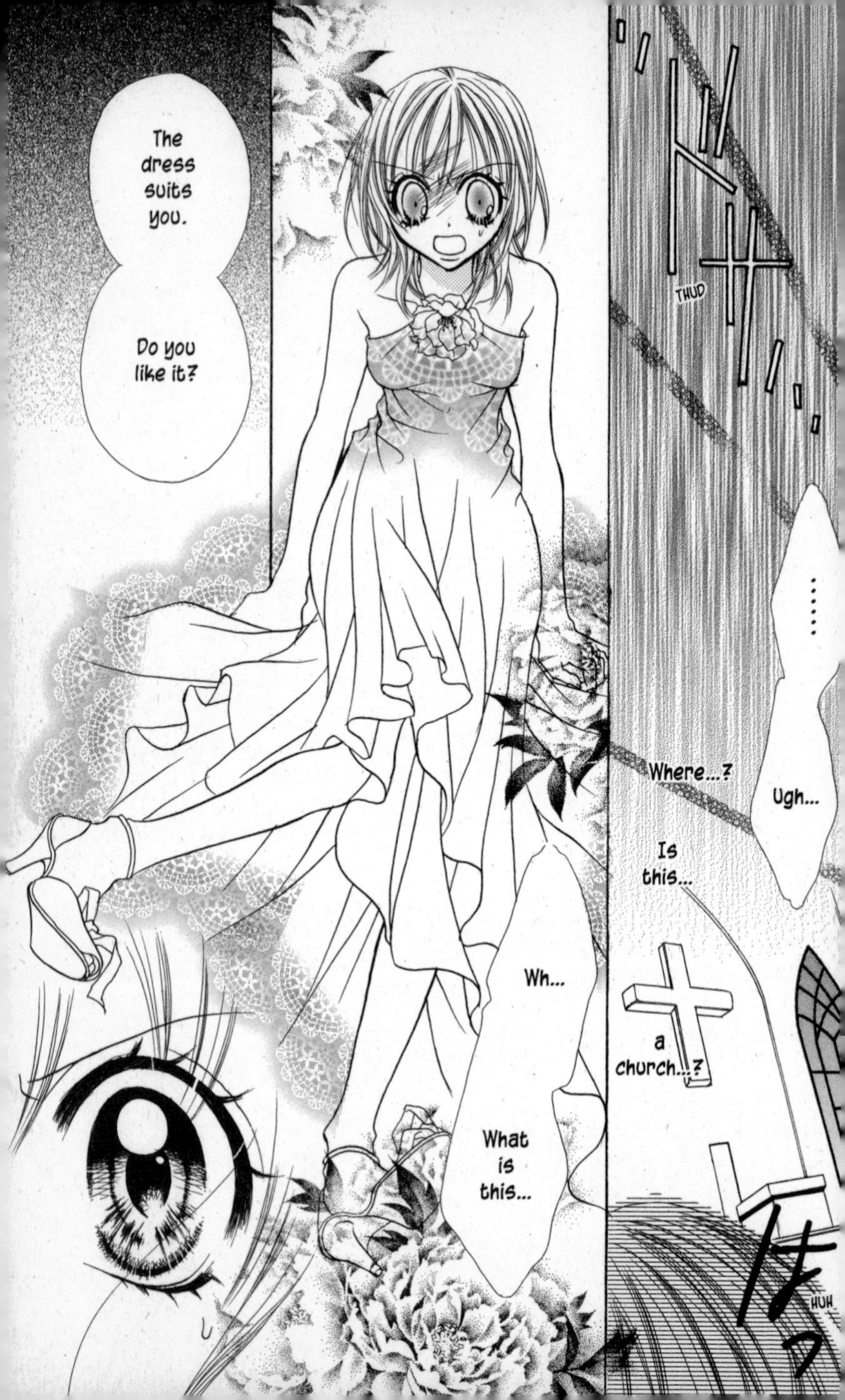

ドサッ
THUD
......
Ugh...
Where...?
Is this...
a church...?
はっ
HUH
Wh...
What is this...
The dress suits you.
Do you like it?

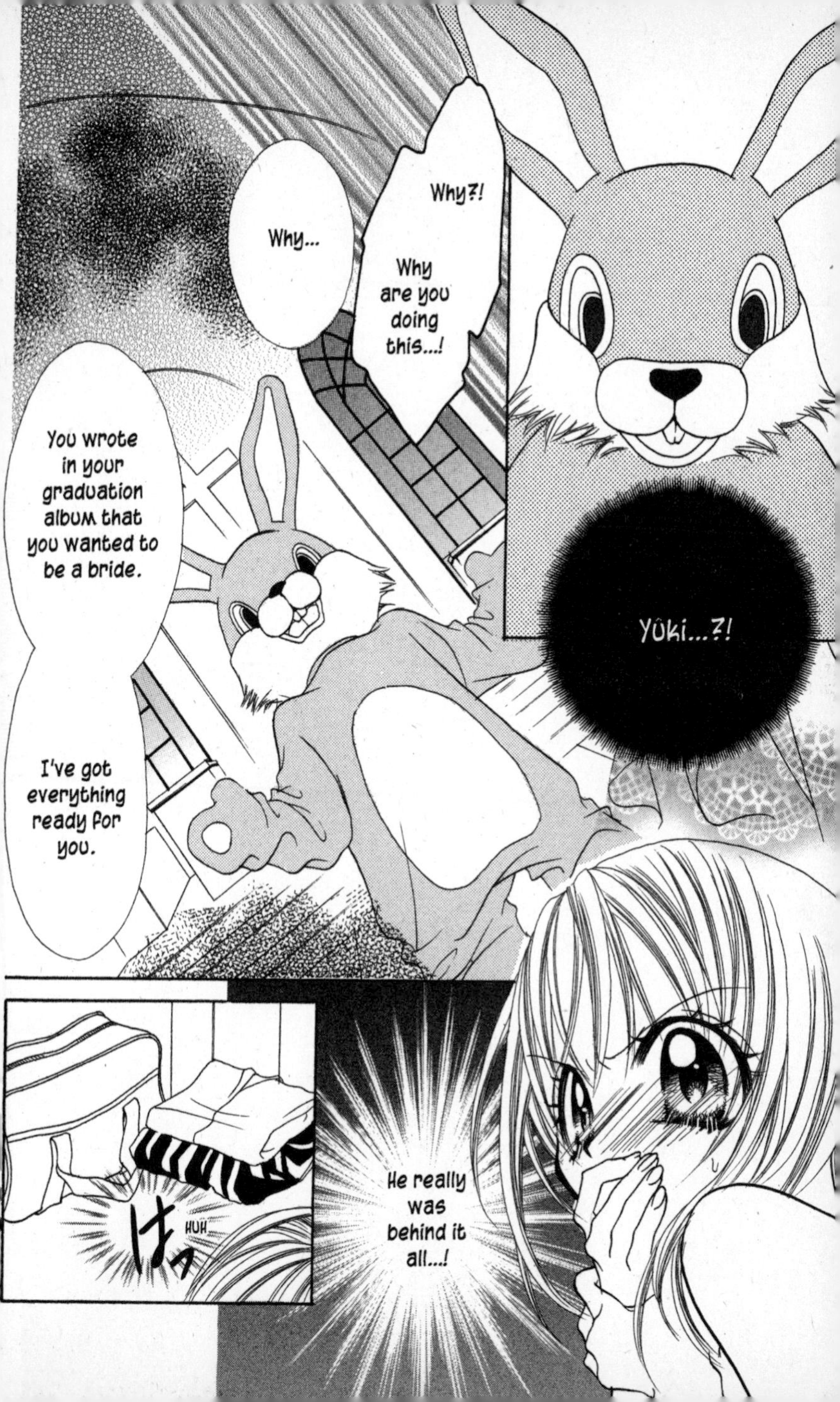

Yûki...?!
Why?!
Why are you doing this...!
Why...
You wrote in your graduation album that you wanted to be a bride.
I've got everything ready for you.
He really was behind it all...!
はっ
HUH

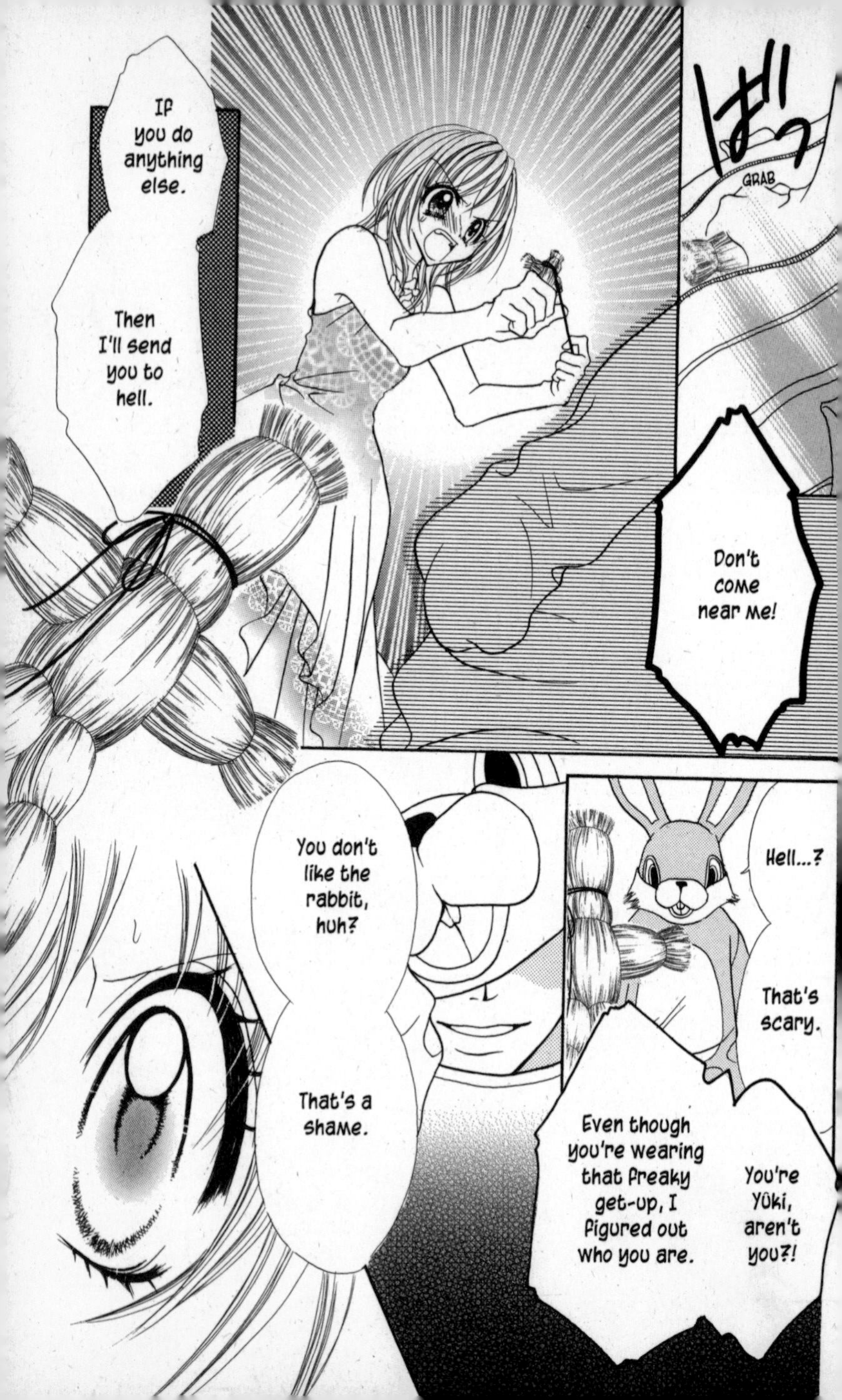
ぱっ
GRAB
Don't come near me!
If you do anything else.
Then I'll send you to hell.
Hell...?
That's scary.
You're Yûki, aren't you?!
Even though you're wearing that freaky get-up, I figured out who you are.
You don't like the rabbit, huh?
That's a shame.

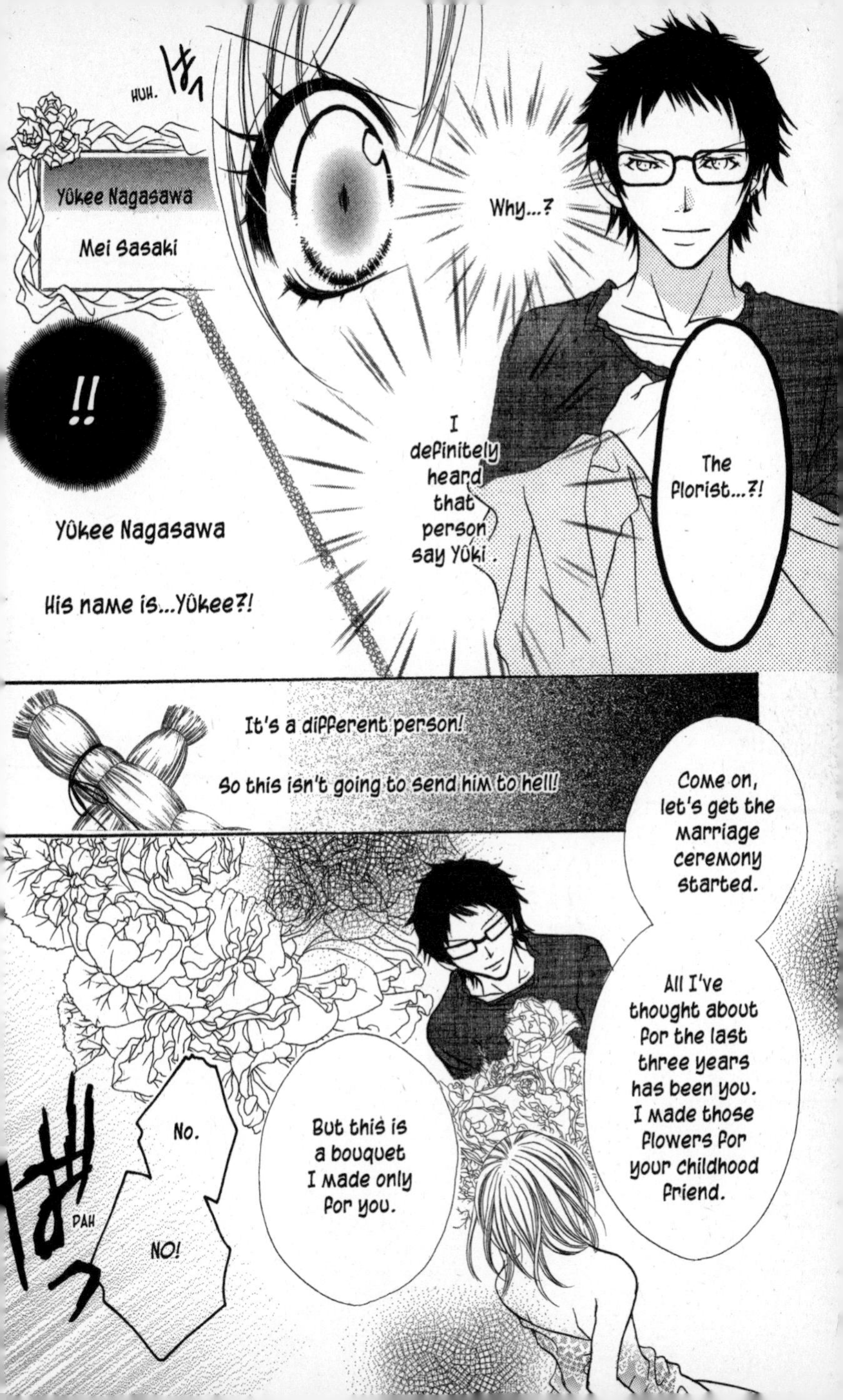
Why...?
The florist...?!
I definitely heard that person say Yûki.
HUH.
Yûkee Nagasawa
Mei Sasaki
!!
Yûkee Nagasawa
His name is...Yûkee?!
It's a different person!
So this isn't going to send him to hell!
Come on, let's get the marriage ceremony started.
All I've thought about for the last three years has been you. I made those flowers for your childhood friend.
But this is a bouquet I made only for you.
No.
PAH
NO!

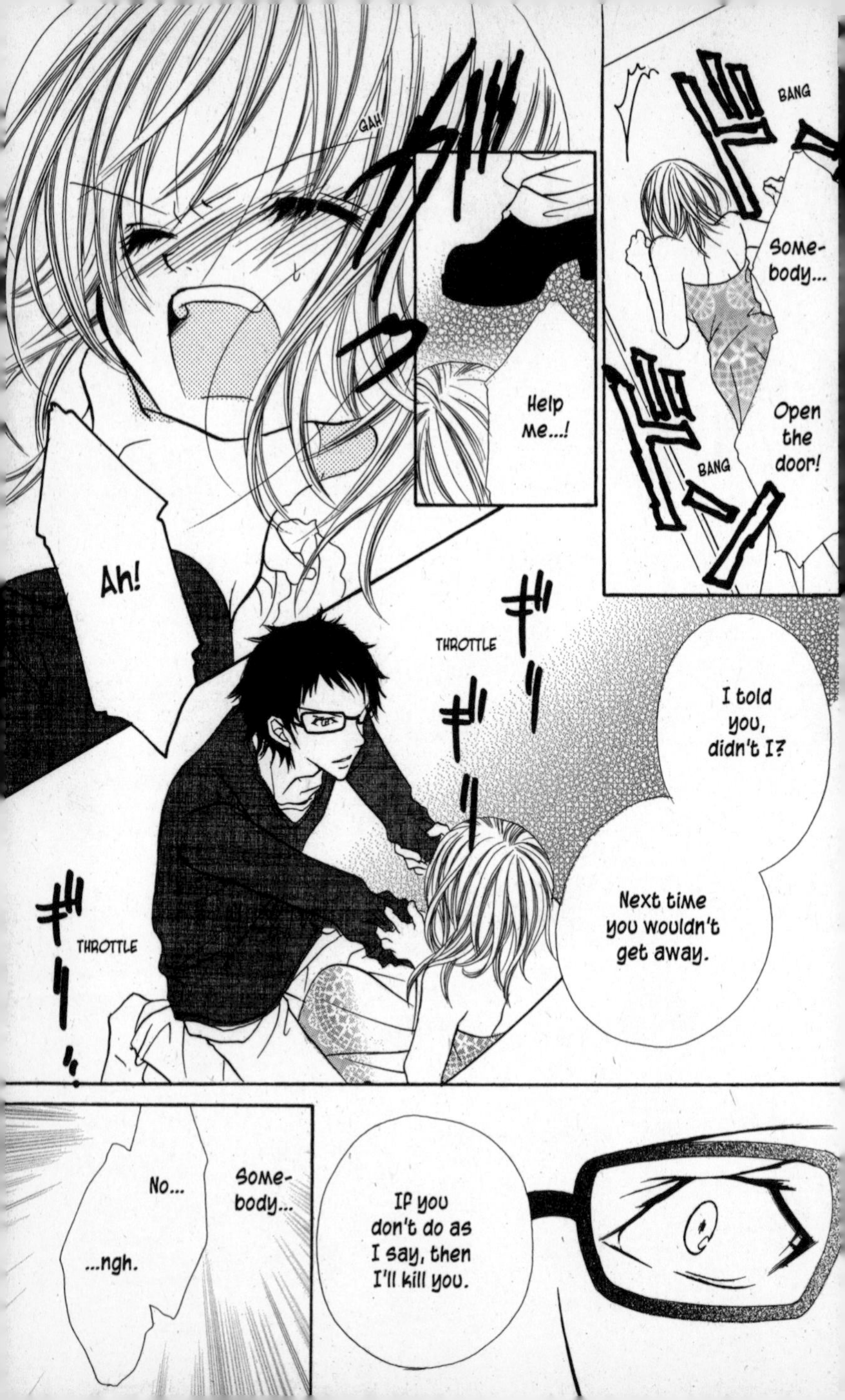
BANG
Some-body...
Open the door!
BANG
Help me...!
GAH
Ah!
I told you, didn't I?
Next time you wouldn't get away.
THROTTLE
THROTTLE
If you don't do as I say, then I'll kill you.
Some-body...
No...
...ngh.

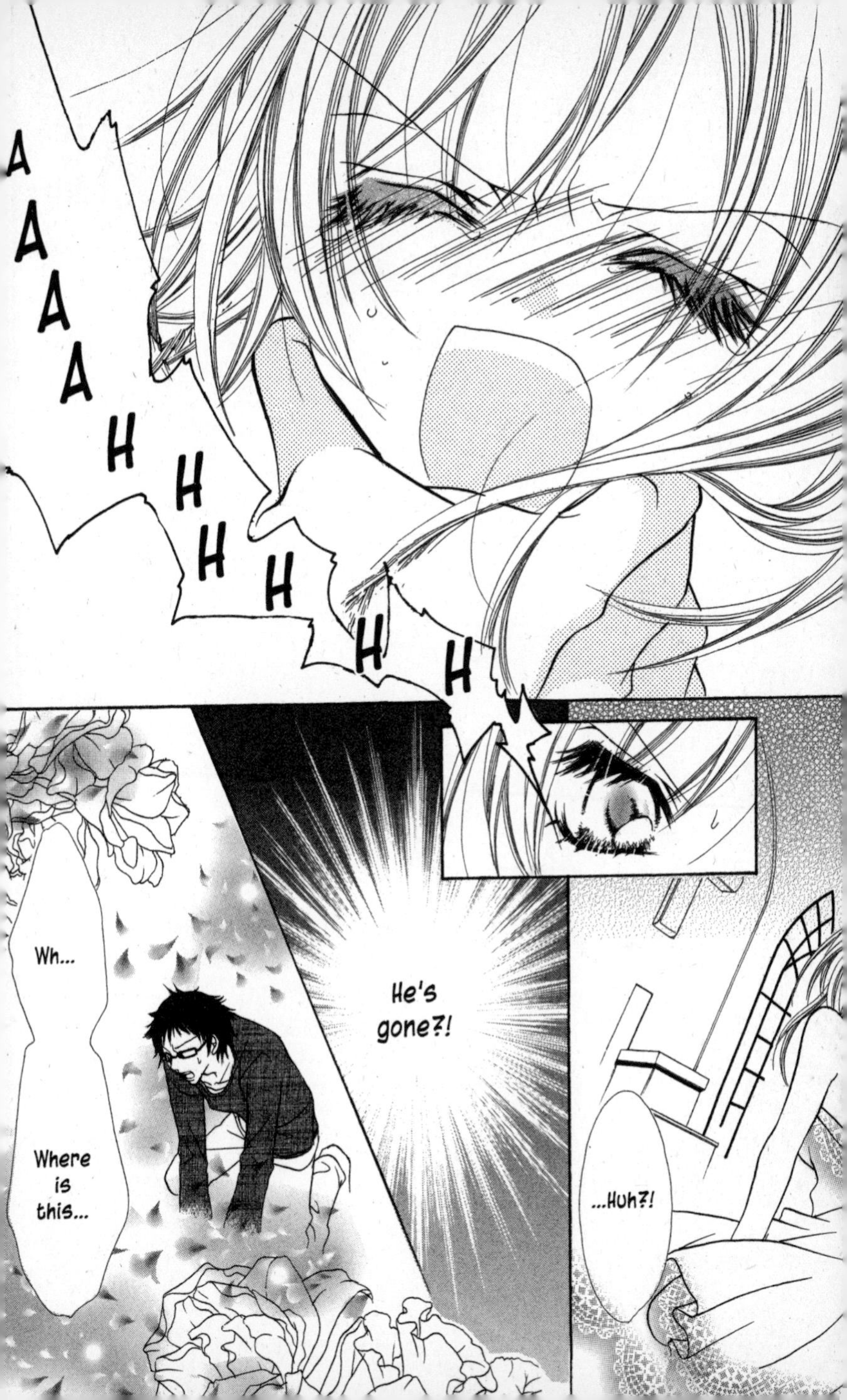
AAAAHHHHHH
...Huh?!
He's gone?!
Wh...
Where is this...

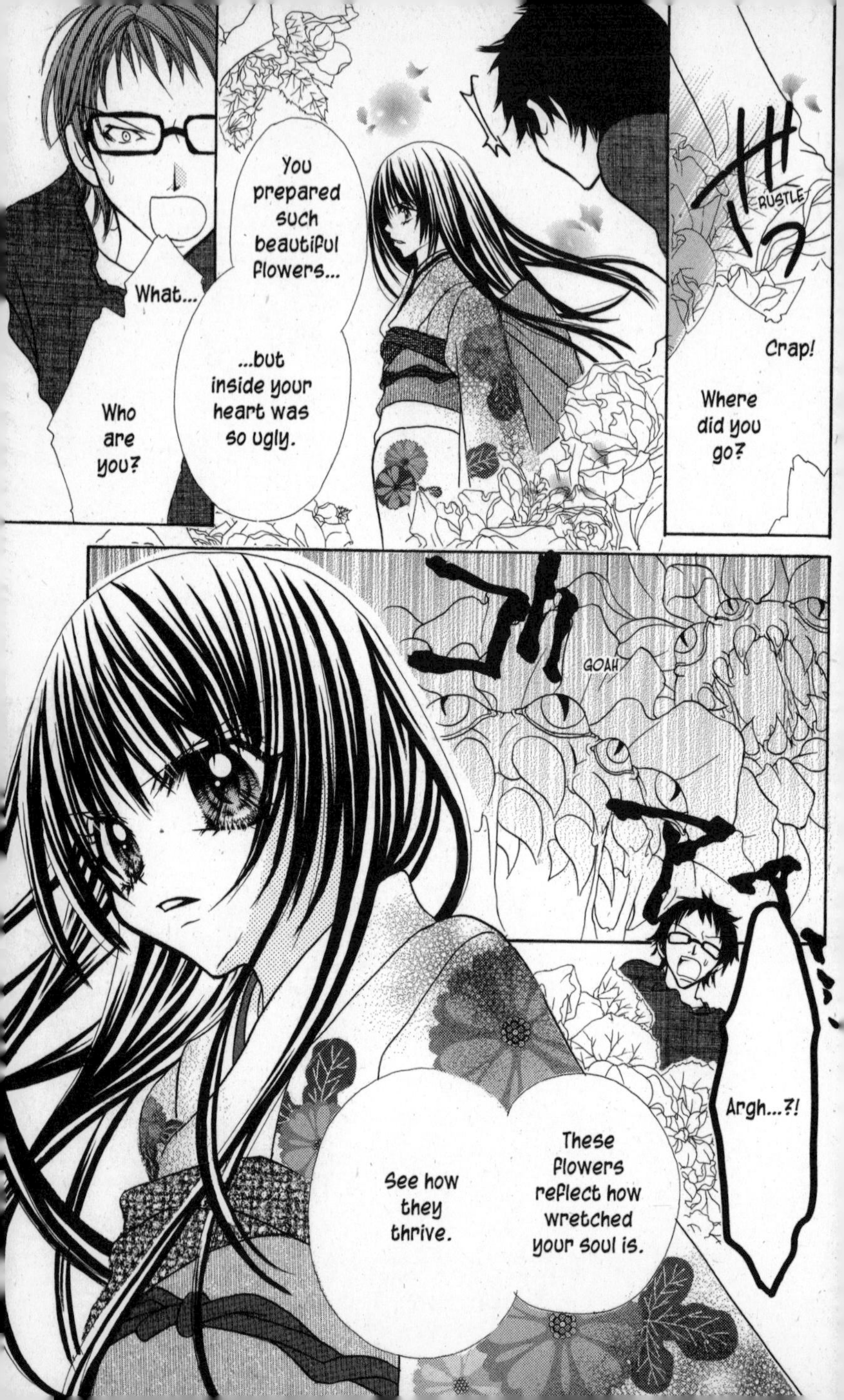
RUSTLE
Crap!
Where did you go?
You prepared such beautiful flowers...
...but inside your heart was so ugly.
What...
Who are you?
GOAH
Argh...?!
These flowers reflect how wretched your soul is.
See how they thrive.

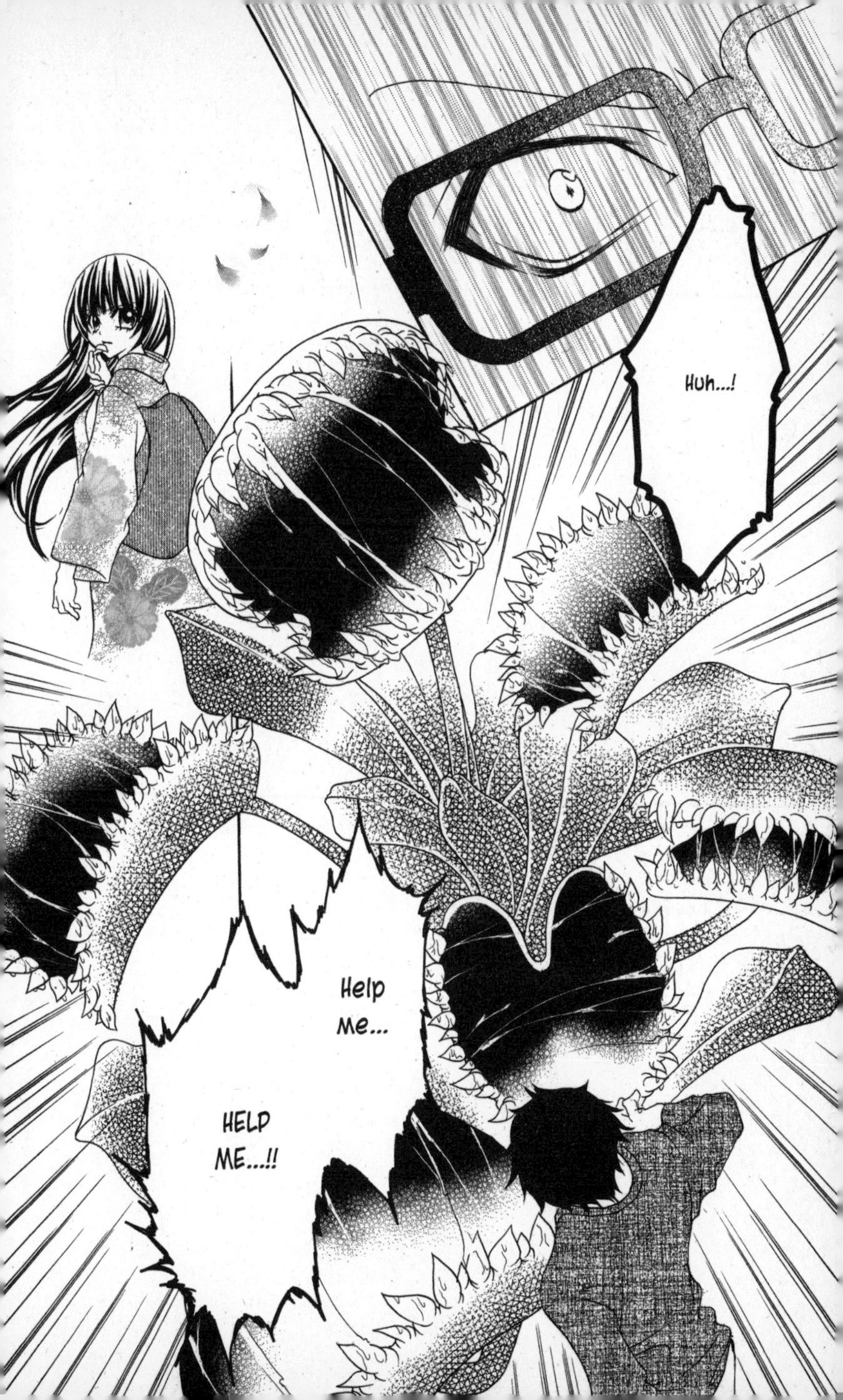
Huh...!
Help me...
HELP ME...!!

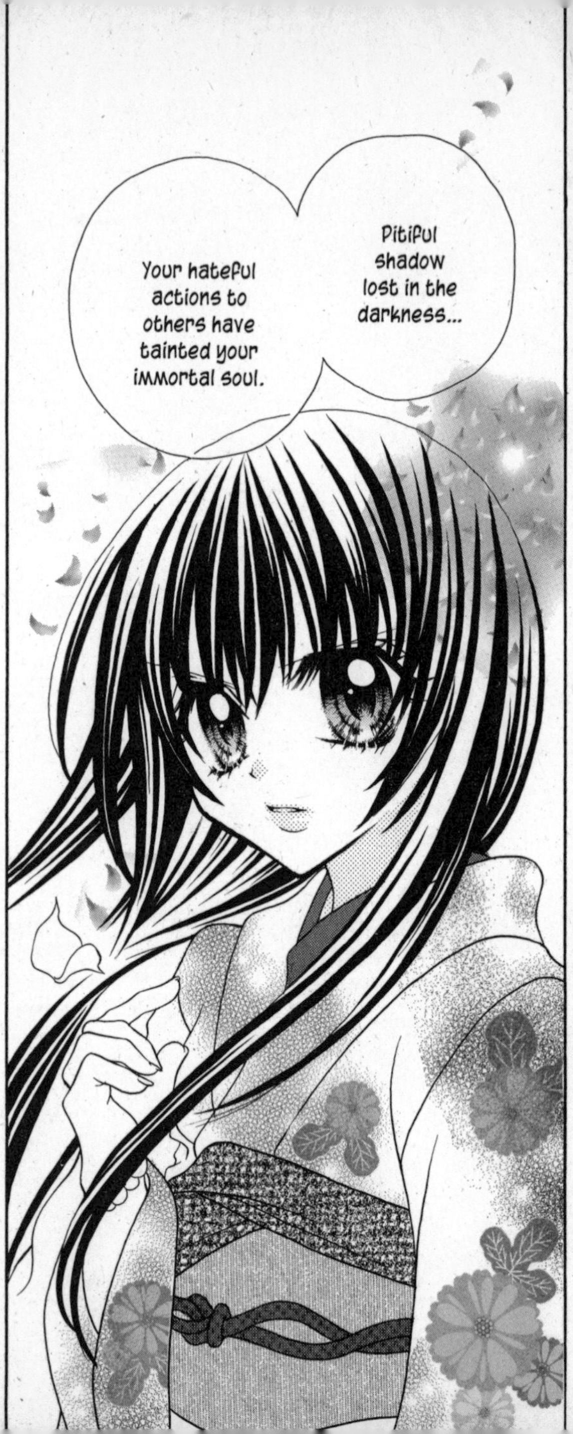
Pitiful shadow lost in the darkness...
Your hateful actions to others have tainted your immortal soul.

Author's Note

This chapter was tough. I was short two pages!

So many things happened, and so I rushed out pages 106 and 107.

The line work wasn't very good, but when it was collected into a volume I got to redraw it.

If you look at the *Nakayoshi* May issue, then I think you'll see how bad the work is.

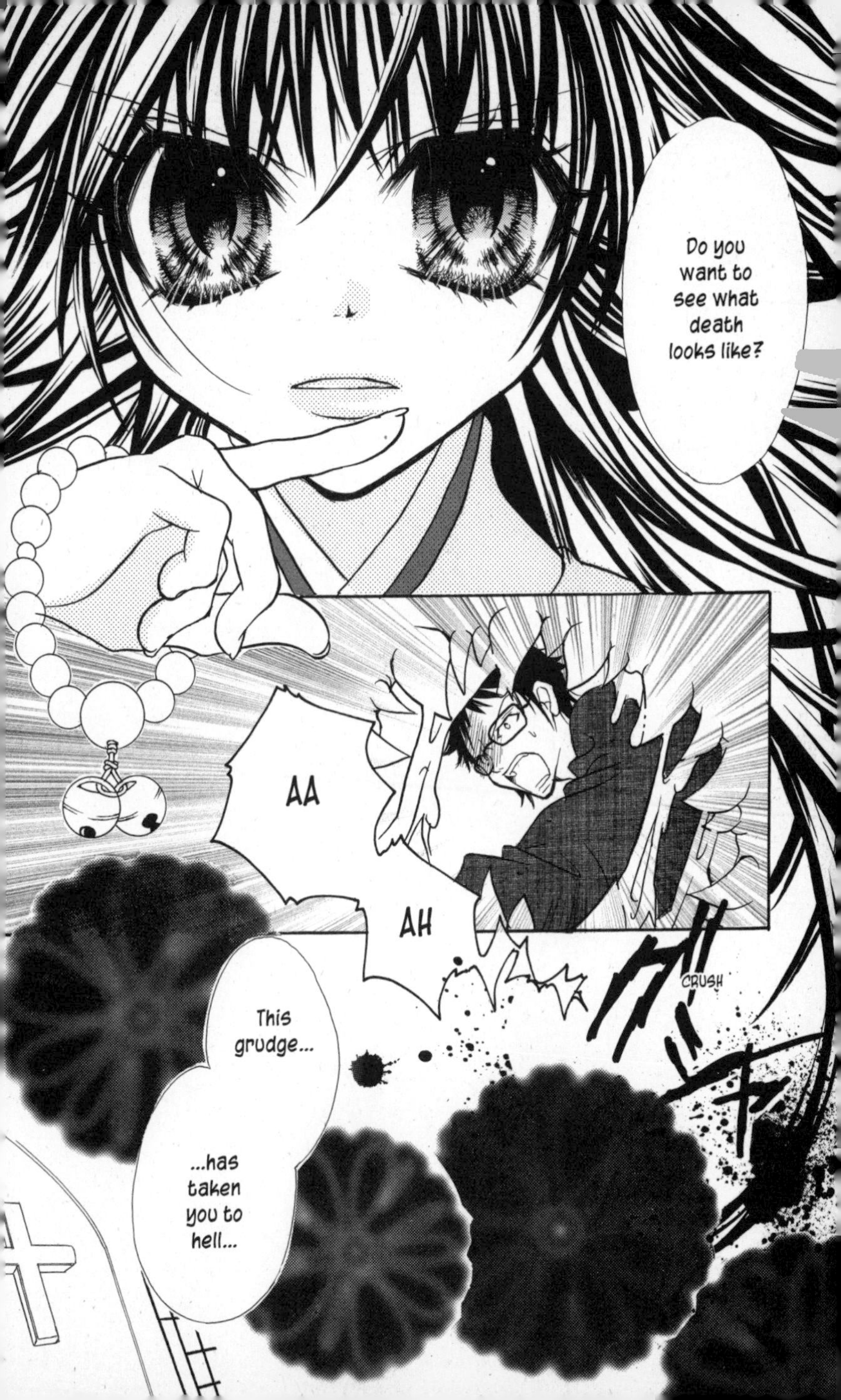
Do you want to see what death looks like?
AA
AH
CRUSH
This grudge...
...has taken you to hell...

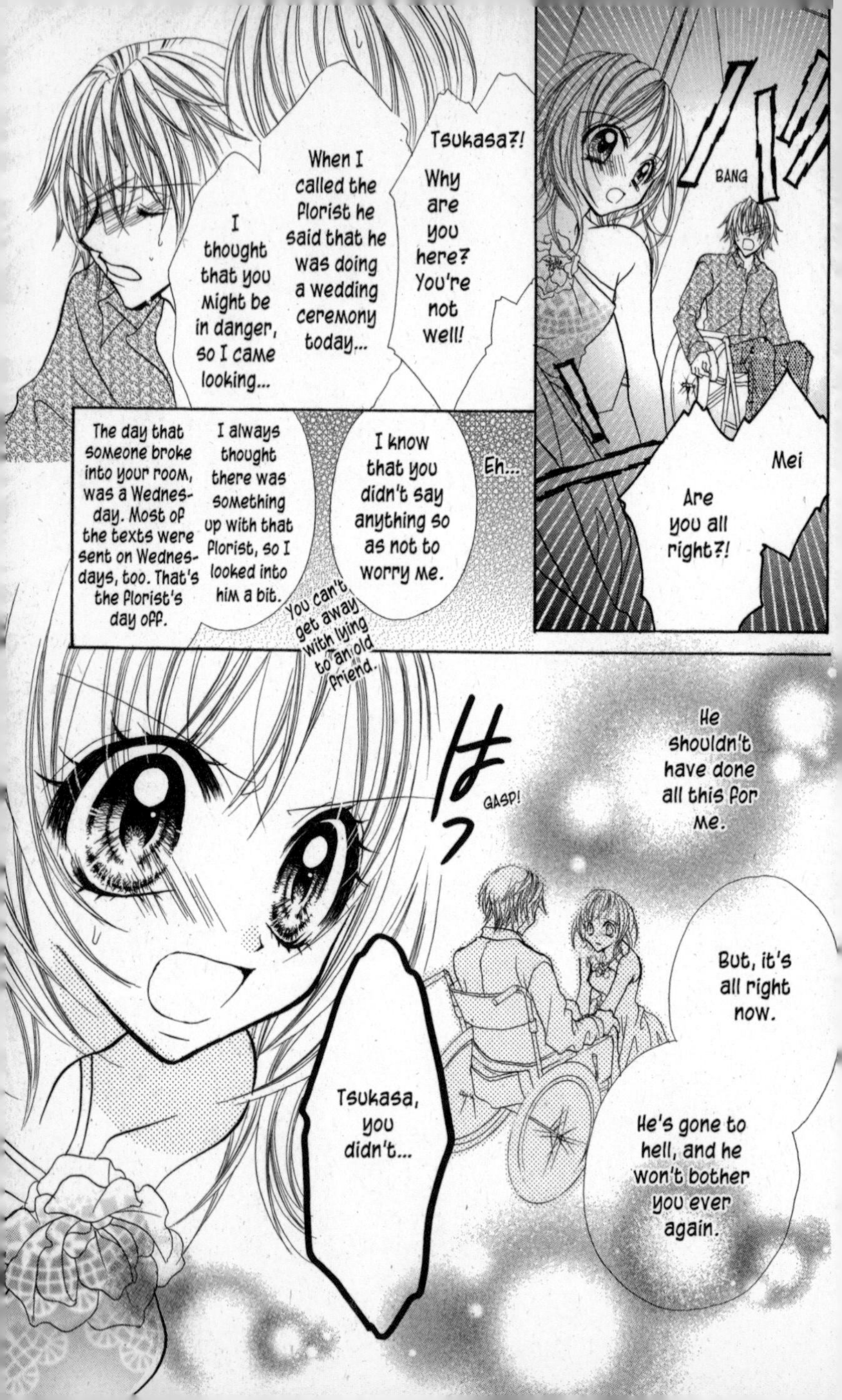
BANG
Mei
Are you all right?!
Tsukasa?!
Why are you here? You're not well!
When I called the florist he said that he was doing a wedding ceremony today...
I thought that you might be in danger, so I came looking...
Eh...
I know that you didn't say anything so as not to worry me.
I always thought there was something up with that florist, so I looked into him a bit.
The day that someone broke into your room, was a Wednesday. Most of the texts were sent on Wednesdays, too. That's the florist's day off.
You can't get away with lying to an old friend.
He shouldn't have done all this for me.
GASP!
But, it's all right now.
He's gone to hell, and he won't bother you ever again.
Tsukasa, you didn't...

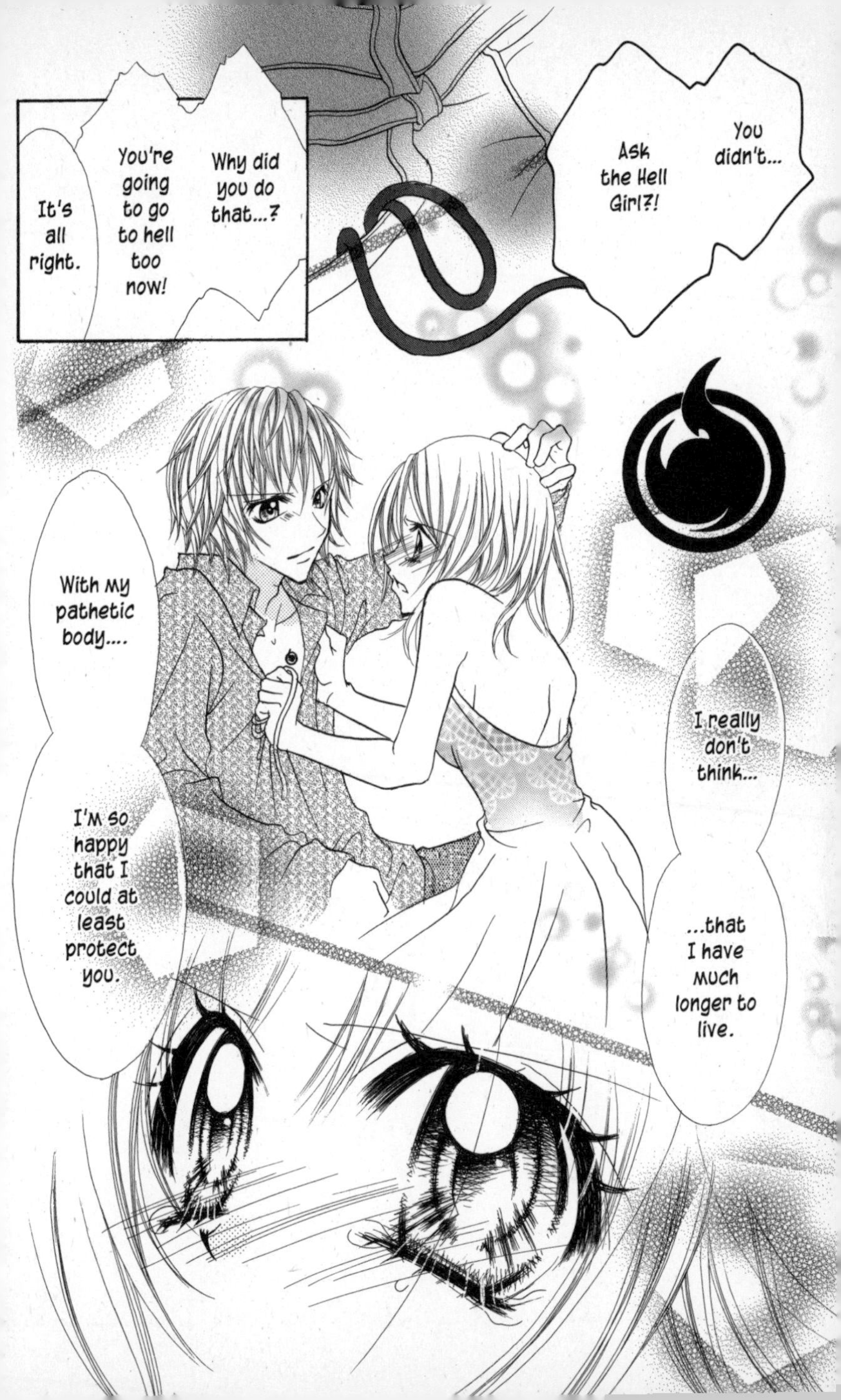
You didn't...
Ask the Hell Girl?!
Why did you do that...?
You're going to go to hell too now!
It's all right.
I really don't think...
...that I have much longer to live.
With my pathetic body....
I'm so happy that I could at least protect you.

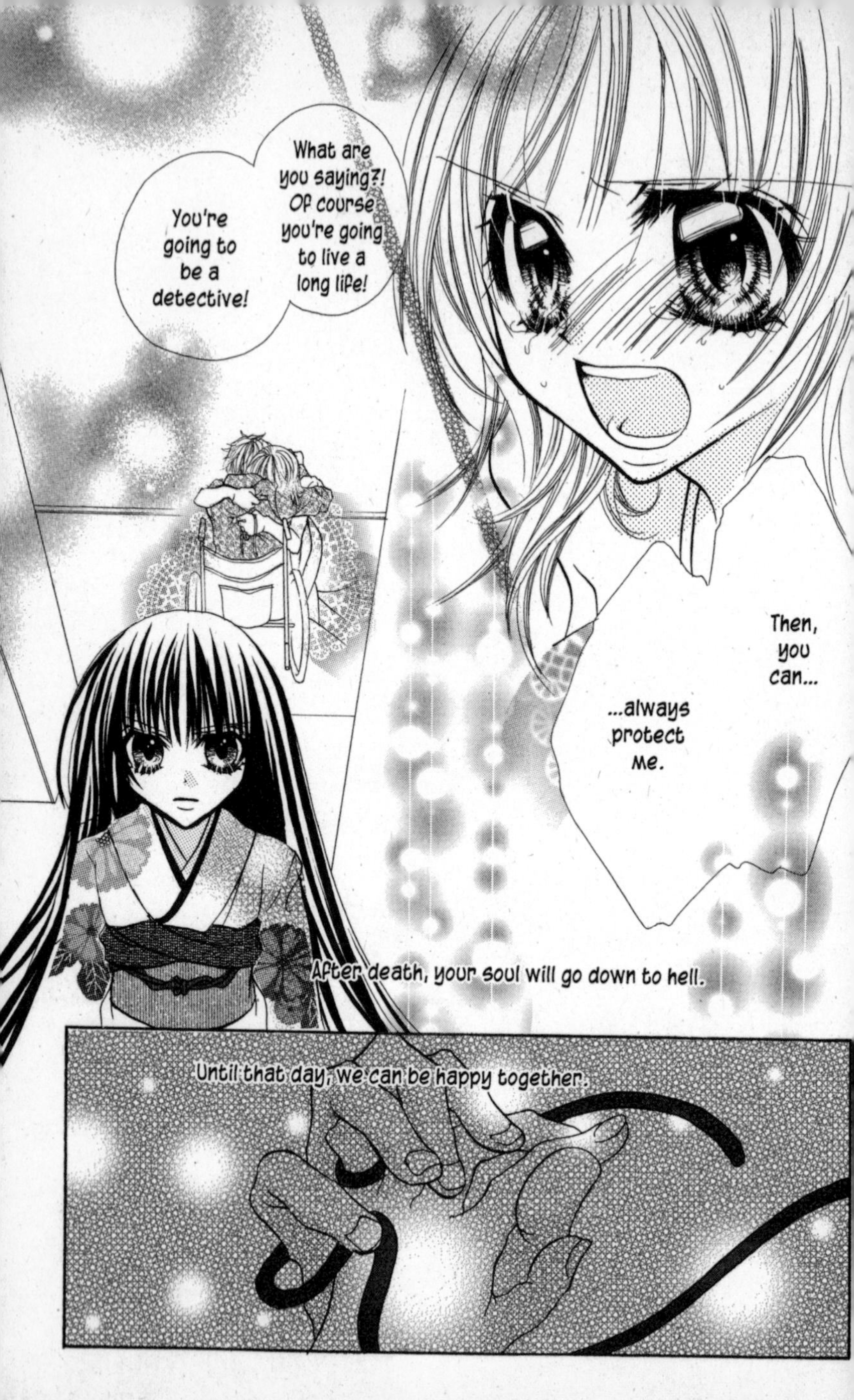
What are you saying?! Of course you're going to live a long life!
You're going to be a detective!
Then, you can...
...always protect me.
After death, your soul will go down to hell.
Until that day, we can be happy together.

Author's Note

At the end of the book, there are short comics for the *Nakayoshi* Gag Festival that are also included with each of the anime DVDs.

When I was drawing them I thought there was no way you could make a joke out of *Hell Girl*.

I was surprised when they got such a good reception.

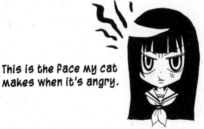

Annoyed Ai-chan
This is the face my cat makes when it's angry.

Big Thank You

The people at Aniplex

Chisano-sama Maruyama-sama Oriuchi-sama
All those involved and all those who helped.

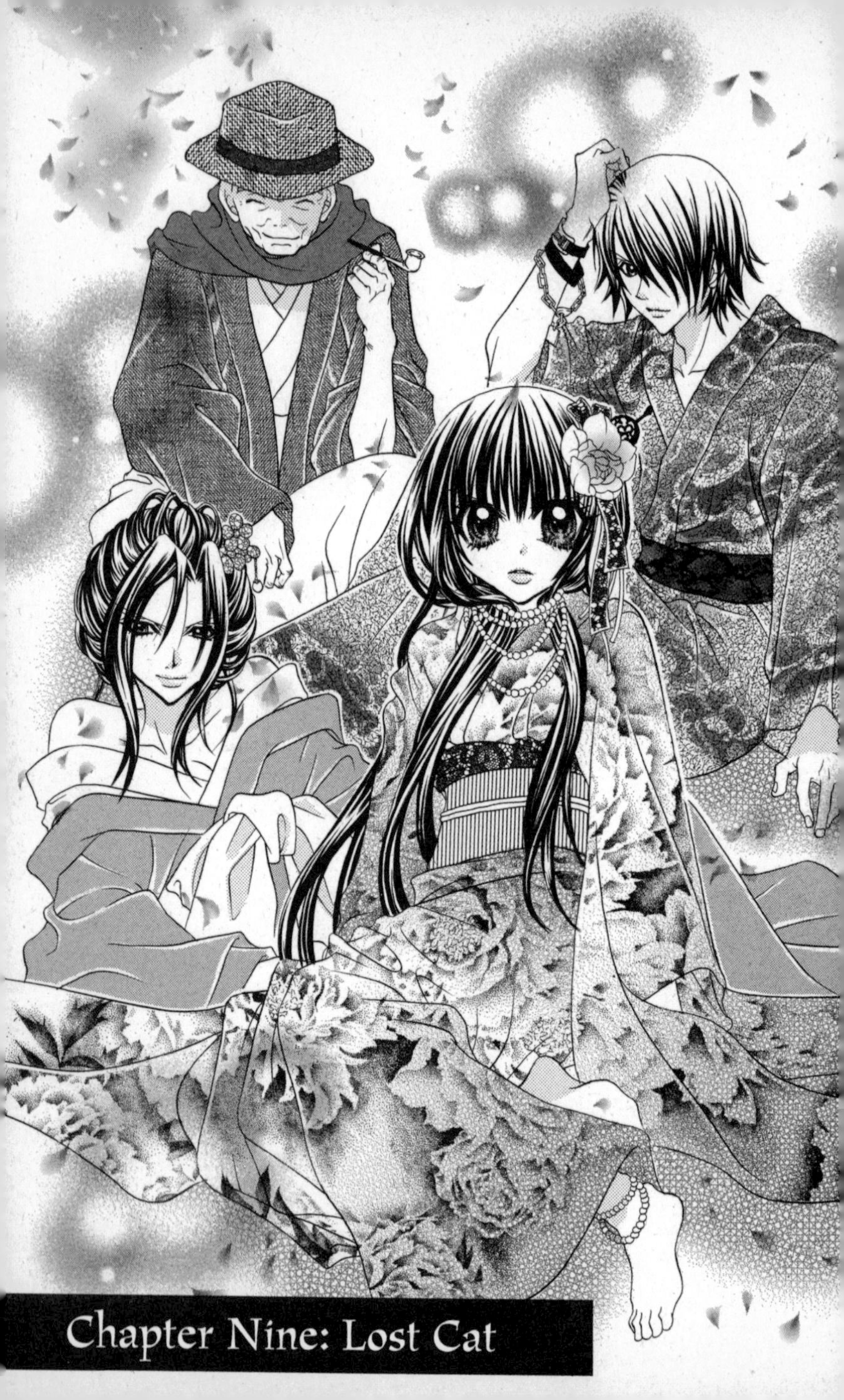

Chapter Nine: Lost Cat

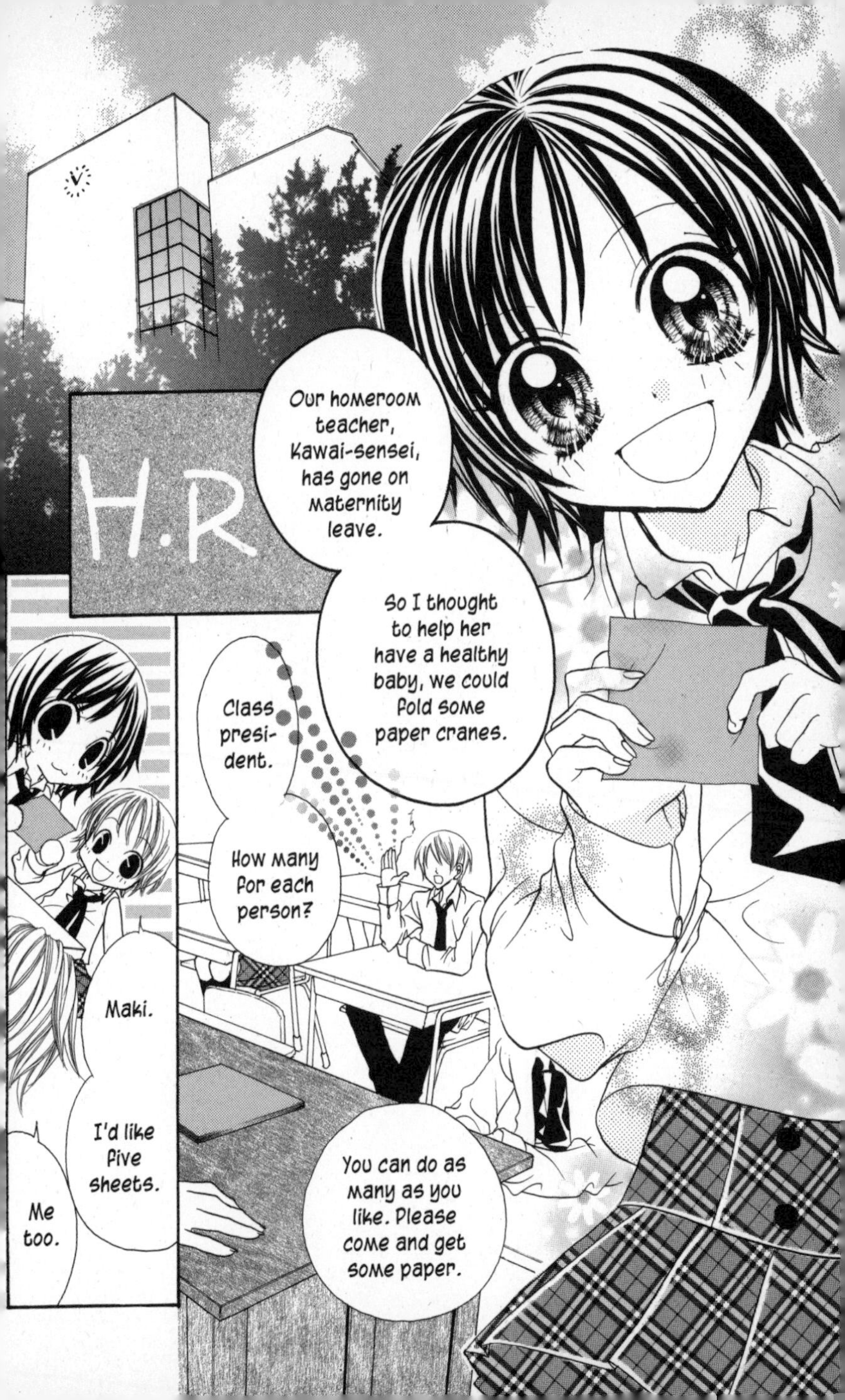
H.R
Our homeroom teacher, Kawai-sensei, has gone on maternity leave.
So I thought to help her have a healthy baby, we could fold some paper cranes.
Class president.
How many for each person?
You can do as many as you like. Please come and get some paper.
Maki.
I'd like five sheets.
Me too.

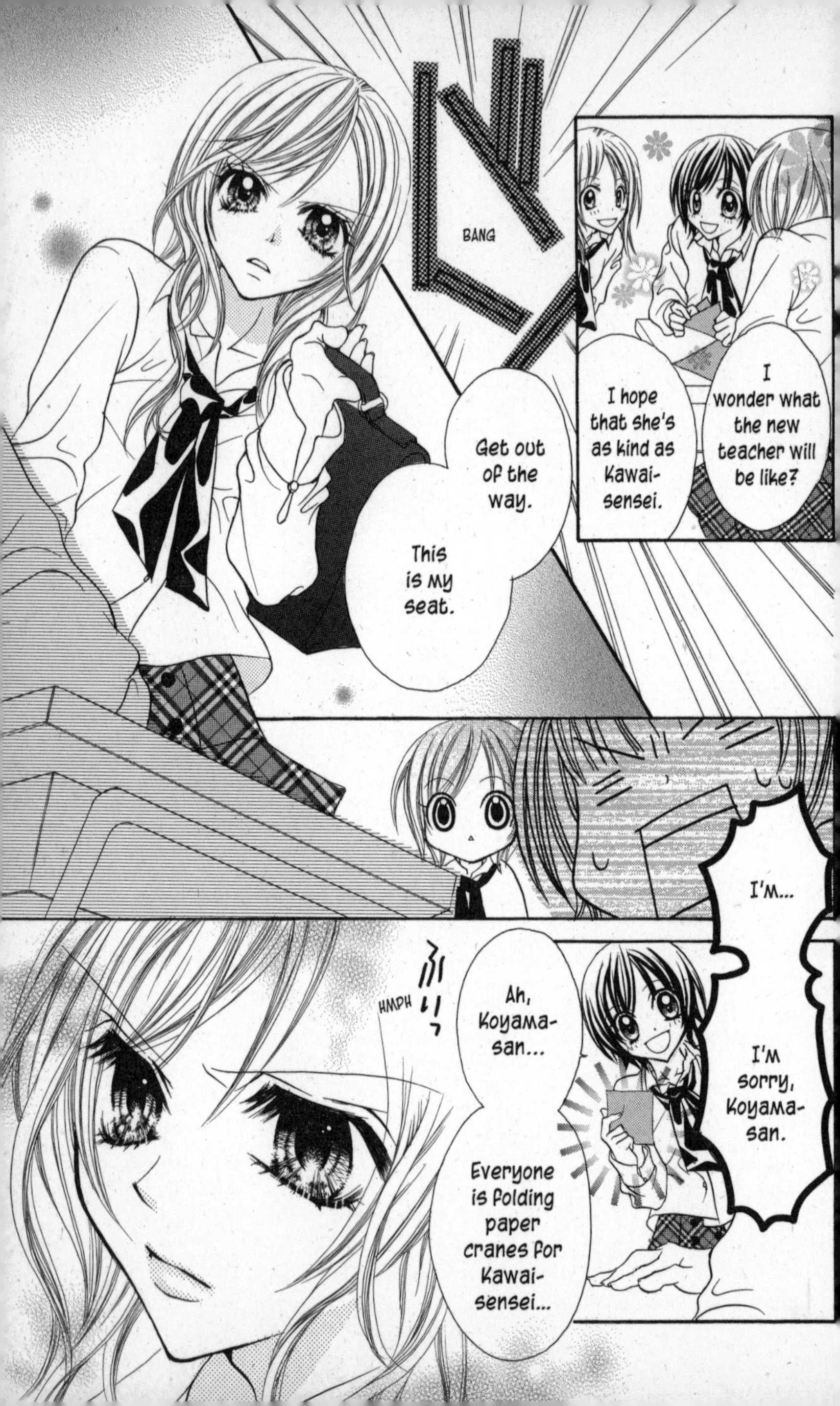

I wonder what the new teacher will be like?
I hope that she's as kind as Kawai-sensei.
BANG
Get out of the way.
This is my seat.
I'm...
I'm sorry, Koyama-san.
Ah, Koyama-san...
Everyone is folding paper cranes for Kawai-sensei...
HMPH

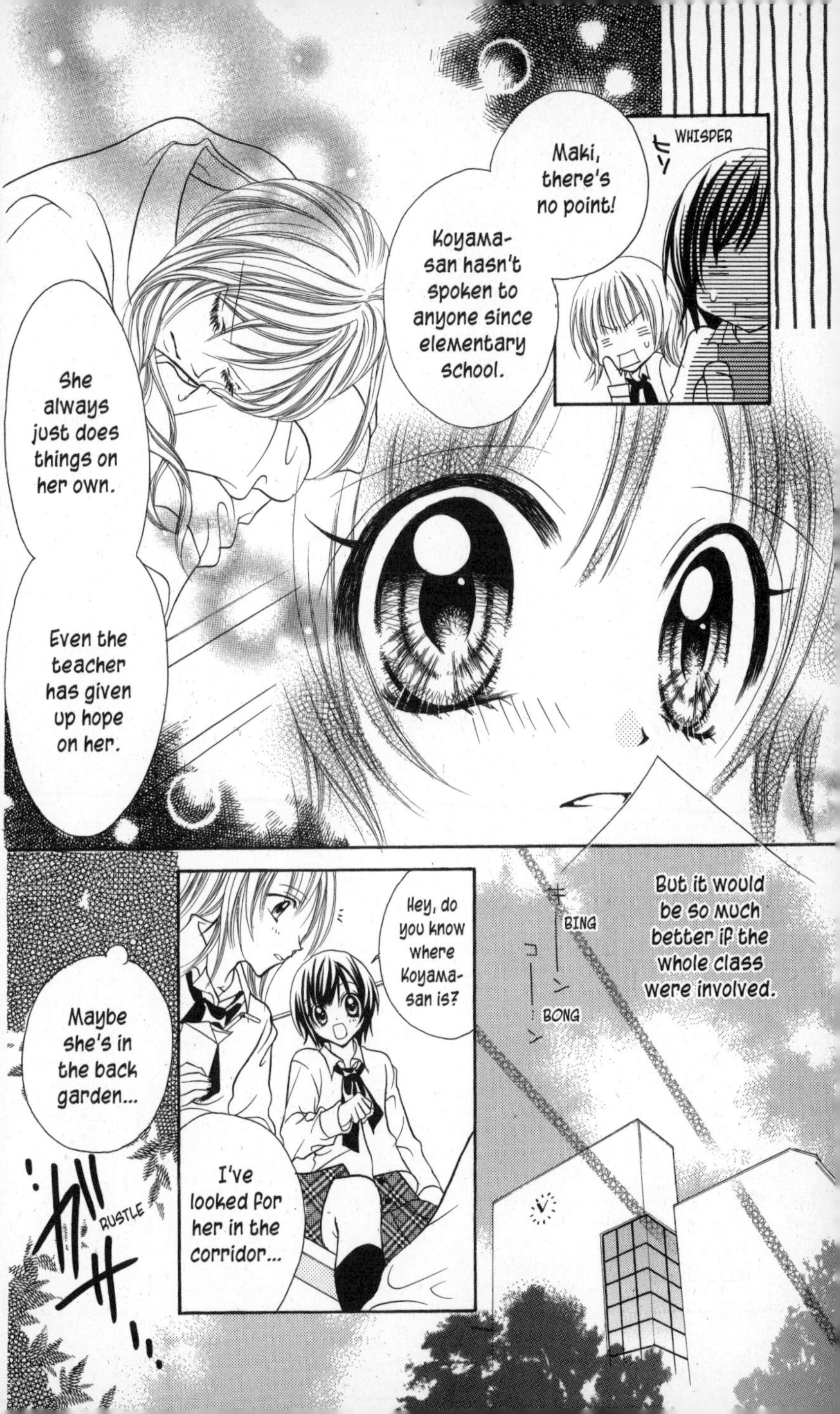
WHISPER
Maki, there's no point!
Koyama-san hasn't spoken to anyone since elementary school.
She always just does things on her own.
Even the teacher has given up hope on her.
But it would be so MUCH better if the whole class were involved.
BING
BONG
Hey, do you know where Koyama-san is?
I've looked for her in the corridor...
Maybe she's in the back garden...
RUSTLE

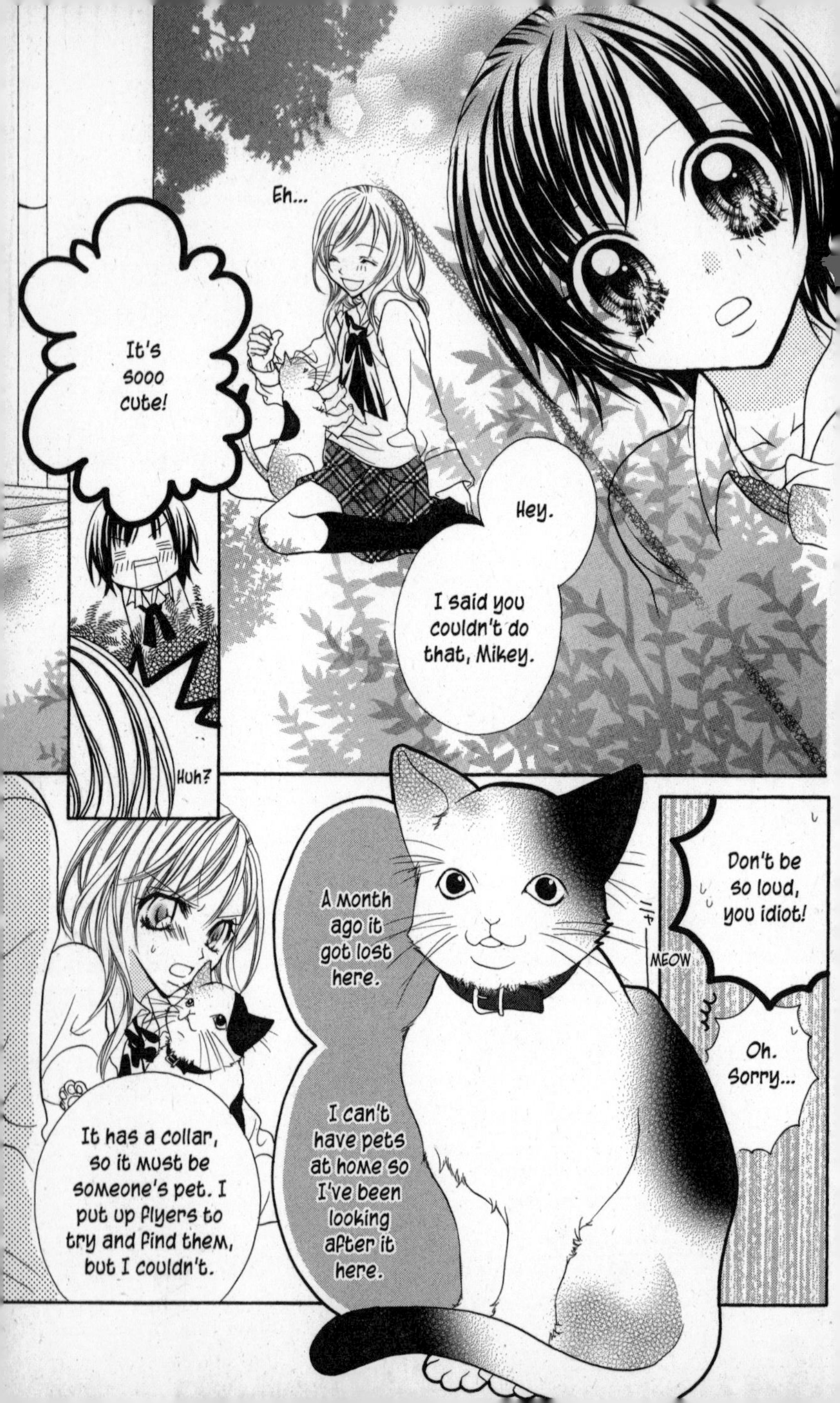
Eh...
Hey.
I said you couldn't do that, Mikey.
It's sooo cute!
Huh?
Don't be so loud, you idiot!
MEOW
Oh. Sorry...
A month ago it got lost here.
It has a collar, so it must be someone's pet. I put up flyers to try and find them, but I couldn't.
I can't have pets at home so I've been looking after it here.

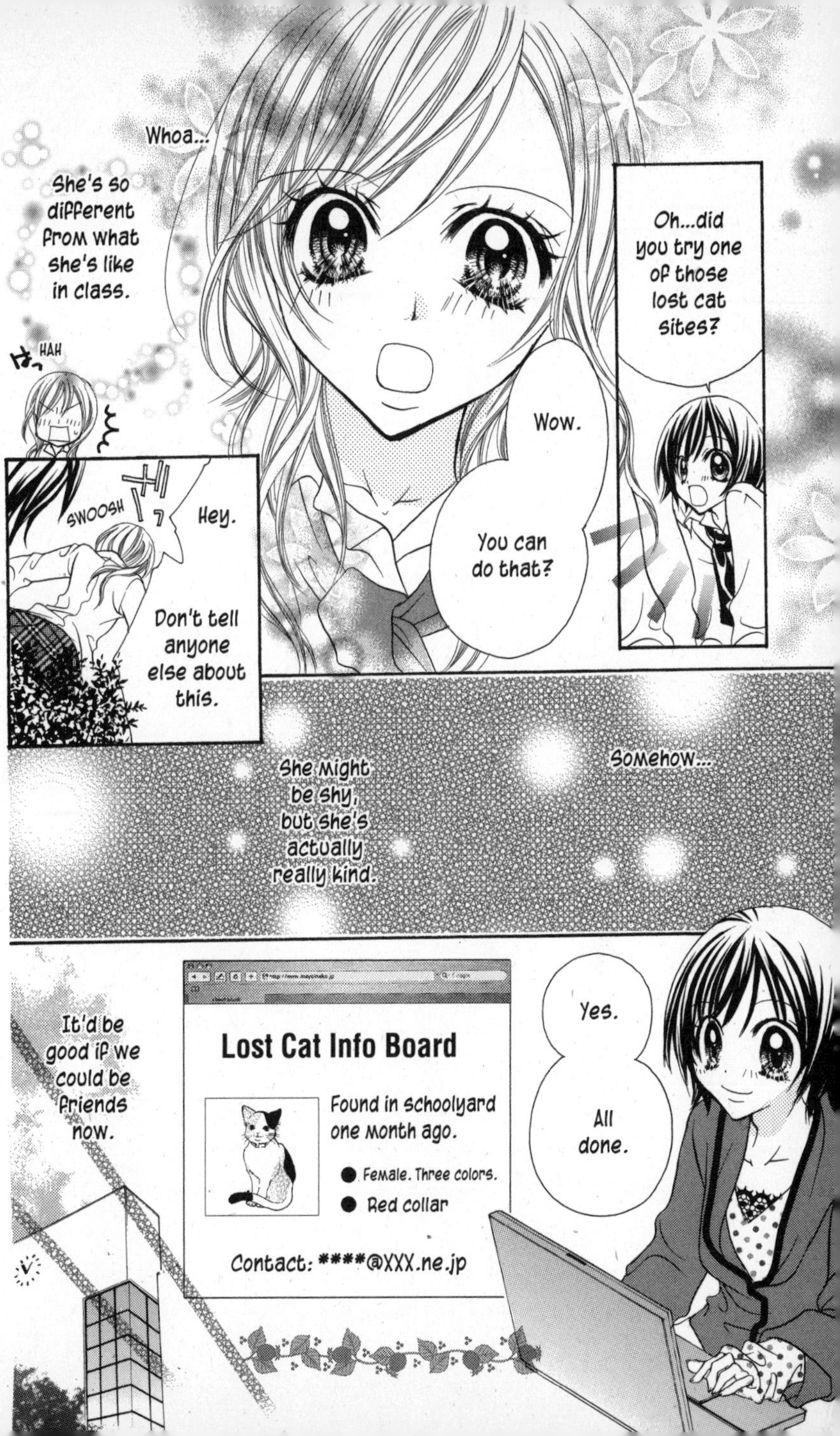
Oh...did you try one of those lost cat sites?
Wow.
You can do that?
Whoa...
She's so different from what she's like in class.
HAH
Hey.
SWOOSH
Don't tell anyone else about this.
Somehow...
She might be shy, but she's actually really kind.
Yes.
All done.
Lost Cat Info Board
Found in schoolyard one month ago.
Female. Three colors.
Red collar
Contact: ****@XXX.ne.jp
It'd be good if we could be friends now.

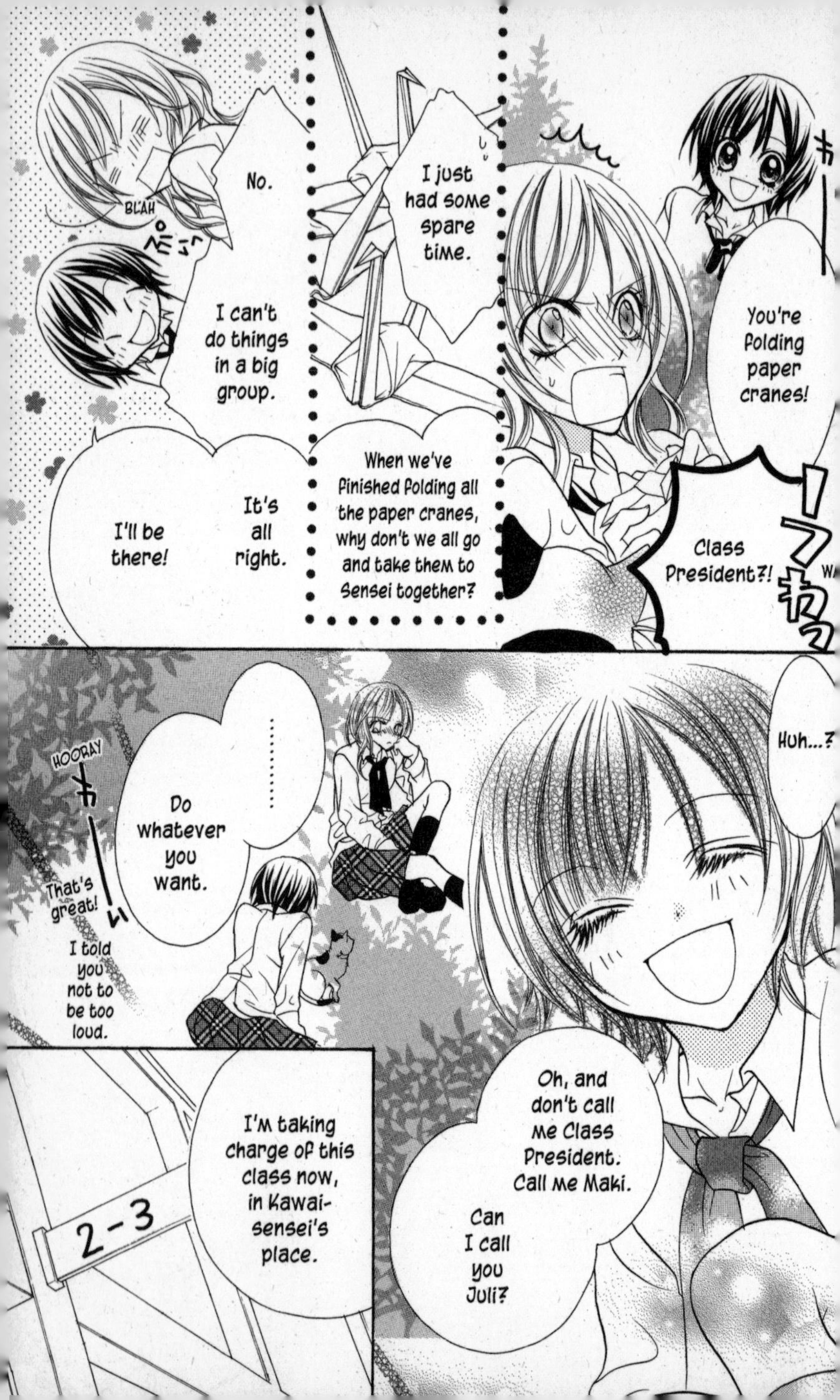
You're folding paper cranes!
Class President?!
I just had some spare time.
When we've finished folding all the paper cranes, why don't we all go and take them to Sensei together?
No.
I can't do things in a big group.
BLAH
It's all right.
I'll be there!
Huh...?
Oh, and don't call me Class President. Call me Maki.
Can I call you Juli?
......
Do whatever you want.
HOORAY
That's great!
I told you not to be too loud.
2-3
I'm taking charge of this class now, in Kawai-sensei's place.

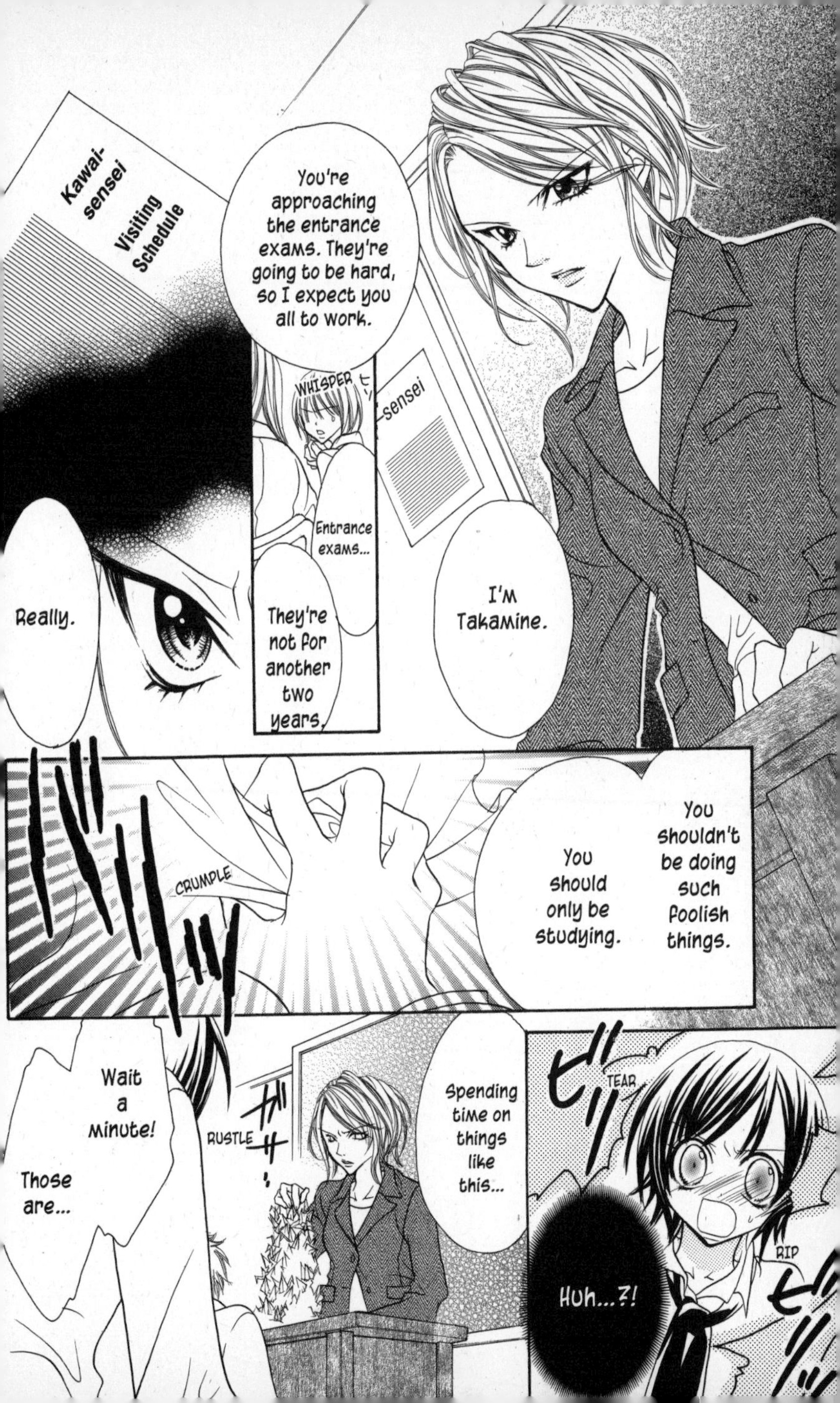
I'm Takamine.
You're approaching the entrance exams. They're going to be hard, so I expect you all to work.
WHISPER
sensei
Entrance exams...
They're not for another two years.
Kawai-sensei Visiting Schedule
Really.
You shouldn't be doing such foolish things.
You should only be studying.
CRUMPLE
TEAR
RIP
Huh...?!
Spending time on things like this...
RUSTLE
Wait a minute!
Those are...

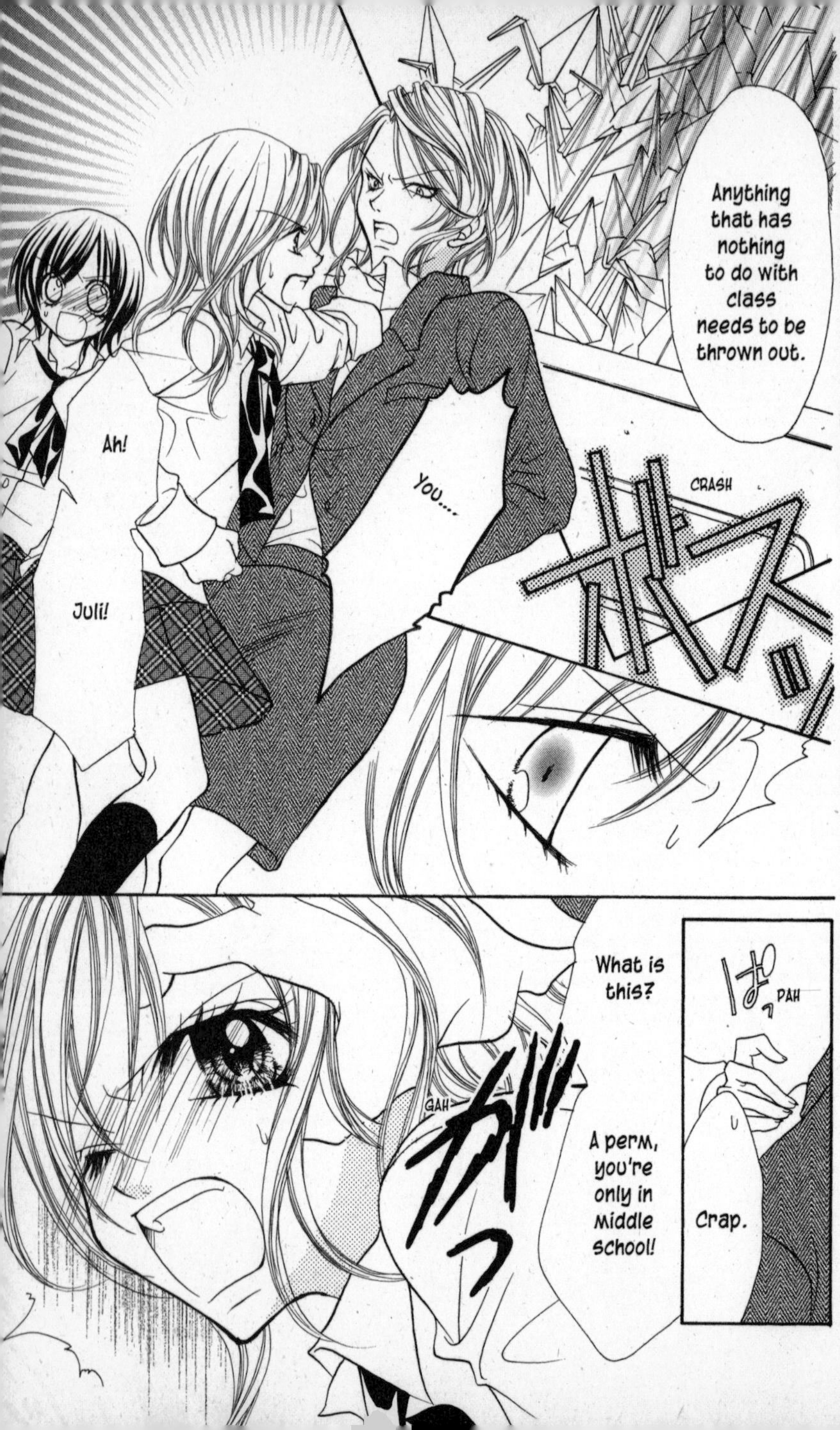
Anything that has nothing to do with class needs to be thrown out.
CRASH
You....
Ah!
Juli!
PAH
Crap.
What is this?
A perm, you're only in middle school!
GAH

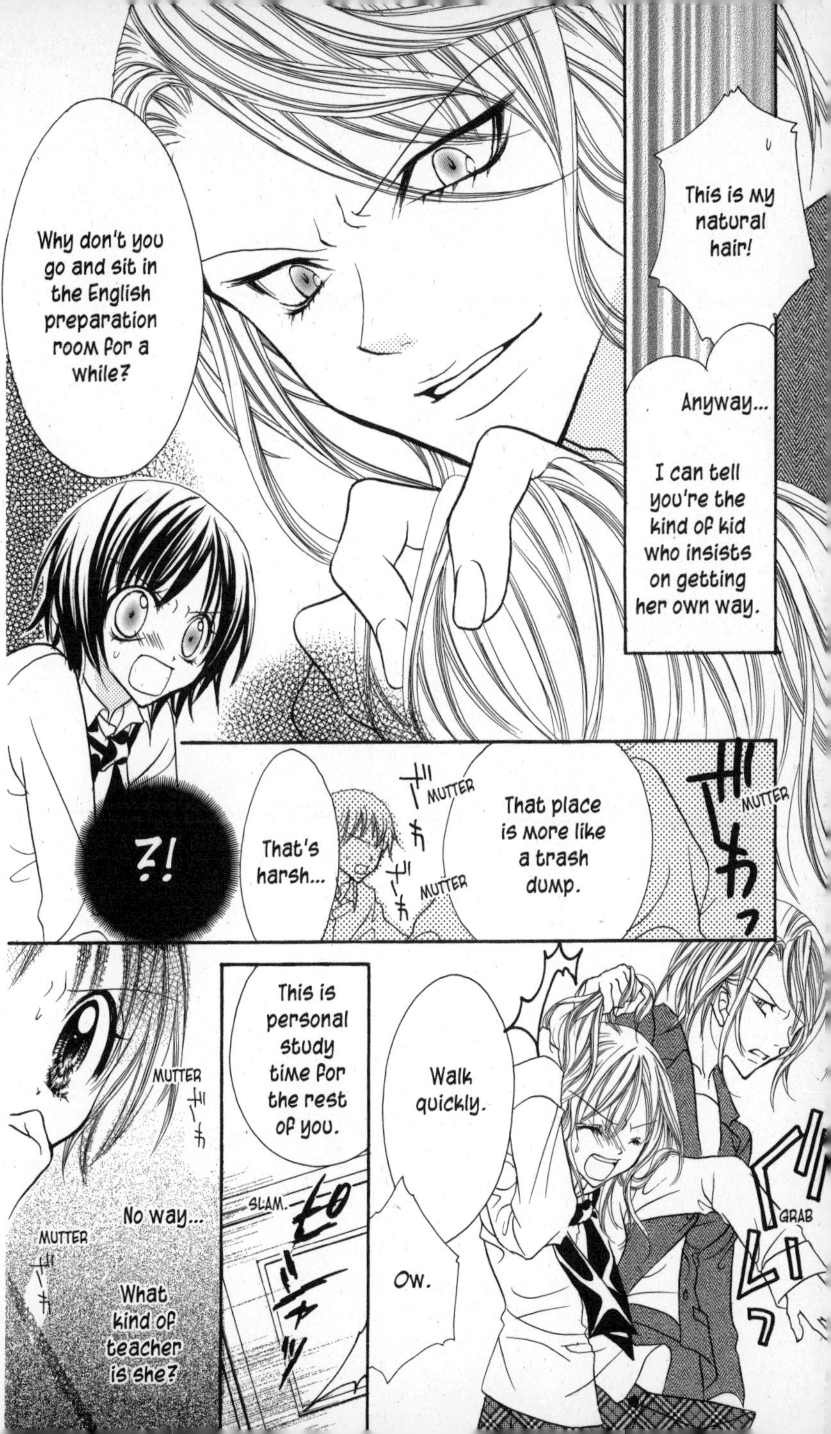
This is my natural hair!
Anyway...
I can tell you're the kind of kid who insists on getting her own way.
Why don't you go and sit in the English preparation room for a while?
?!
MUTTER
That place is more like a trash dump.
MUTTER
MUTTER
That's harsh...
GRAB
Walk quickly.
Ow.
This is personal study time for the rest of you.
SLAM.
MUTTER
No way...
MUTTER
What kind of teacher is she?

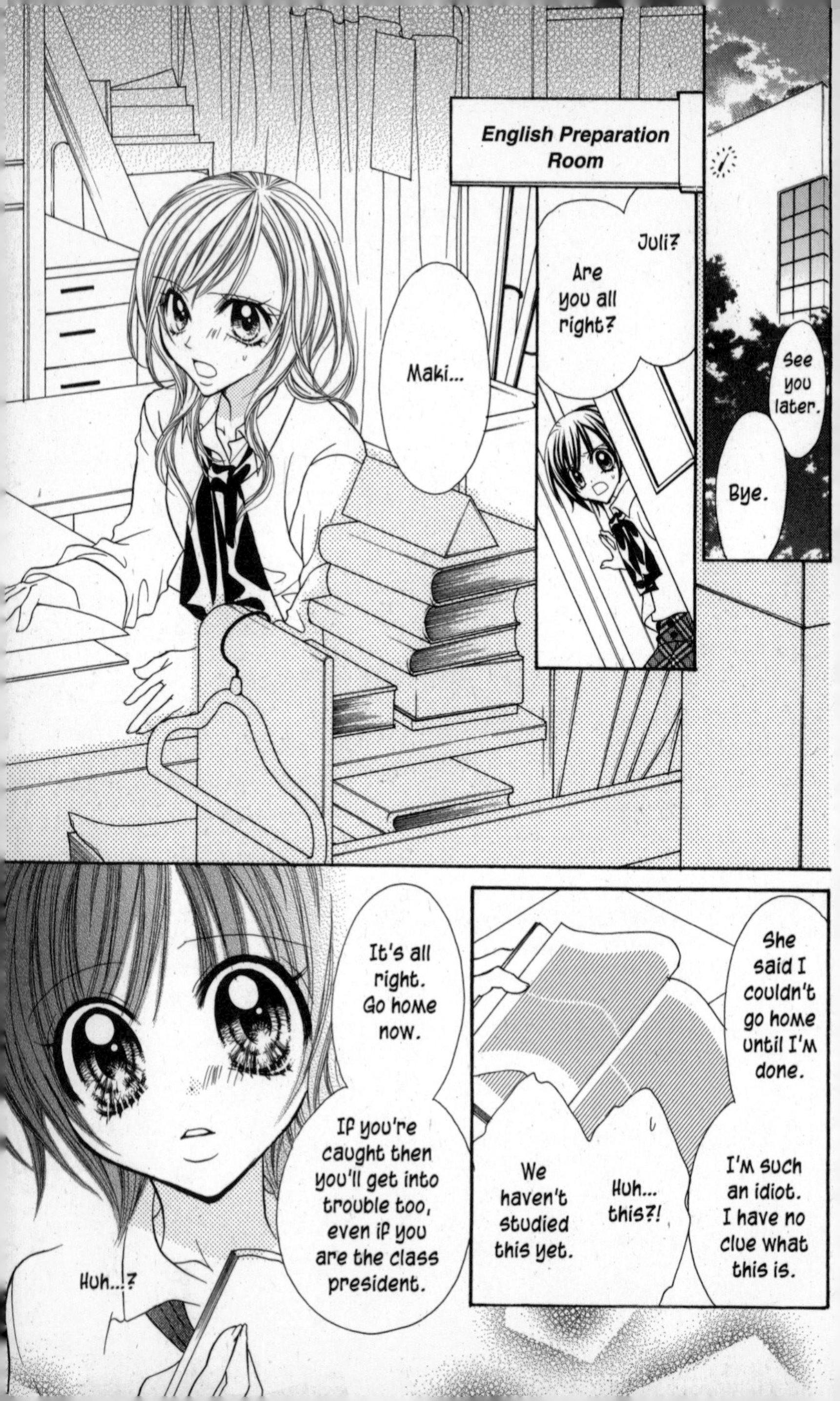

See you later.
Bye.
English Preparation Room
Juli? Are you all right?
Maki...
She said I couldn't go home until I'm done.
I'm such an idiot. I have no clue what this is.
Huh... this?!
We haven't studied this yet.
It's all right. Go home now.
If you're caught then you'll get into trouble too, even if you are the class president.
Huh...?

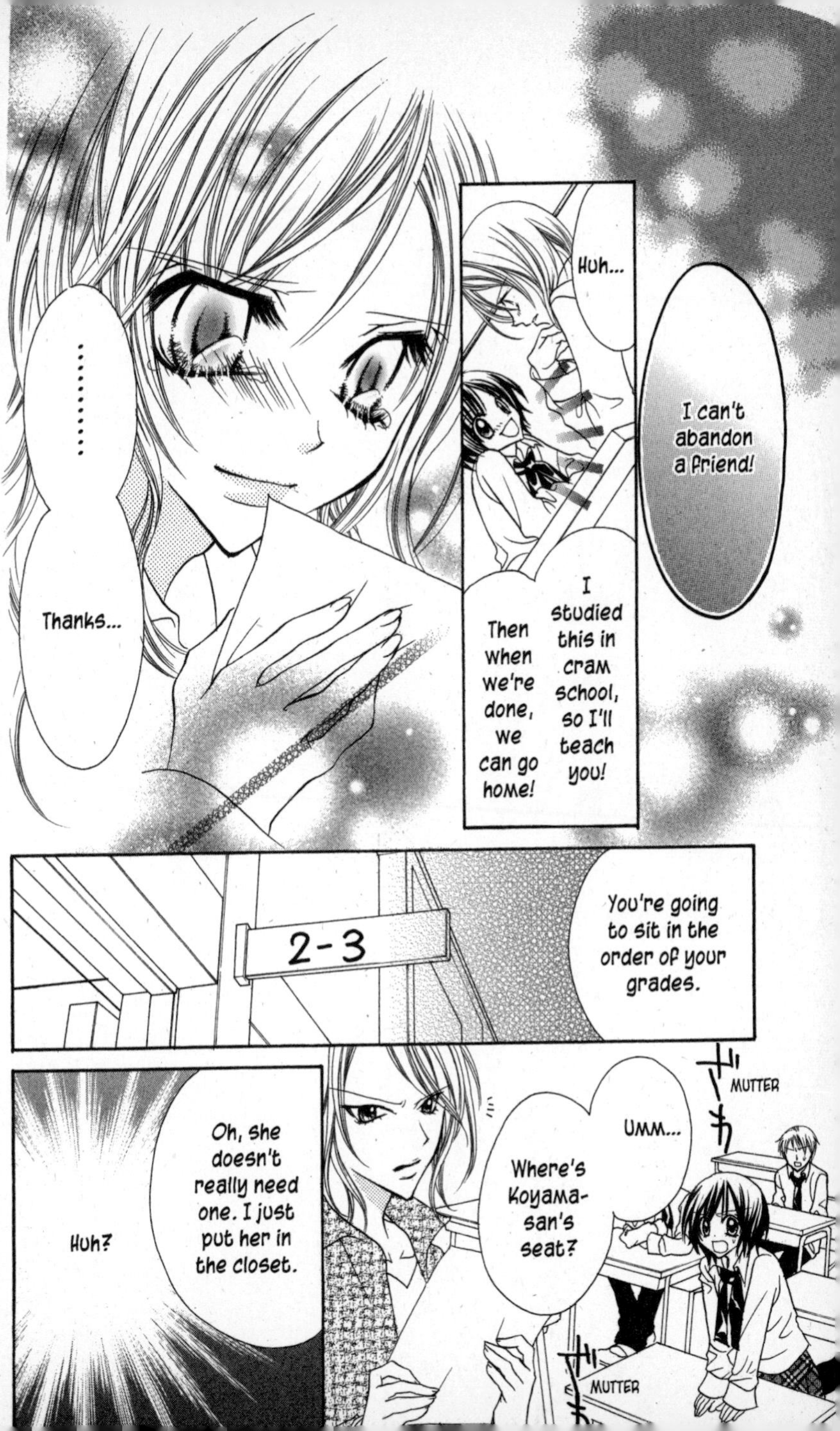
I can't abandon a friend!
Huh...
I studied this in cram school, so I'll teach you!
Then when we're done, we can go home!
......
Thanks...
2-3
You're going to sit in the order of your grades.
MUTTER
Umm...
Where's Koyama-san's seat?
MUTTER
Oh, she doesn't really need one. I just put her in the closet.
Huh?

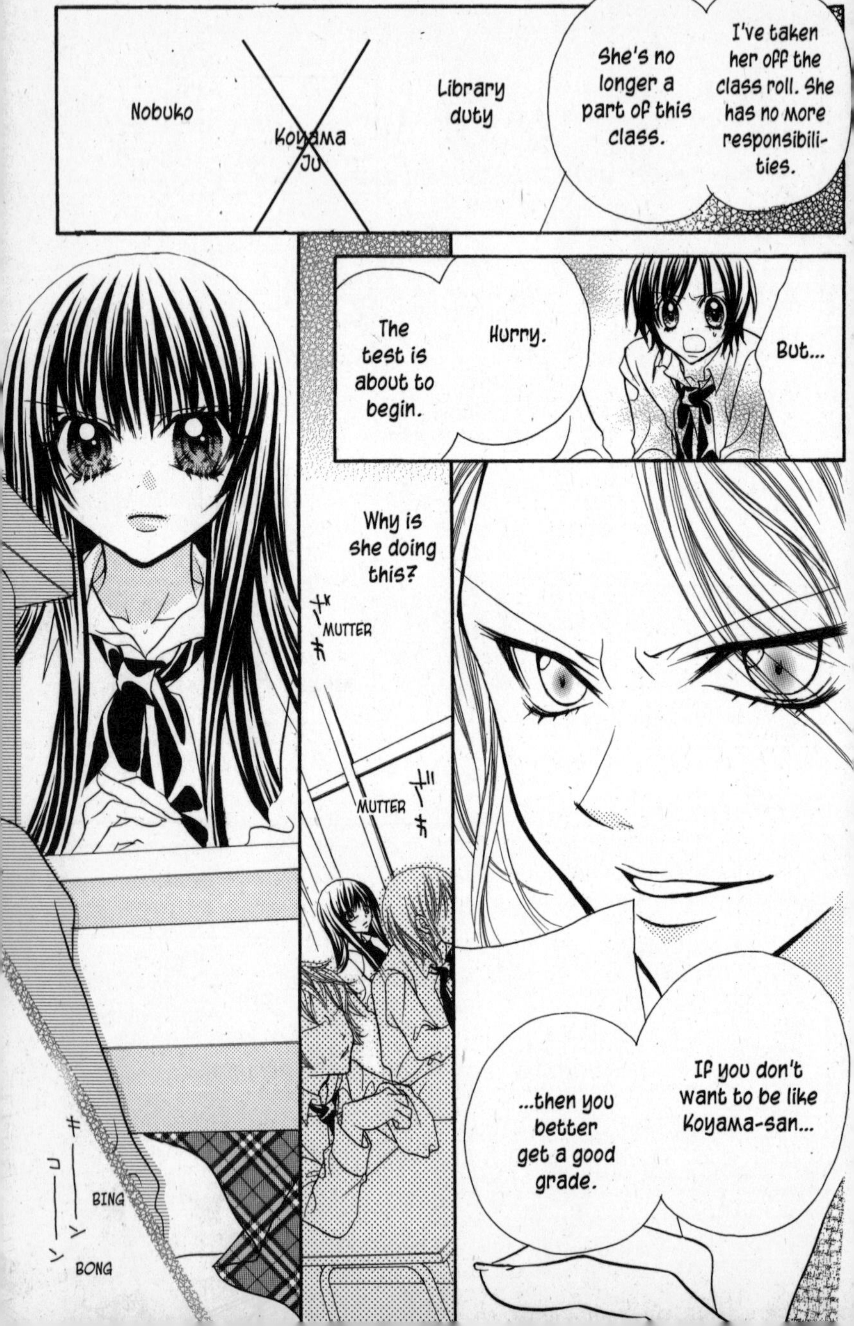
I've taken her off the class roll. She has no more responsibilities.
She's no longer a part of this class.
Library duty
Koyama Ju
Nobuko
But...
Hurry.
The test is about to begin.
If you don't want to be like Koyama-san...
...then you better get a good grade.
Why is she doing this?
MUTTER
MUTTER
BING
BONG

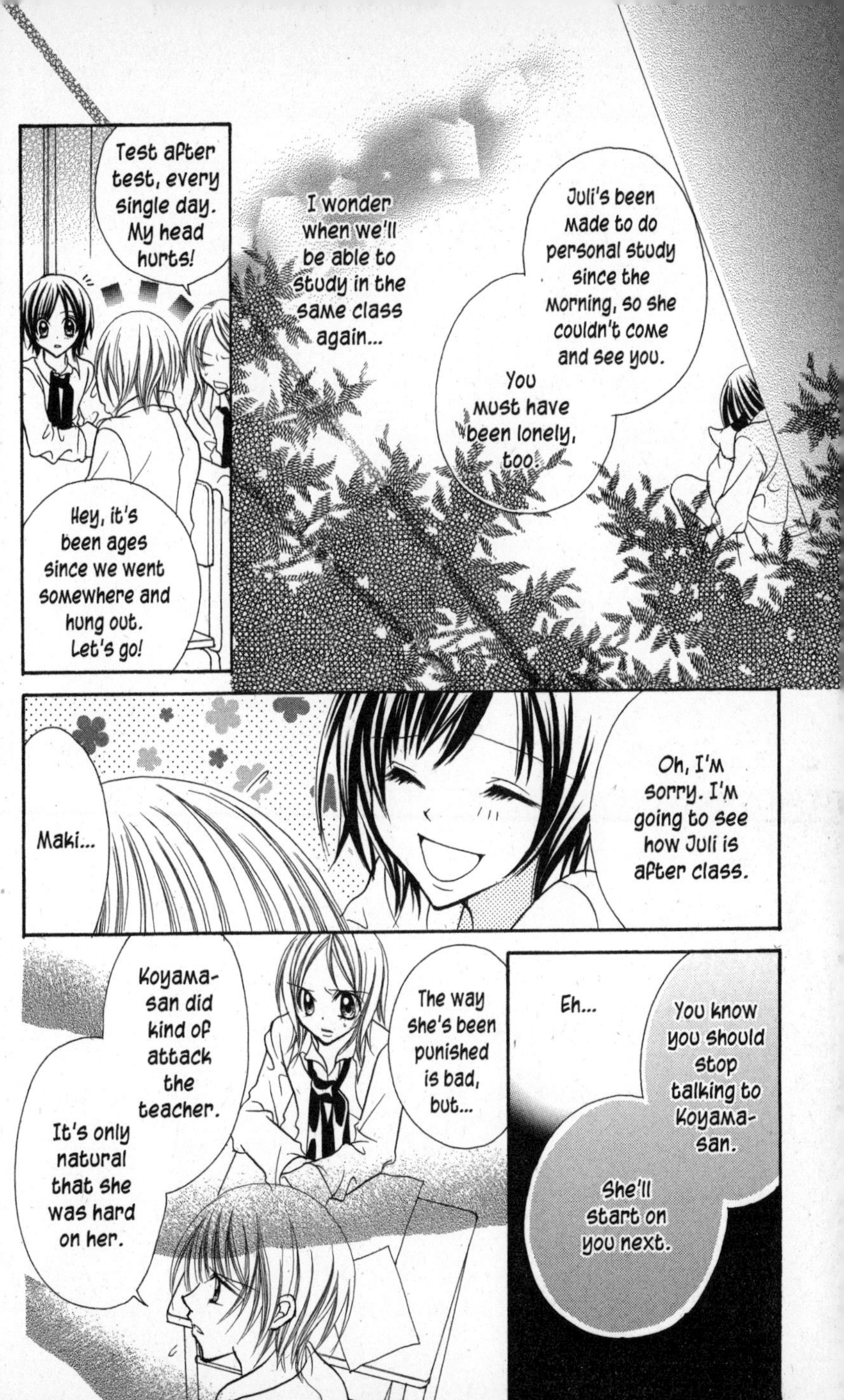
Juli's been made to do personal study since the morning, so she couldn't come and see you.
You must have been lonely, too.
I wonder when we'll be able to study in the same class again...
Test after test, every single day. My head hurts!
Hey, it's been ages since we went somewhere and hung out. Let's go!
Oh, I'm sorry. I'm going to see how Juli is after class.
Maki...
You know you should stop talking to Koyama-san.
She'll start on you next.
Eh...
The way she's been punished is bad, but...
Koyama-san did kind of attack the teacher.
It's only natural that she was hard on her.

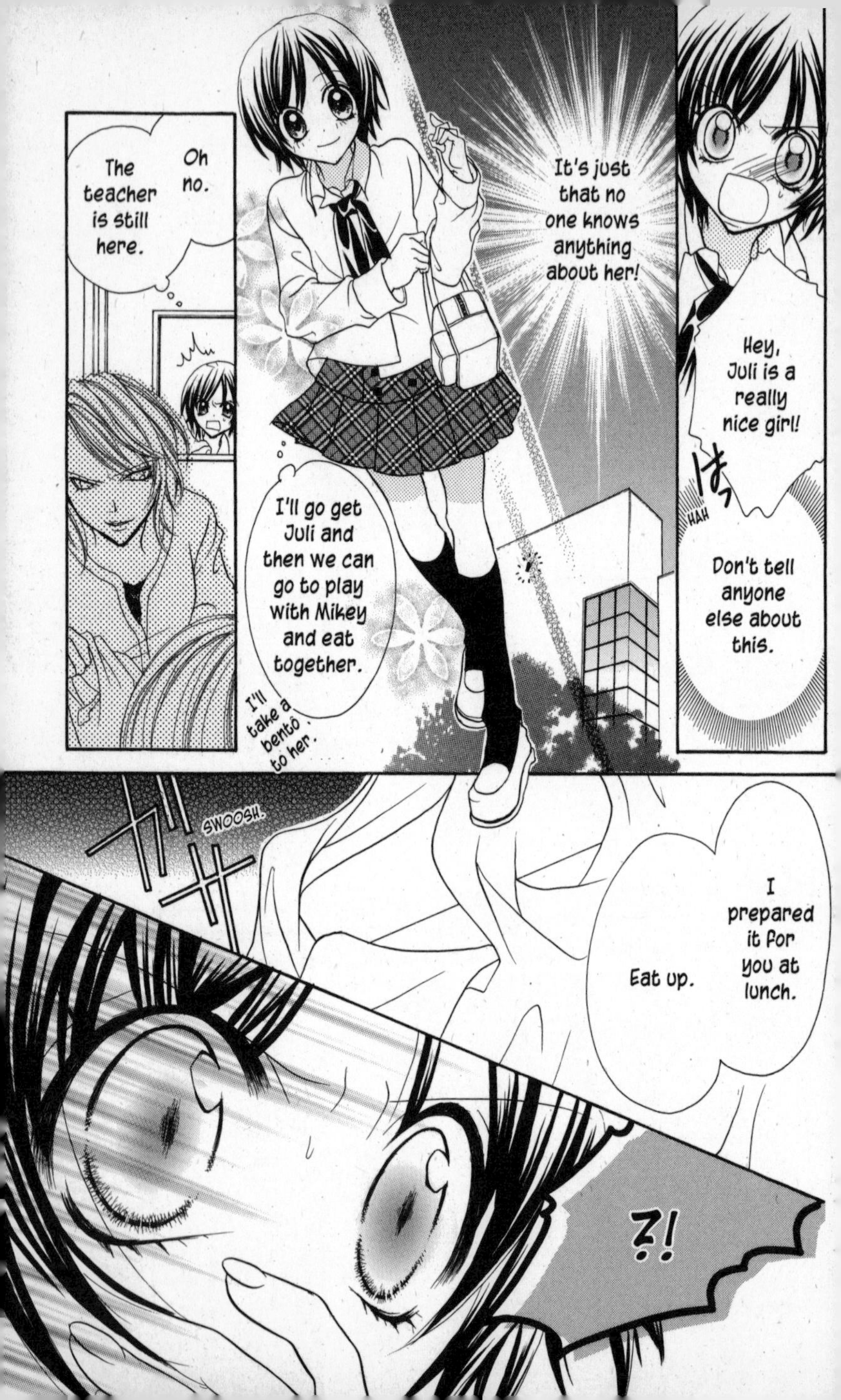
Hey, Juli is a really nice girl!
はっ
HAH
Don't tell anyone else about this.
It's just that no one knows anything about her!
I'll go get Juli and then we can go to play with Mikey and eat together.
I'll take a bentô to her.
Oh no. The teacher is still here.
SWOOSH.
I prepared it for you at lunch.
Eat up.
?!

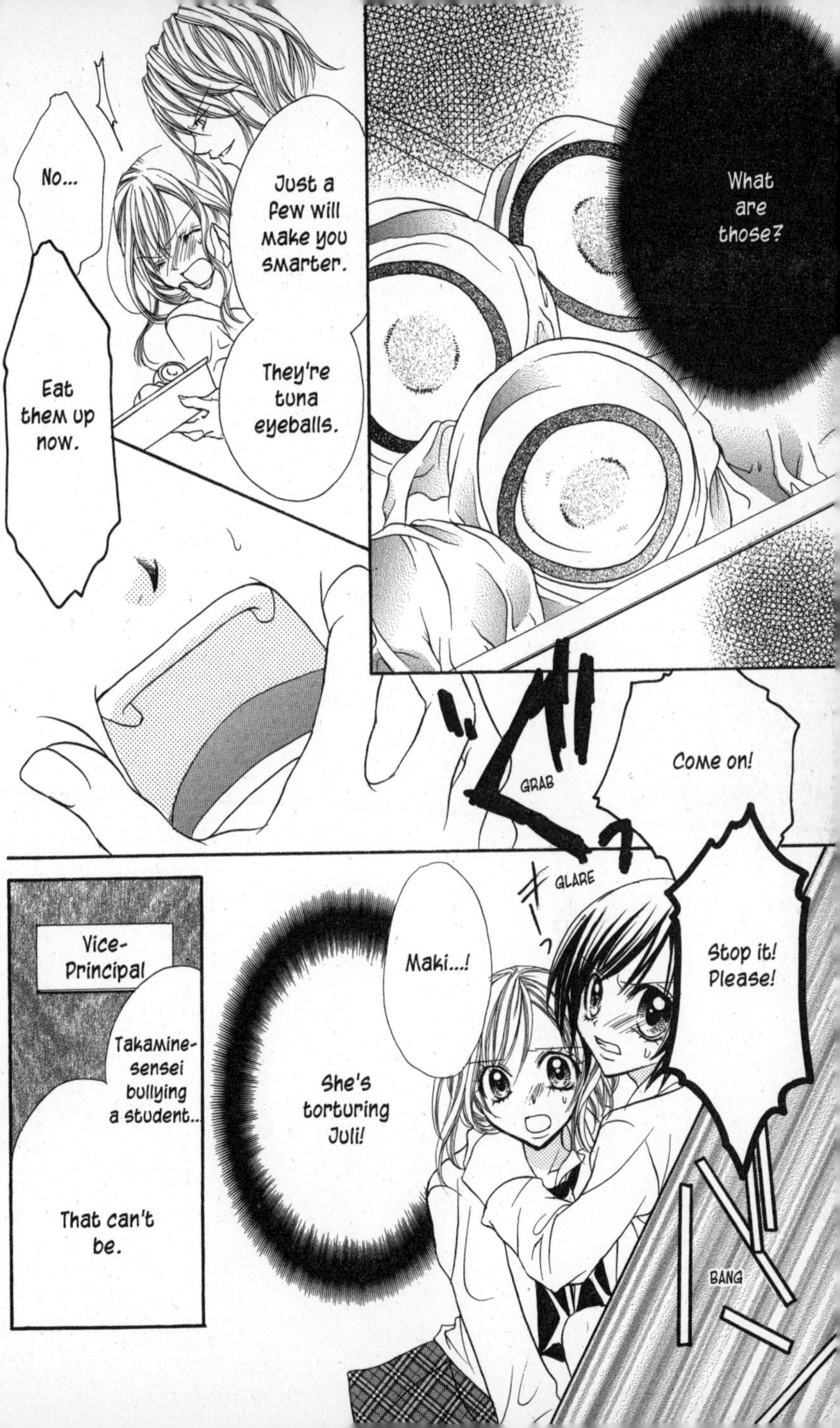
What are those?
Come on!
GRAB
Just a few will make you smarter.
They're tuna eyeballs.
No...
Eat them up now.
Stop it! Please!
GLARE
Maki...!
She's torturing Juli!
BANG
Vice-Principal
Takamine-sensei bullying a student...
That can't be.

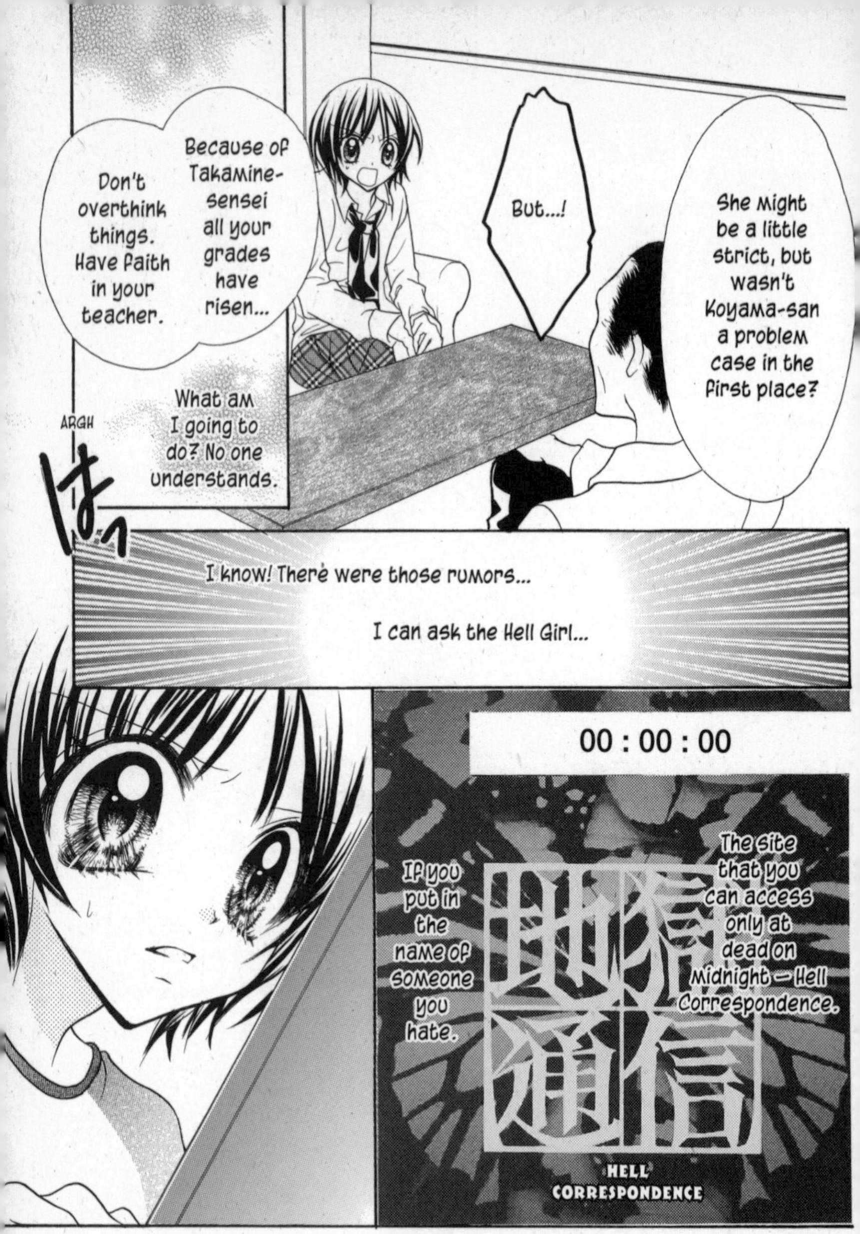
She might be a little strict, but wasn't Koyama-san a problem case in the first place?
But...!
Because of Takamine-sensei all your grades have risen...
Don't overthink things. Have faith in your teacher.
What am I going to do? No one understands.
ARGH
は
I know! There were those rumors...
I can ask the Hell Girl...
00 : 00 : 00
The site that you can access only at dead on Midnight — Hell Correspondence.
If you put in the name of someone you hate.
地獄通信
HELL CORRESPONDENCE

Please send Takamine to hell.

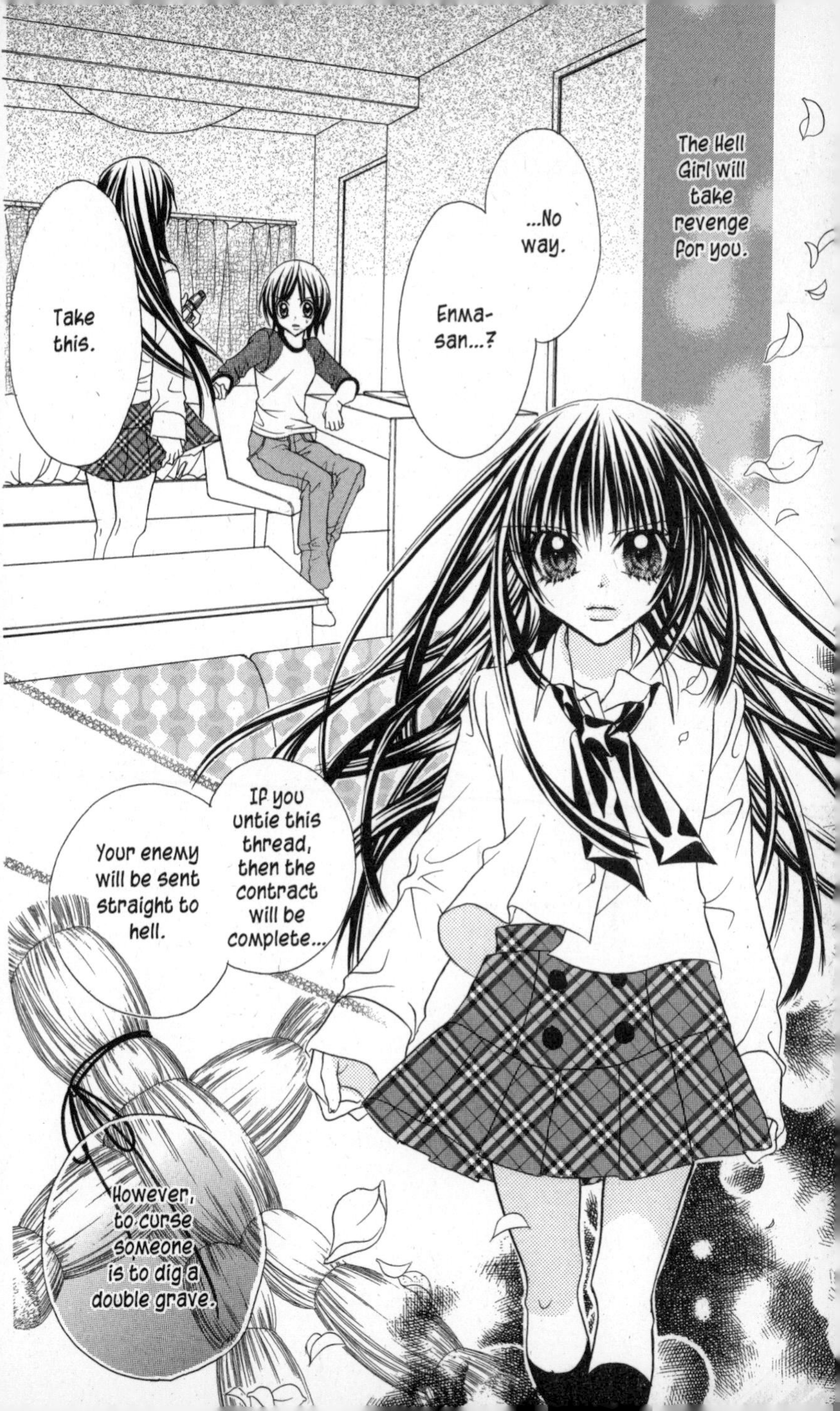
The Hell Girl will take revenge for you.
...No way.
Enma-san...?
Take this.
If you untie this thread, then the contract will be complete...
Your enemy will be sent straight to hell.
However, to curse someone is to dig a double grave.

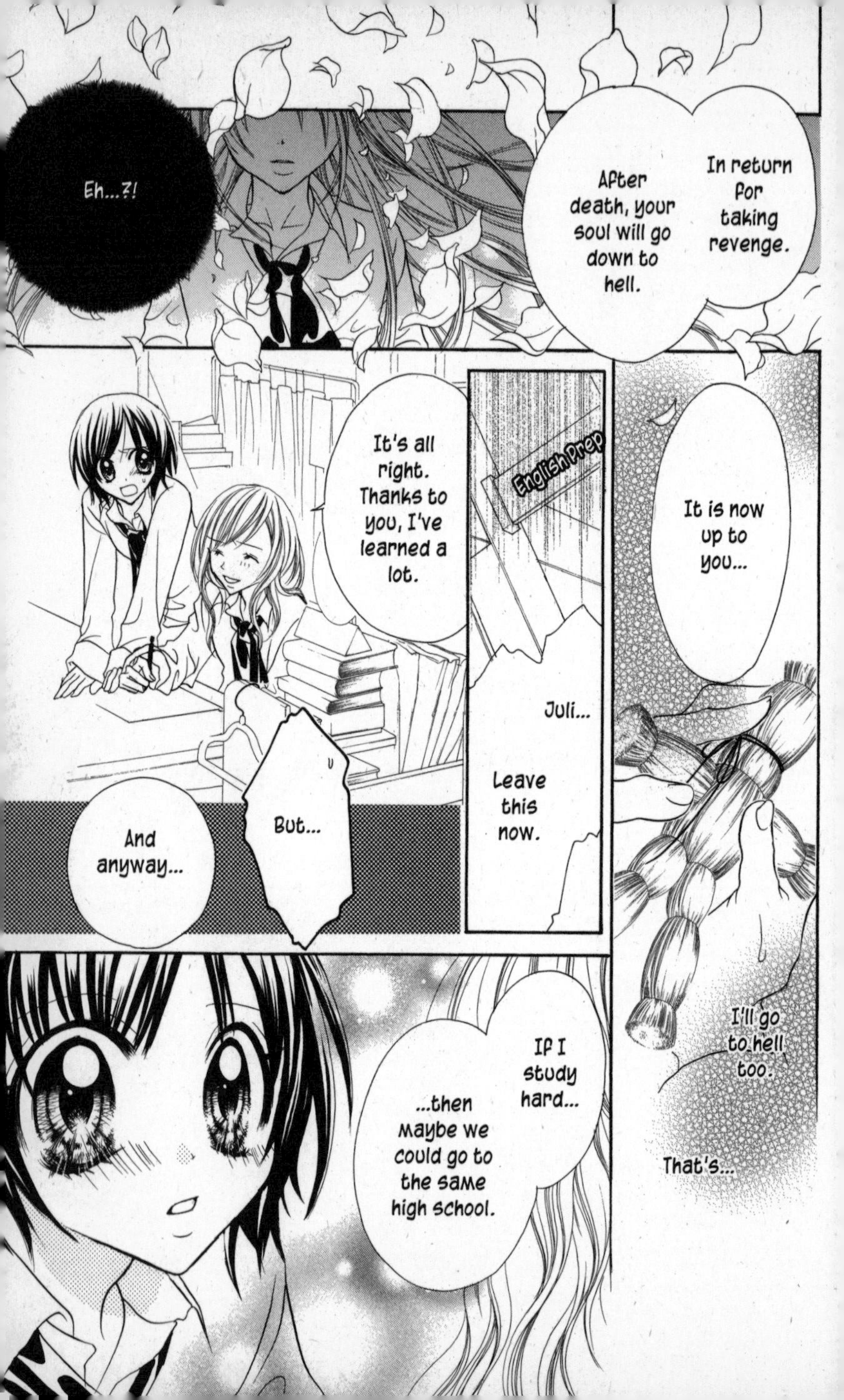
In return for taking revenge.
After death, your soul will go down to hell.
Eh...?!
It is now up to you...
I'll go to hell too.
That's...
English Prep
Juli...
Leave this now.
It's all right. Thanks to you, I've learned a lot.
But...
And anyway...
If I study hard...
...then maybe we could go to the same high school.

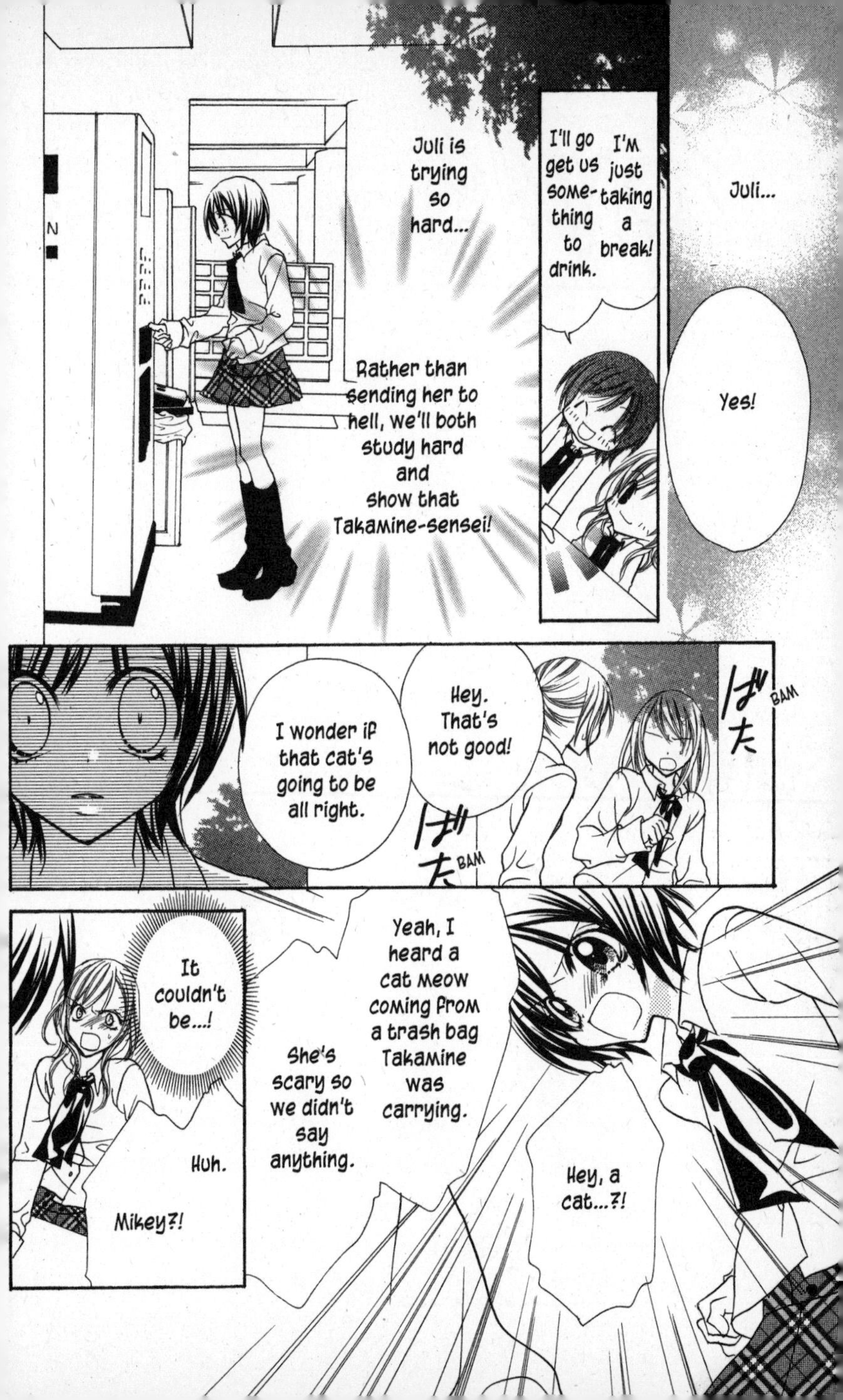

Juli...
Yes!
I'm just taking a break!
I'll go get us something to drink.
Juli is trying so hard...
Rather than sending her to hell, we'll both study hard and show that Takamine-sensei!
ばた
BAM
Hey. That's not good!
I wonder if that cat's going to be all right.
ばた
BAM
Hey, a cat...?!
Yeah, I heard a cat meow coming from a trash bag Takamine was carrying.
She's scary so we didn't say anything.
It couldn't be...!
Huh.
Mikey?!

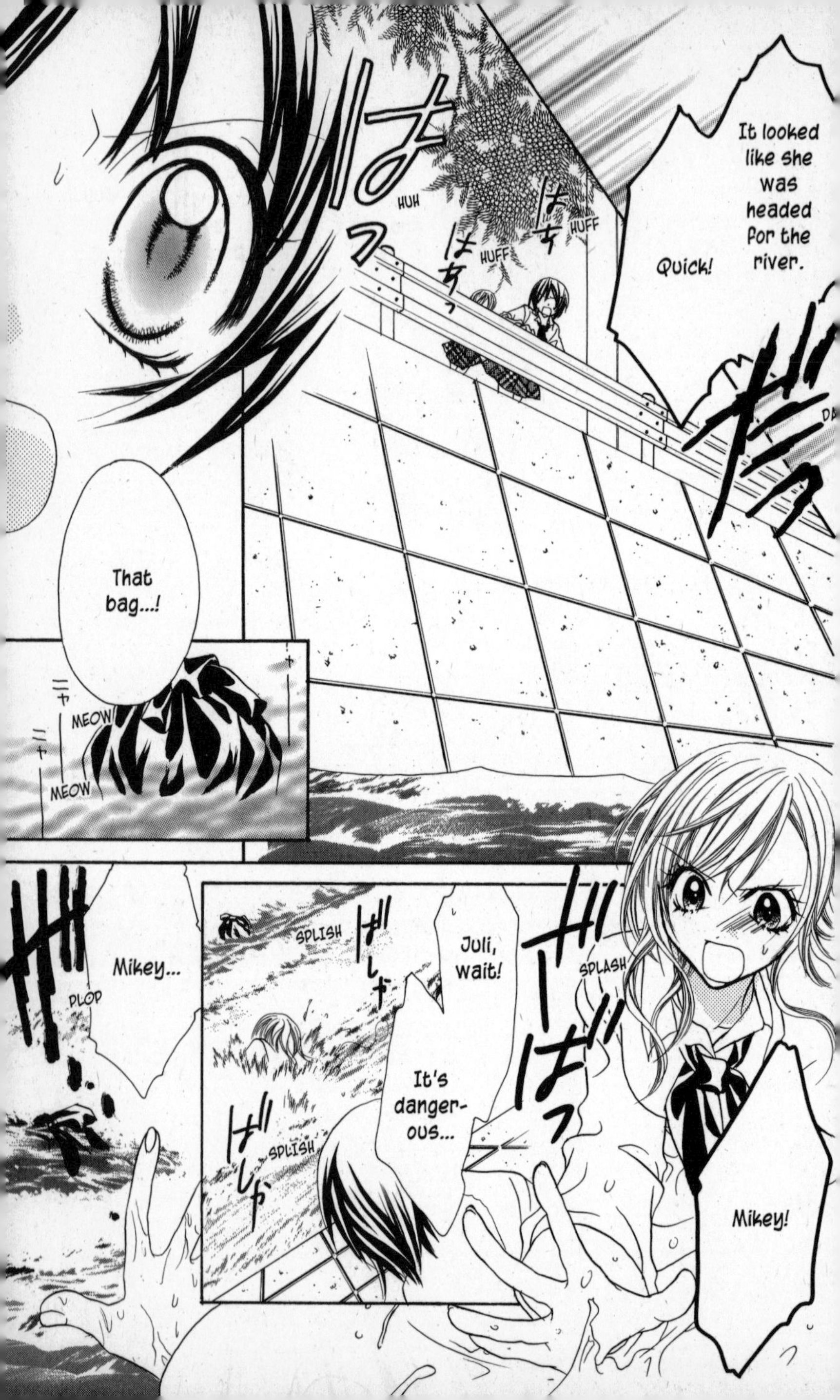
It looked like she was headed for the river.
Quick!
DA
HUFF
HUFF
HUH
That bag...!
MEOW
MEOW
Mikey!
SPLASH
Juli, wait!
It's danger-ous...
SPLISH
SPLISH
Mikey...
PLOP

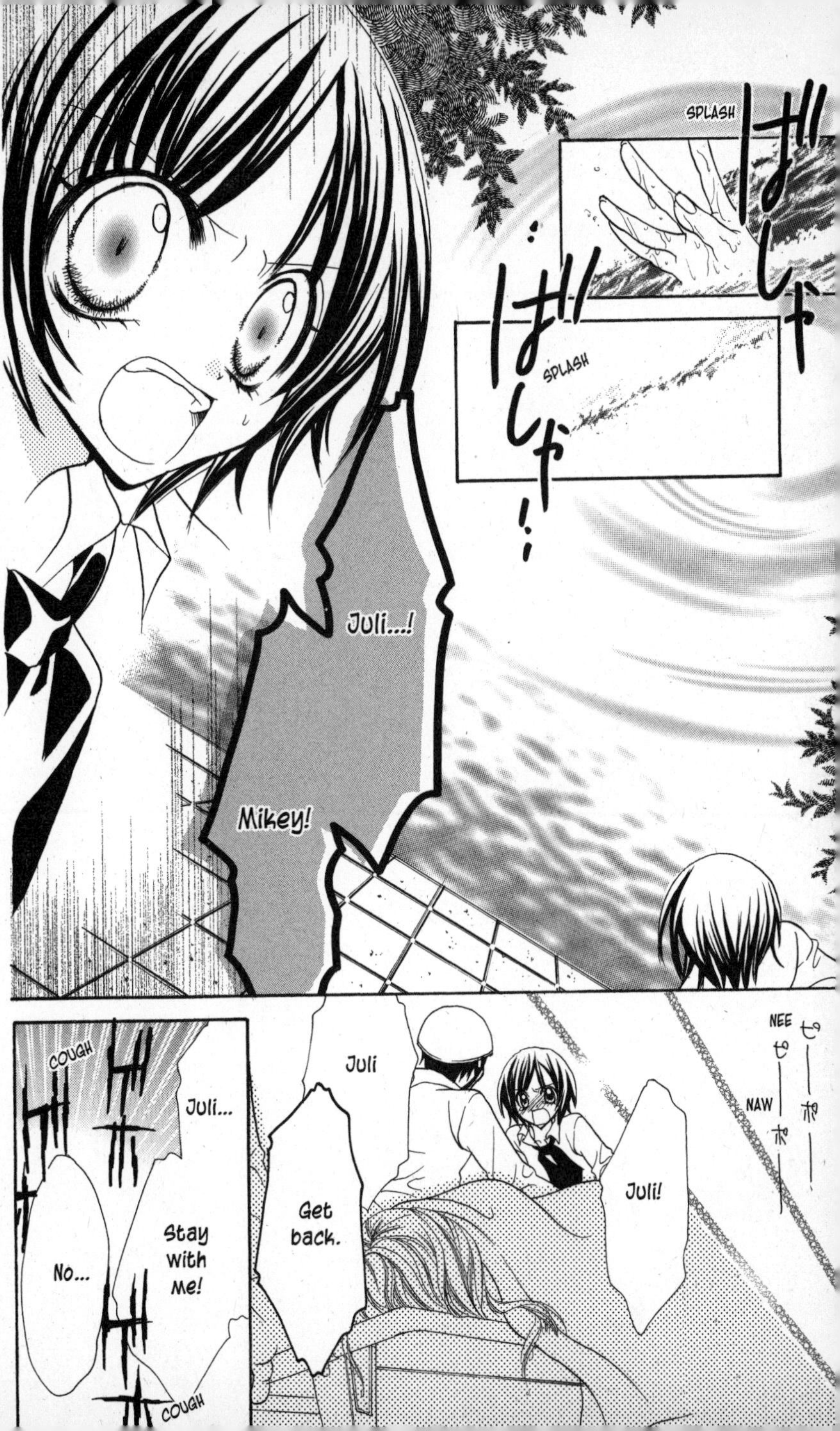
SPLASH
ばしゃ
SPLASH
ばしゃ!!
Juli...!
Mikey!
NEE
NAW
ピーポー!
ピーポー
Juli!
Juli
Get back.
COUGH
Juli...
Stay with me!
No...
COUGH

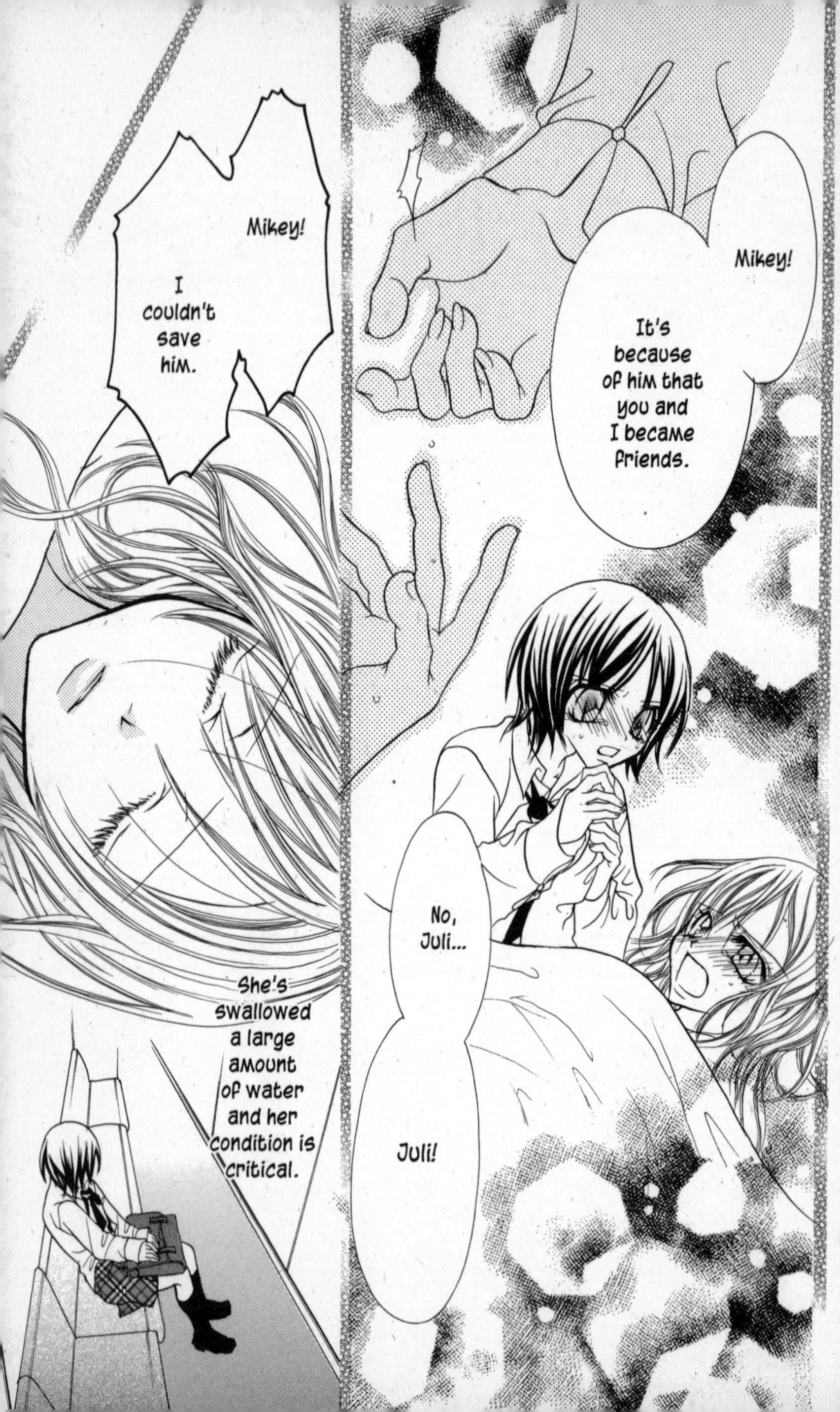
Mikey! It's because of him that you and I became friends.
No, Juli...
Juli!
Mikey! I couldn't save him.
She's swallowed a large amount of water and her condition is critical.

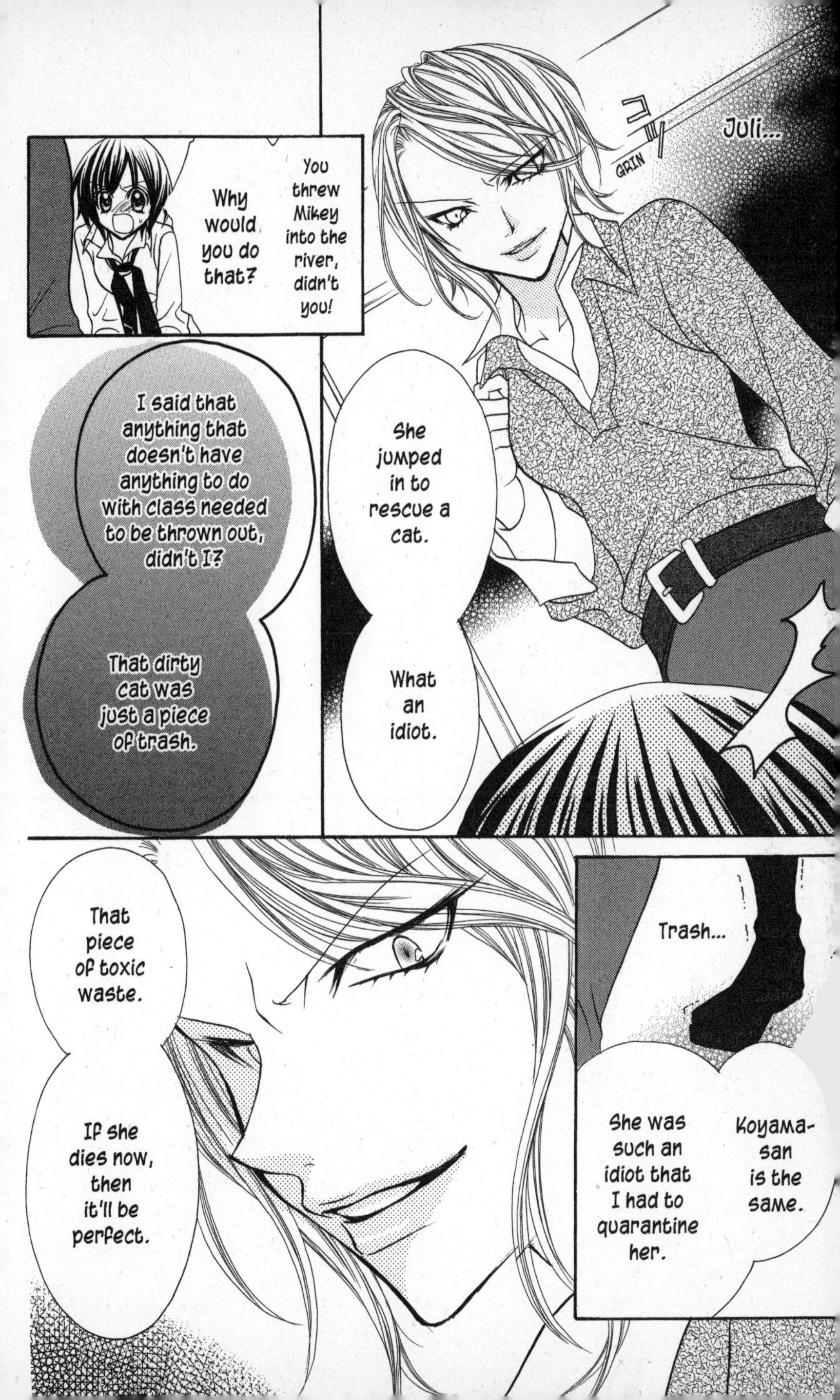
Juli...
ニッ
GRIN
She jumped in to rescue a cat.
What an idiot.
You threw Mikey into the river, didn't you!
Why would you do that?
I said that anything that doesn't have anything to do with class needed to be thrown out, didn't I?
That dirty cat was just a piece of trash.
Trash...
Koyama-san is the same.
She was such an idiot that I had to quarantine her.
That piece of toxic waste.
If she dies now, then it'll be perfect.

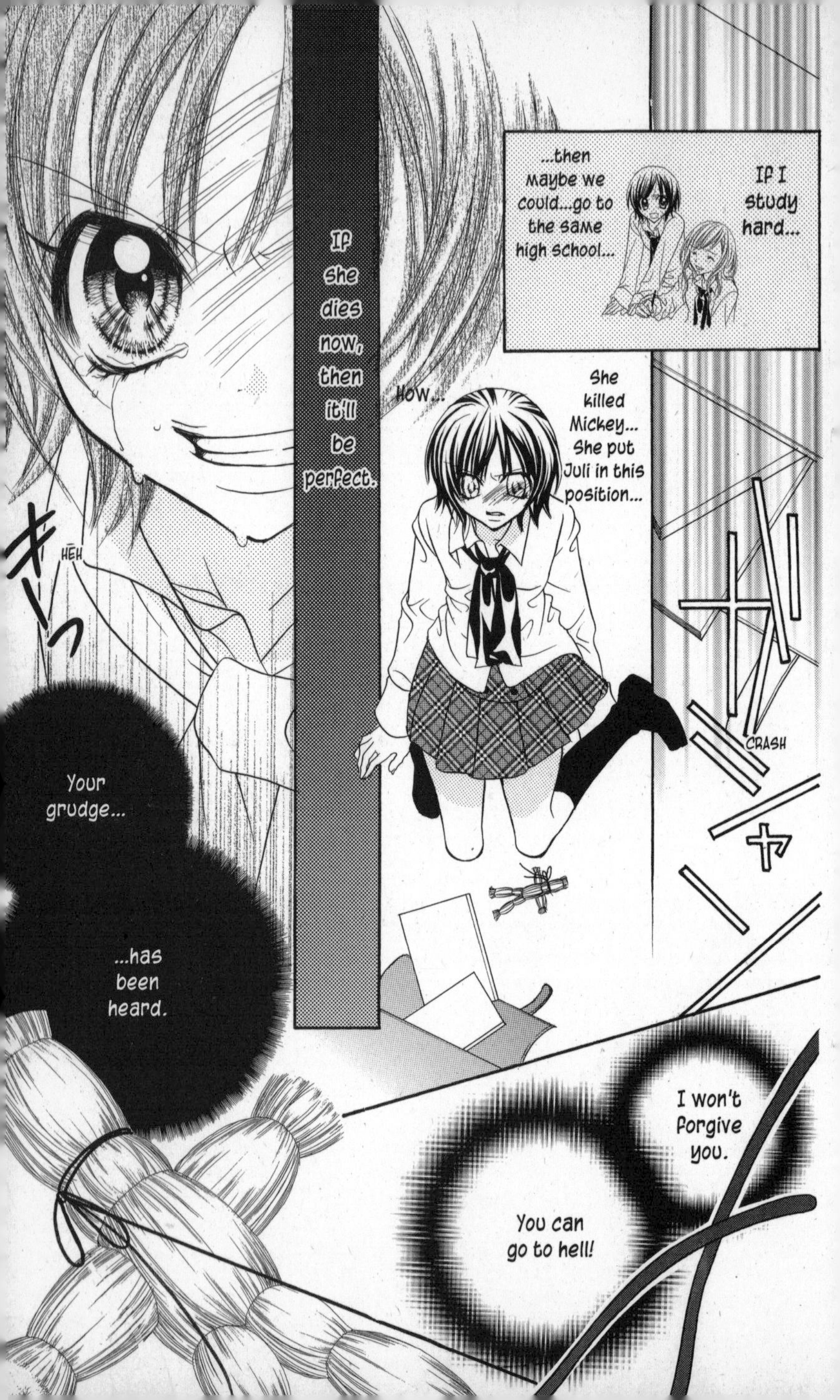

If I study hard...
...then maybe we could...go to the same high school...
She killed Mickey... She put Juli in this position...
How...
CRASH
I won't forgive you.
You can go to hell!
If she dies now, then it'll be perfect.
HEH
Your grudge...
...has been heard.

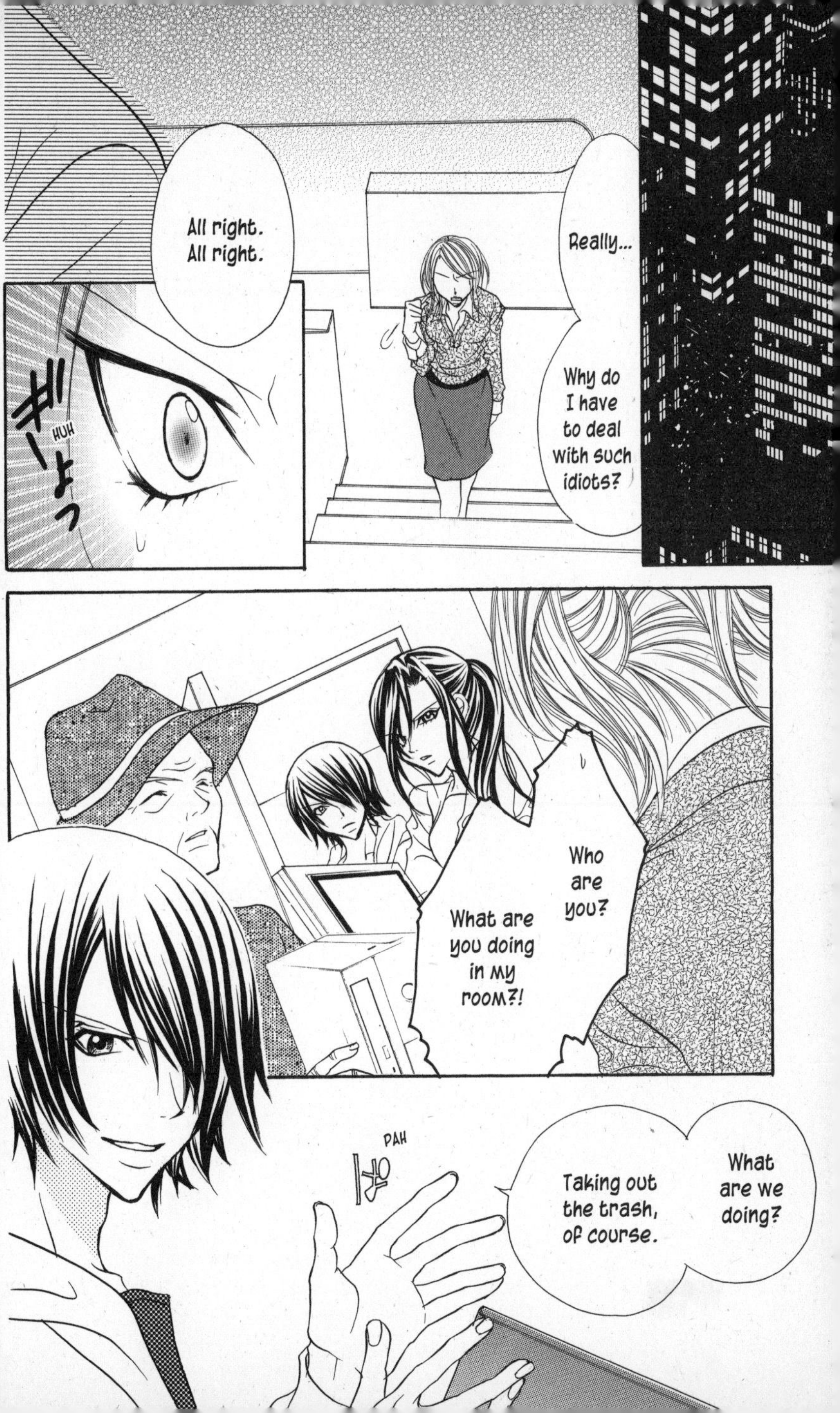

Really...
Why do I have to deal with such idiots?
All right. All right.
ぎょっ
HUH
Who are you?
What are you doing in my room?!
What are we doing?
Taking out the trash, of course.
PAH

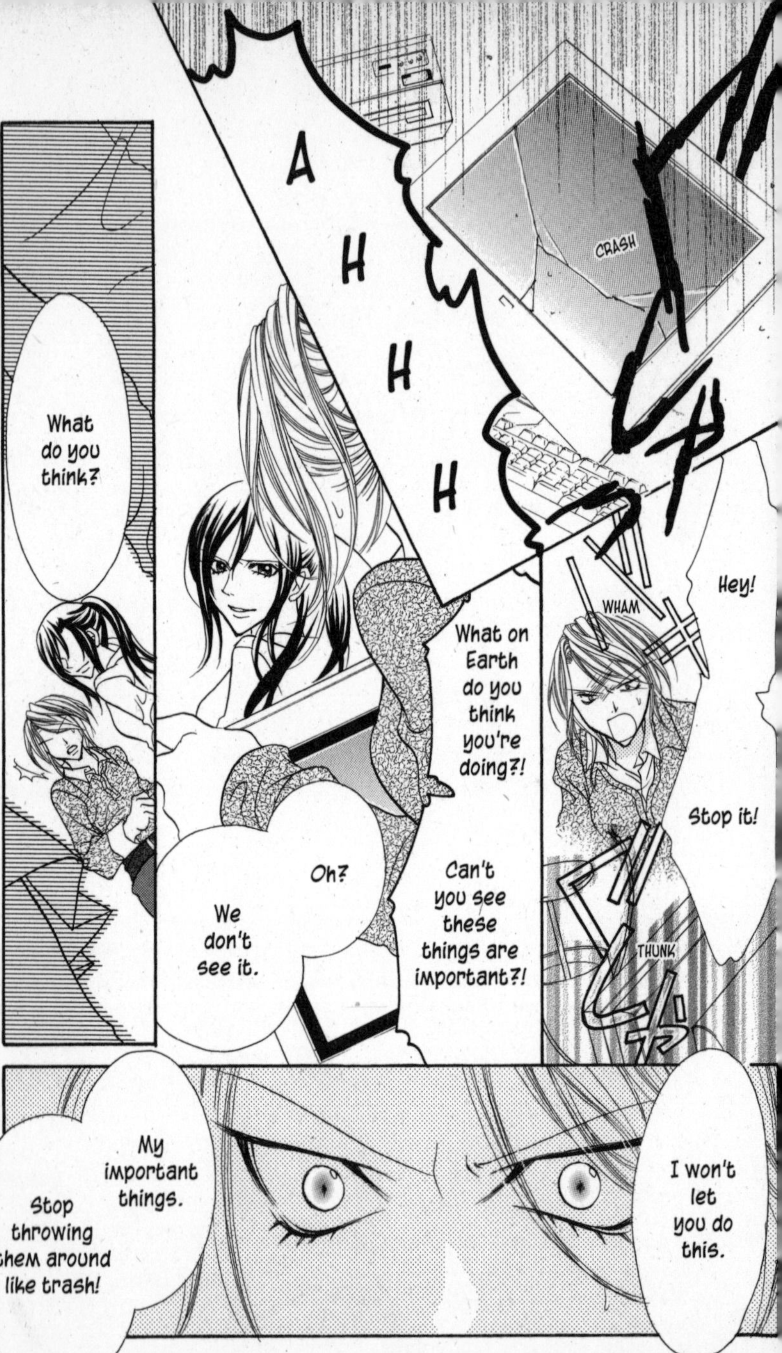
AHHHH
CRASH
Hey!
WHAM
Stop it!
THUNK
What on Earth do you think you're doing?!
Can't you see these things are important?!
Oh?
We don't see it.
What do you think?
I won't let you do this.
My important things.
Stop throwing them around like trash!

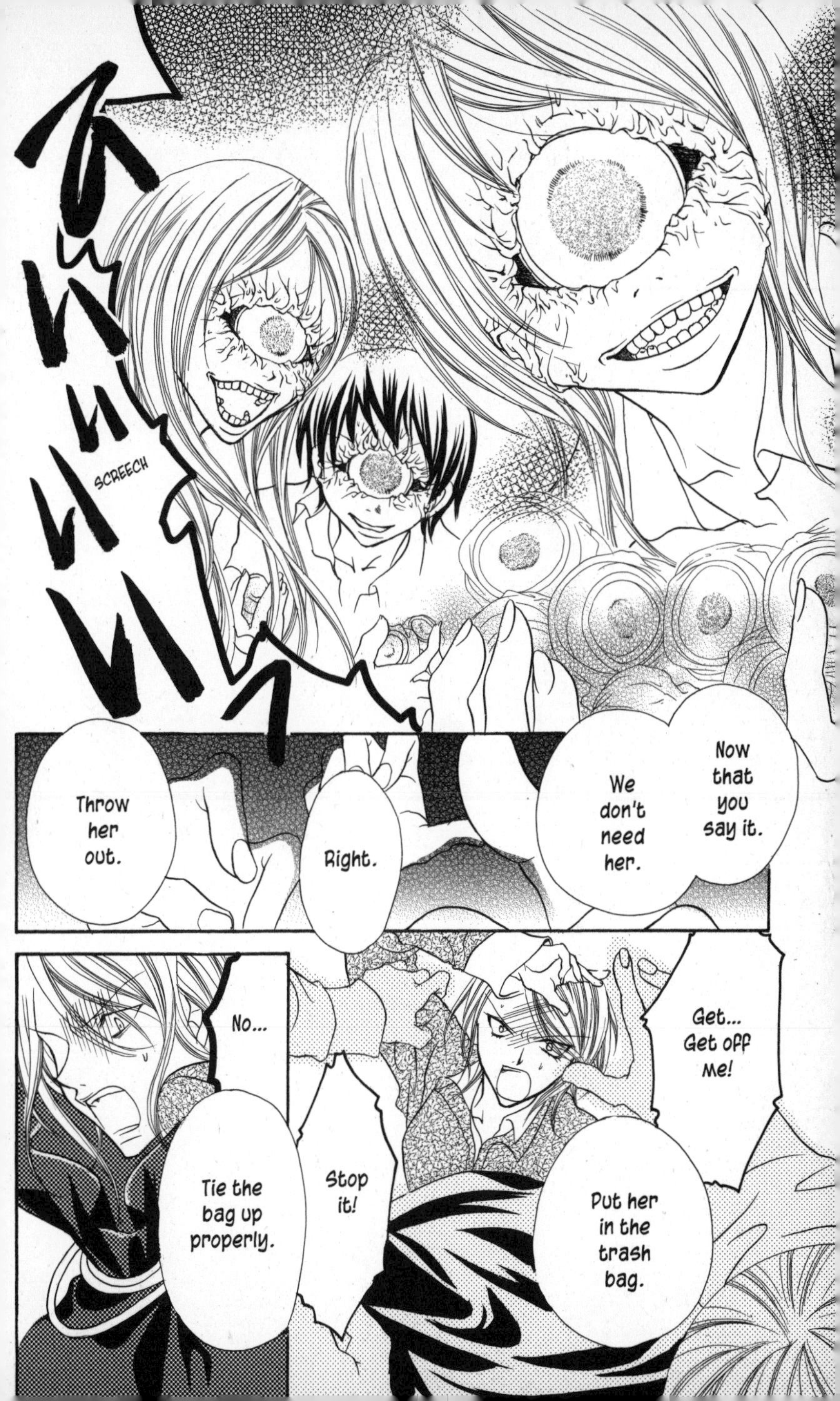
SCREECH
Now that you say it.
We don't need her.
Right.
Throw her out.
Get... Get off me!
Put her in the trash bag.
Stop it!
No...
Tie the bag up properly.

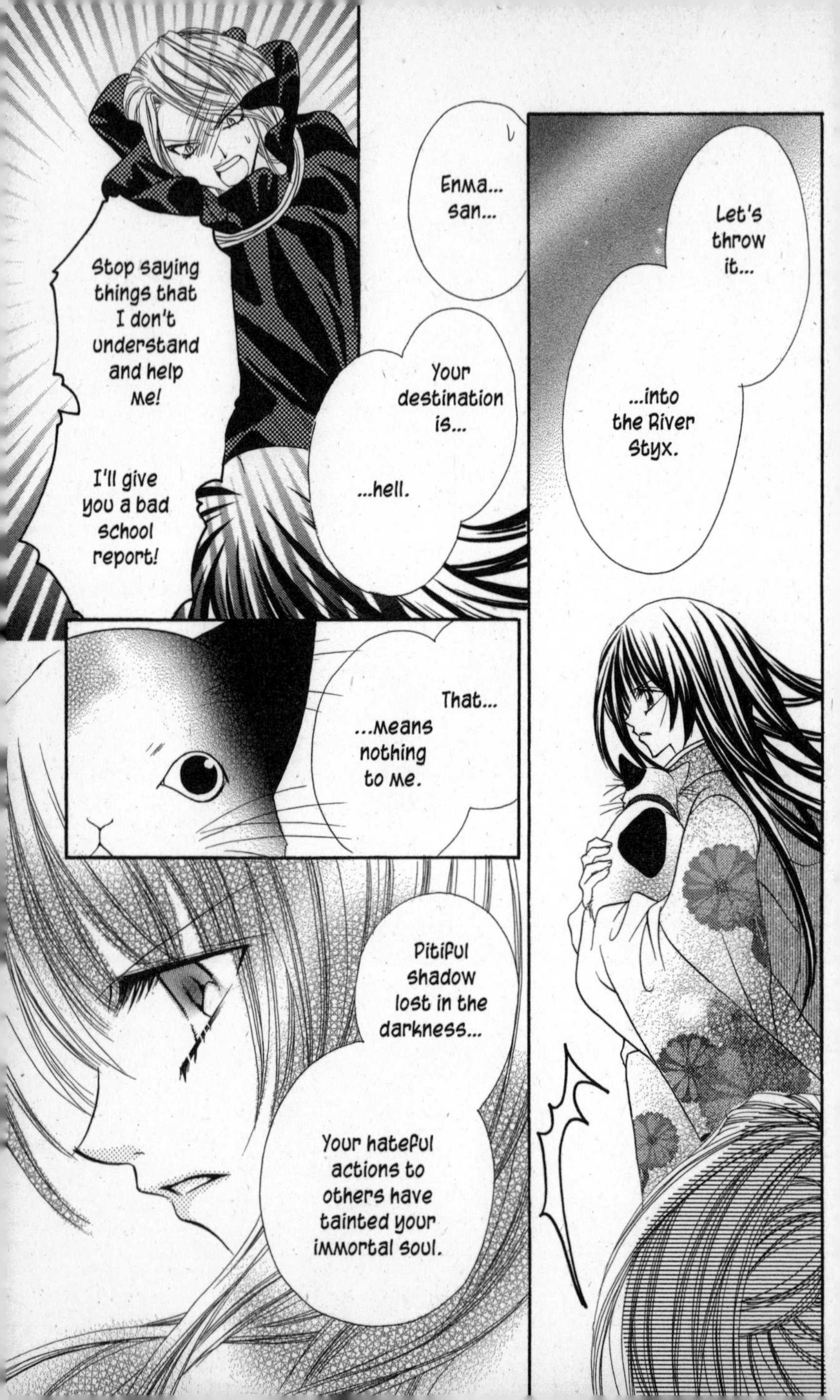
Let's throw it...
...into the River Styx.
Enma... san...
Stop saying things that I don't understand and help me!
I'll give you a bad school report!
Your destination is...
...hell.
That...
...means nothing to me.
Pitiful shadow lost in the darkness...
Your hateful actions to others have tainted your immortal soul.

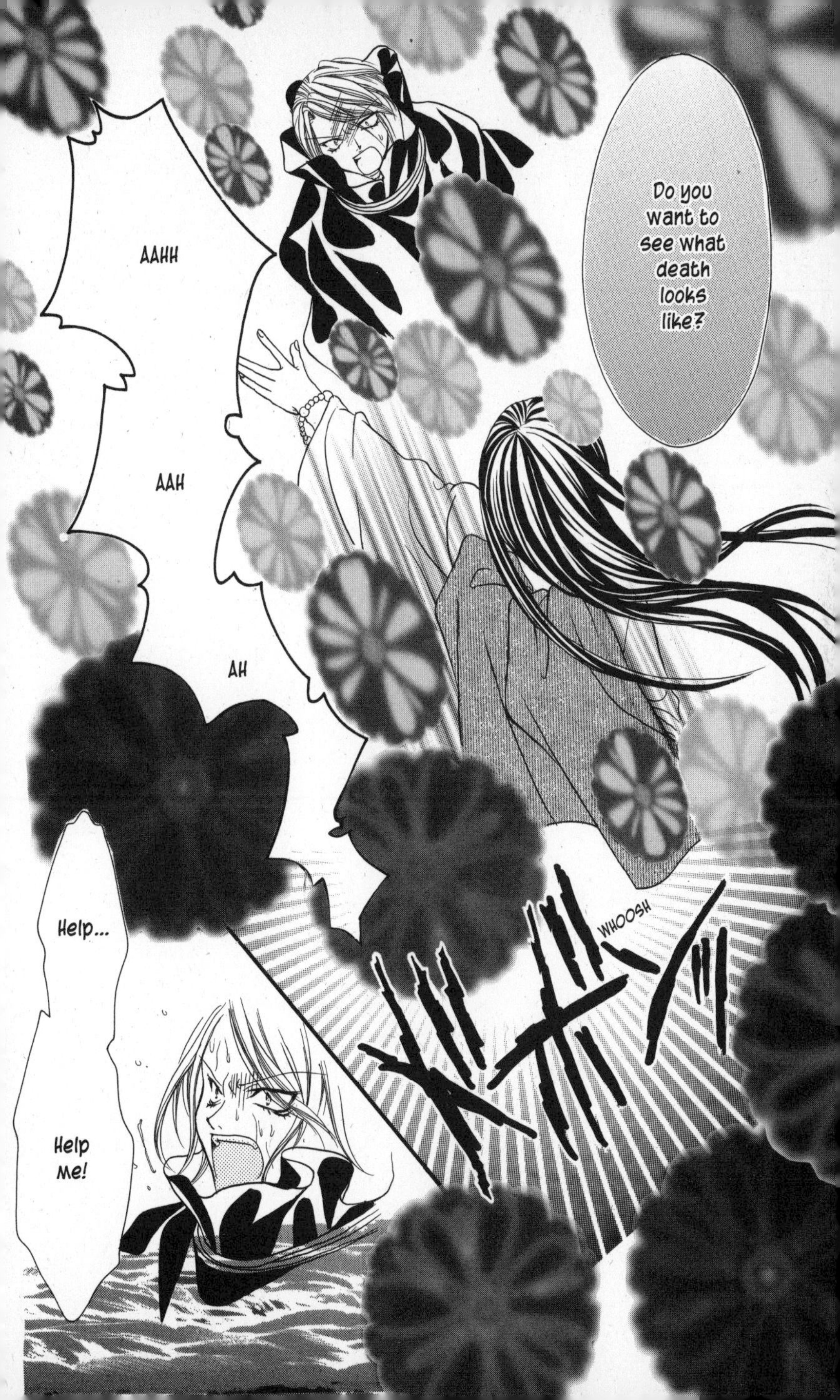
Do you want to see what death looks like?
AAHH AAH AH
WHOOSH
Help... Help me!

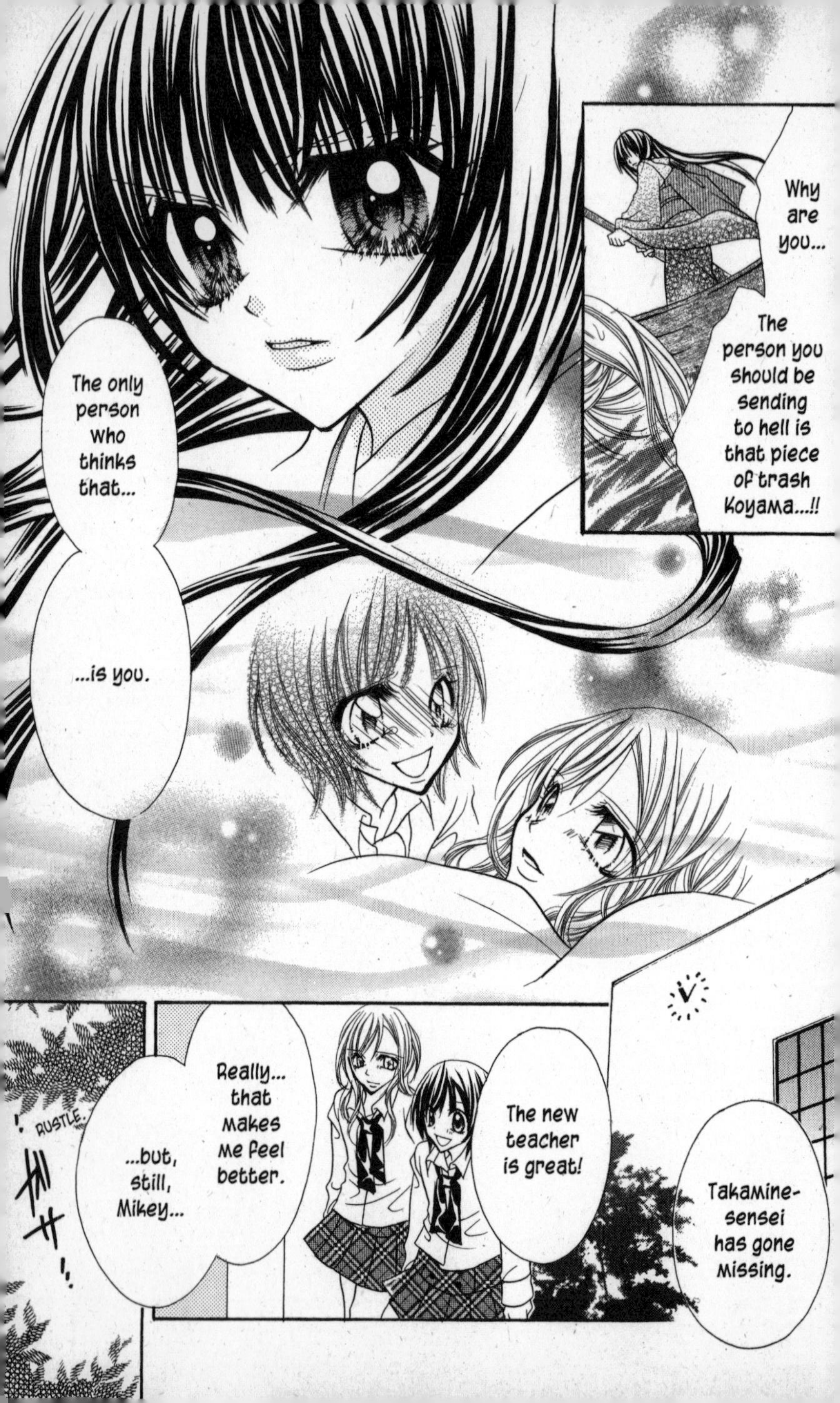
Why are you...
The person you should be sending to hell is that piece of trash Koyama...!!
The only person who thinks that...
...is you.
Takamine-sensei has gone missing.
The new teacher is great!
Really... that makes me feel better.
...but, still, Mikey...
RUSTLE.

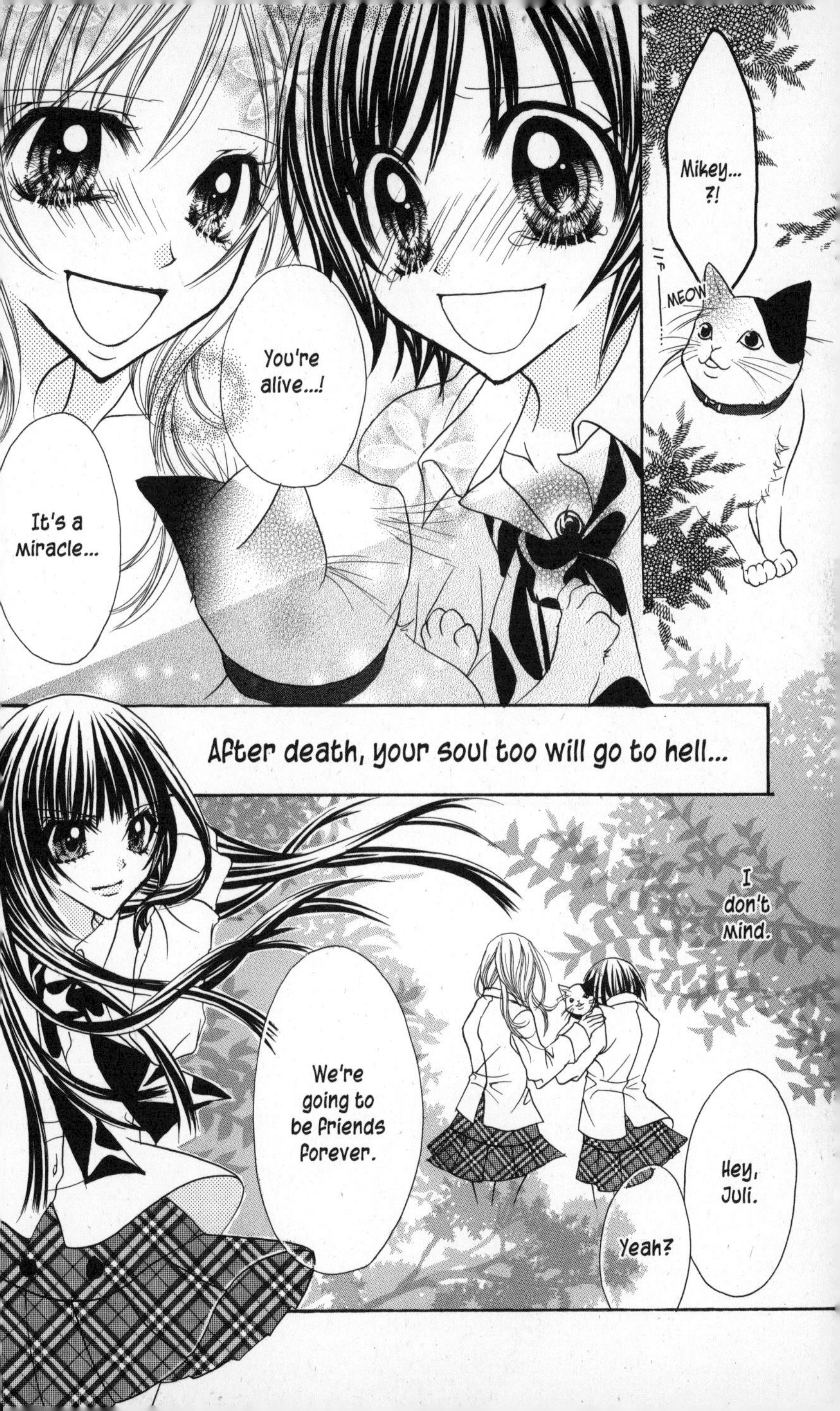
Mikey... ?!
MEOW
You're alive...!
It's a miracle...
After death, your soul too will go to hell...
I don't mind.
Hey, Juli.
Yeah?
We're going to be friends forever.

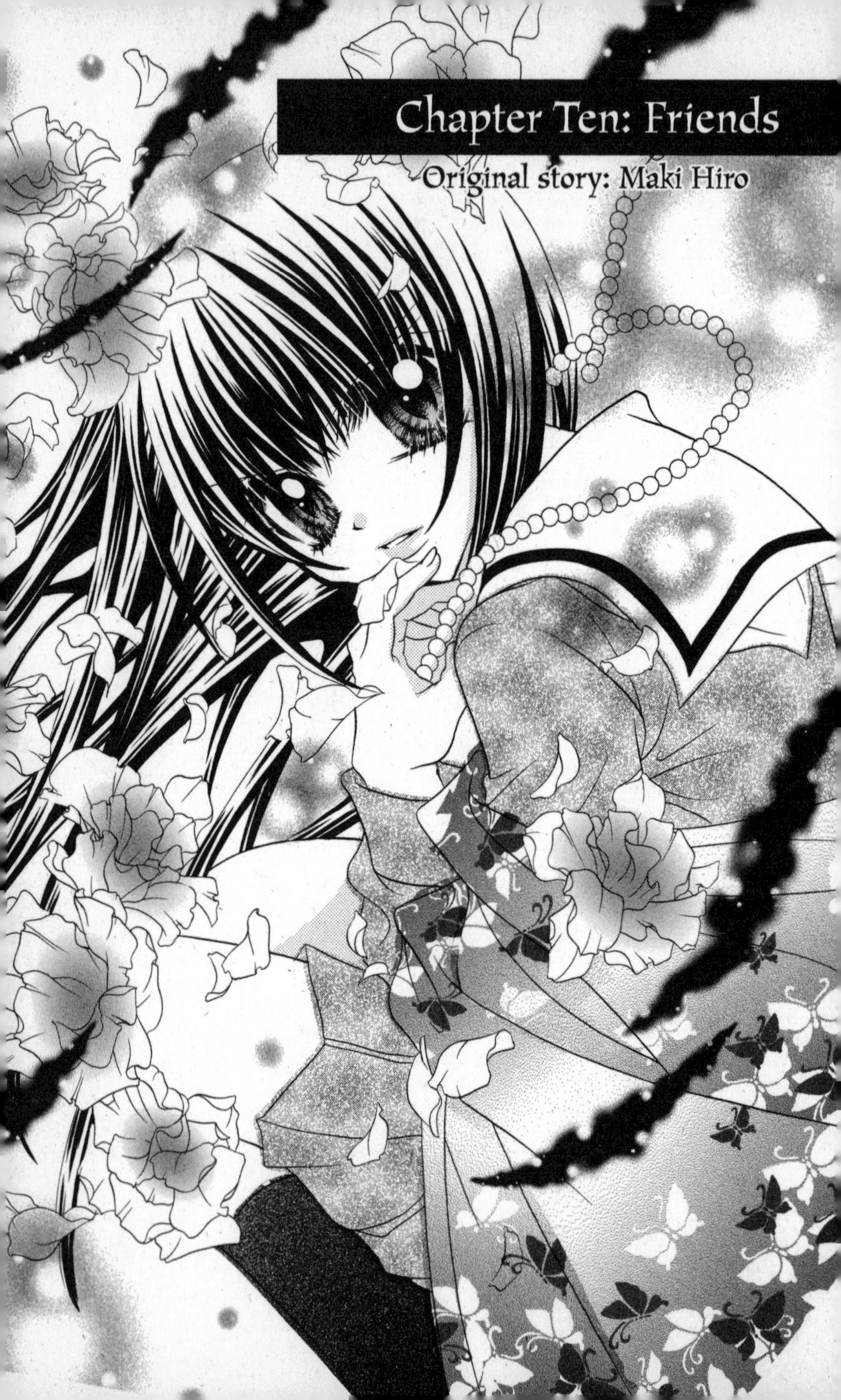
Chapter Ten: Friends
Original story: Maki Hiro

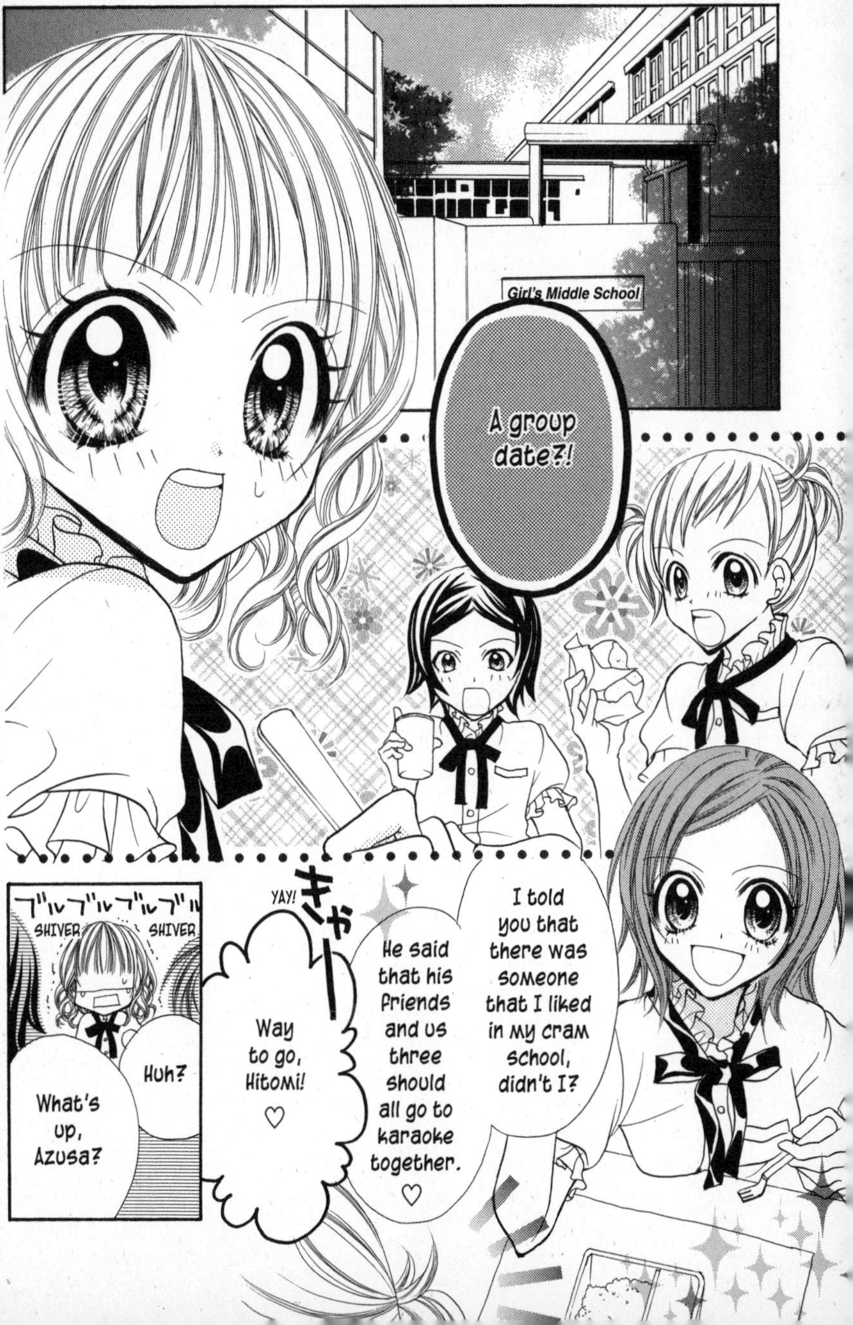
Girl's Middle School
A group date?!
I told you that there was someone that I liked in my cram school, didn't I?
He said that his friends and us three should all go to karaoke together. ♡
YAY! きゃー
Way to go, Hitomi! ♡
ブルブルブル SHIVER SHIVER
Huh?
What's up, Azusa?

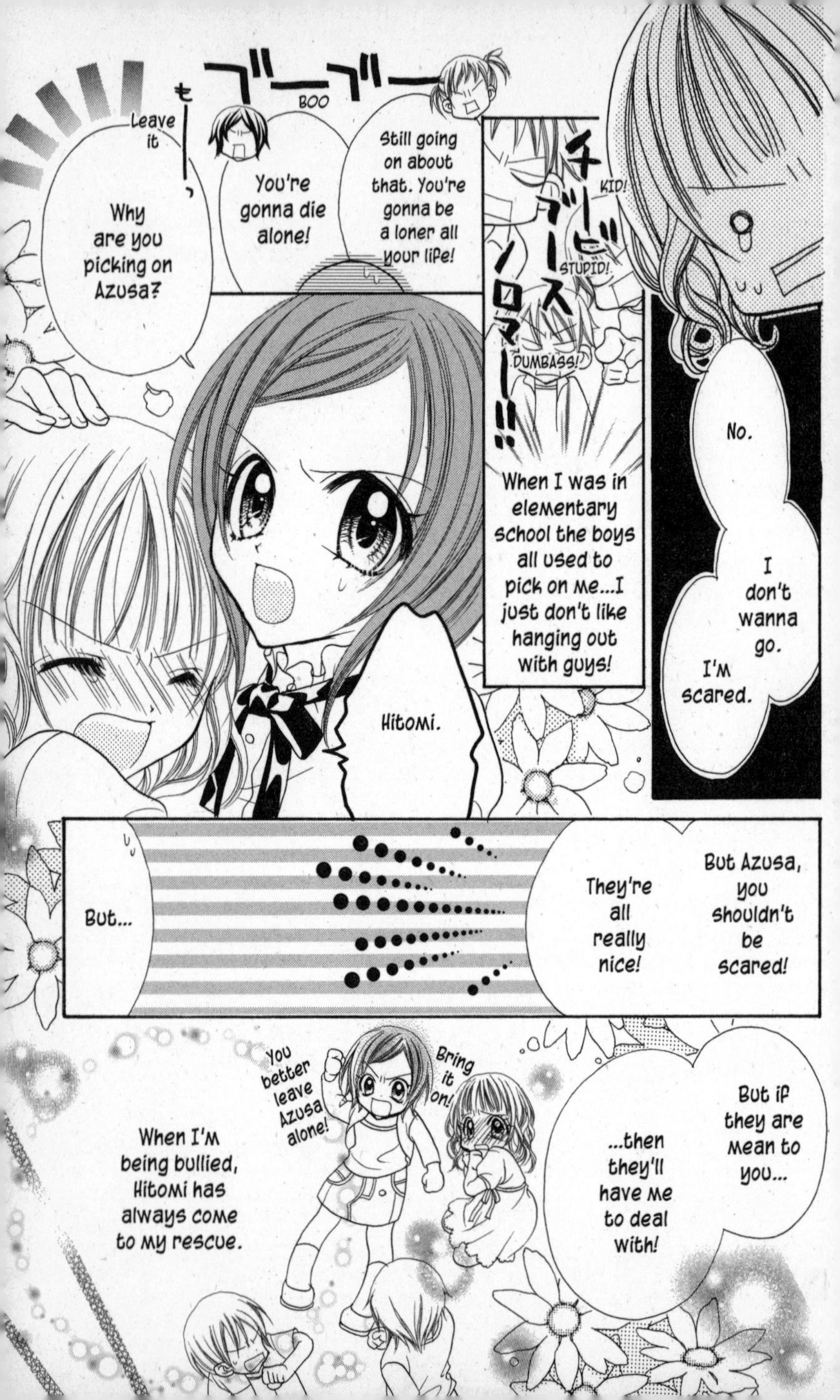

No.
I don't wanna go.
I'm scared.
チービ
KID!
ブース
STUPID!
ノロマー!!
DUMBASS!
When I was in elementary school the boys all used to pick on me...I just don't like hanging out with guys!
ブーブー
BOO
Still going on about that. You're gonna be a loner all your life!
You're gonna die alone!
Leave it
Why are you picking on Azusa?
Hitomi.
But Azusa, you shouldn't be scared!
They're all really nice!
But...
But if they are mean to you...
...then they'll have me to deal with!
Bring it on!
You better leave Azusa alone!
When I'm being bullied, Hitomi has always come to my rescue.

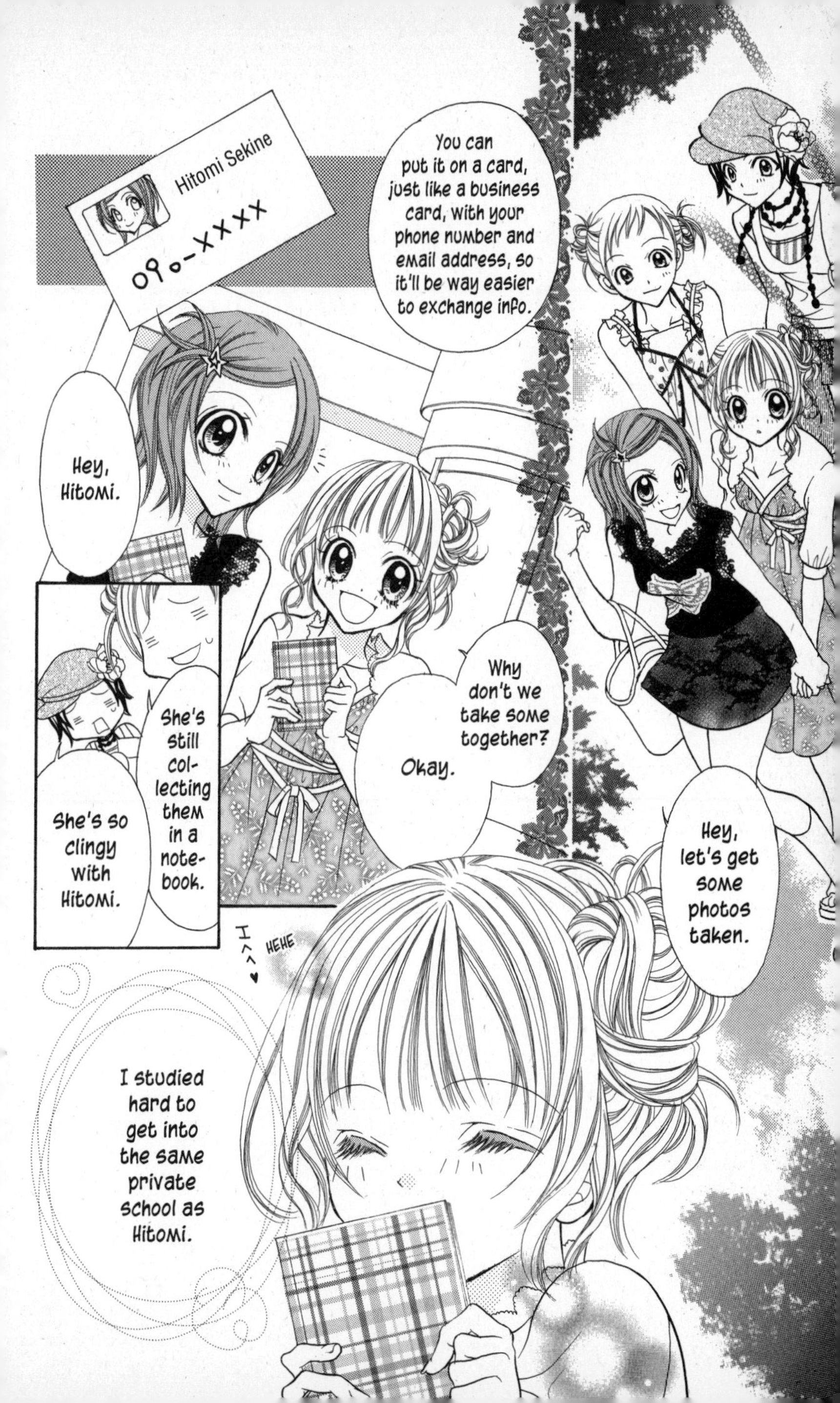
Hey, let's get some photos taken.
Hitomi Sekine
090-XXXX
You can put it on a card, just like a business card, with your phone number and email address, so it'll be way easier to exchange info.
Hey, Hitomi.
Why don't we take some together?
Okay.
She's still collecting them in a notebook.
She's so clingy with Hitomi.
HEHE
I studied hard to get into the same private school as Hitomi.

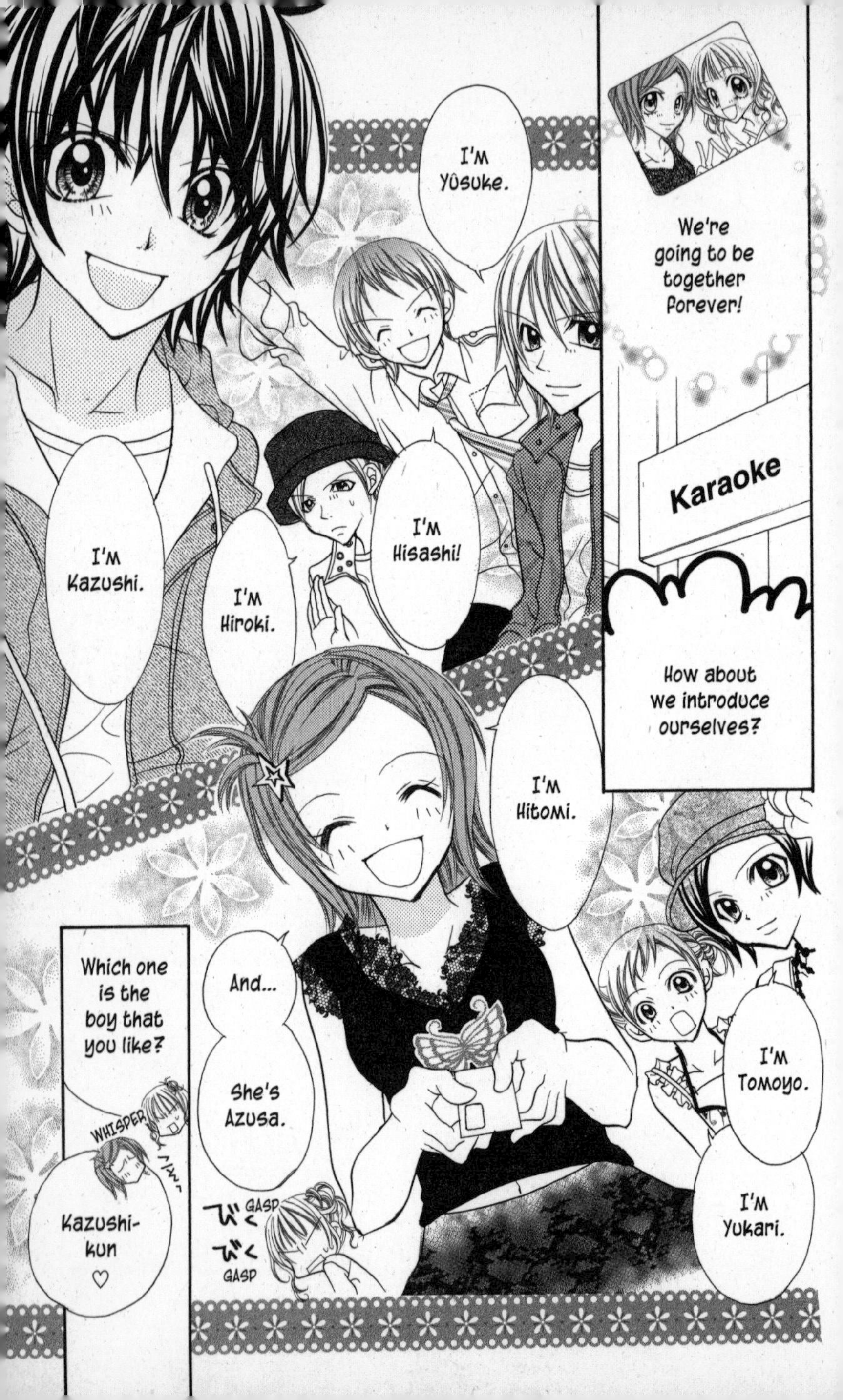
We're going to be together forever!
Karaoke
How about we introduce ourselves?
I'm Yûsuke.
I'm Hisashi!
I'm Hiroki.
I'm Kazushi.
I'm Hitomi.
I'm Tomoyo.
I'm Yukari.
And...
She's Azusa.
びく GASP
びく GASP
Which one is the boy that you like?
WHISPER
Kazushi-kun ♡

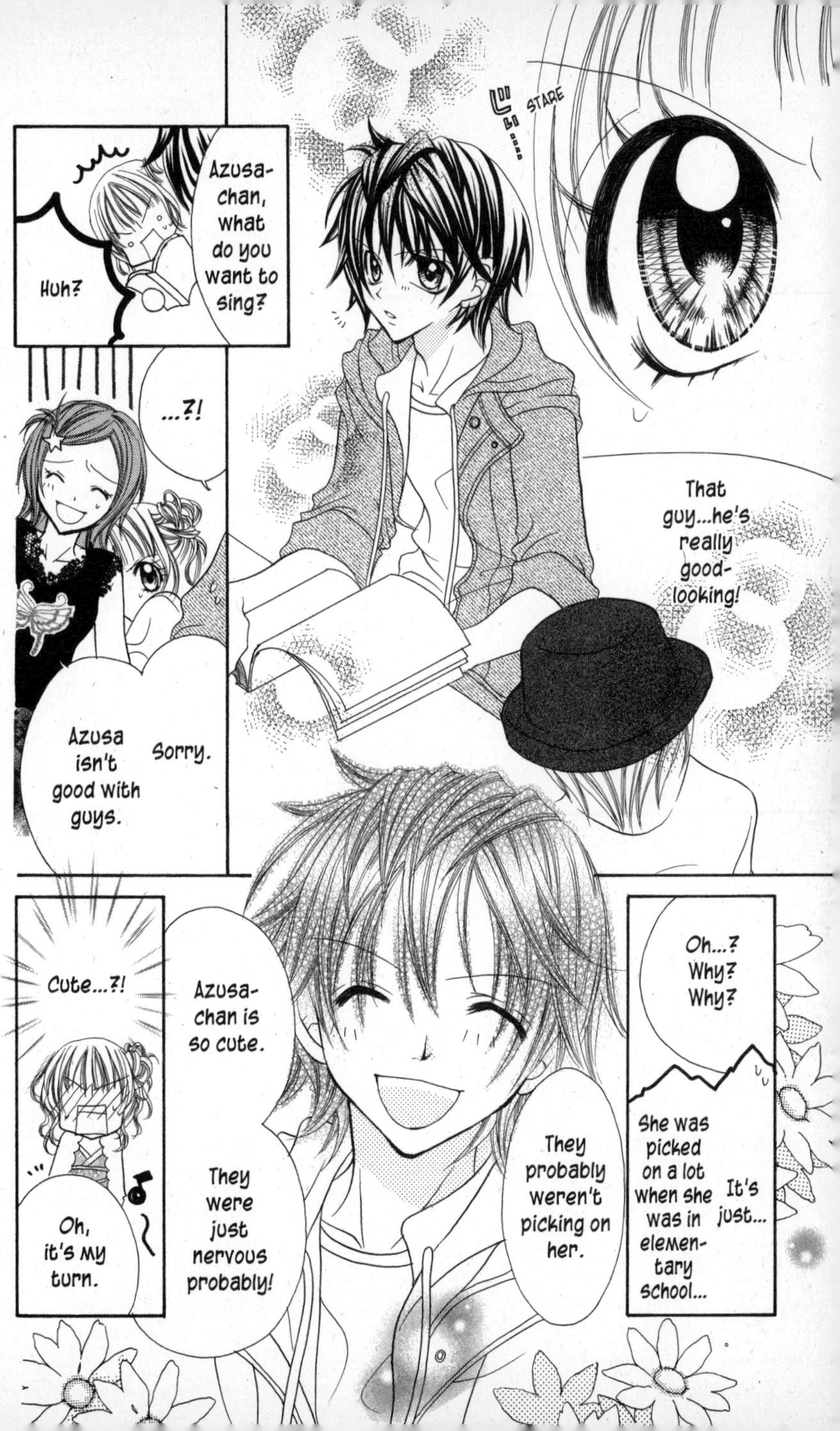
STARE
That guy...he's really good-looking!
Azusa-chan, what do you want to sing?
Huh?
...?!
Sorry.
Azusa isn't good with guys.
Oh...? Why? Why?
It's just...
She was picked on a lot when she was in elementary school...
They probably weren't picking on her.
They were just nervous probably!
Azusa-chan is so cute.
Cute...?!
Oh, it's my turn.

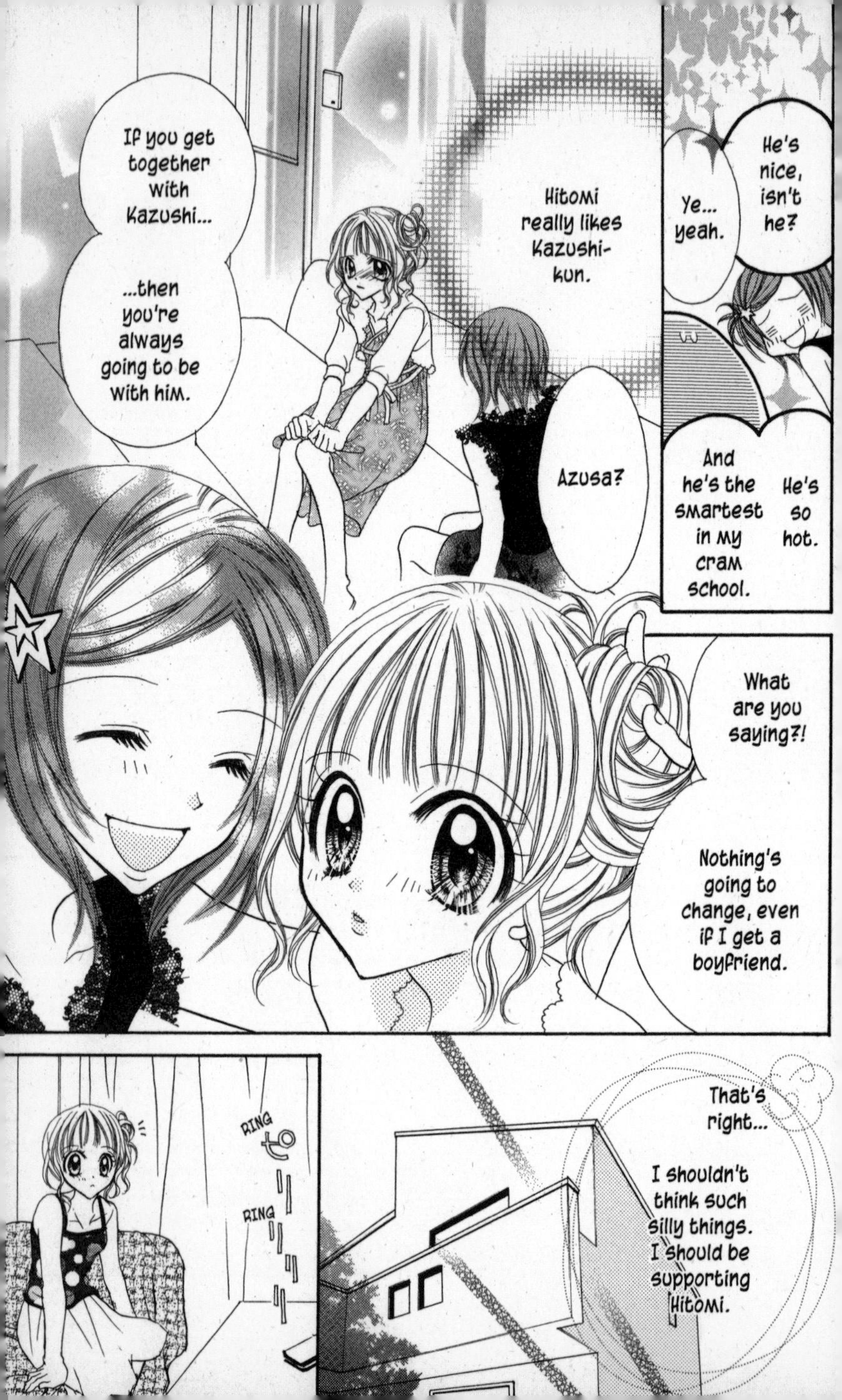
He's nice, isn't he?
Ye... yeah.
He's so hot.
And he's the smartest in my cram school.
Hitomi really likes Kazushi-kun.
Azusa?
If you get together with Kazushi...
...then you're always going to be with him.
What are you saying?!
Nothing's going to change, even if I get a boyfriend.
That's right...
I shouldn't think such silly things. I should be supporting Hitomi.
RING
RING

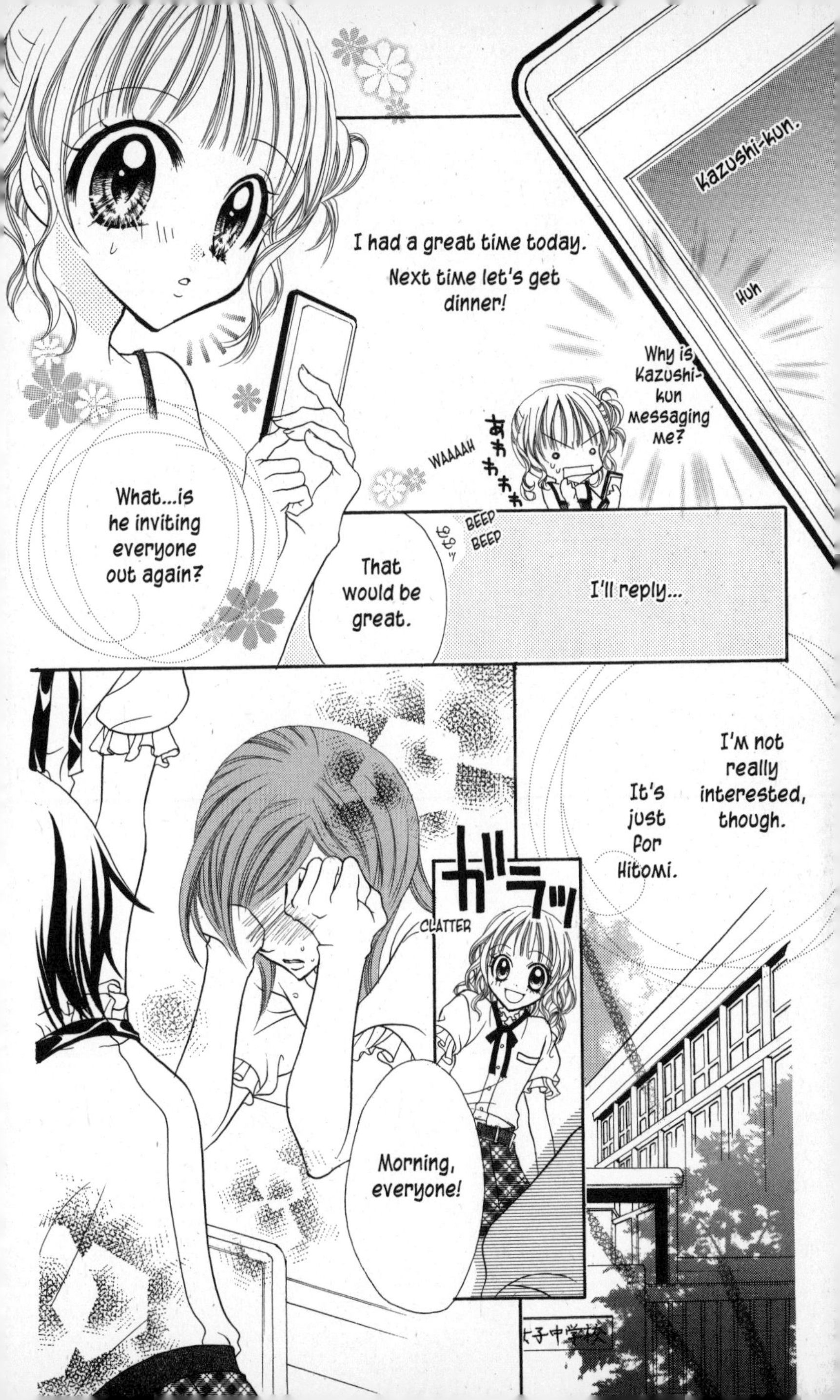
Kazushi-kun.
I had a great time today.
Next time let's get dinner!
Huh
Why is Kazushi-kun messaging me?
WAAAAH
BEEP BEEP
I'll reply...
That would be great.
What...is he inviting everyone out again?
I'm not really interested, though.
It's just for Hitomi.
ガラッ
CLATTER
Morning, everyone!

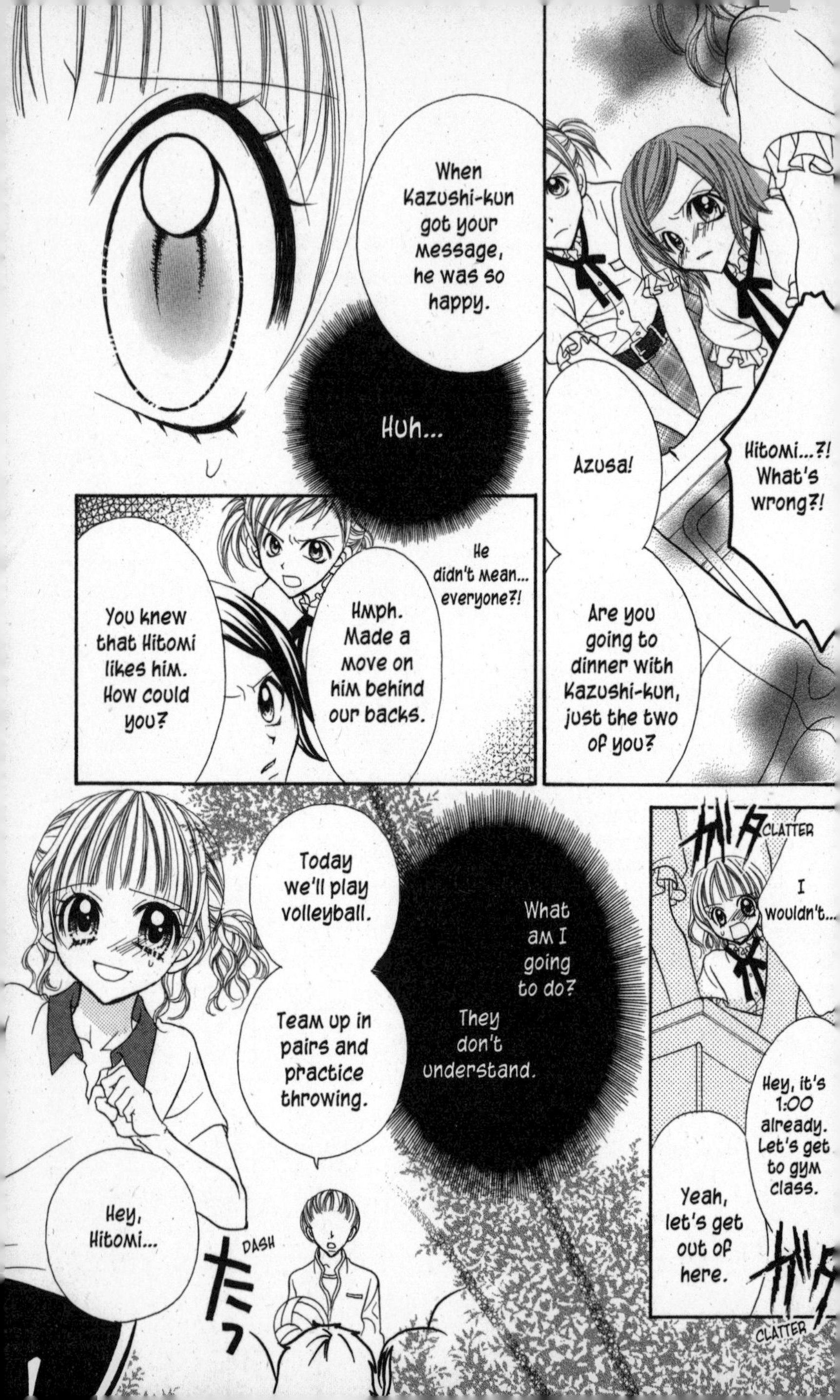
Hitomi...?! What's wrong?!
Azusa!
Are you going to dinner with Kazushi-kun, just the two of you?
When Kazushi-kun got your message, he was so happy.
Huh...
He didn't mean... everyone?!
Hmph. Made a move on him behind our backs.
You knew that Hitomi likes him. How could you?
CLATTER
I wouldn't...
Hey, it's 1:00 already. Let's get to gym class.
Yeah, let's get out of here.
CLATTER
What am I going to do?
They don't understand.
Today we'll play volleyball.
Team up in pairs and practice throwing.
Hey, Hitomi...
DASH

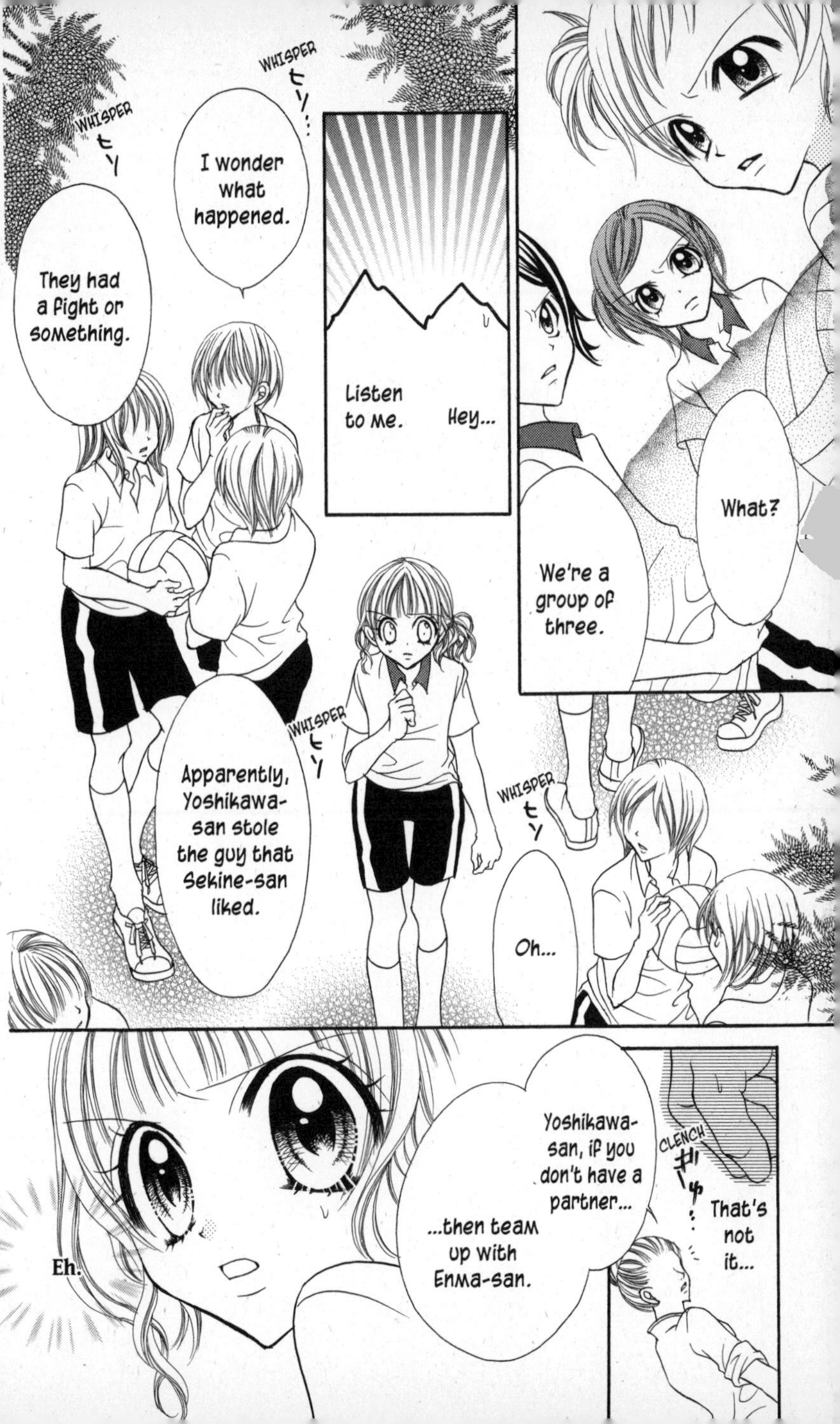
What?
We're a group of three.
Hey...
Listen to me.
WHISPER
I wonder what happened.
WHISPER
They had a fight or something.
WHISPER
Apparently, Yoshikawa-san stole the guy that Sekine-san liked.
WHISPER
Oh...
CLENCH
That's not it...
Yoshikawa-san, if you don't have a partner...
...then team up with Enma-san.
Eh.

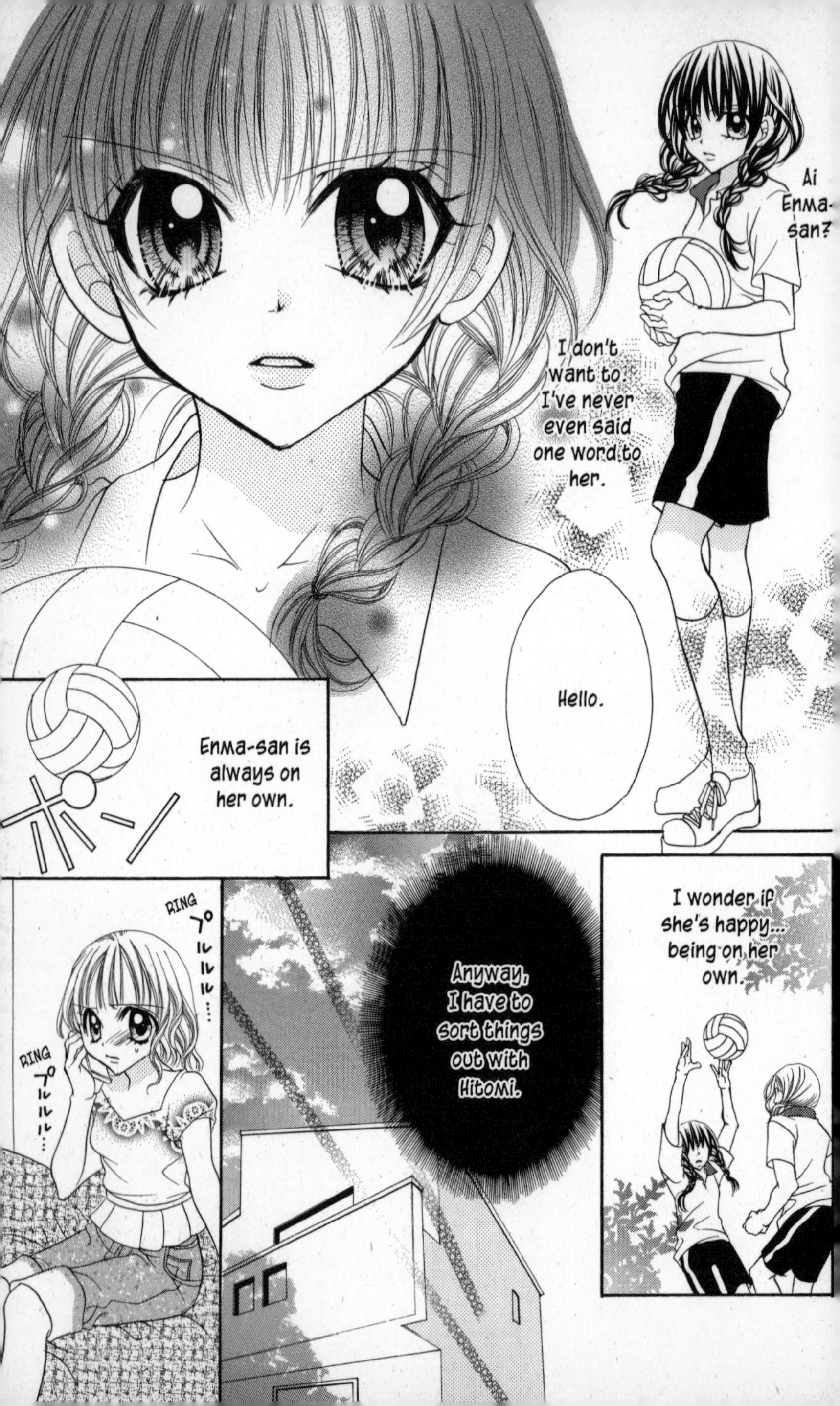
Ai Enma-san?
I don't want to. I've never even said one word to her.
Hello.
Enma-san is always on her own.
ポーン
I wonder if she's happy... being on her own.
Anyway, I have to sort things out with Hitomi.
RING
プルルル…
RING
プルルル…

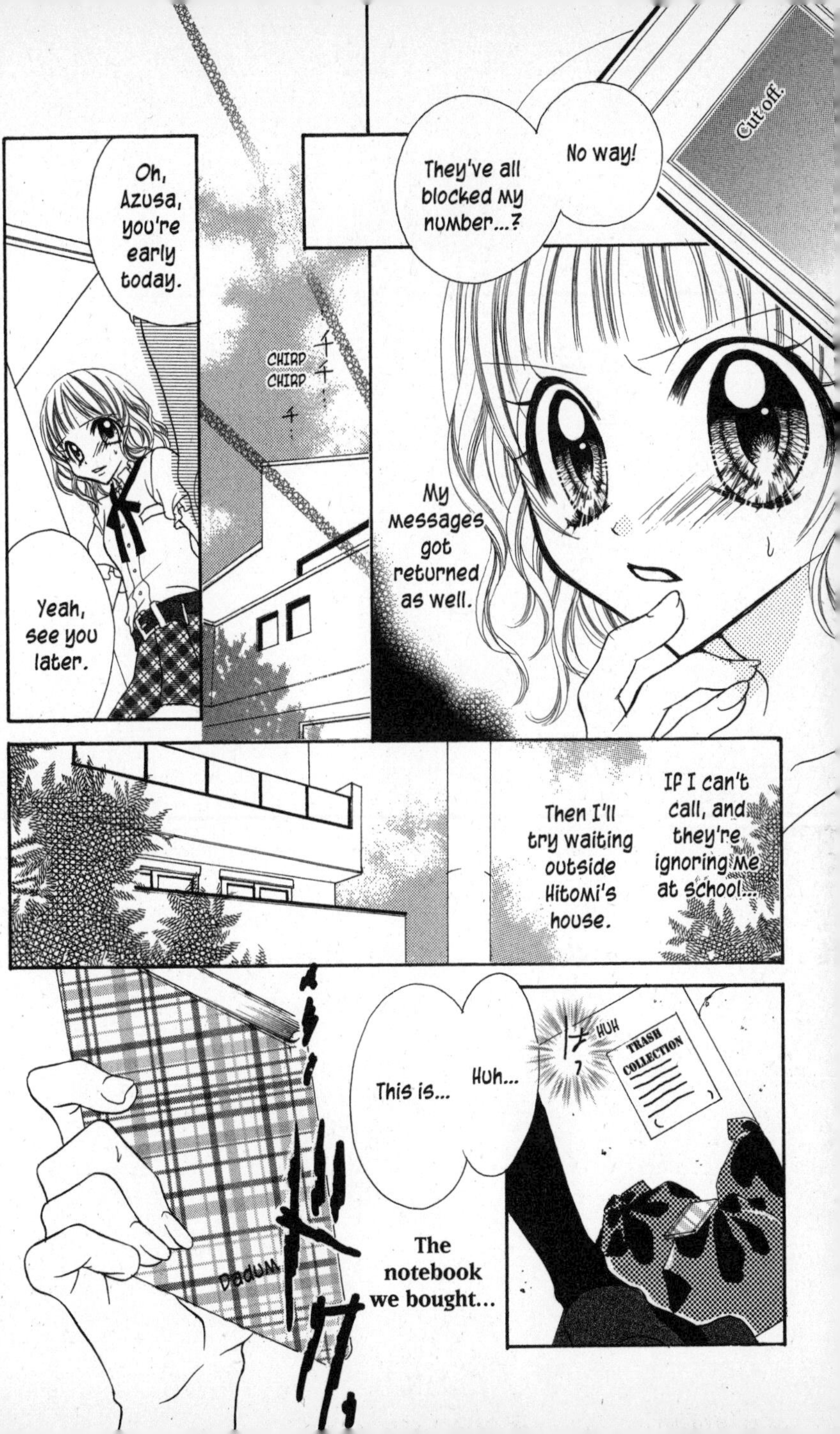
Cut off.
No way!
They've all blocked my number...?
My messages got returned as well.
CHIRP CHIRP
Oh, Azusa, you're early today.
Yeah, see you later.
If I can't call, and they're ignoring me at school...
Then I'll try waiting outside Hitomi's house.
HUH
TRASH COLLECTION
Huh...
This is...
The notebook we bought...
Dadum

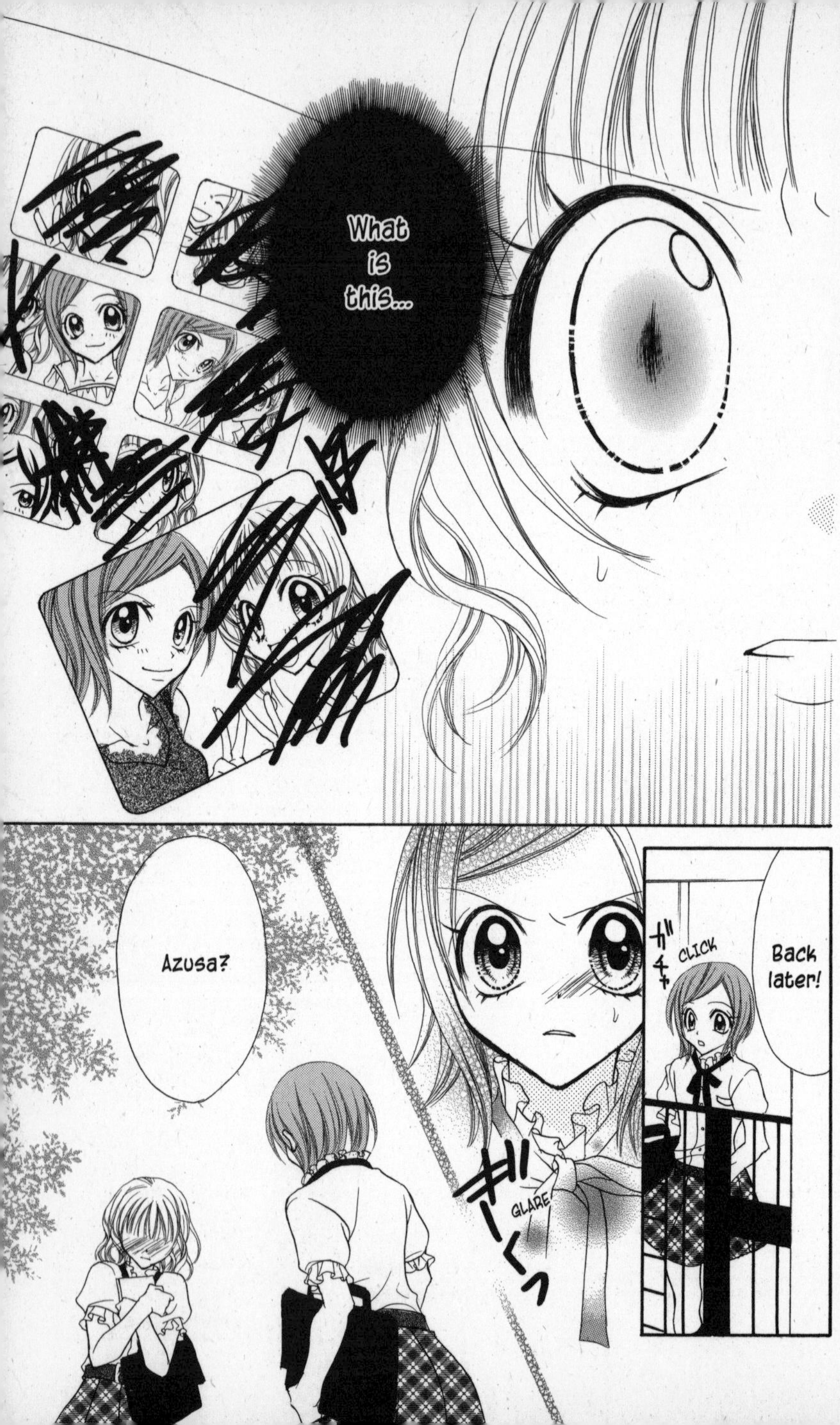
What is this...
CLICK
Back later!
GLARE
Azusa?

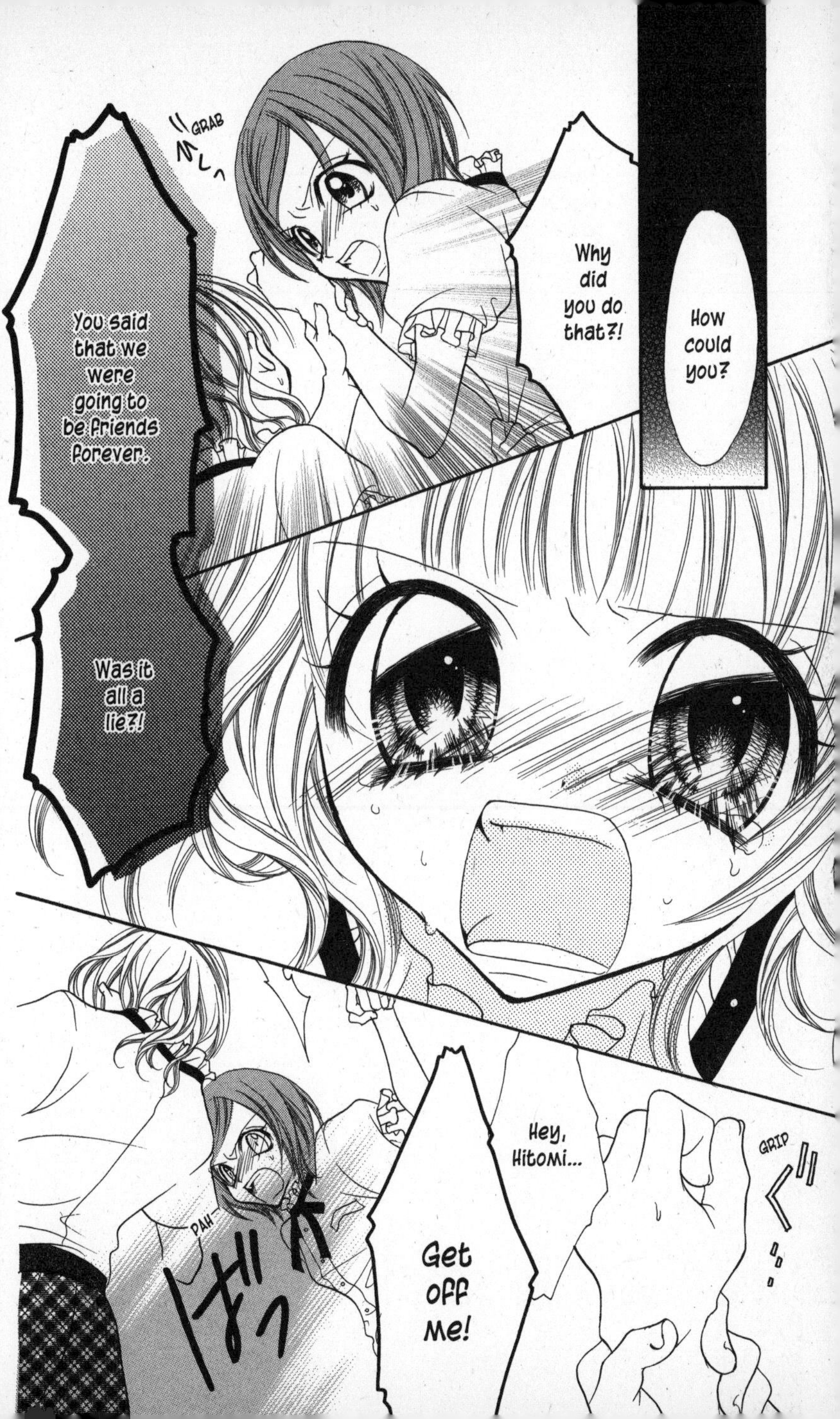

How could you?
Why did you do that?!
GRAB
You said that we were going to be friends forever.
Was it all a lie?!
GRIP
Hey, Hitomi...
Get off me!
PAH

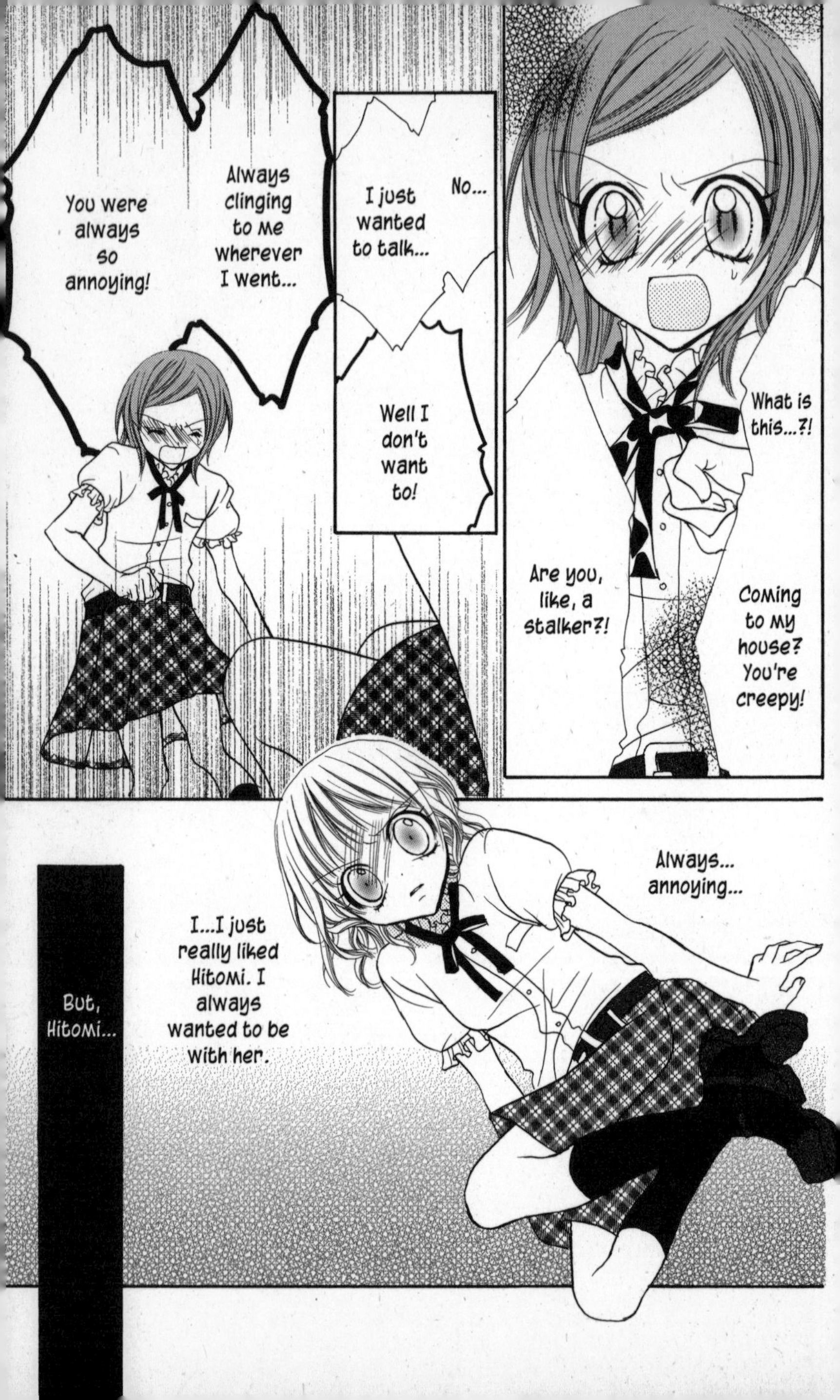
What is this...?!
Coming to my house? You're creepy!
Are you, like, a stalker?!
No...
I just wanted to talk...
Well I don't want to!
Always clinging to me wherever I went...
You were always so annoying!
Always... annoying...
I...I just really liked Hitomi. I always wanted to be with her.
But, Hitomi...

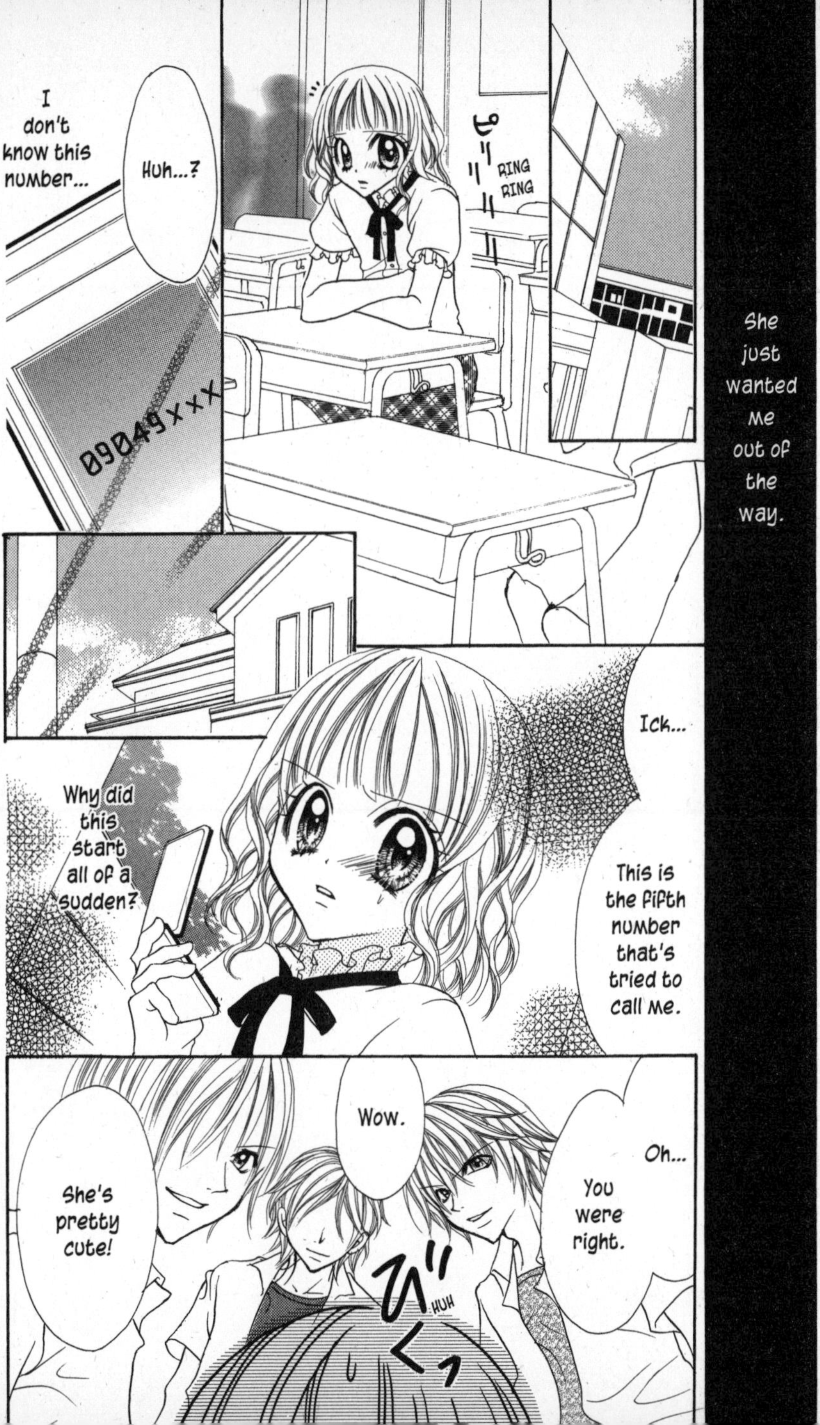
She just wanted me out of the way.
RING RING
Huh...?
I don't know this number...
09049xxx
Ick...
This is the fifth number that's tried to call me.
Why did this start all of a sudden?
Oh...
You were right.
Wow.
She's pretty cute!
HUH

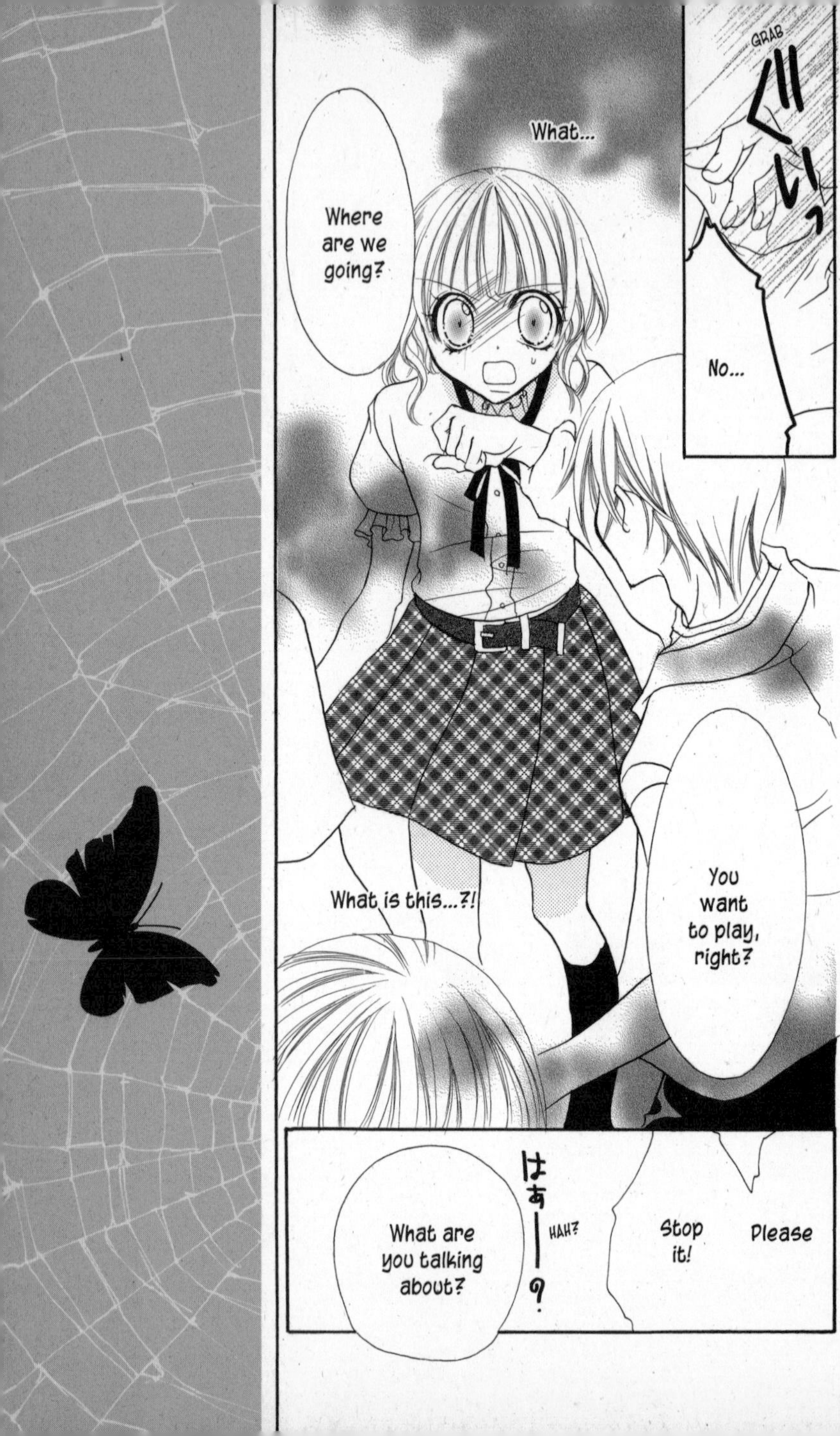
GRAB
ぐいっ
No...
What...
Where are we going?
You want to play, right?
What is this...?!
Please
Stop it!
はあーっ?
HAH?
What are you talking about?

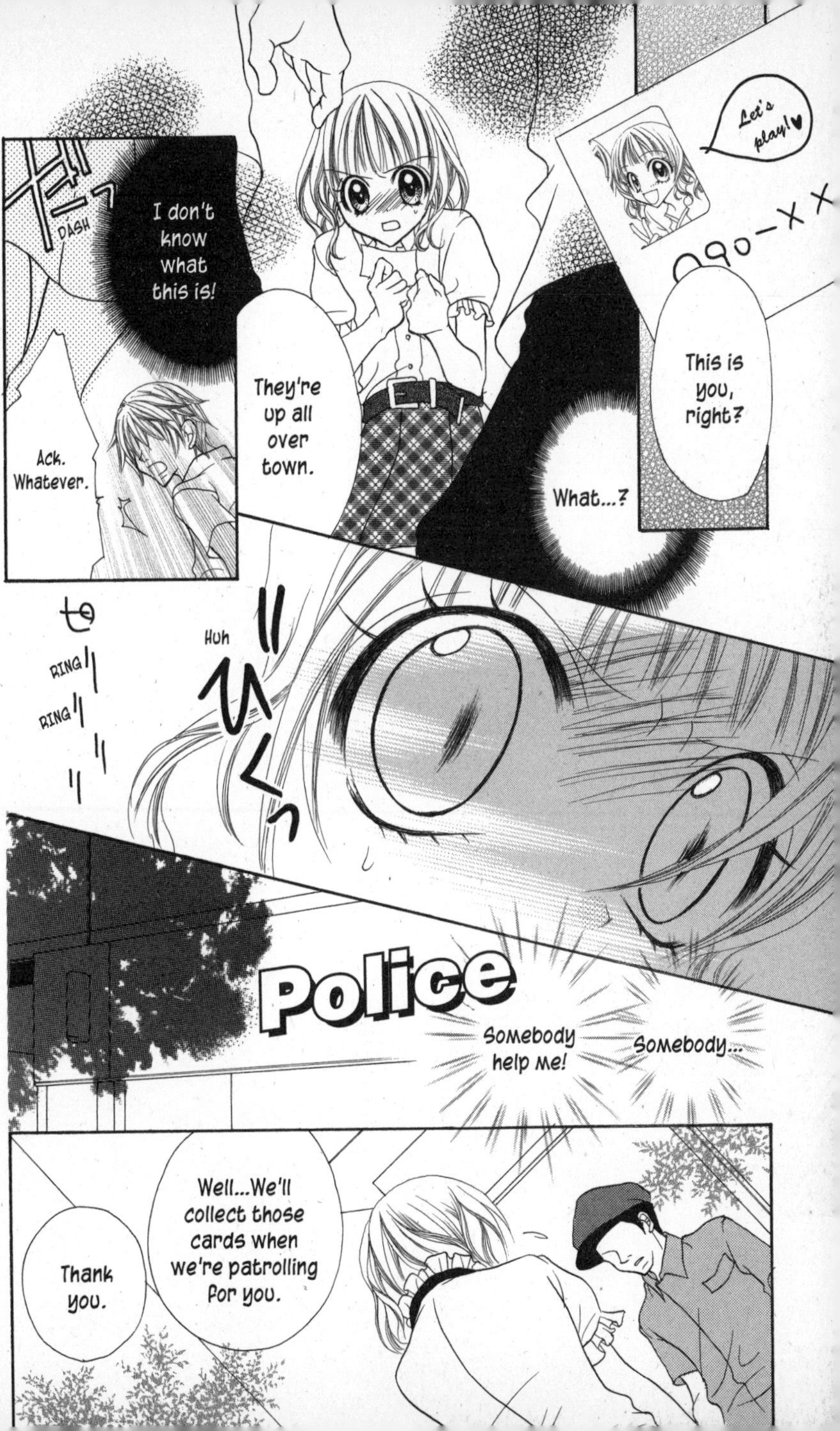
Let's play!♥
090-XX
This is you, right?
What...?
They're up all over town.
I don't know what this is!
DASH
Ack. Whatever.
Huh
RING
RING
Police
Somebody...
Somebody help me!
Well...We'll collect those cards when we're patrolling for you.
Thank you.

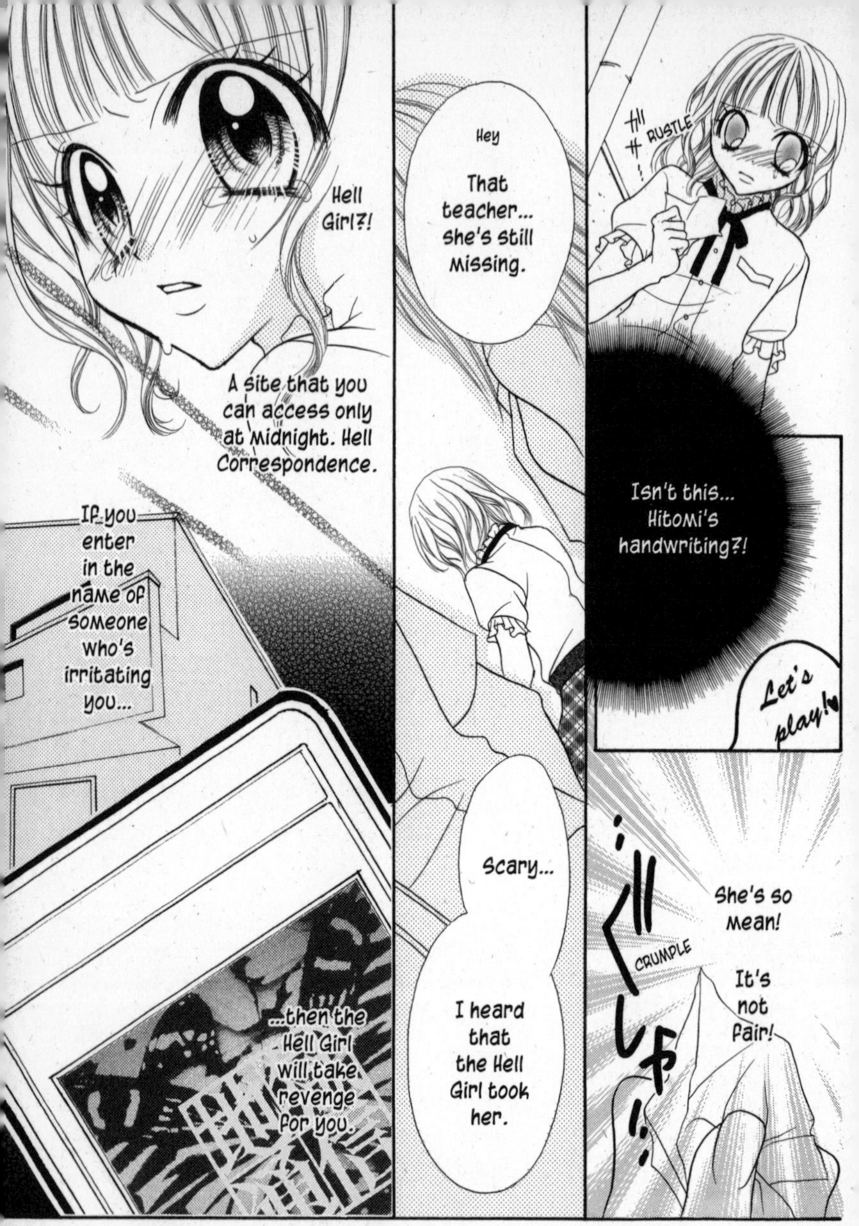
RUSTLE
Isn't this... Hitomi's handwriting?!
Let's play!♥
She's so mean!
It's not fair!
CRUMPLE
Hey
That teacher... she's still missing.
Scary...
I heard that the Hell Girl took her.
Hell Girl?!
A site that you can access only at midnight. Hell Correspondence.
If you enter in the name of someone who's irritating you...
...then the Hell Girl will take revenge for you.

Send Hitomi Sekine to hell.

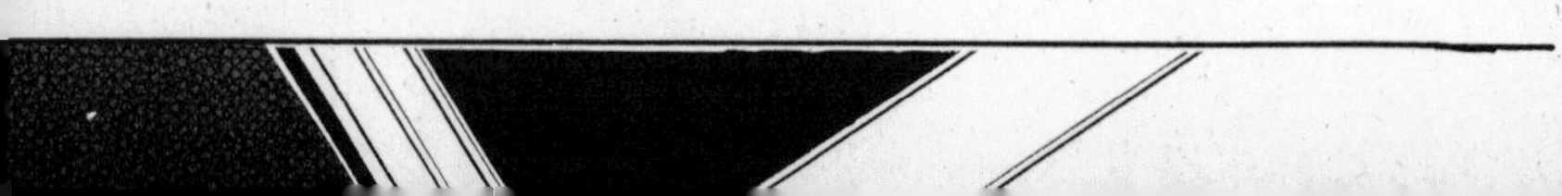

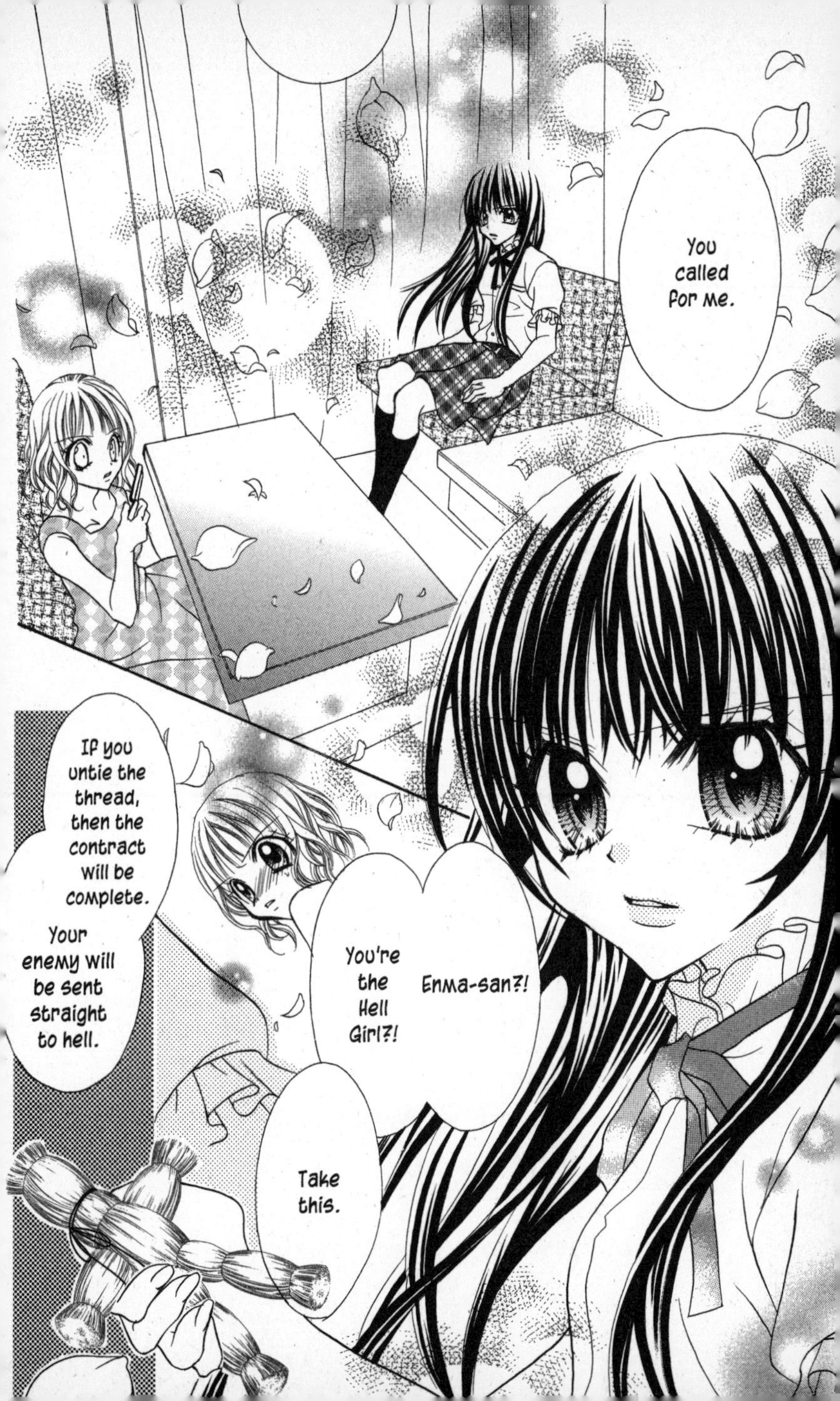
You called for me.
You're the Hell Girl?!
Enma-san?!
Take this.
If you untie the thread, then the contract will be complete.
Your enemy will be sent straight to hell.

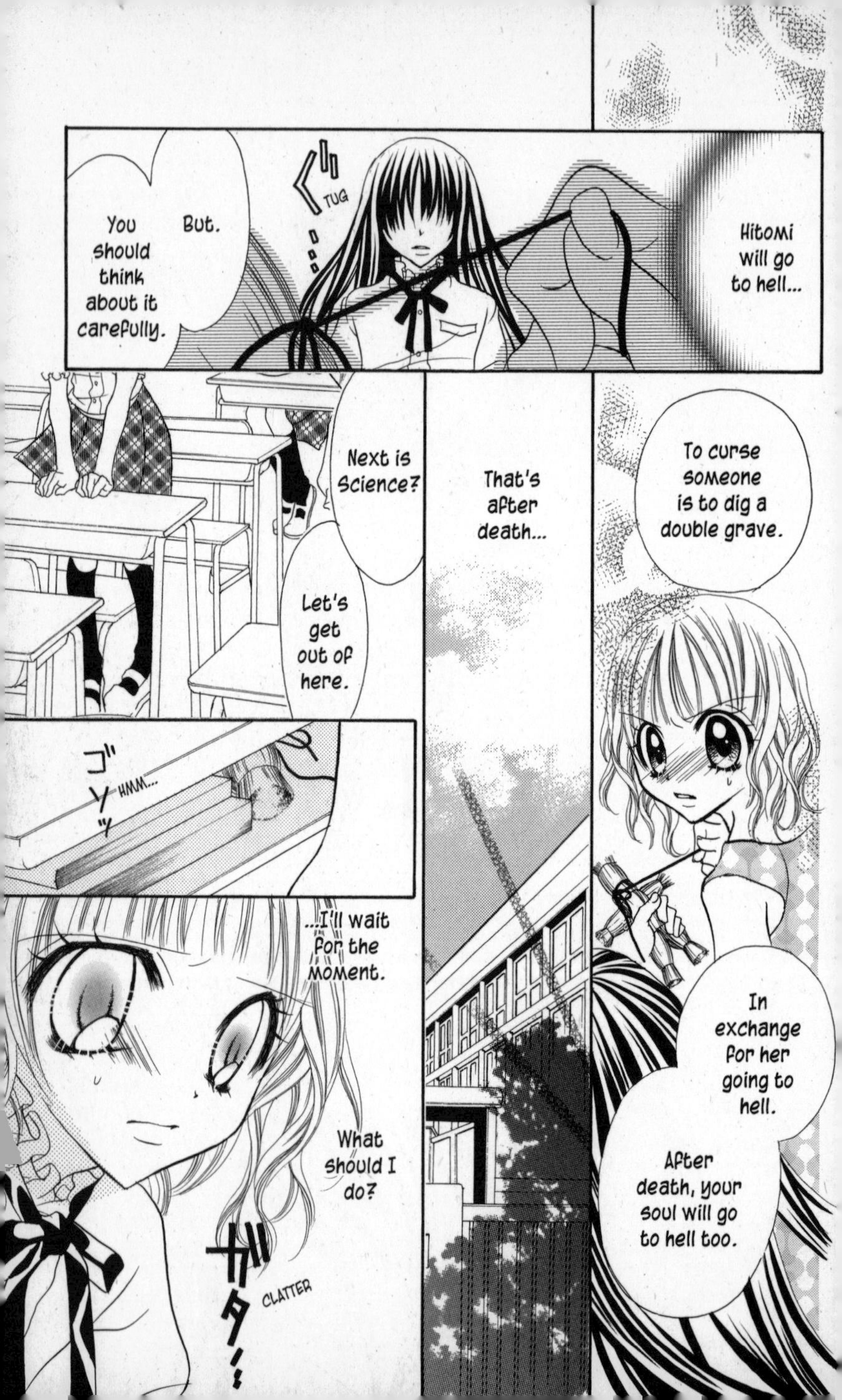
Hitomi will go to hell...
TUG
But.
You should think about it carefully.
To curse someone is to dig a double grave.
In exchange for her going to hell.
After death, your soul will go to hell too.
That's after death...
Next is Science?
Let's get out of here.
HMM...
...I'll wait for the moment.
What should I do?
CLATTER

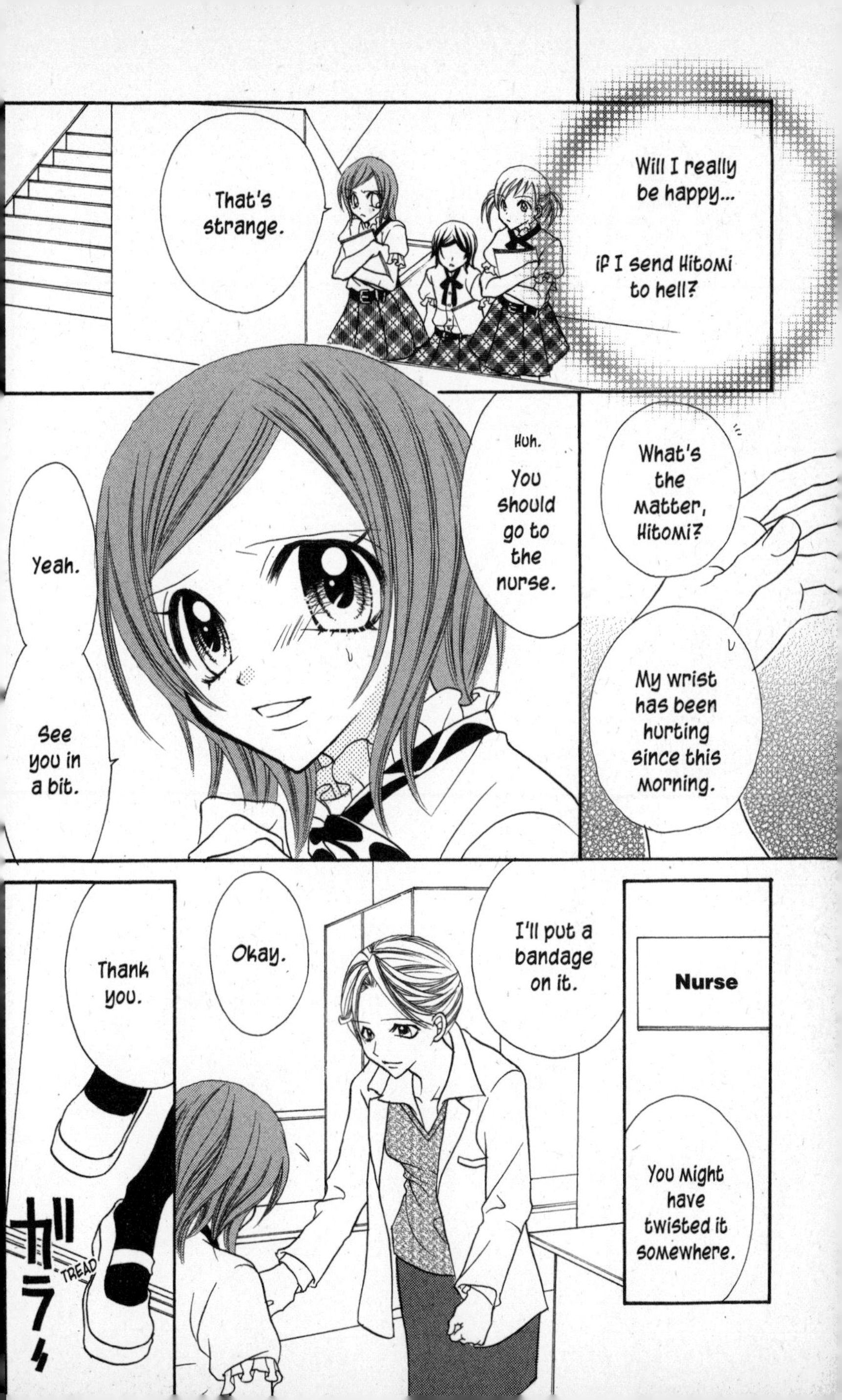

Will I really be happy...
if I send Hitomi to hell?
That's strange.
What's the matter, Hitomi?
My wrist has been hurting since this morning.
Huh.
You should go to the nurse.
Yeah.
See you in a bit.
Nurse
I'll put a bandage on it.
You might have twisted it somewhere.
Okay.
Thank you.
TREAD

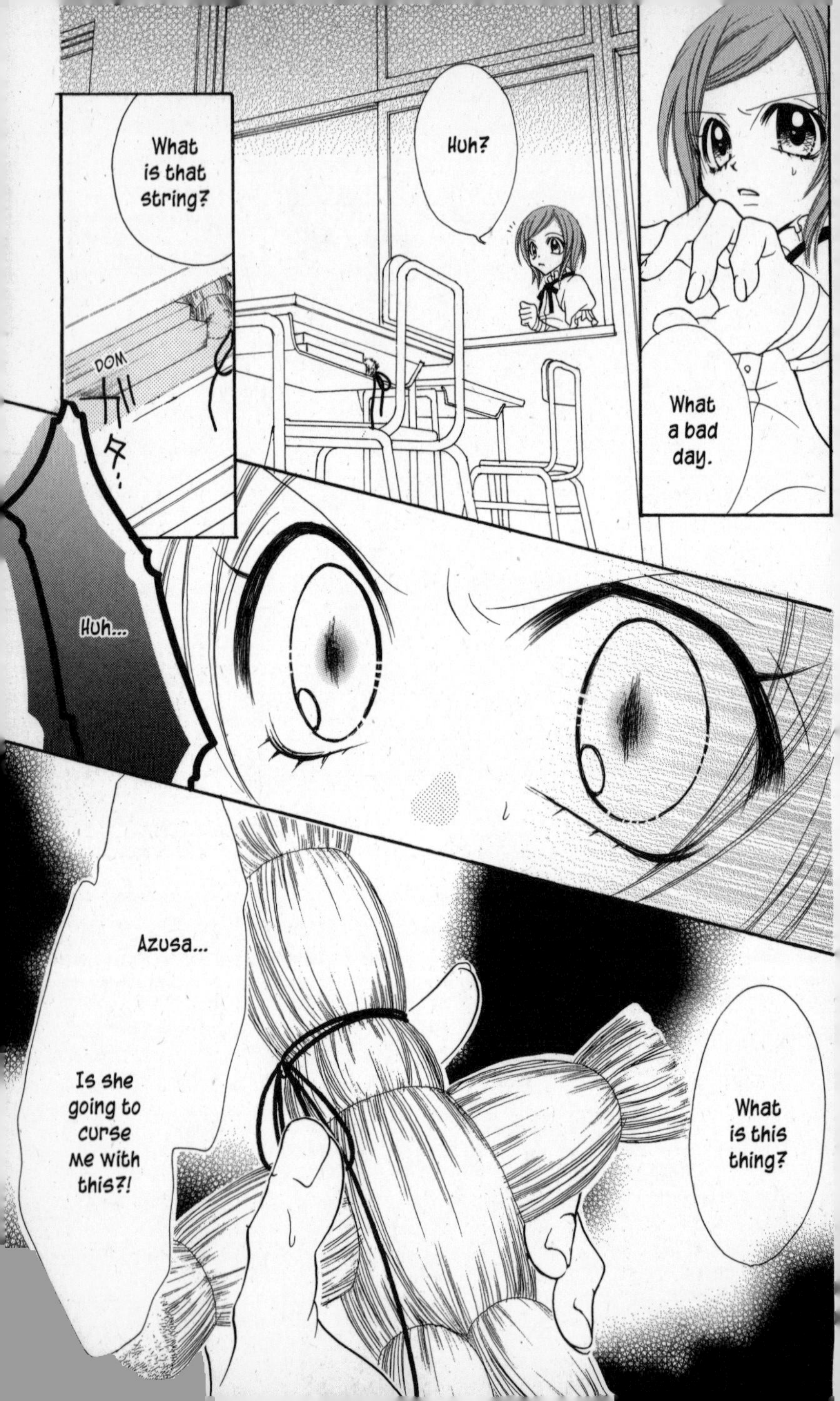

What a bad day.
Huh?
What is that string?
DOM
ガタ…
Huh...
What is this thing?
Azusa...
Is she going to curse me with this?!

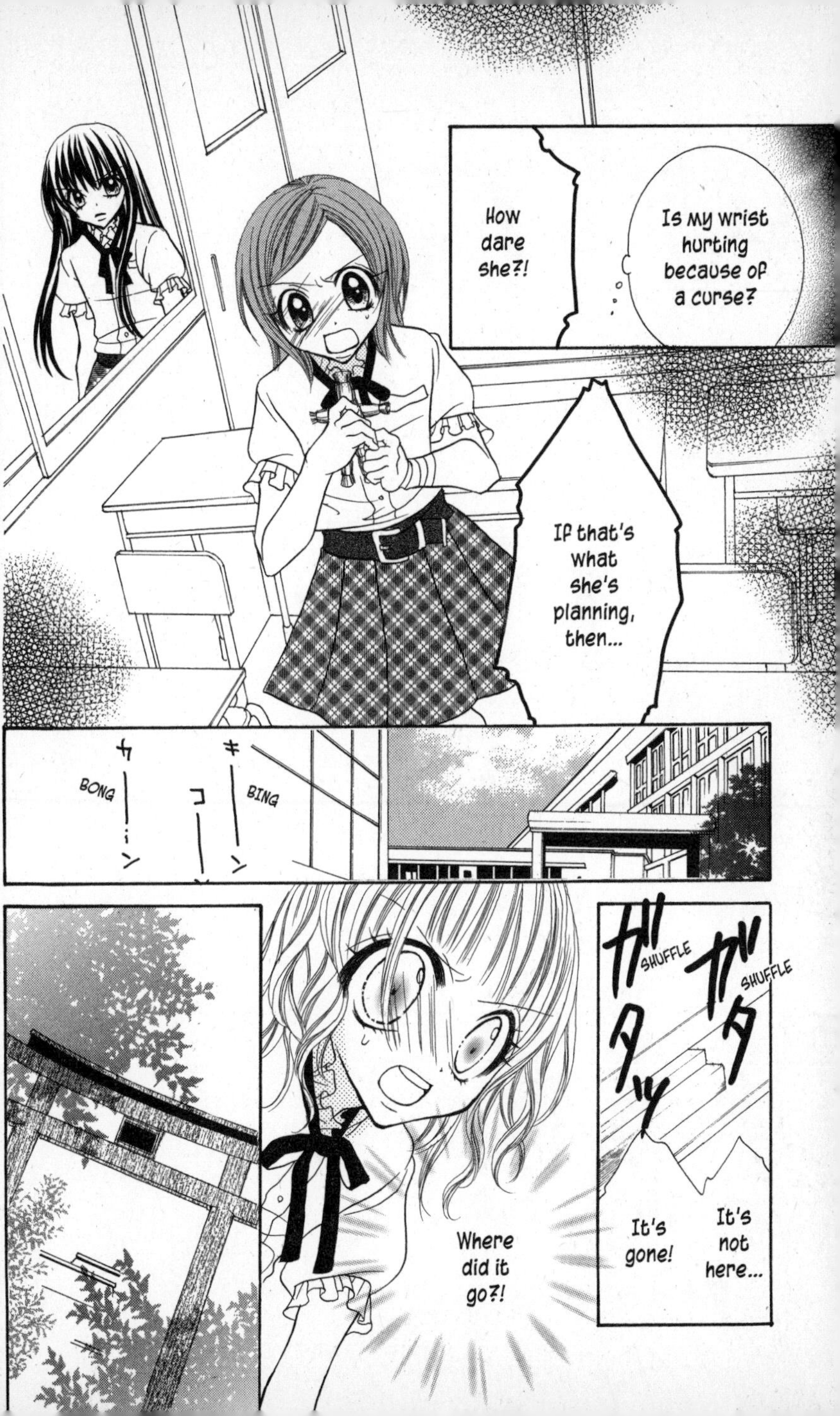

Is my wrist hurting because of a curse?
How dare she?!
If that's what she's planning, then...
キーン
BING
コーン
カーン
BONG
ガタ
SHUFFLE
ガタッ
SHUFFLE
It's not here...
It's gone!
Where did it go?!

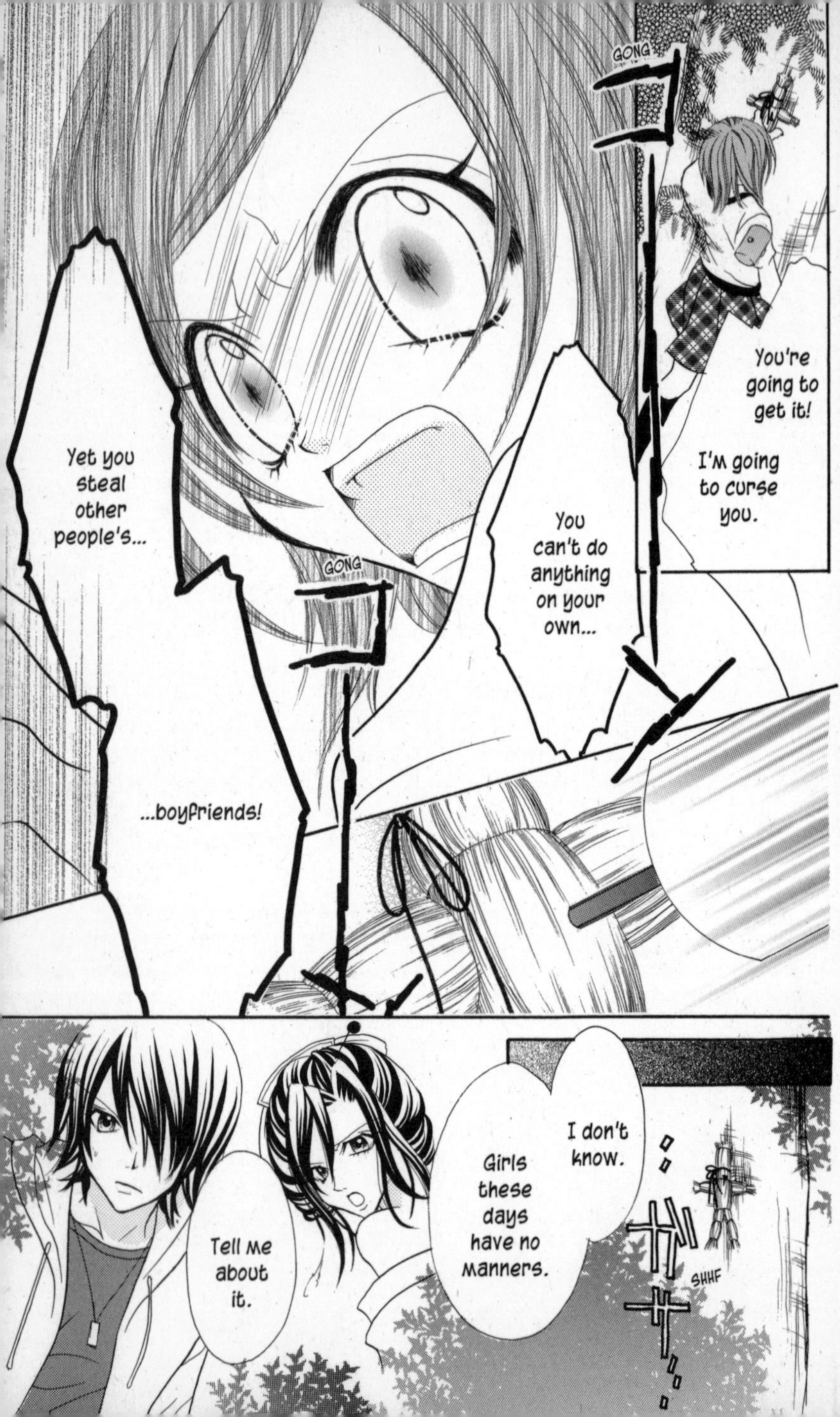
GONG
You're going to get it!
I'm going to curse you.
You can't do anything on your own...
GONG
Yet you steal other people's...
...boyfriends!
SHUF
I don't know.
Girls these days have no manners.
Tell me about it.

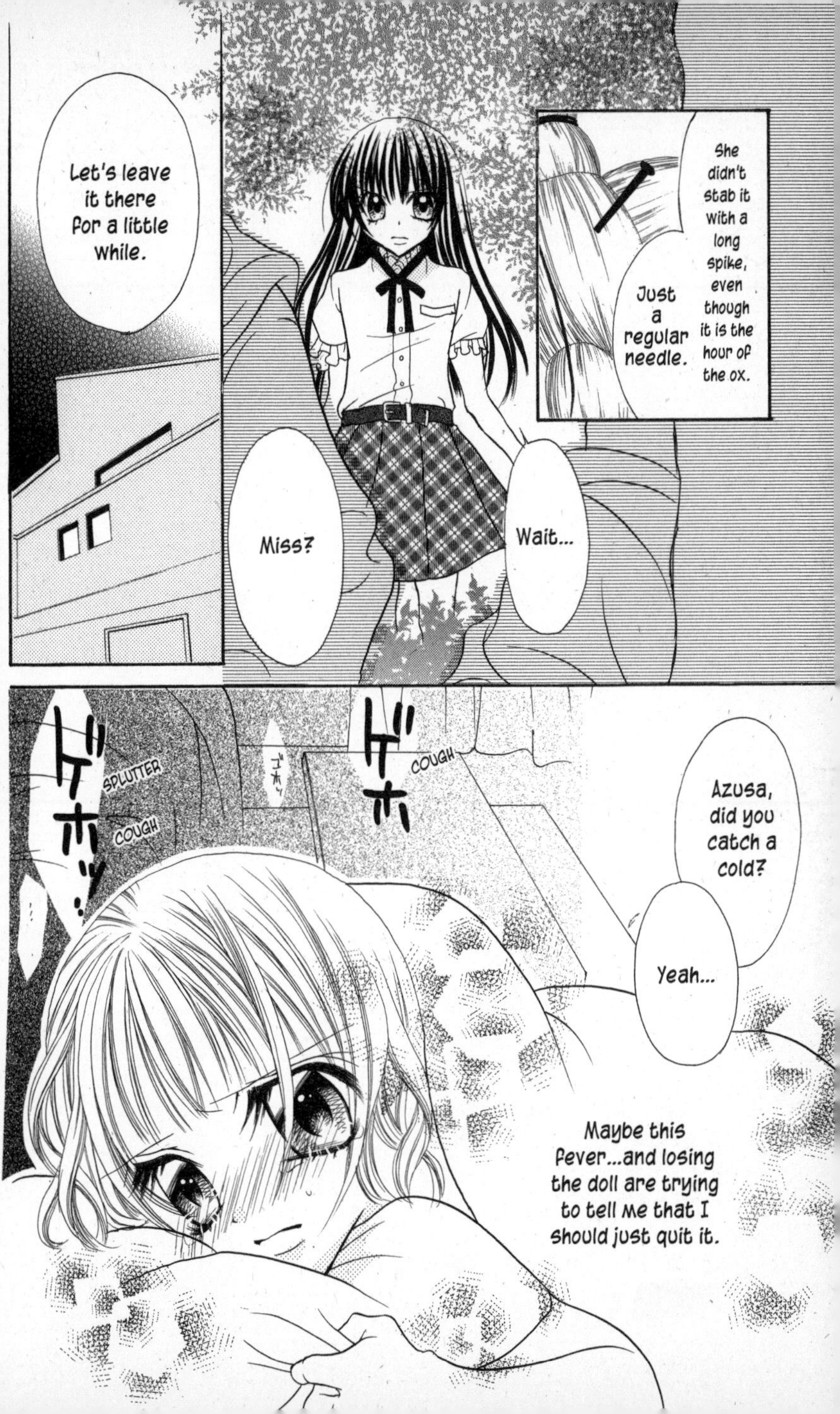
She didn't stab it with a long spike, even though it is the hour of the ox.
Just a regular needle.
Wait...
Miss?
Let's leave it there for a little while.
ゲホ
COUGH
ゴホッ
ゲホッ..
SPLUTTER
COUGH
Azusa, did you catch a cold?
Yeah...
Maybe this fever...and losing the doll are trying to tell me that I should just quit it.

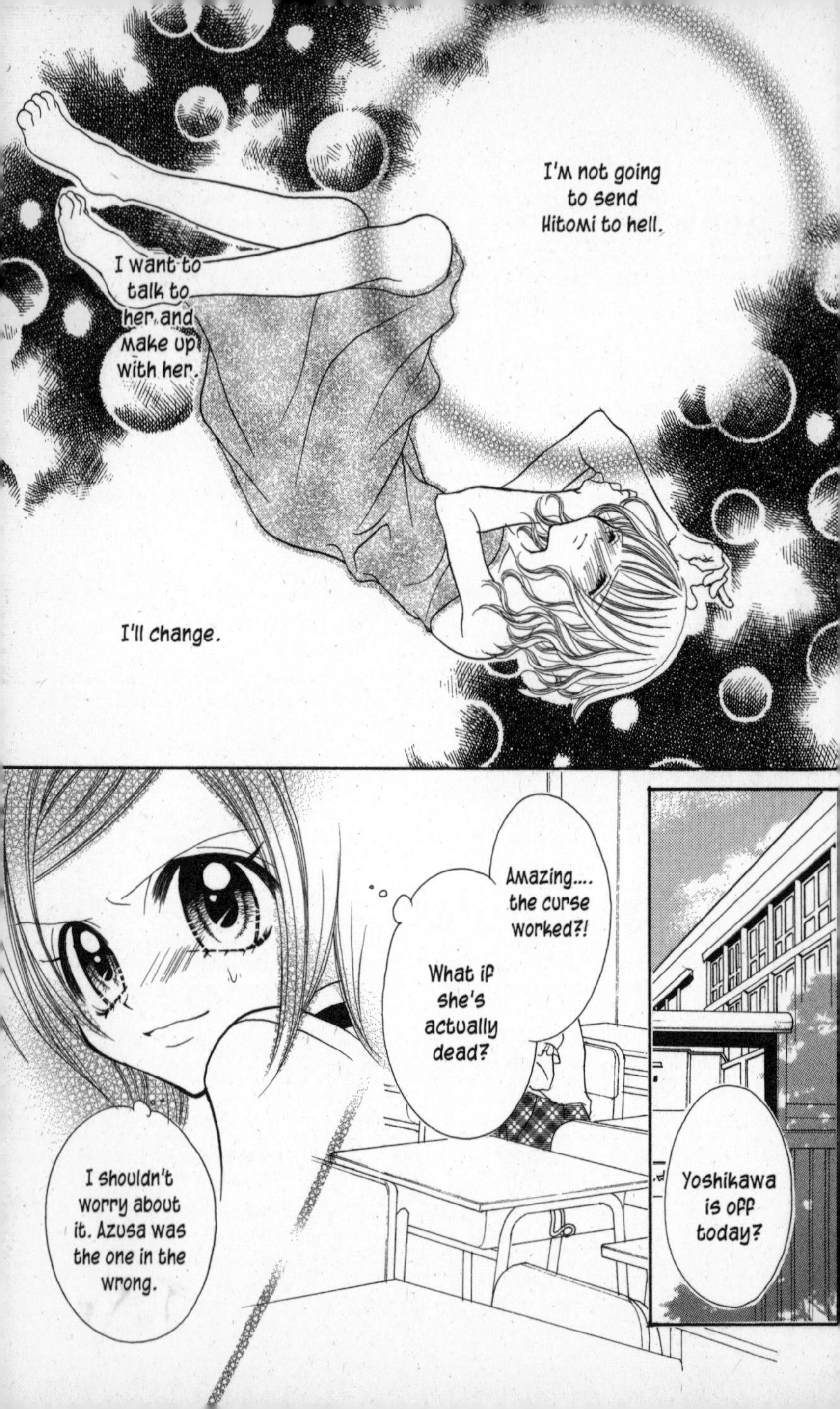
I'm not going to send Hitomi to hell.
I want to talk to her and make up with her.
I'll change.
Yoshikawa is off today?
Amazing.... the curse worked?!
What if she's actually dead?
I shouldn't worry about it. Azusa was the one in the wrong.

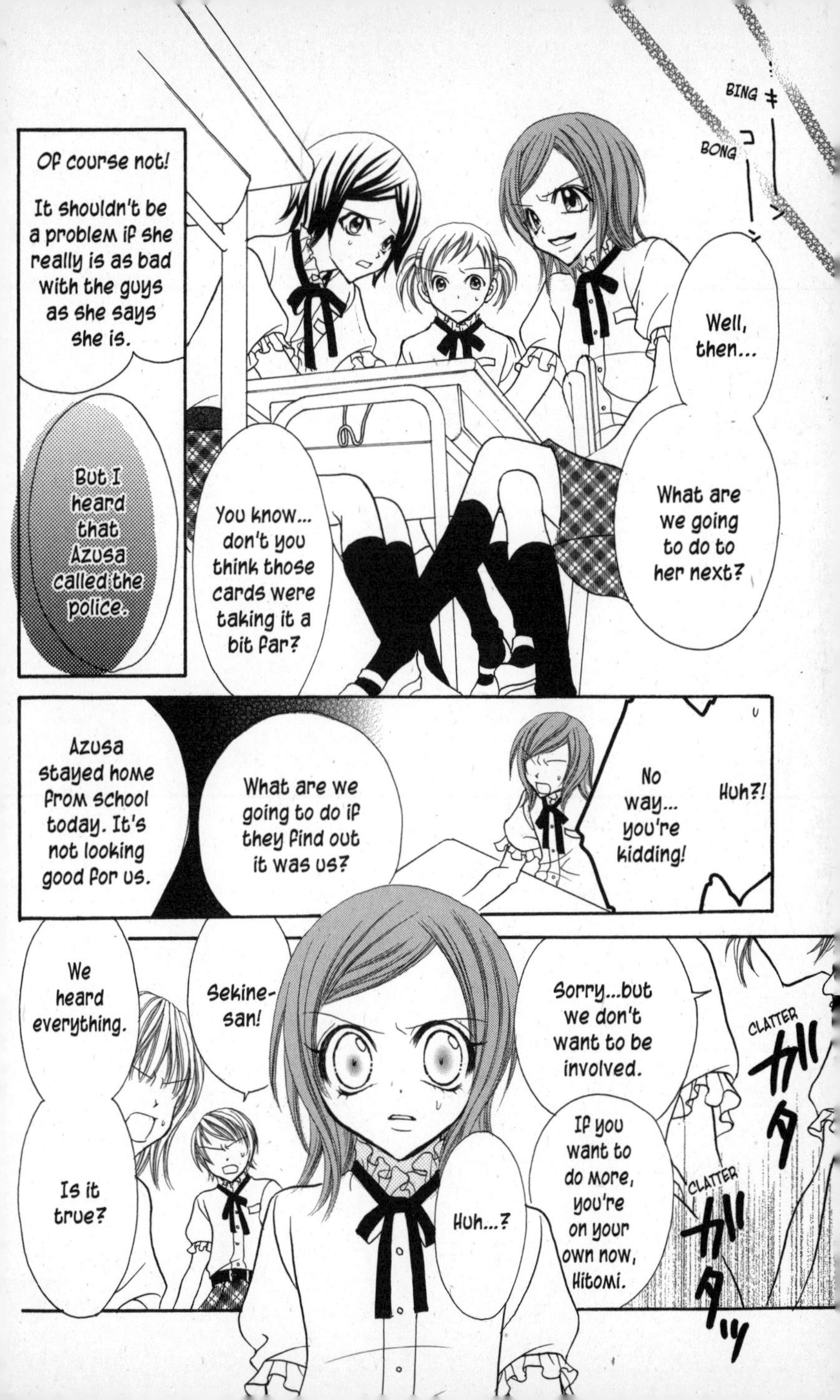
BING
キ
BONG
コーン
Well, then...
What are we going to do to her next?
You know... don't you think those cards were taking it a bit far?
Of course not!
It shouldn't be a problem if she really is as bad with the guys as she says she is.
But I heard that Azusa called the police.
Huh?!
No way... you're kidding!
What are we going to do if they find out it was us?
Azusa stayed home from school today. It's not looking good for us.
CLATTER
ガタ
CLATTER
ガタッ
Sorry...but we don't want to be involved.
If you want to do more, you're on your own now, Hitomi.
Huh...?
Sekine-san!
We heard everything.
Is it true?

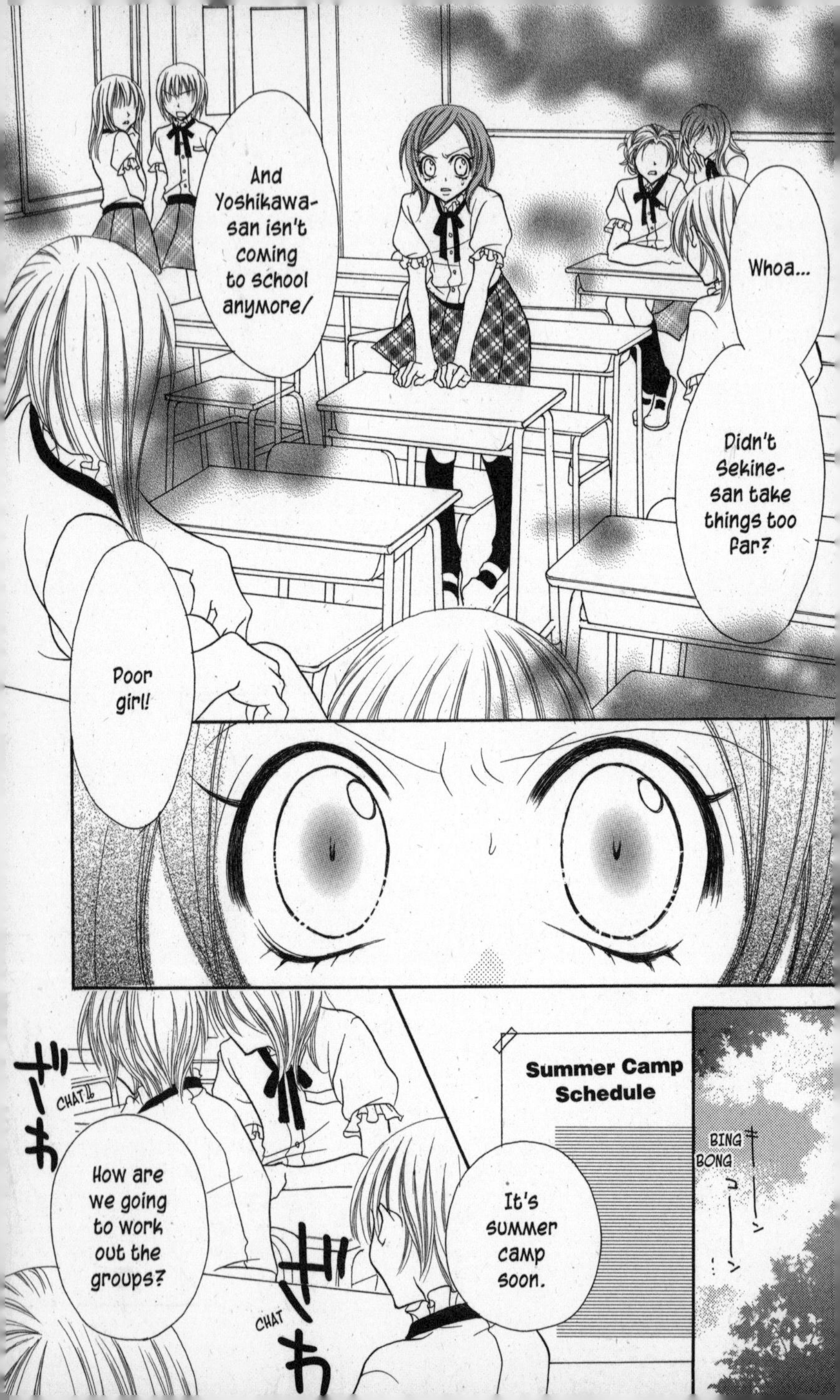

Whoa...
Didn't Sekine-san take things too far?
And Yoshikawa-san isn't coming to school anymore!
Poor girl!
Summer Camp Schedule
BING BONG
It's summer camp soon.
CHAT
How are we going to work out the groups?
CHAT

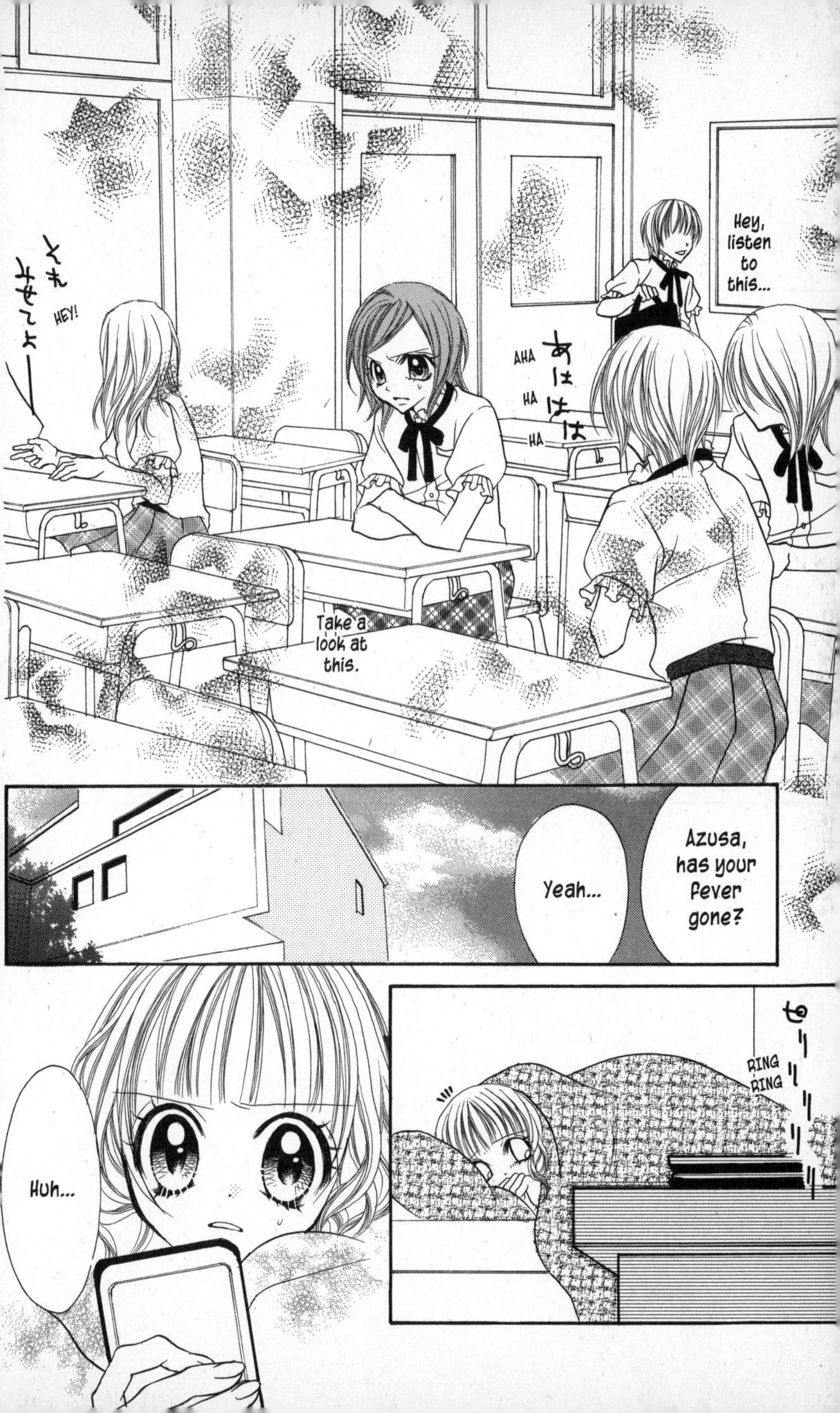
Hey, listen to this...
あははは
AHA HA HA
それみせてよー
HEY!
Take a look at this.
Azusa, has your fever gone?
Yeah...
ピリリリリ
RING RING
Huh...

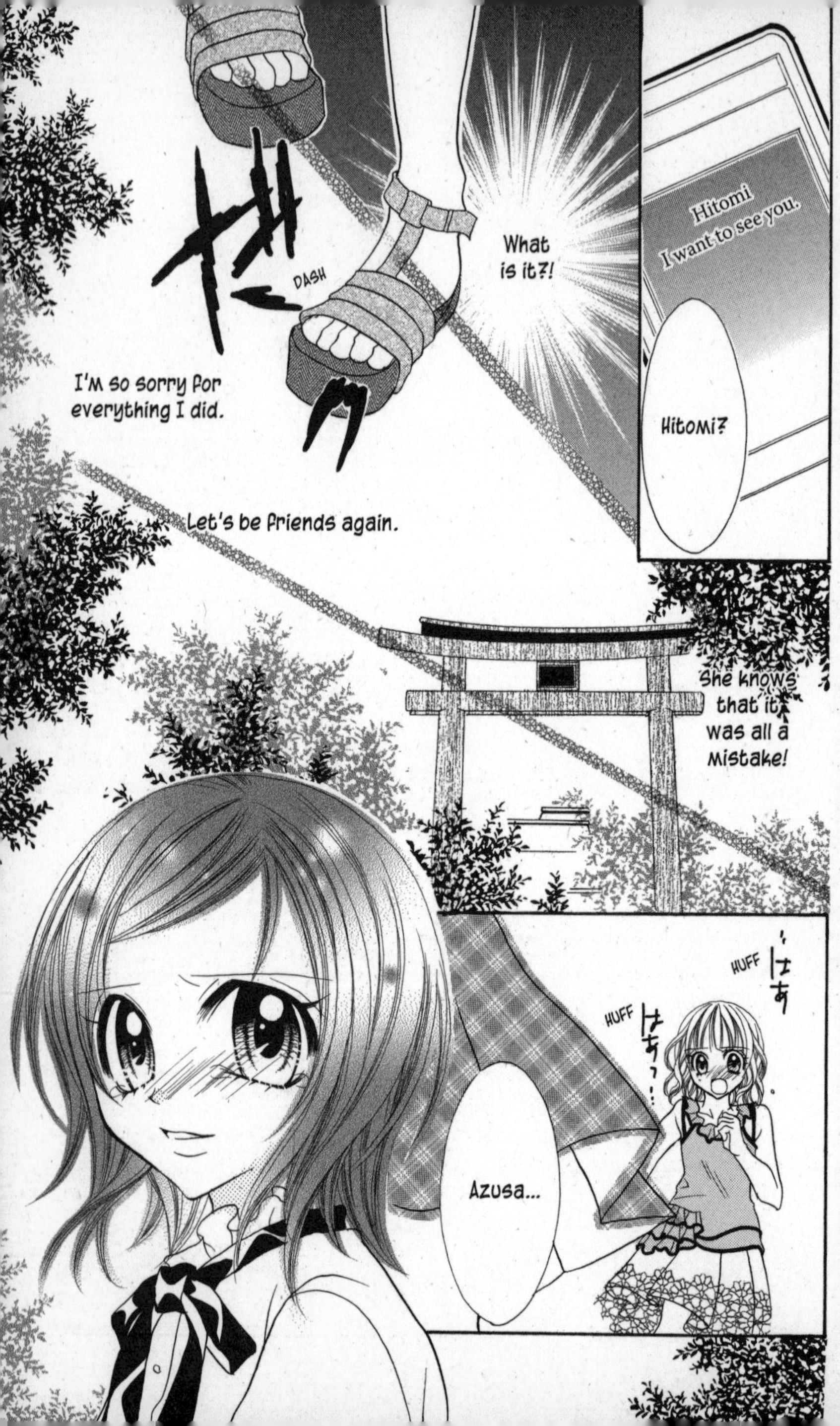

Hitomi
I want to see you.
Hitomi?
What is it?!
DASH
I'm so sorry for everything I did.
Let's be friends again.
She knows that it was all a mistake!
HUFF
はぁ
HUFF
はぁっ…
Azusa...

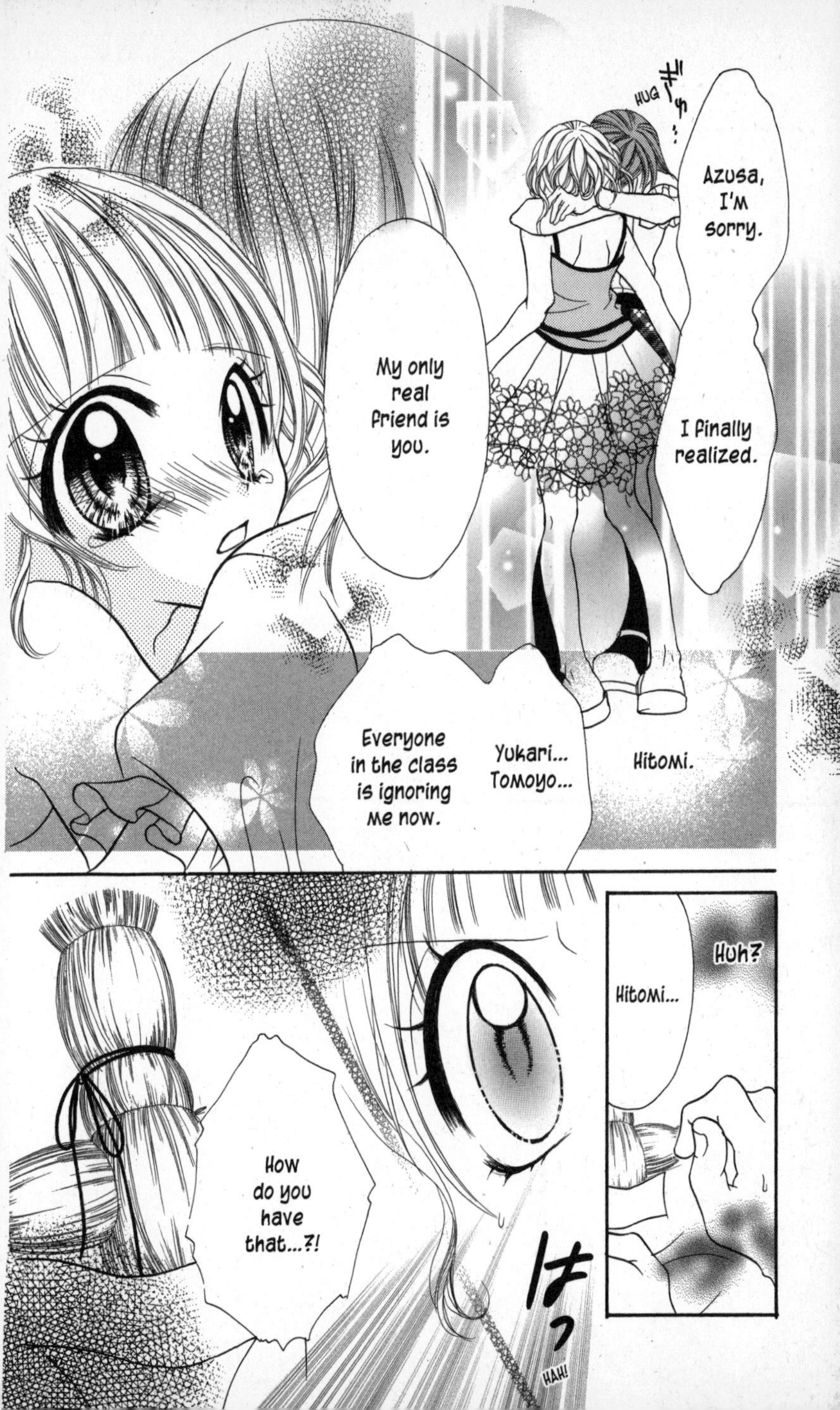
HUG
Azusa, I'm sorry.
I finally realized.
My only real friend is you.
Hitomi.
Yukari... Tomoyo...
Everyone in the class is ignoring me now.
Huh?
Hitomi...
HAH!
How do you have that...?!

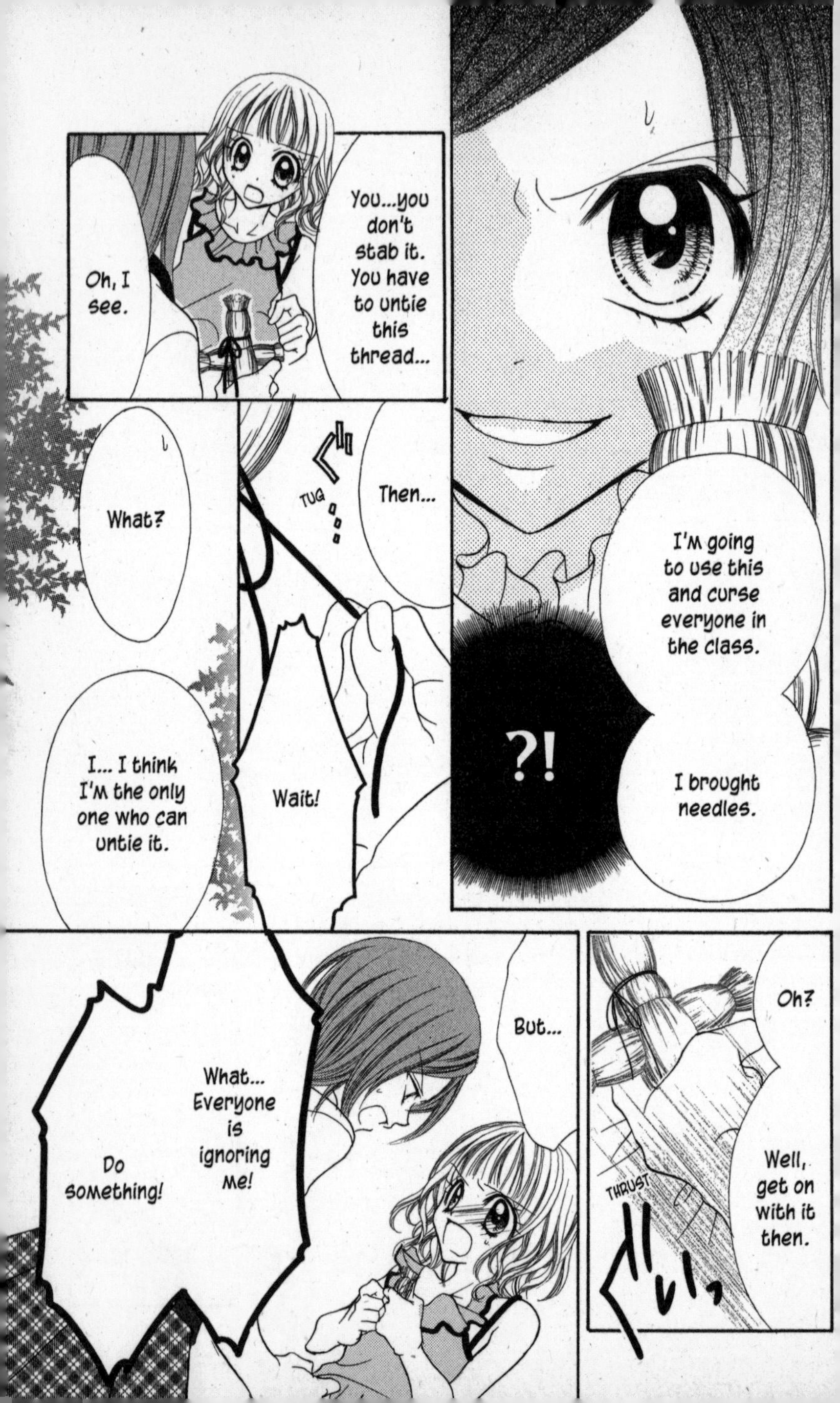
I'm going to use this and curse everyone in the class.
?!
I brought needles.
You...you don't stab it. You have to untie this thread...
Oh, I see.
Then...
TUG
Wait!
What?
I... I think I'm the only one who can untie it.
Oh?
THRUST
Well, get on with it then.
But...
What... Everyone is ignoring me!
Do something!

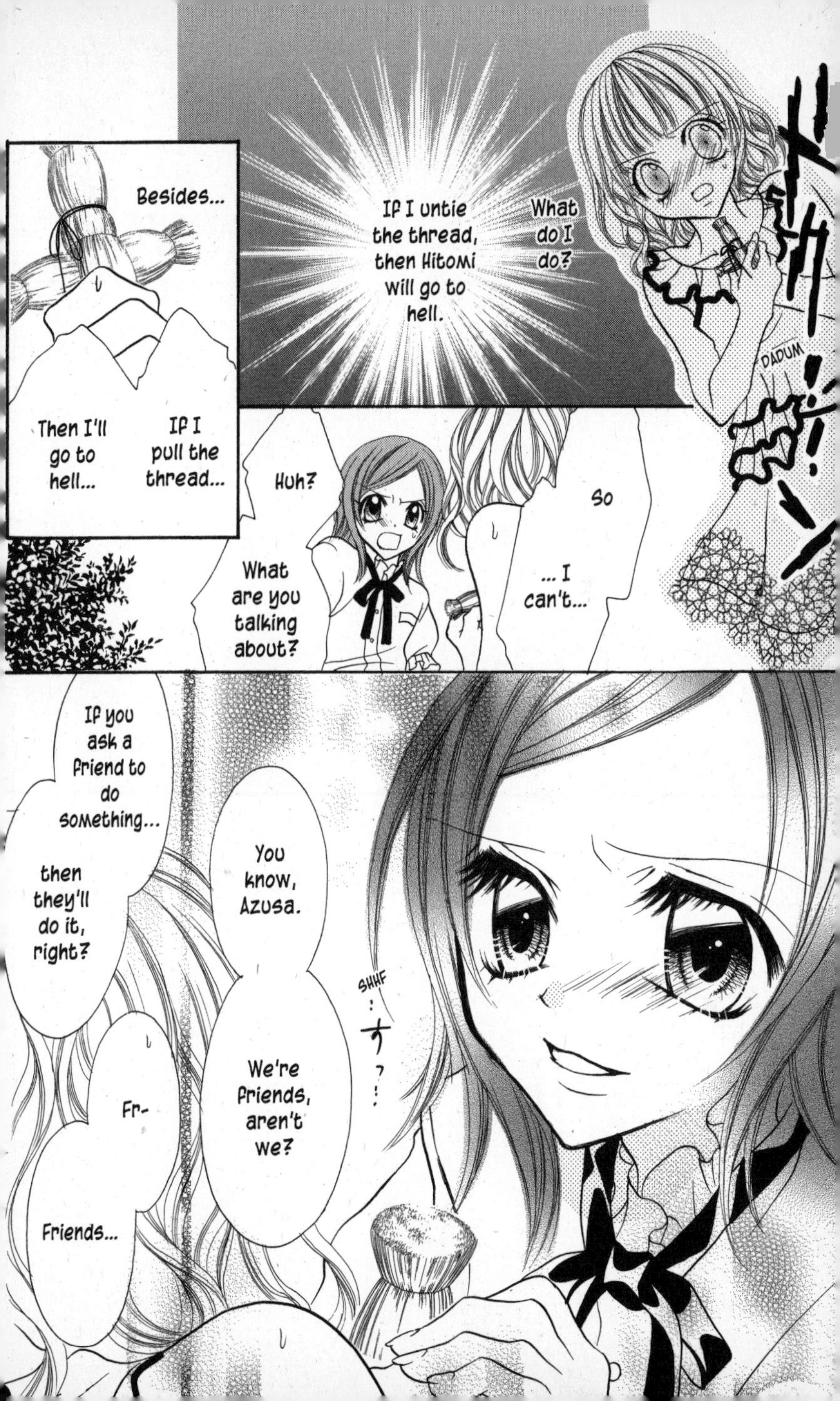

What do I do?
DADUM
If I untie the thread, then Hitomi will go to hell.
Besides...
If I pull the thread...
Then I'll go to hell...
So
... I can't...
Huh?
What are you talking about?
You know, Azusa.
If you ask a friend to do something...
then they'll do it, right?
SHHF
We're friends, aren't we?
Fr-
Friends...

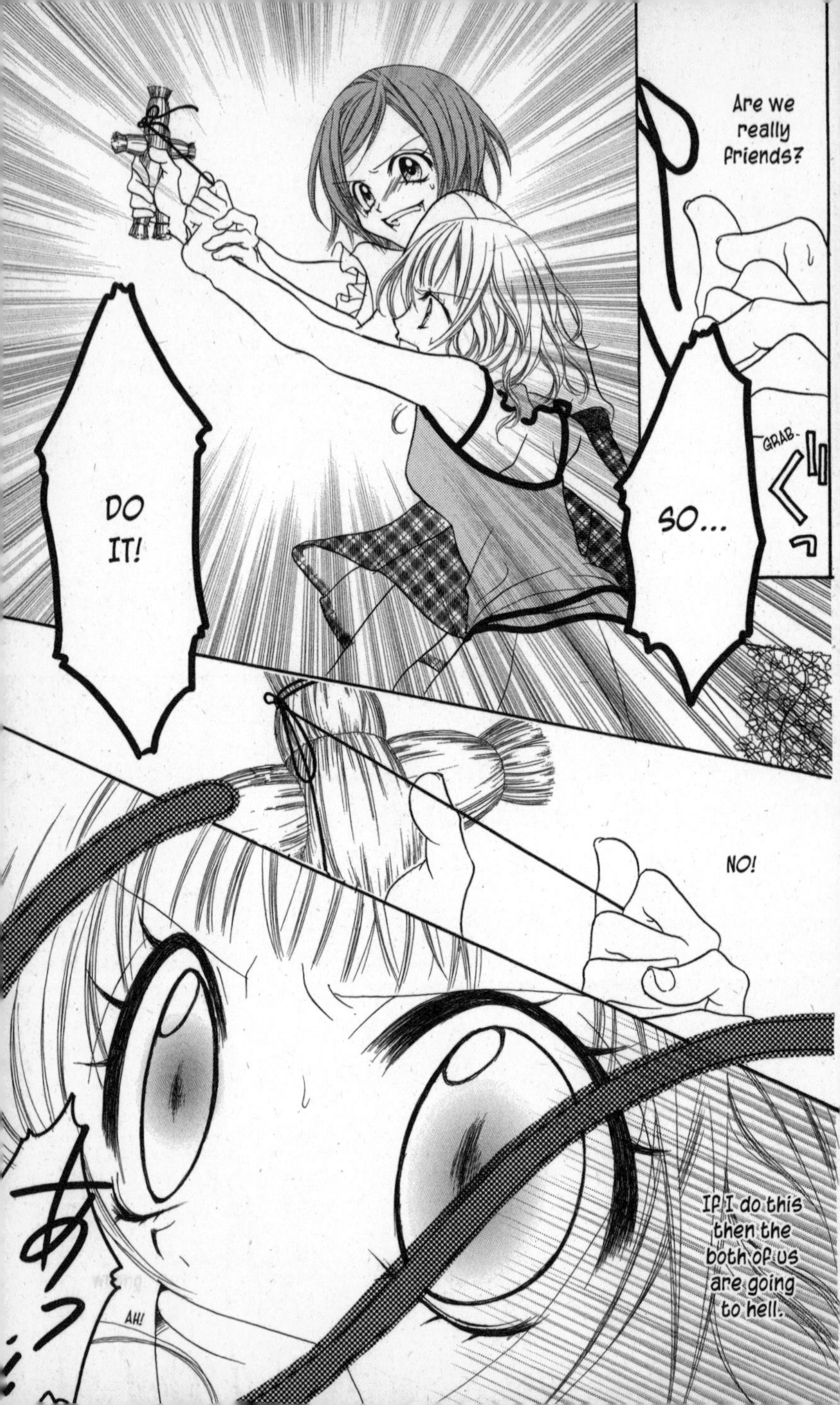
Are we really friends?
GRAB
SO...
DO IT!
NO!
If I do this then the both of us are going to hell.
AH!
あっ

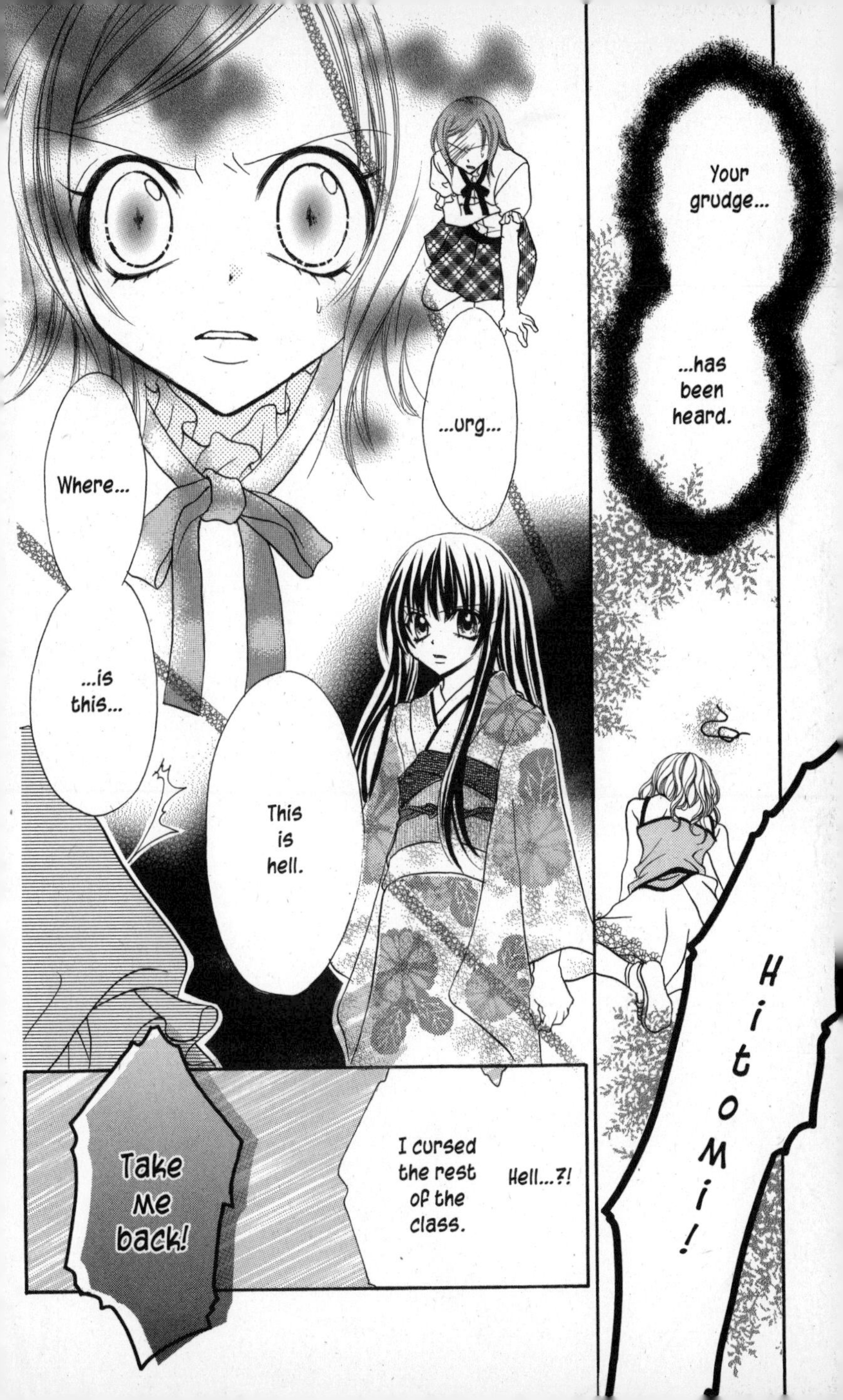
Your grudge...
...has been heard.
Hitomi!
...urg...
Where...
...is this...
This is hell.
Hell...?!
I cursed the rest of the class.
Take me back!

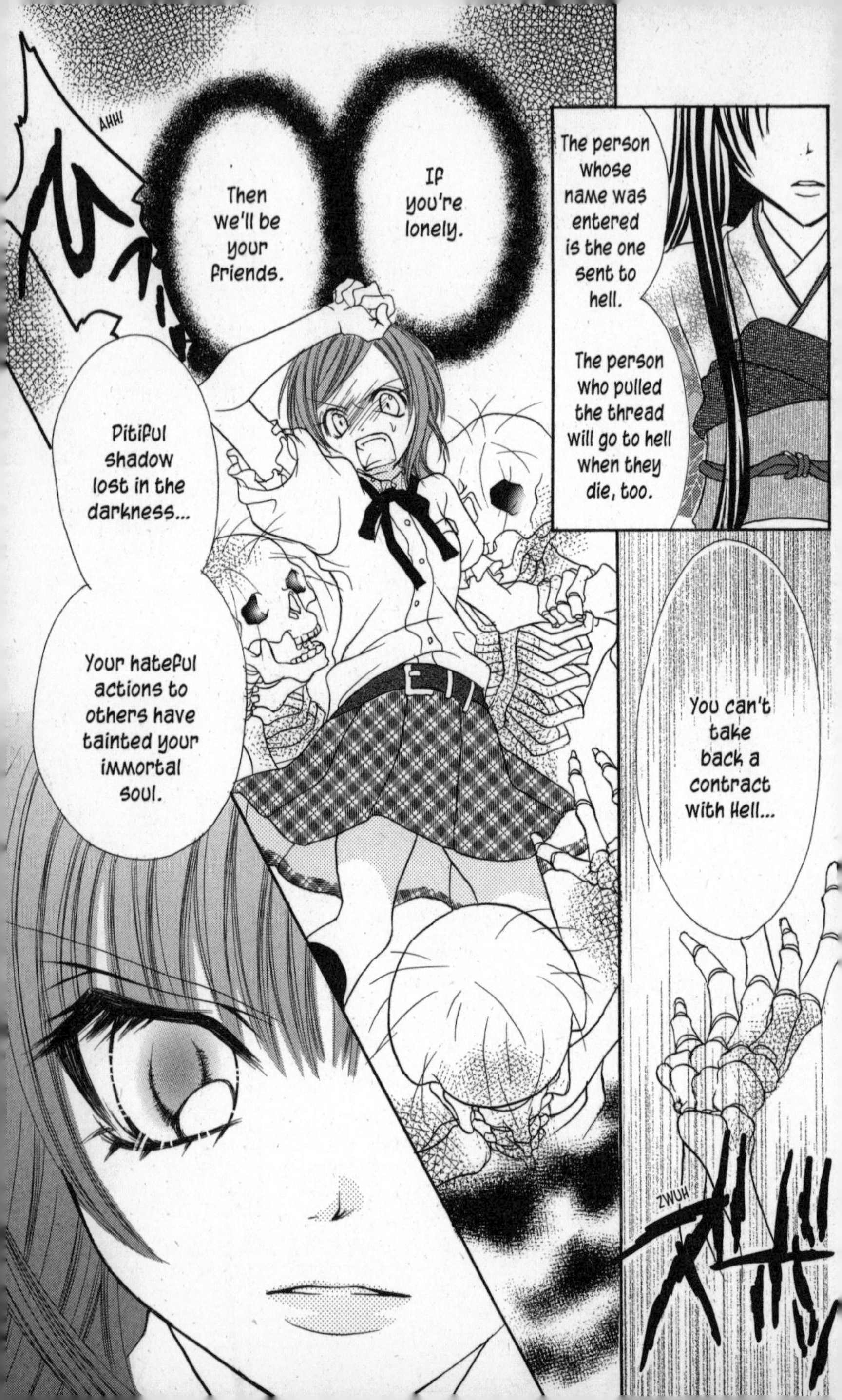
The person whose name was entered is the one sent to hell.
The person who pulled the thread will go to hell when they die, too.
You can't take back a contract with Hell...
ZWUH
AHH!
If you're lonely.
Then we'll be your friends.
Pitiful shadow lost in the darkness...
Your hateful actions to others have tainted your immortal soul.

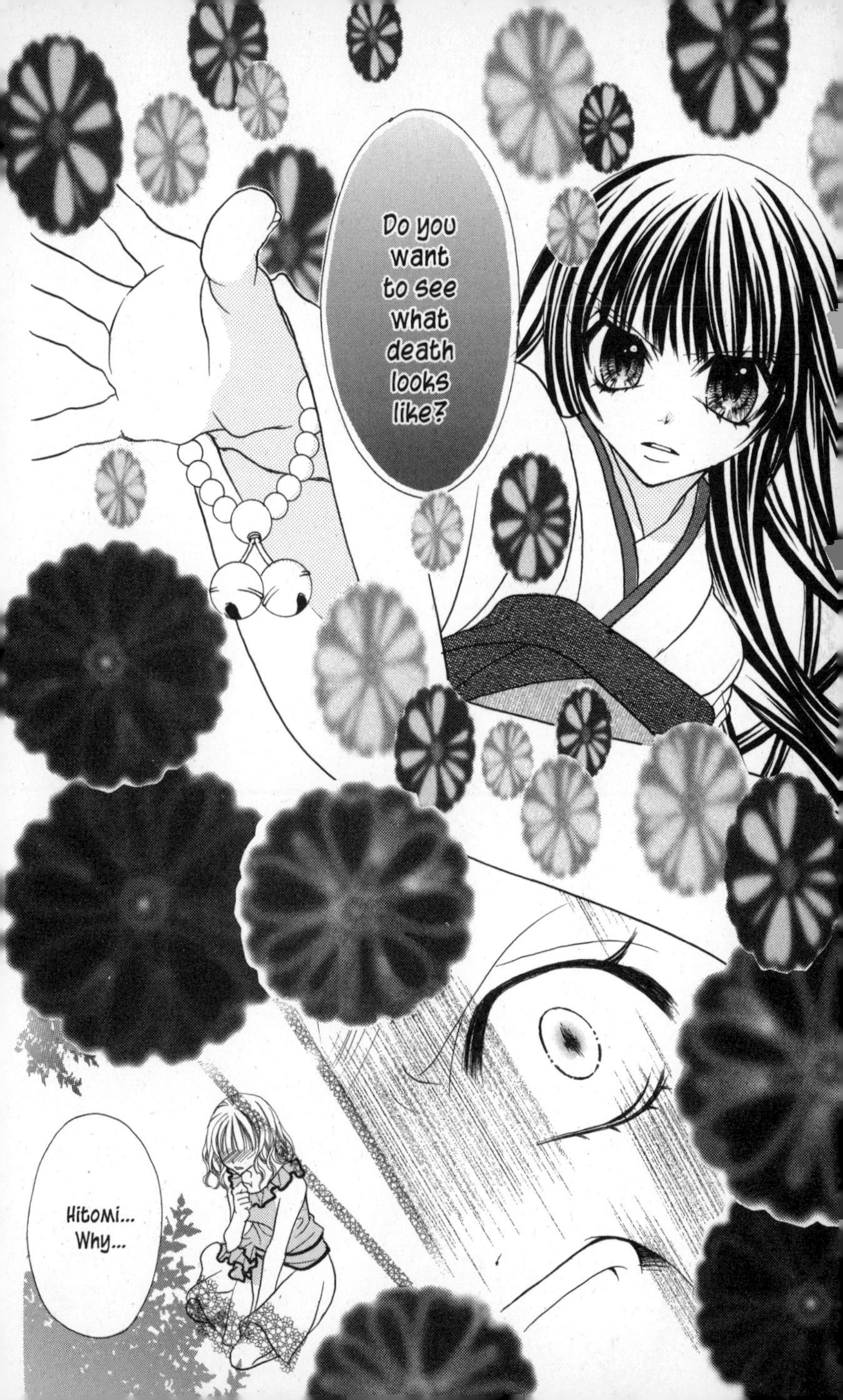
Do you want to see what death looks like?
Hitomi... Why...

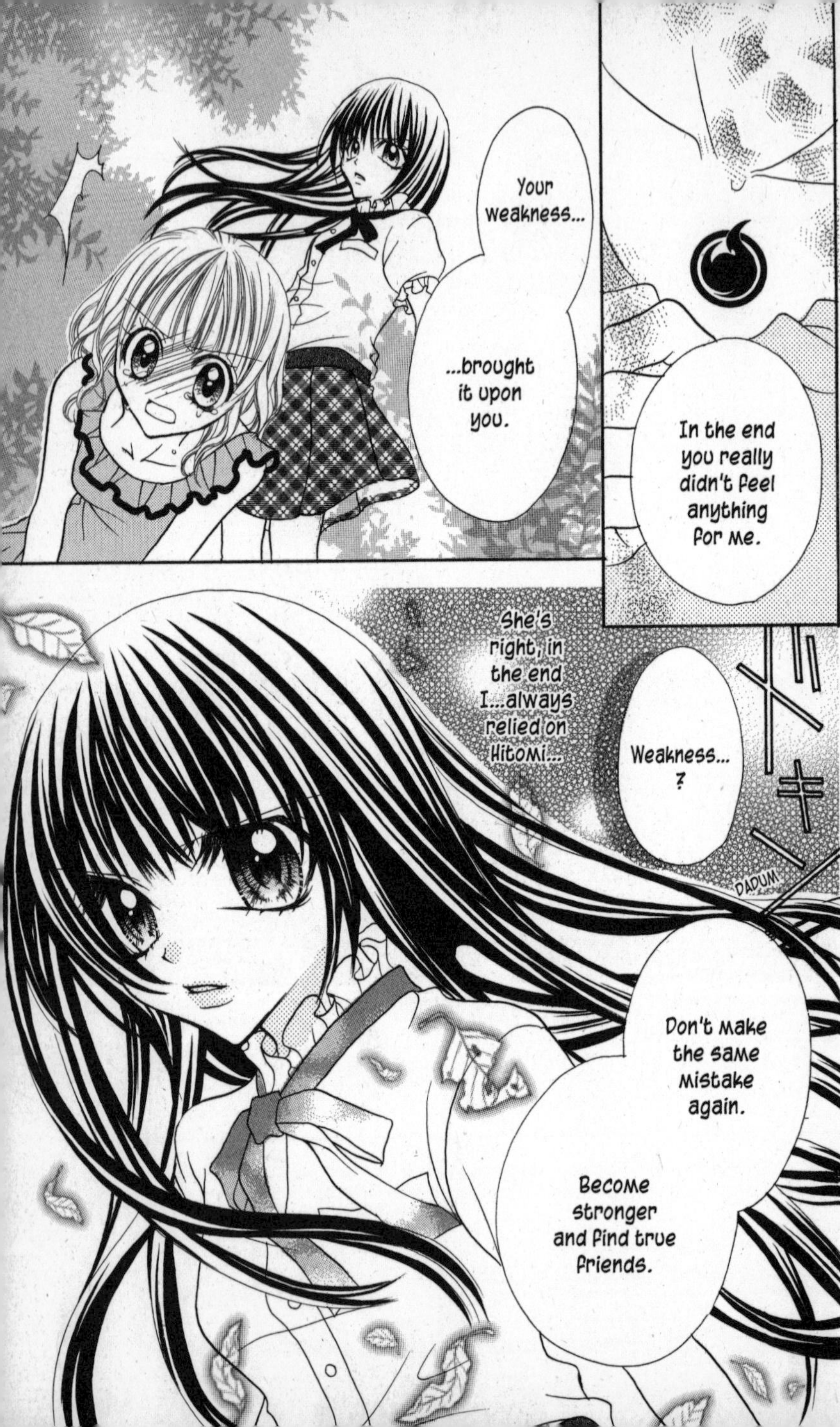
In the end you really didn't feel anything for me.
Your weakness...
...brought it upon you.
Weakness...?
She's right, in the end I...always relied on Hitomi...
DADUM
Don't make the same mistake again.
Become stronger and find true friends.

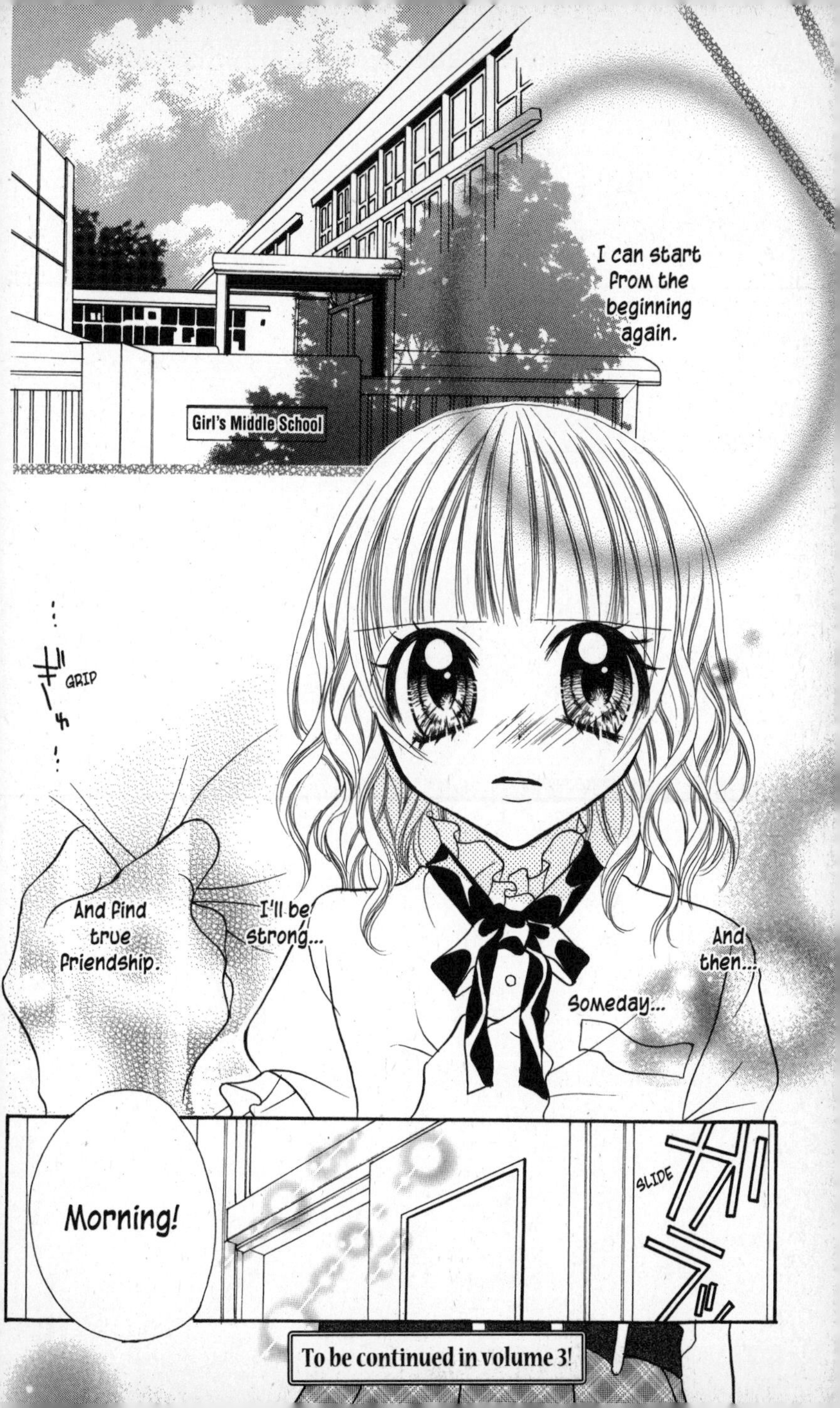
I can start from the beginning again.
Girl's Middle School
And then...
Someday...
I'll be strong...
And find true friendship.
GRIP
SLIDE
Morning!
To be continued in volume 3!

Hell Girl Special

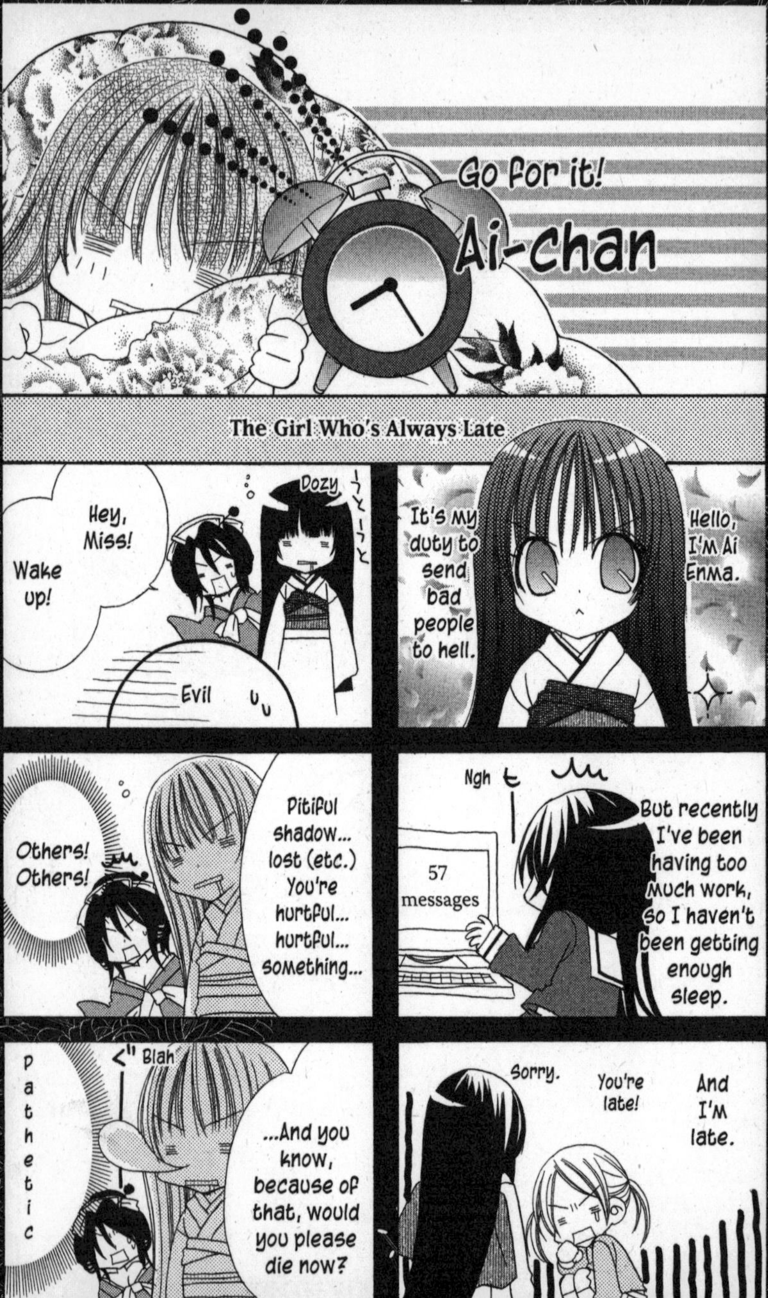
Go for it!
Ai-chan
The Girl Who's Always Late
Hello, I'm Ai Enma.
It's my duty to send bad people to hell.
Dozy
Hey, Miss!
Wake up!
Evil
Ngh
But recently I've been having too much work, so I haven't been getting enough sleep.
57 messages
Pitiful shadow... lost (etc.) You're hurtful... hurtful... something...
Others! Others!
And I'm late.
You're late!
Sorry.
...And you know, because of that, would you please die now?
Blah
pathetic

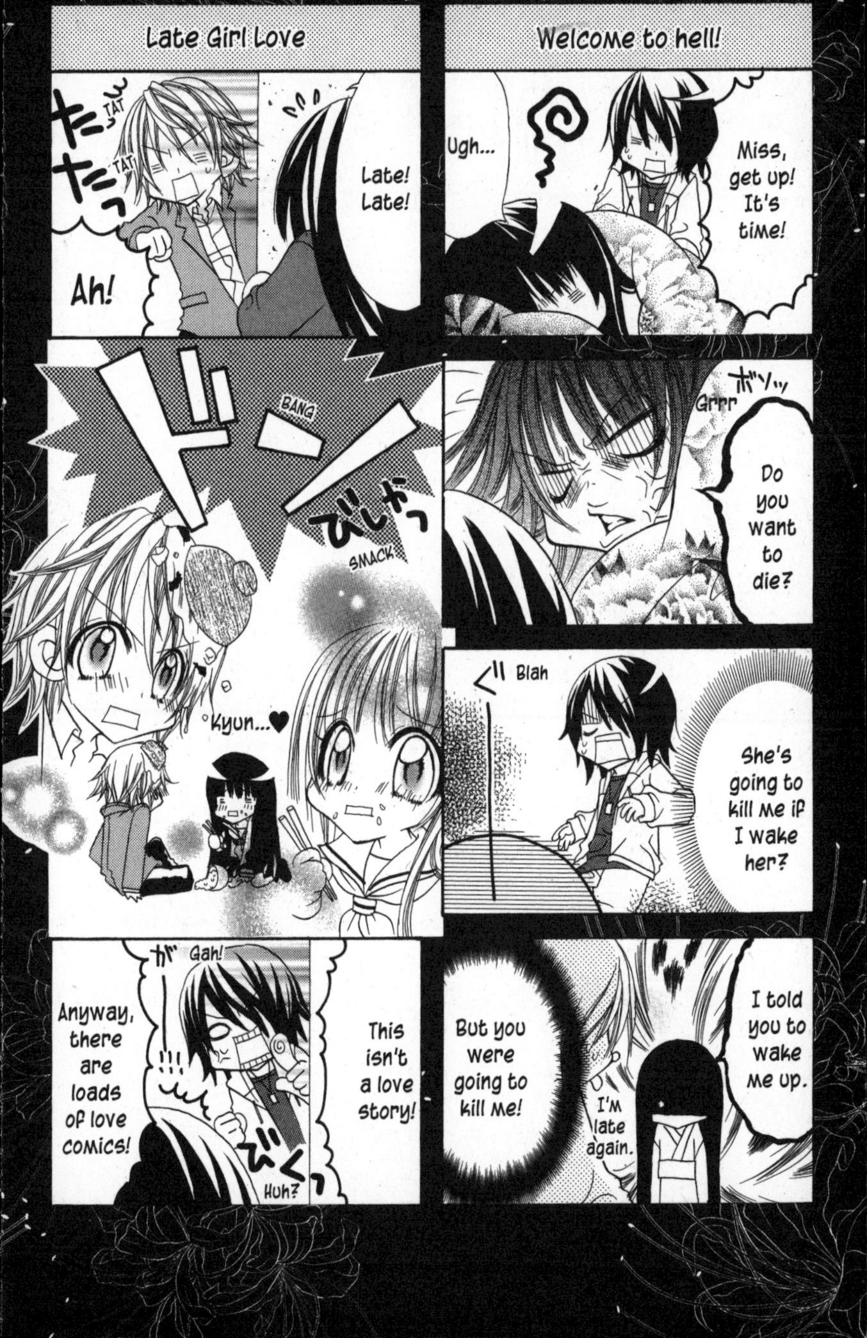
Welcome to hell!
Miss, get up! It's time!
Ugh...
Grrr
Do you want to die?
Blah
She's going to kill me if I wake her?
I told you to wake me up.
I'm late again.
But you were going to kill me!
Late Girl Love
Late! Late!
TAT
TAT
Ah!
BANG
SMACK
Kyun...♥
This isn't a love story!
Gah!
Anyway, there are loads of love comics!
Huh?

Mail

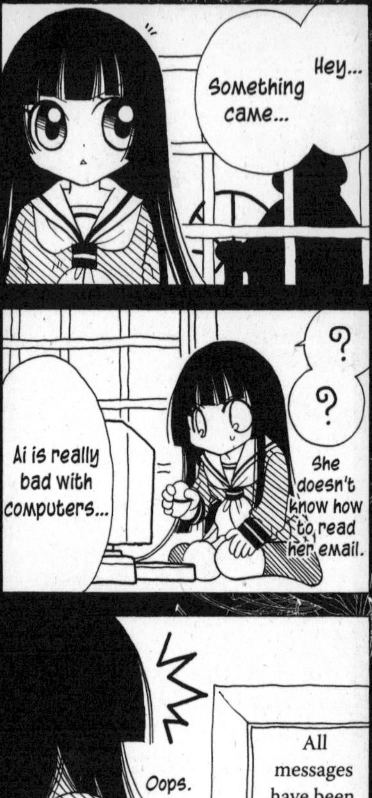
Hey... Something came...
?
?
She doesn't know how to read her email.
Ai is really bad with computers...
All messages have been deleted.
Oops.
Crap
Why isn't she coming?!
Don't do it!
AHH!
She's going to jump!

Ichimokuren

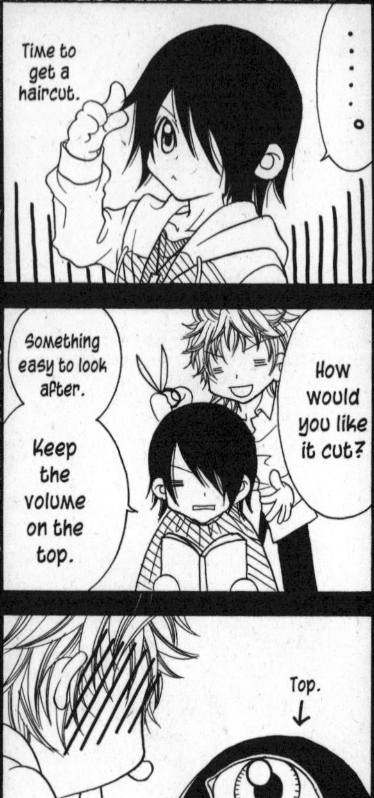
.....
Time to get a haircut.
How would you like it cut?
Something easy to look after.
Keep the volume on the top.
Top.
I can't cut that!
STARE

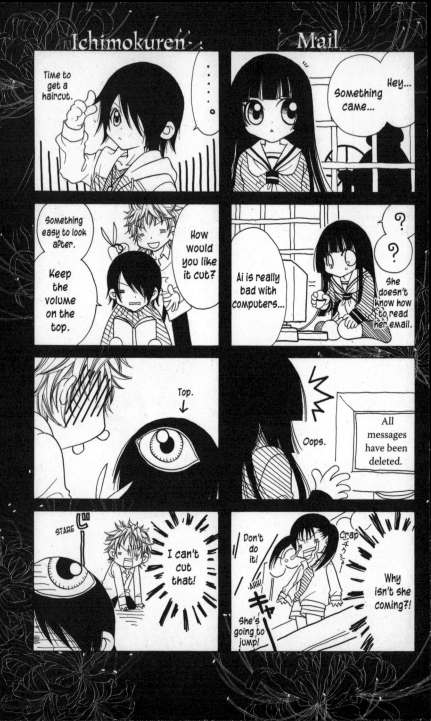

Hone Onna

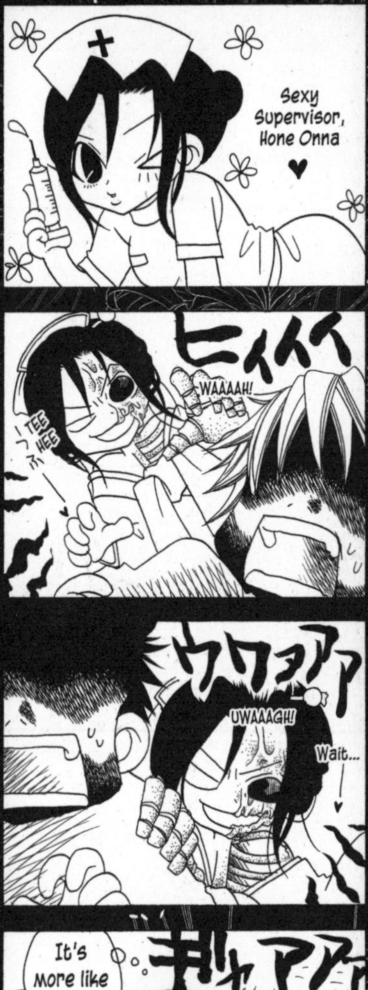
Sexy Supervisor, Hone Onna ♥
WAAAAH!
TEE HEE
Wait... ♥
UWAAAGH!
WAAAAH!!
It's more like you're the...
scary supervisor!

Wanyuudou

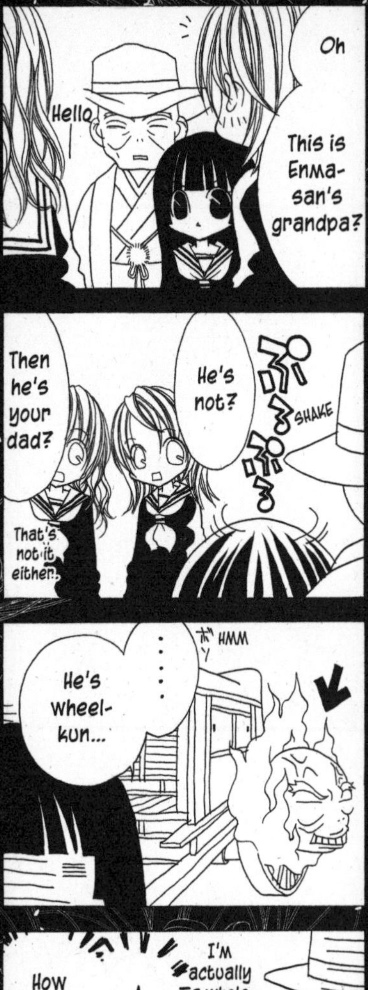
Oh
This is Enma-san's grandpa?
Hello
SHAKE
He's not?
Then he's your dad?
That's not it either.
HMM
......
He's wheel-kun...
Miss...
I'm actually a whole coach.
A wheel...
How old are you?!

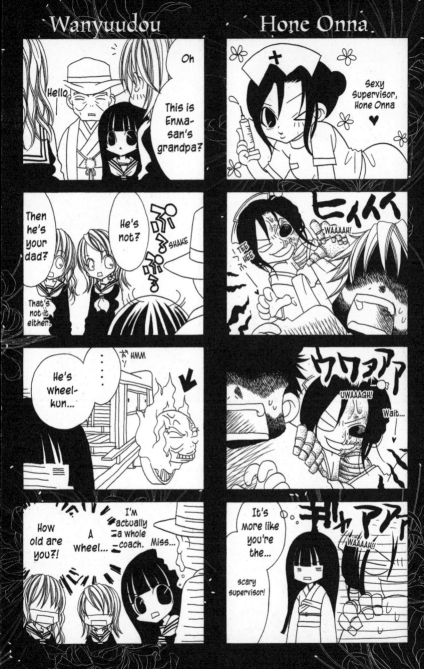

Sweet Trap

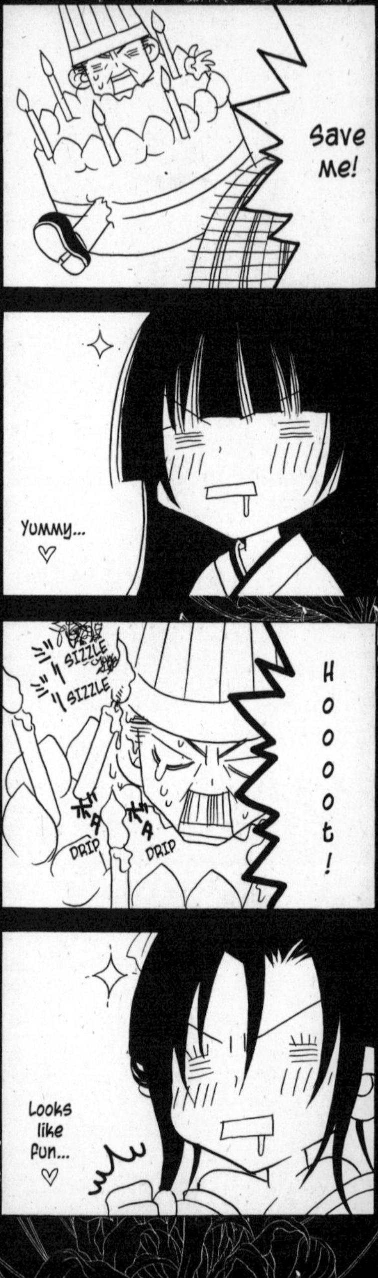
Save me!
Yummy... ♡
Hoooot!
SIZZLE
SIZZLE
DRIP
DRIP
Looks like fun... ♡

Problem Mail

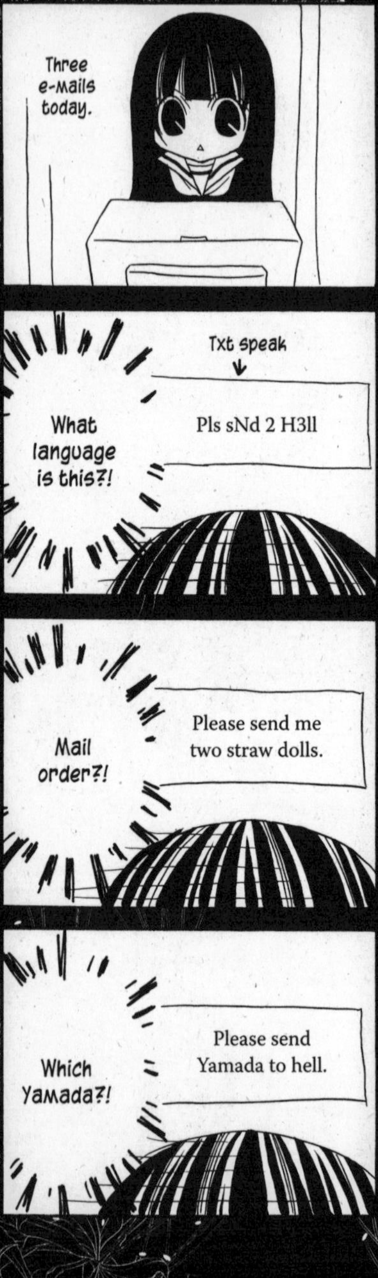
Three e-mails today.
Txt speak
Pls sNd 2 H3ll
What language is this?!
Please send me two straw dolls.
Mail order?!
Please send Yamada to hell.
Which Yamada?!

Friends

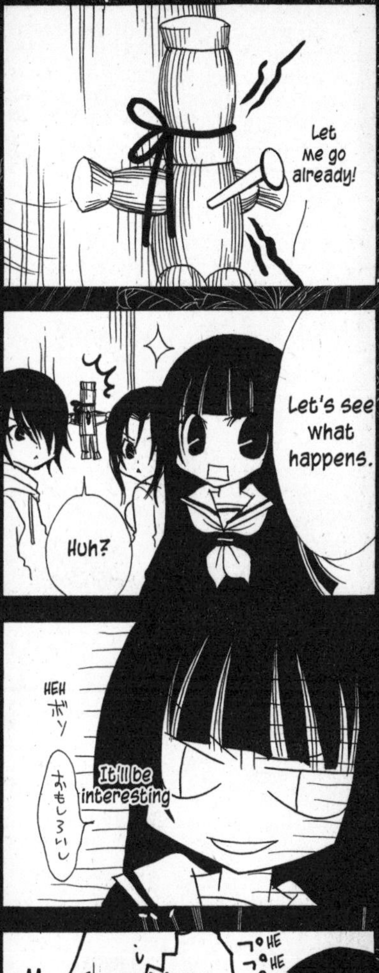

Let me go already!
Let's see what happens.
Huh?
HEH
ボソ
It'll be interesting
おもしろいし
HE HE HE
プフフー
But...
Miss?!
TEE HEE HEE
クスクスクス

Out of Area

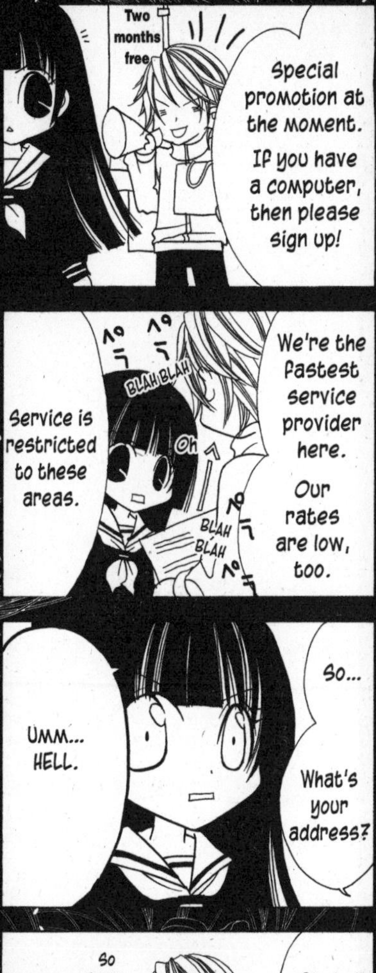

Special promotion at the moment.
If you have a computer, then please sign up!
Two months free
We're the fastest service provider here.
Our rates are low, too.
BLAH BLAH
ペラペラ
Oh
BLAH BLAH
Service is restricted to these areas.
So...
What's your address?
UMM... HELL.
Oh, hell isn't in our service area.
So sorry.
That's a shame.

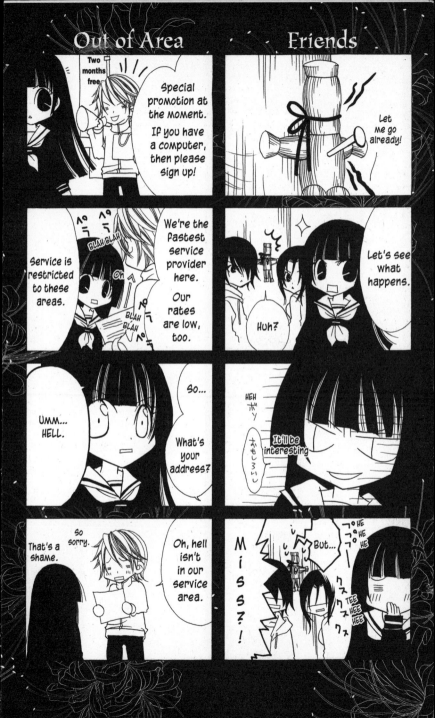

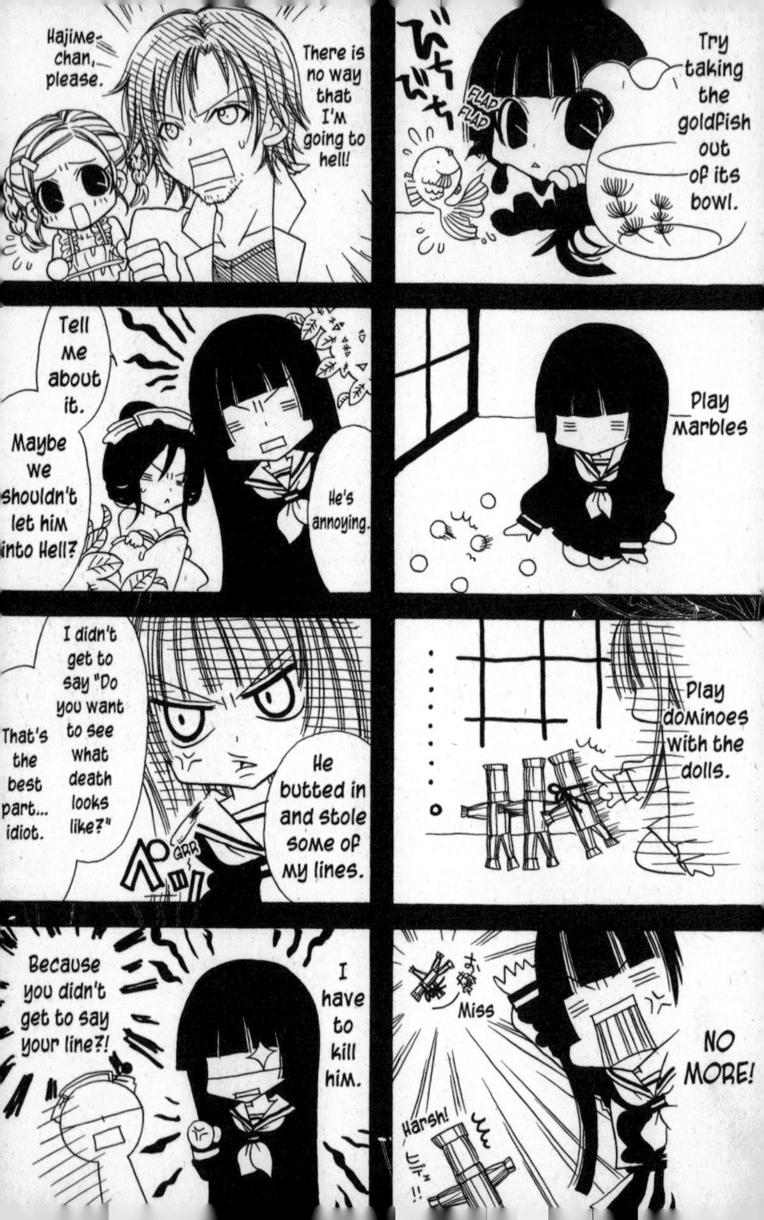

FLAP FLAP
Try taking the goldfish out of its bowl.
There is no way that I'm going to hell!
Hajime-chan, please.
Play Marbles
He's annoying.
Tell Me about it.
Maybe we shouldn't let him into Hell?
Play dominoes with the dolls.
He butted in and stole some of my lines.
I didn't get to say "Do you want to see what death looks like?"
That's the best part... idiot.
GRR
NO MORE!
Miss
Harsh!
I have to kill him.
Because you didn't get to say your line?!

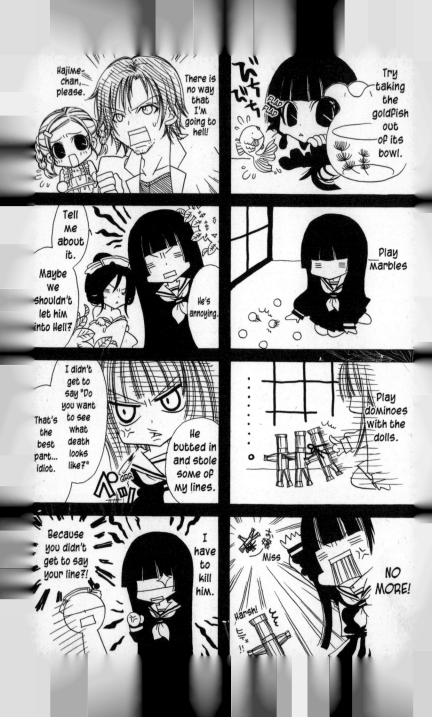

About the Creator

Miyuki Eto

Birth date: July 3
Astrological sign: Cancer
Blood type: A

Born in Hiroshima prefecture, Miyuki Eto made her
manga debut in *Nakayoshi* magazine's
"Summer Vacationland" special issue with the story "Lila's
Flower Language." That story won her the 25th Annual
Nakayoshi New Manga Artist Award.
To date, *Hell Girl* may be her best-known work. Her
hobby is taking care of her cats!

Translation Notes

Japanese is a tricky language for most Westerners, and translation is often more an art than a science. For your edification and reading pleasure, here are notes on some of the places where we could have gone in a different direction, or where a Japanese cultural reference is used.

Nakayoshi, page 11

Nakayoshi is the name of the Japenese magazine in which *Hell Girl* was serialized. This magazine is aimed at young girls and usually features such sweet, lighthearted manga series as *Kitchen Princess*. *Hell Girl*'s dark subject matter is a real departure for *Nakayoshi*'s pages, as the author points out here!

Cram school, page 124

Cram schools are private institutions that run after-school classes for students who want or need extra preparation for Japan's infamously tough school entrance exams. In this case, cram school has given Maki an extra edge—she's studied material in advance of her regular English class.

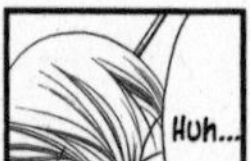

Huh...
I studied this in cram school, so I'll teach you!
Then when we're done, we can go home!

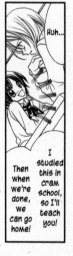

River Styx, page 141

The River Styx is a reference to Greek mythology. It is the river that separates the world of the living from that of the dead.

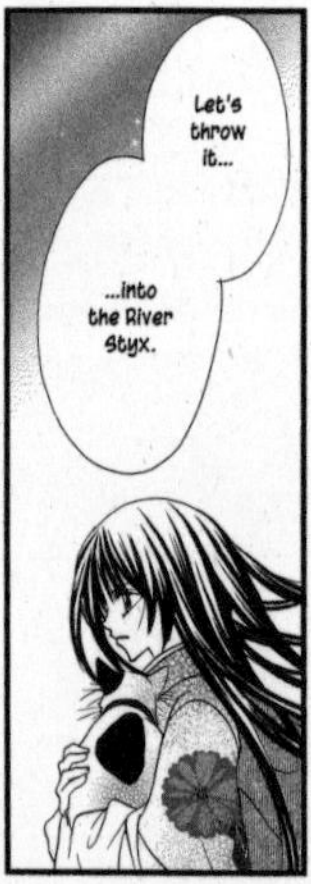

Let's throw it...
...into the River Styx.

The Girl Who's Always Late, page 185

The original Japanese title for this section contained a play on words. The word for "to be late" is *chikoku*, which sounds an awful lot like *jigoku*, the word for "hell."

Preview of Volume 3

We're pleased to present you with a preview of volume 3.
Please check our website (www.delreymanga.com) to see when this volume
will be available in English. For now you'll have to make do with Japanese!

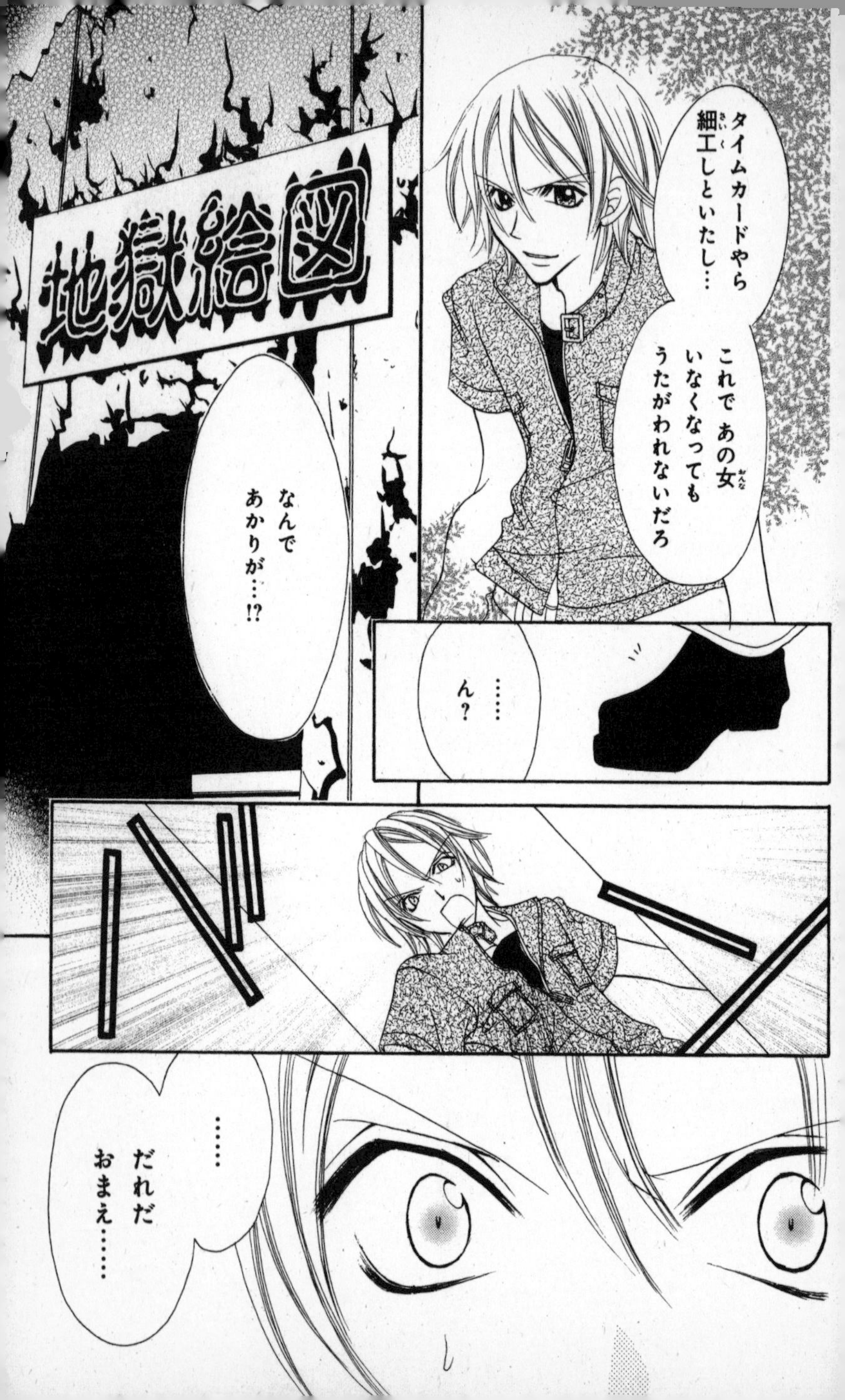
タイムカードやら細工しといたしし…
これであの女いなくなってもうたがわれないだろ
……ん?
地獄絵図
なんであかりが…!?
……
だれだおまえ……

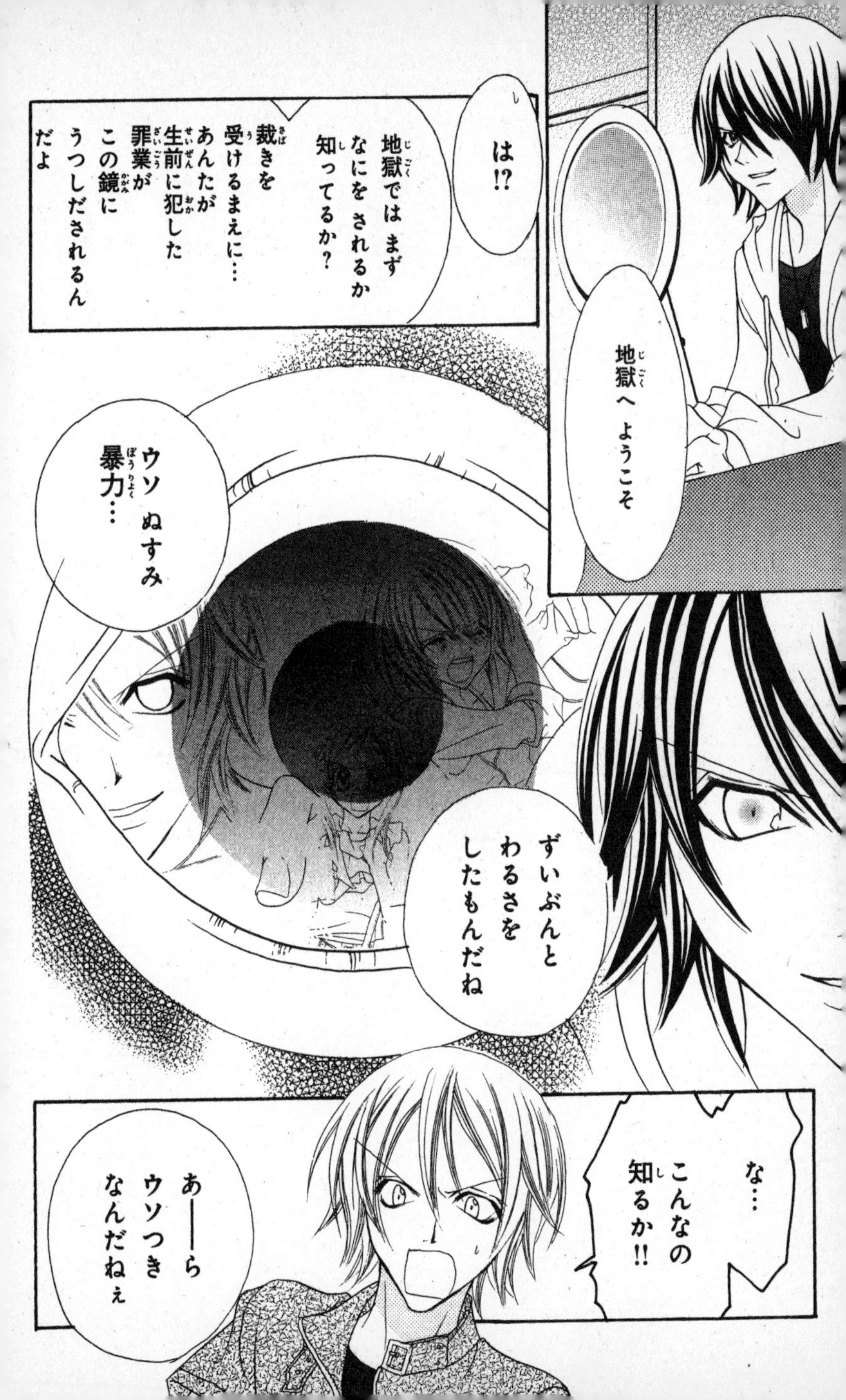

地獄へ ようこそ
は!?
地獄では まず なにを されるか 知ってるか?
裁きを 受けるまえに… あんたが 生前に犯した 罪業が この鏡に うつしだされるんだよ
ウソ ぬすみ 暴力…
ずいぶんと わるさを したもんだね
な… こんなの 知るか!!
あーーら ウソつき なんだねぇ

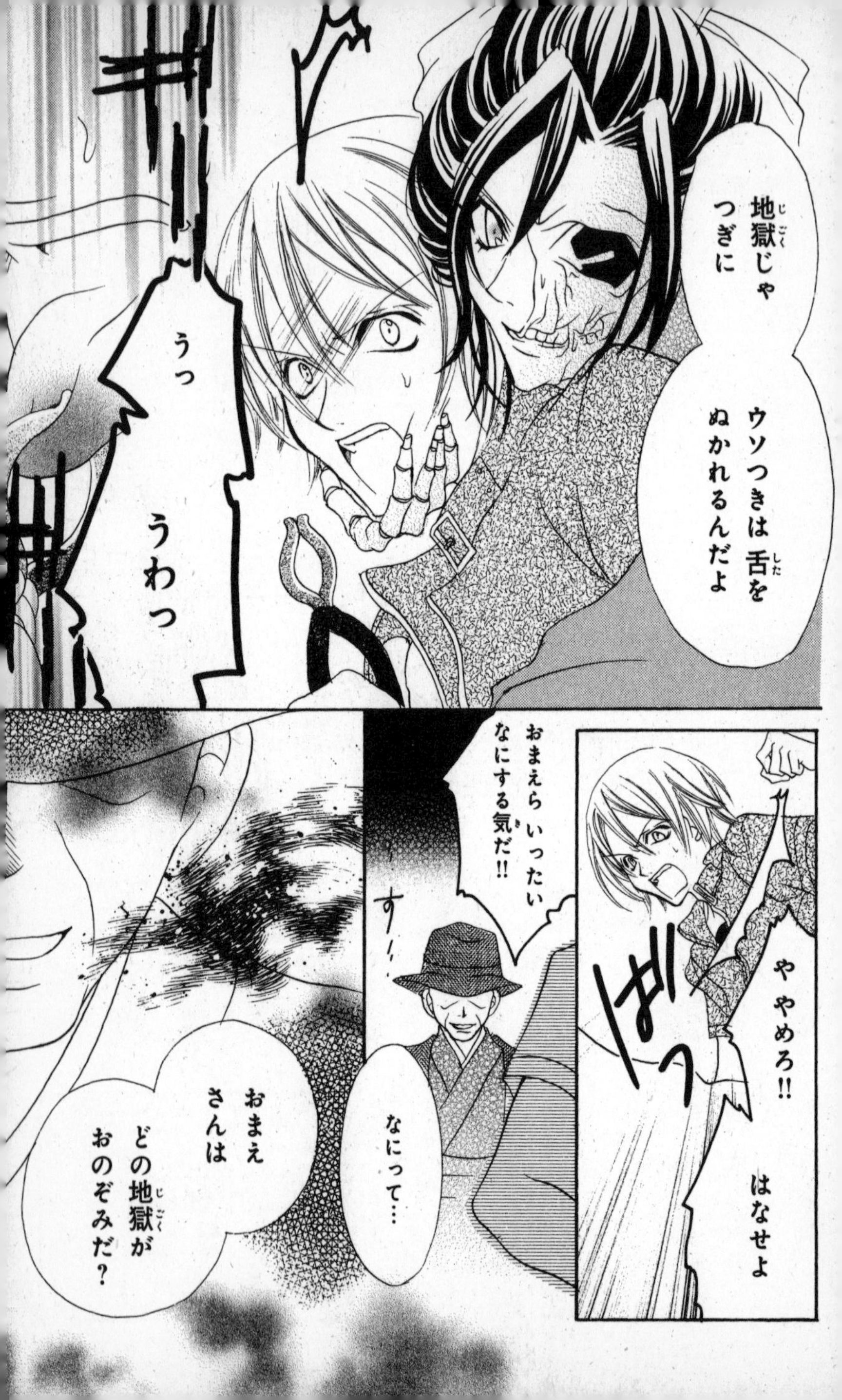
地獄じゃ
つぎに
ウソつきは舌を
ぬかれるんだよ
うっ
うわっ
ややめろ!!
はなせよ
おまえら いったい
なにする気だ!!
なにって…
おまえさんは
どの地獄が
おのぞみだ?

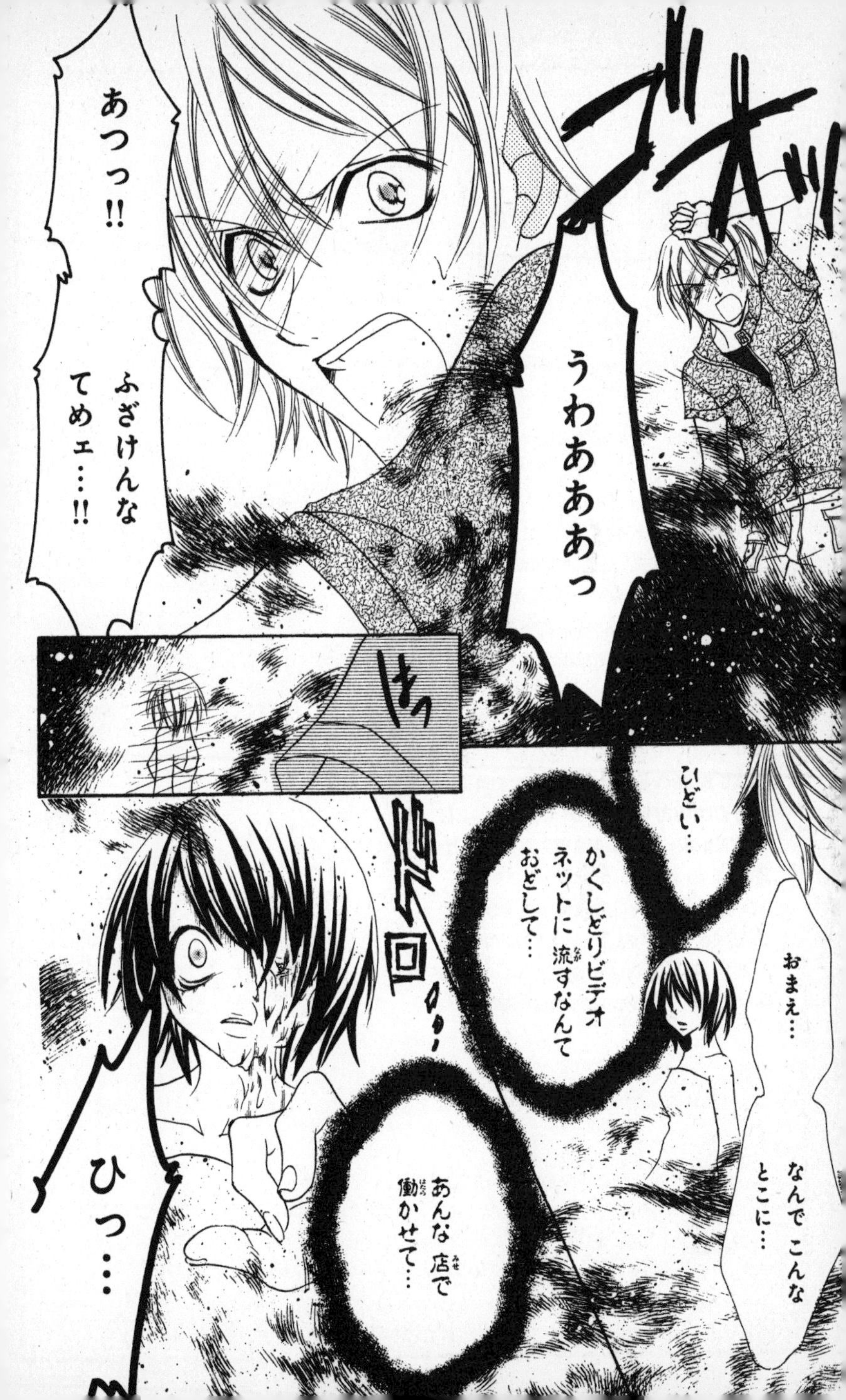
ゴオッ
うわあああっ
あつっ!!
ふざけんなてめェ…!!
はっ
おまえ…なんでこんなとこに…
ひどい…
かくしどりビデオネットに流すなんておどして…
あんな店で働かせて…
ひっ…

BY CLAMP

Watanuki Kimihiro is haunted by visions. When he finds himself irresistibly drawn into a shop owned by Yûko, a mysterious witch, he is offered the chance to rid himself of the spirits that plague him. He accepts, but soon realizes that he's just been tricked into working for the shop to pay off the cost of Yûko's services! But this isn't any ordinary kind of shop . . . In this shop, Yûko grants wishes to those in need. But they must have the strength of will not only to truly understand their need, but to give up something incredibly precious in return.

Ages: 13+

Special extras in each volume! Read them all!

VISIT WWW.DELREYMANGA.COM TO:
• View release date calendars for upcoming volumes
• Sign up for Del Rey's free manga e-newsletter
• Find out the latest about new Del Rey Manga series

SHUGO CHARA!

PEACH-PIT

Creators of *Dears* and *Rozen Maiden*

Everybody at Seiyo Elementary thinks that stylish and super-cool Amu has it all. But nobody knows the *real* Amu, a shy girl who wishes she had the courage to truly be herself. Changing Amu's life is going to take more than wishes and dreams—it's going to take a little magic! One morning, Amu finds a surprise in her bed: three strange little eggs. Each egg contains a Guardian Character, an angel-like being who can give her the power to be someone new. With the help of her Guardian Characters, Amu is about to discover that her true self is even more amazing than she ever dreamed.

Special extras in each volume! Read them all!

TOMARE!

止まれ

[STOP]

You're going the wrong way!

Manga is a completely different type of reading experience.

To start at the *beginning*, go to the *end*!

That's right! Authentic manga is read the traditional Japanese way—from right to left, exactly the *opposite* of how American books are read. It's easy to follow: Just go to the other end of the book, and read each page—and each panel—from right side to left side, starting at the top right. Now you're experiencing manga as it was meant to be!